doubt!!™

volume six

story and art by
Kaneyoshi Izumi

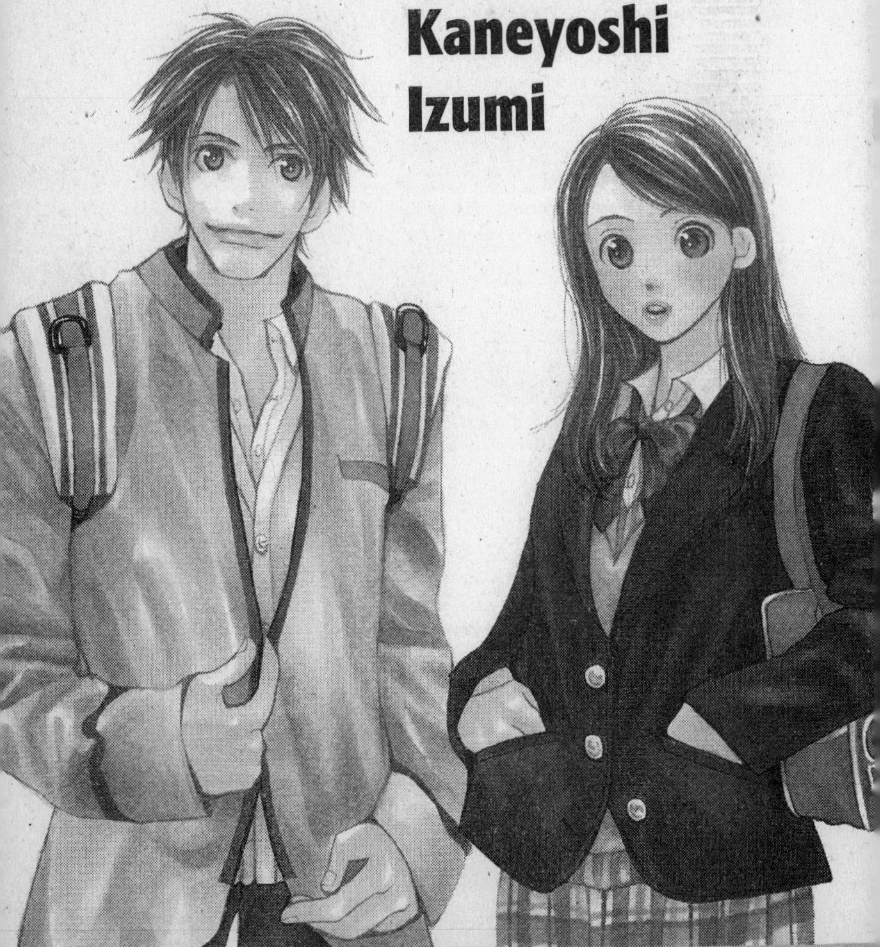

doubt!!™

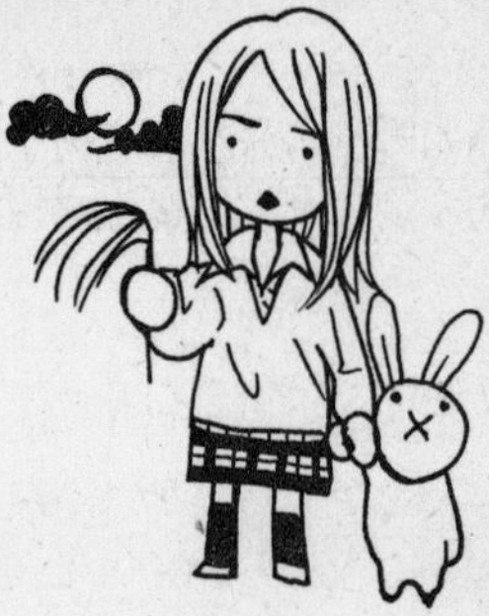

volume six
shôjo edition

Story & Art by Kaneyoshi Izumi

English Adaptation/Kelly Sue DeConnick
Translation/Naomi Kokubo
Touch-up Art & Lettering/Freeman Wong
Design/Amy Martin
Editor/Frances E. Wall

Managing Editor/Annette Roman
Director of Production/Noboru Watanabe
Vice President of Publishing/Alvin Lu
Sr. Director of Acquisitions/Rika Inouye
Vice President of Sales & Marketing/Liza Coppola
Publisher/Hyoe Narita

Printed in the U.S.A.

Published by VIZ Media, LLC
P.O. Box 77010
San Francisco, CA 94107

10 9 8 7 6 5 4 3 2 1
First printing, December 2005

viz media™

www.viz.com

store.viz.com

doubt!!™ 6 contents

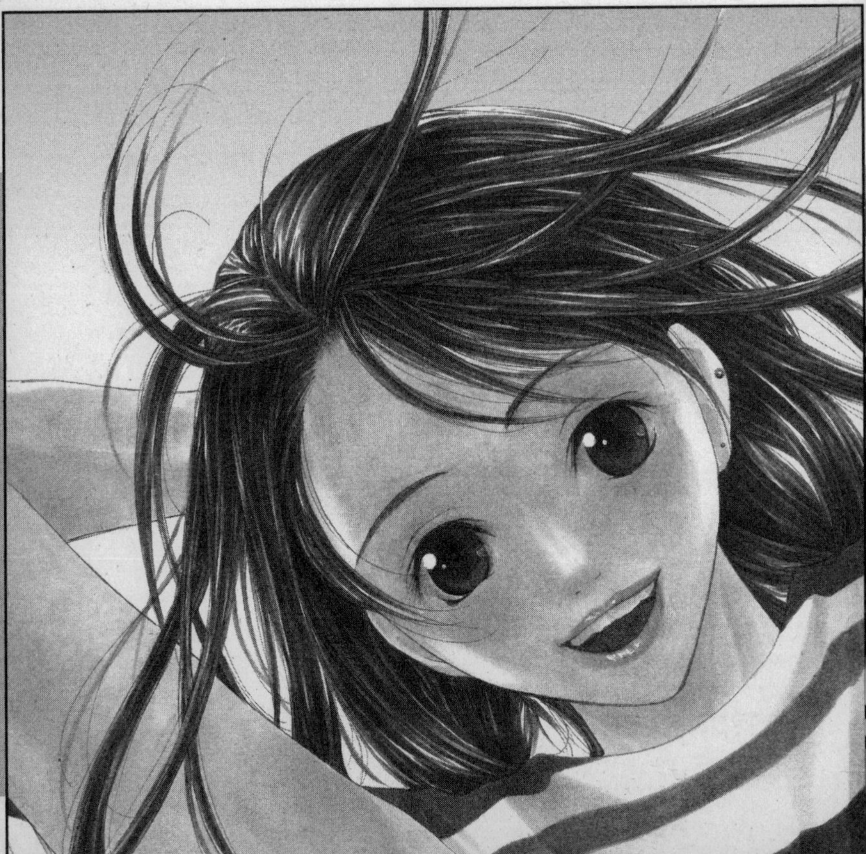

the story so far...

In junior high, Ai Maekawa was a jimi girl -- a plain, nerdy wallflower who never attracted anyone's attention. But after a dramatic incident of public humiliation, Ai vowed to change her life forever. In hopes of getting a fresh start, she made herself over into a slender, gorgeous babe before entering high school. Though Ai has achieved her dream of becoming beautiful, she's still adjusting to the delights and hazards of her new life, including her on-again, off-again relationship with dashing classmate Sô. Ai is wracked with anxiety over her lack of sexual experience -- she feels horribly naive compared to her friends, especially Sô, and fears she'll prove the cruel taunts of her junior high classmates true by remaining a virgin until she's 30. Ai and Sô's romance is complicated further by the appearance of Sakurako, the girl whom Sô's parents want him to marry. Ai has proven her superiority over Sakurako, but her troubles aren't over yet....

Ai Maekawa
Ai, our heroine, is still getting used to life as a popular girl.

Sô Ichinose
Sô, a cool and aloof guy, is now Ai's boyfriend.

Yuichiro Kato
Yuichiro, Sô's best friend since childhood, has a desperate, futile crush on Ai.

Mina Sato
Ai's best friend Mina, a trendy, super-tan Ko-Gal, is madly in love with Yuichiro.

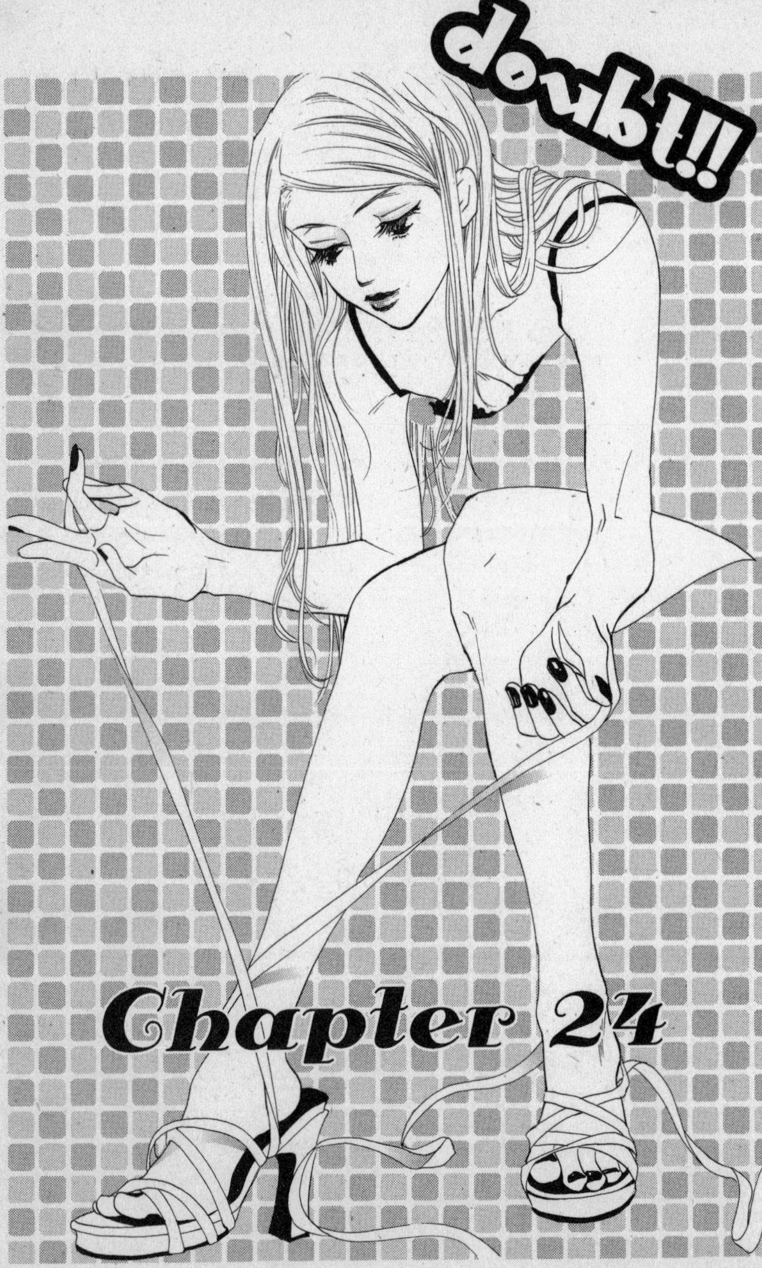
doubt!!
Chapter 24

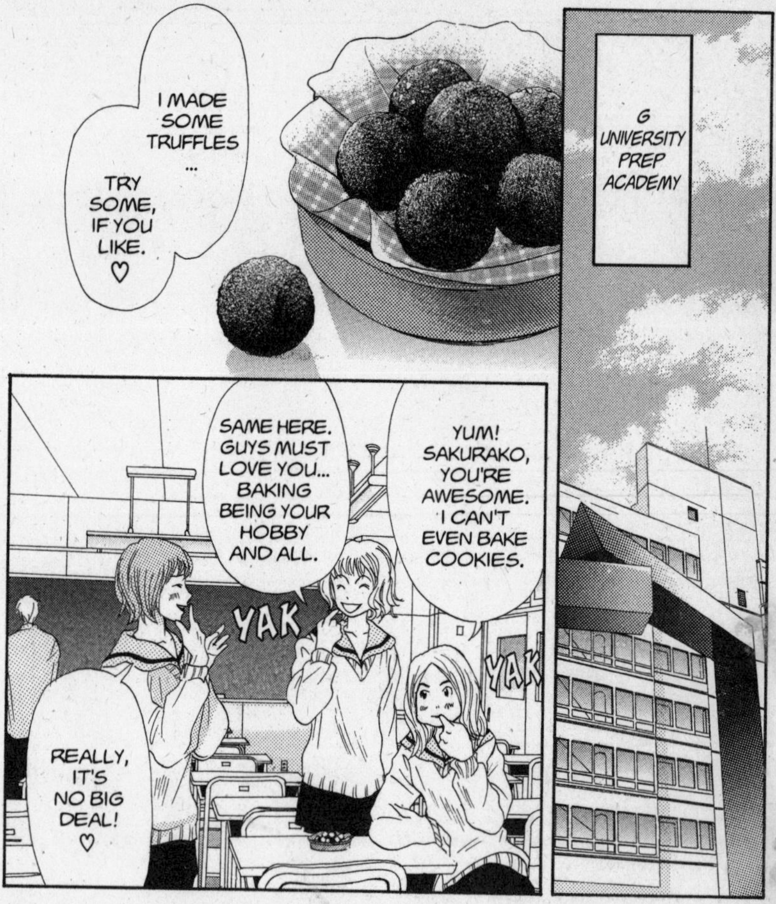
G UNIVERSITY PREP ACADEMY
I MADE SOME TRUFFLES ... TRY SOME, IF YOU LIKE. ♡
YUM! SAKURAKO, YOU'RE AWESOME. I CAN'T EVEN BAKE COOKIES.
SAME HERE. GUYS MUST LOVE YOU... BAKING BEING YOUR HOBBY AND ALL.
YAK
YAK
REALLY, IT'S NO BIG DEAL! ♡

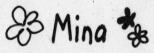

Mina

Her character was so useful that I ended up making her a regular. Plus, she's easy to draw...

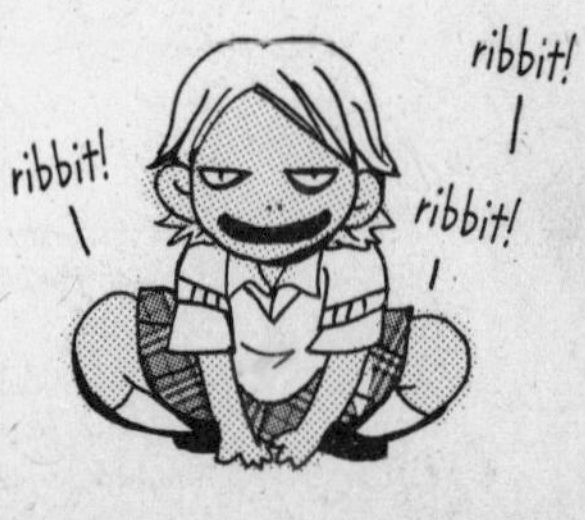
ribbit!
ribbit!
ribbit!

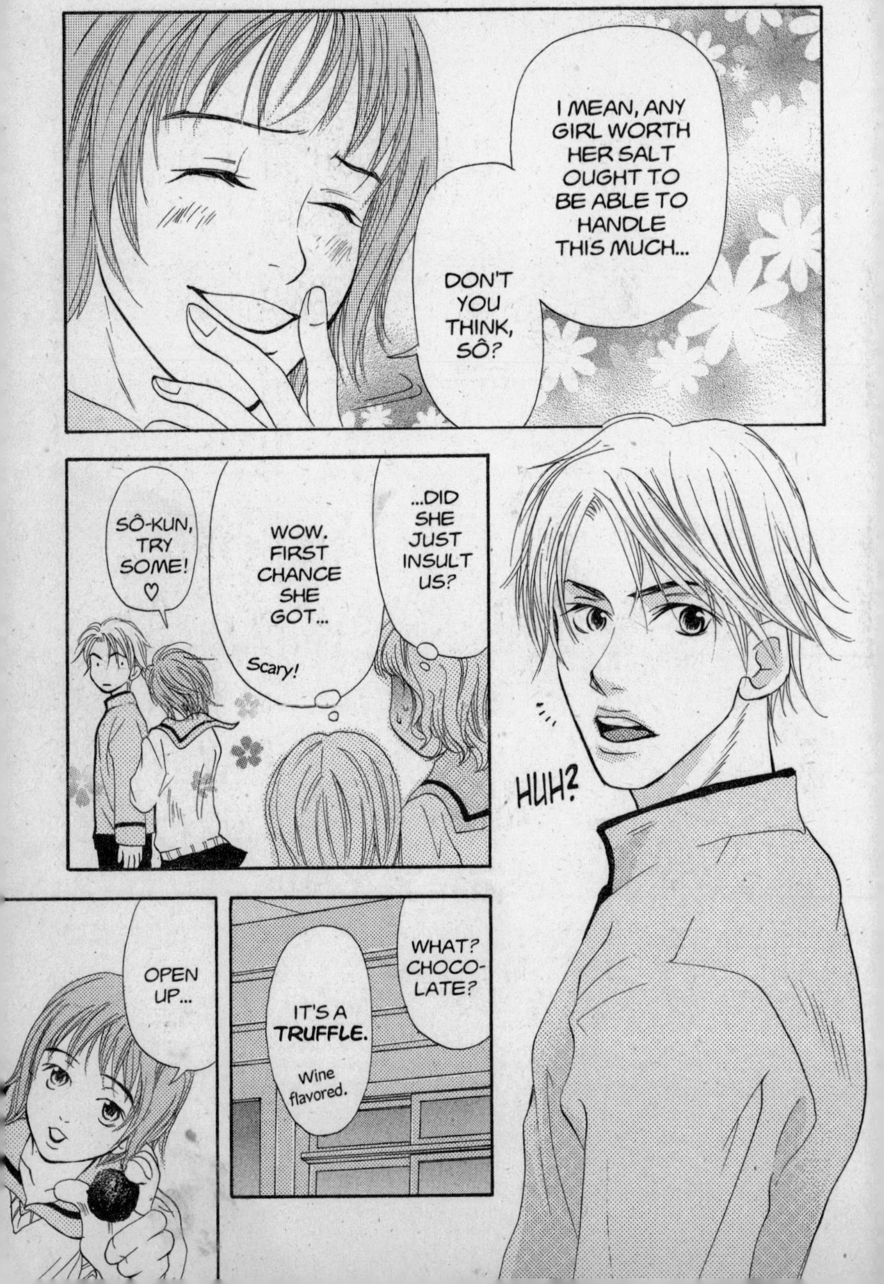
I MEAN, ANY GIRL WORTH HER SALT OUGHT TO BE ABLE TO HANDLE THIS MUCH...
DON'T YOU THINK, SÔ?
HUH?
...DID SHE JUST INSULT US?
WOW. FIRST CHANCE SHE GOT...
Scary!
SÔ-KUN, TRY SOME! ♡
WHAT? CHOCOLATE?
IT'S A **TRUFFLE.**
Wine flavored.
OPEN UP...

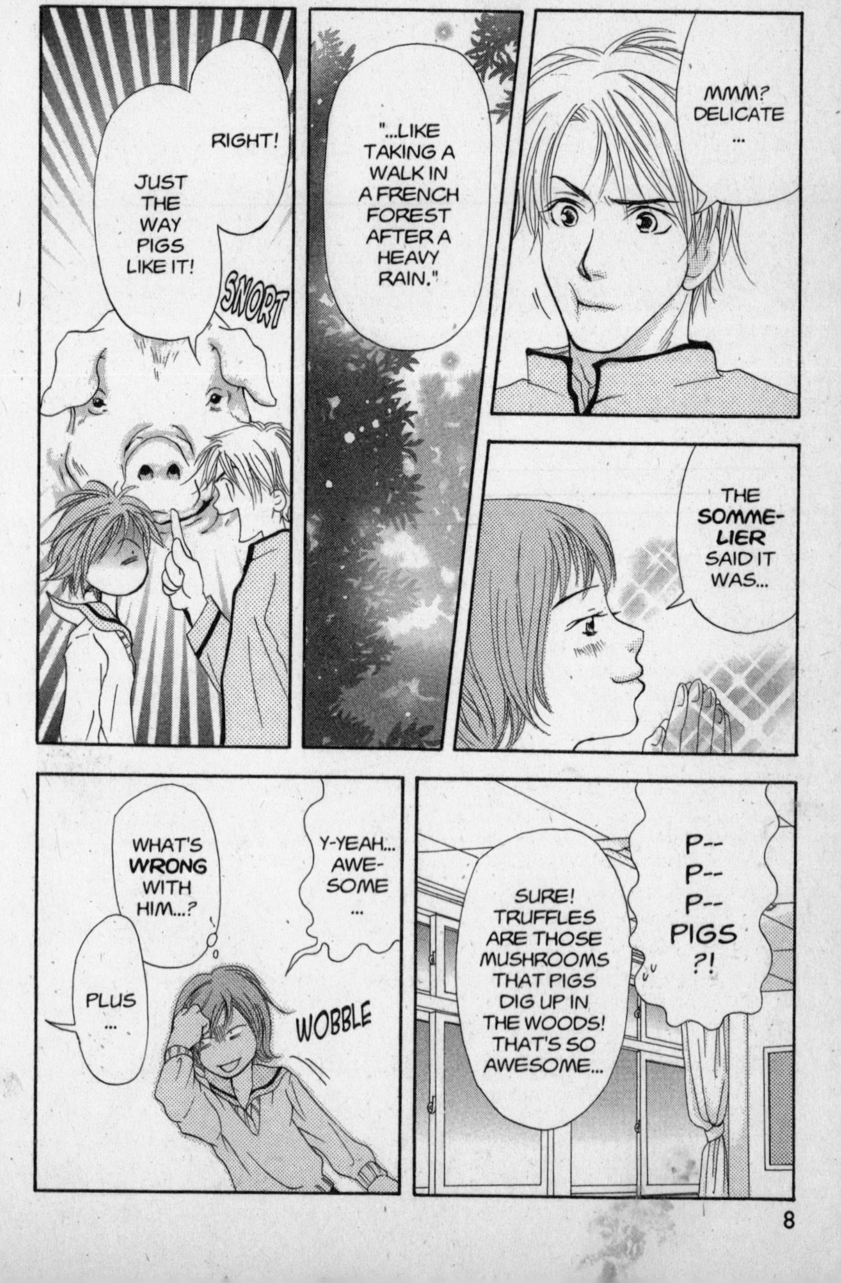
MMM? DELICATE ...
THE **SOMMELIER** SAID IT WAS...
"...LIKE TAKING A WALK IN A FRENCH FOREST AFTER A HEAVY RAIN."
RIGHT!
JUST THE WAY PIGS LIKE IT!
SNORT
P-- P-- P-- PIGS ?!
SURE! TRUFFLES ARE THOSE MUSHROOMS THAT PIGS DIG UP IN THE WOODS! THAT'S SO AWESOME...
Y-YEAH... AWESOME ...
WHAT'S **WRONG** WITH HIM...?
WOBBLE
PLUS ...

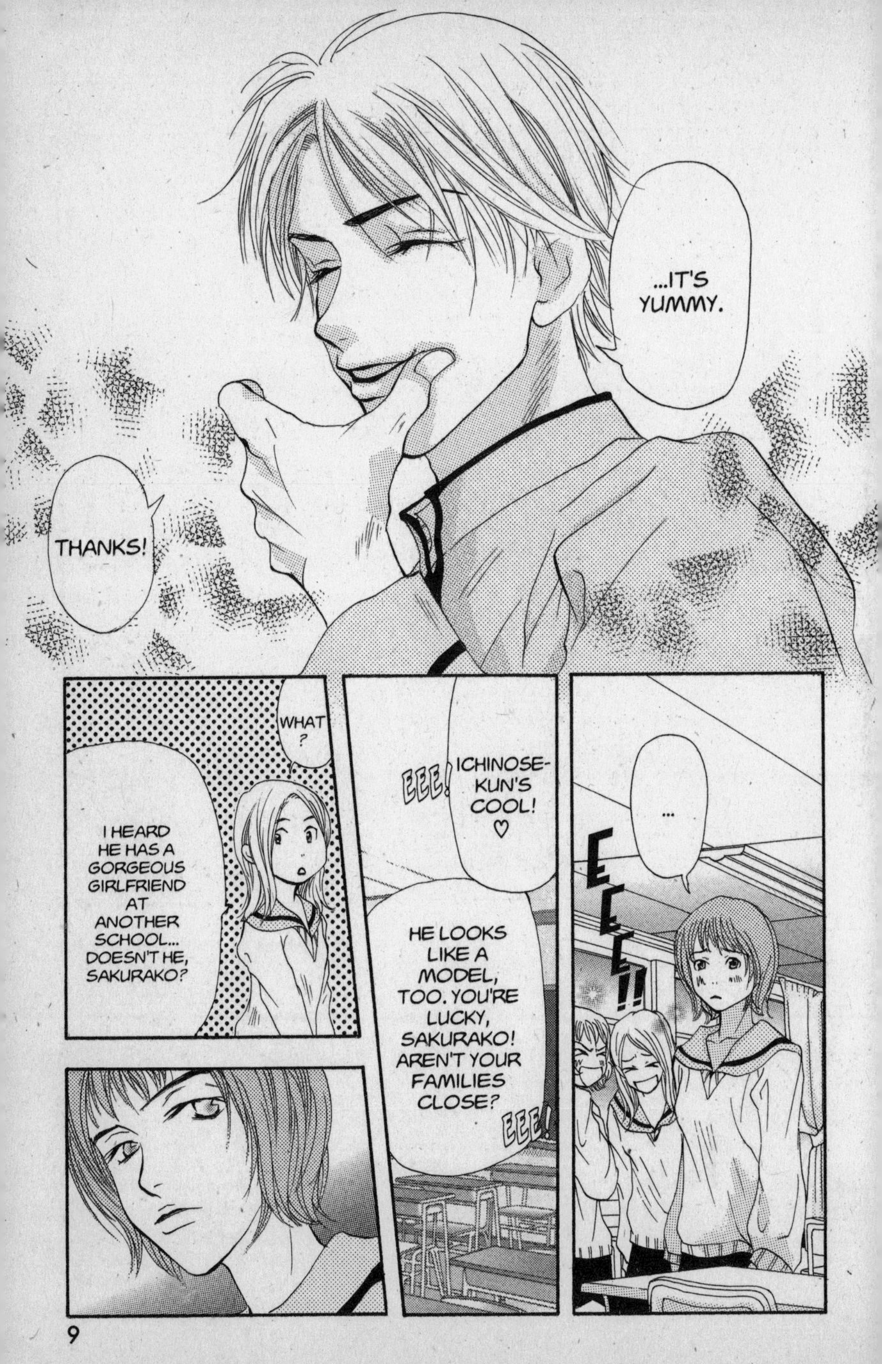
...IT'S YUMMY.
THANKS!
...
EEE!!
EEE!
ICHINOSE-KUN'S COOL! ♡
HE LOOKS LIKE A MODEL, TOO. YOU'RE LUCKY, SAKURAKO! AREN'T YOUR FAMILIES CLOSE?
EEE!
WHAT?
I HEARD HE HAS A GORGEOUS GIRLFRIEND AT ANOTHER SCHOOL... DOESN'T HE, SAKURAKO?

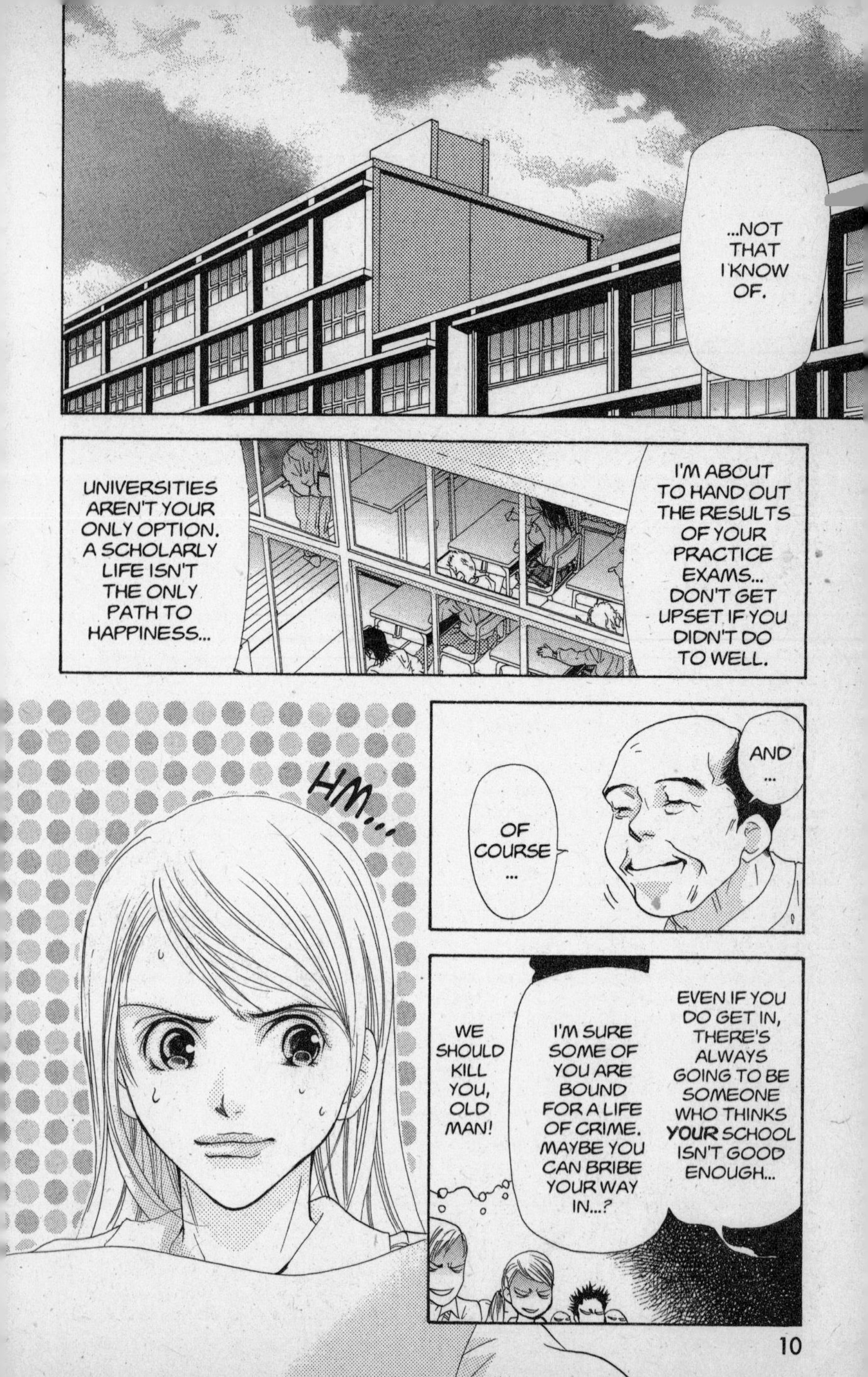
...NOT THAT I KNOW OF.
I'M ABOUT TO HAND OUT THE RESULTS OF YOUR PRACTICE EXAMS... DON'T GET UPSET IF YOU DIDN'T DO TO WELL.
UNIVERSITIES AREN'T YOUR ONLY OPTION. A SCHOLARLY LIFE ISN'T THE ONLY PATH TO HAPPINESS...
AND...
OF COURSE...
EVEN IF YOU DO GET IN, THERE'S ALWAYS GOING TO BE SOMEONE WHO THINKS **YOUR** SCHOOL ISN'T GOOD ENOUGH...
I'M SURE SOME OF YOU ARE BOUND FOR A LIFE OF CRIME. MAYBE YOU CAN BRIBE YOUR WAY IN...?
WE SHOULD KILL YOU, OLD MAN!
HM...

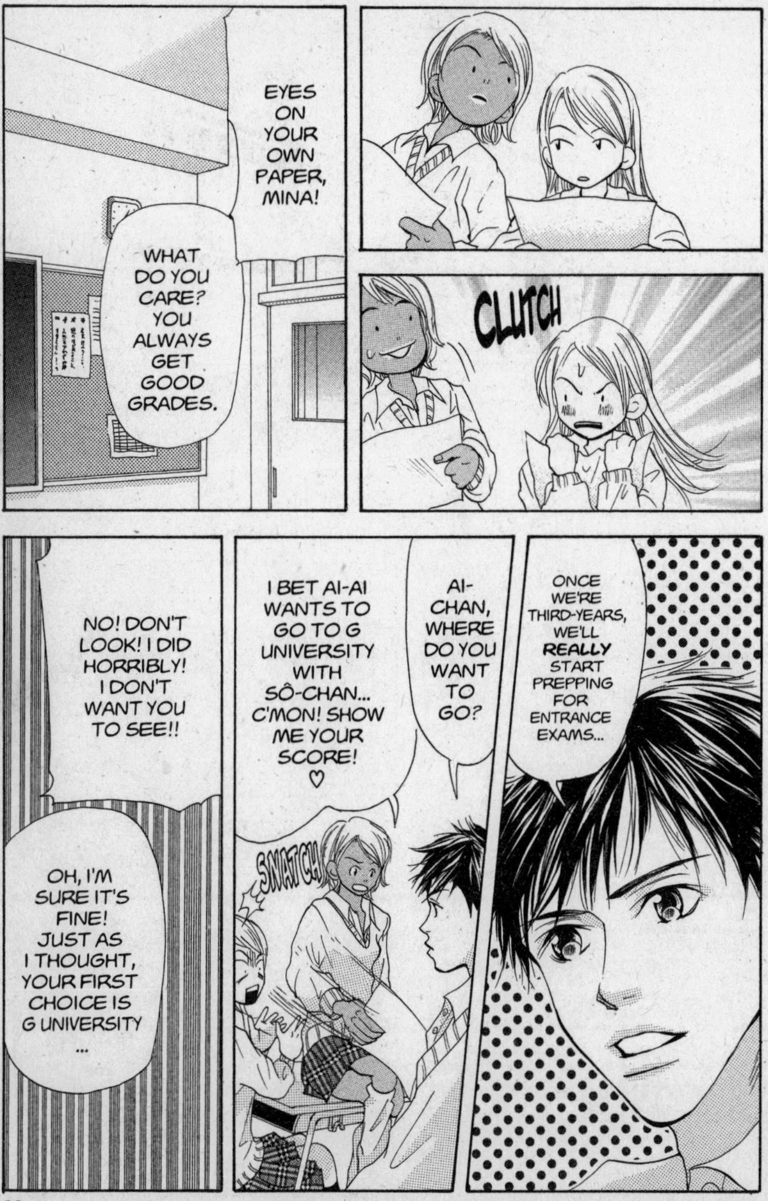
CLUTCH
EYES ON YOUR OWN PAPER, MINA!
WHAT DO YOU CARE? YOU ALWAYS GET GOOD GRADES.
ONCE WE'RE THIRD-YEARS, WE'LL **REALLY** START PREPPING FOR ENTRANCE EXAMS...
AI-CHAN, WHERE DO YOU WANT TO GO?
I BET AI-AI WANTS TO GO TO G UNIVERSITY WITH SÔ-CHAN... C'MON! SHOW ME YOUR SCORE! ♡
SNATCH
NO! DON'T LOOK! I DID HORRIBLY! I DON'T WANT YOU TO SEE!!
OH, I'M SURE IT'S FINE! JUST AS I THOUGHT, YOUR FIRST CHOICE IS G UNIVERSITY ...

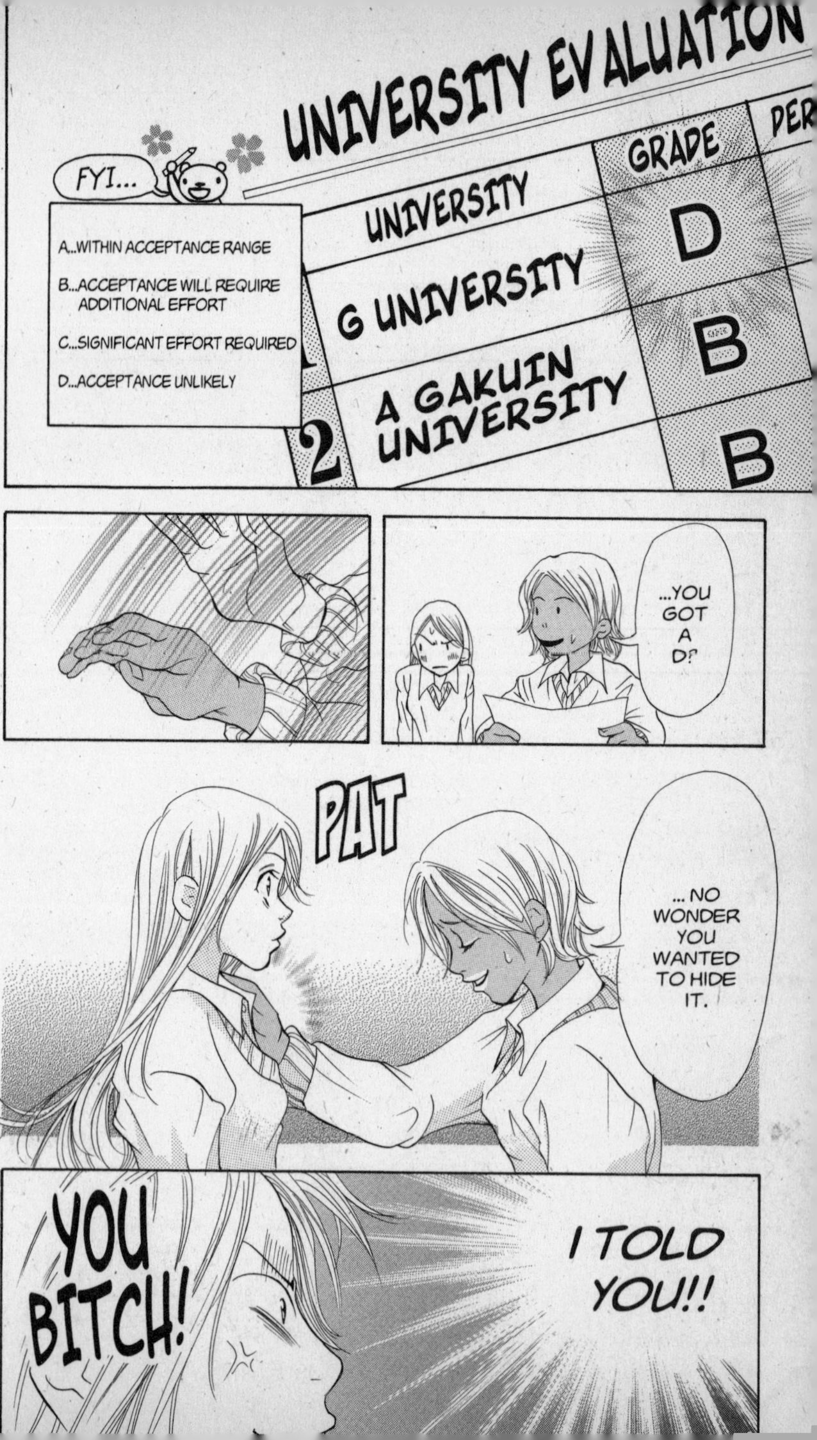
UNIVERSITY EVALUATION
GRADE
PER
UNIVERSITY
1 G UNIVERSITY
D
B
2 A GAKUIN UNIVERSITY
B
FYI...
A...WITHIN ACCEPTANCE RANGE
B...ACCEPTANCE WILL REQUIRE ADDITIONAL EFFORT
C...SIGNIFICANT EFFORT REQUIRED
D...ACCEPTANCE UNLIKELY
...YOU GOT A D?
PAT
... NO WONDER YOU WANTED TO HIDE IT.
I TOLD YOU!!
YOU BITCH!

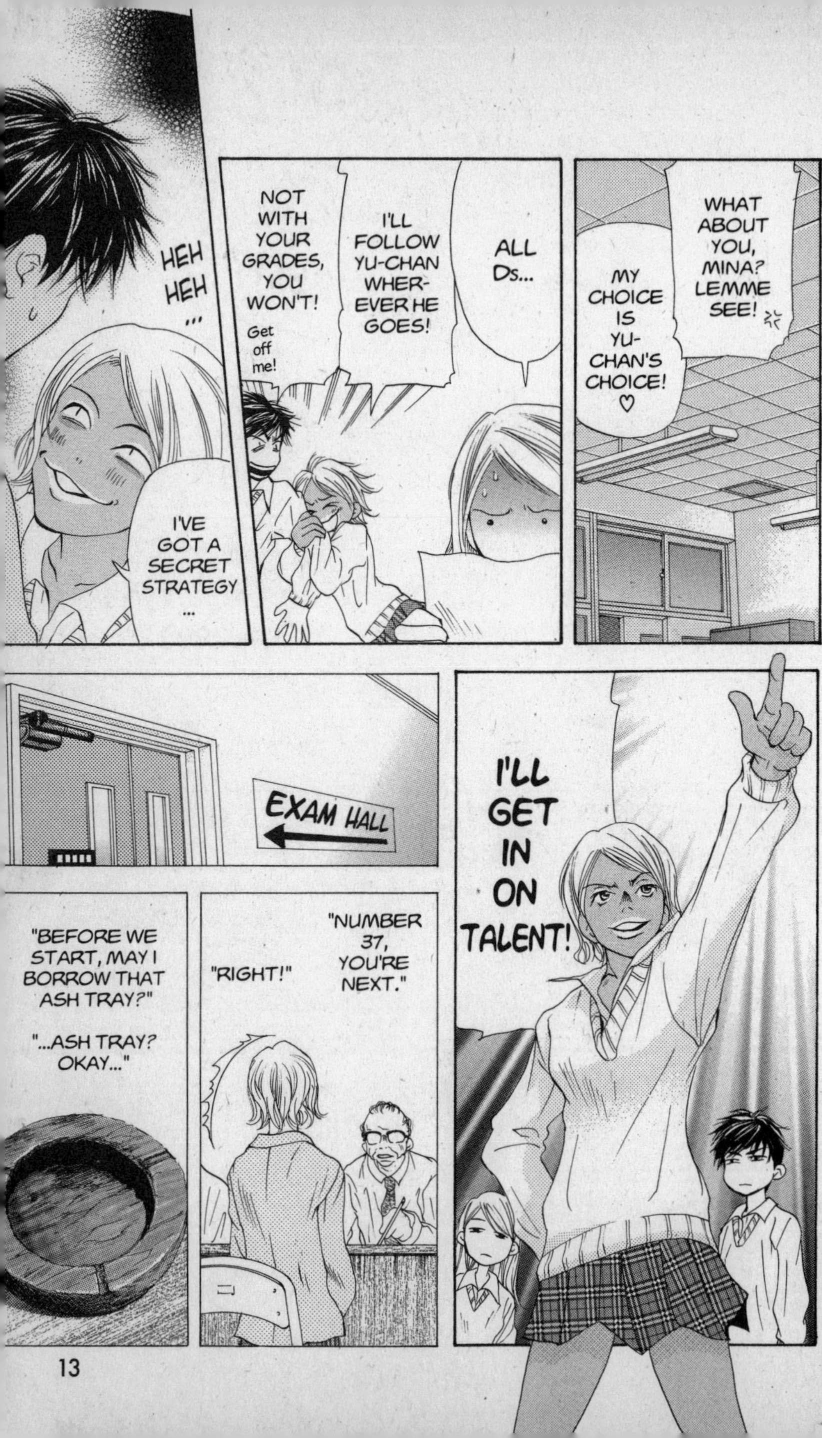
WHAT ABOUT YOU, MINA? LEMME SEE!
MY CHOICE IS YU-CHAN'S CHOICE! ♡
ALL Ds...
I'LL FOLLOW YU-CHAN WHER-EVER HE GOES!
NOT WITH YOUR GRADES, YOU WON'T!
Get off me!
HEH HEH ...
I'VE GOT A SECRET STRATEGY ...
I'LL GET IN ON TALENT!
EXAM HALL
"NUMBER 37, YOU'RE NEXT."
"RIGHT!"
"BEFORE WE START, MAY I BORROW THAT ASH TRAY?"
"...ASH TRAY? OKAY..."

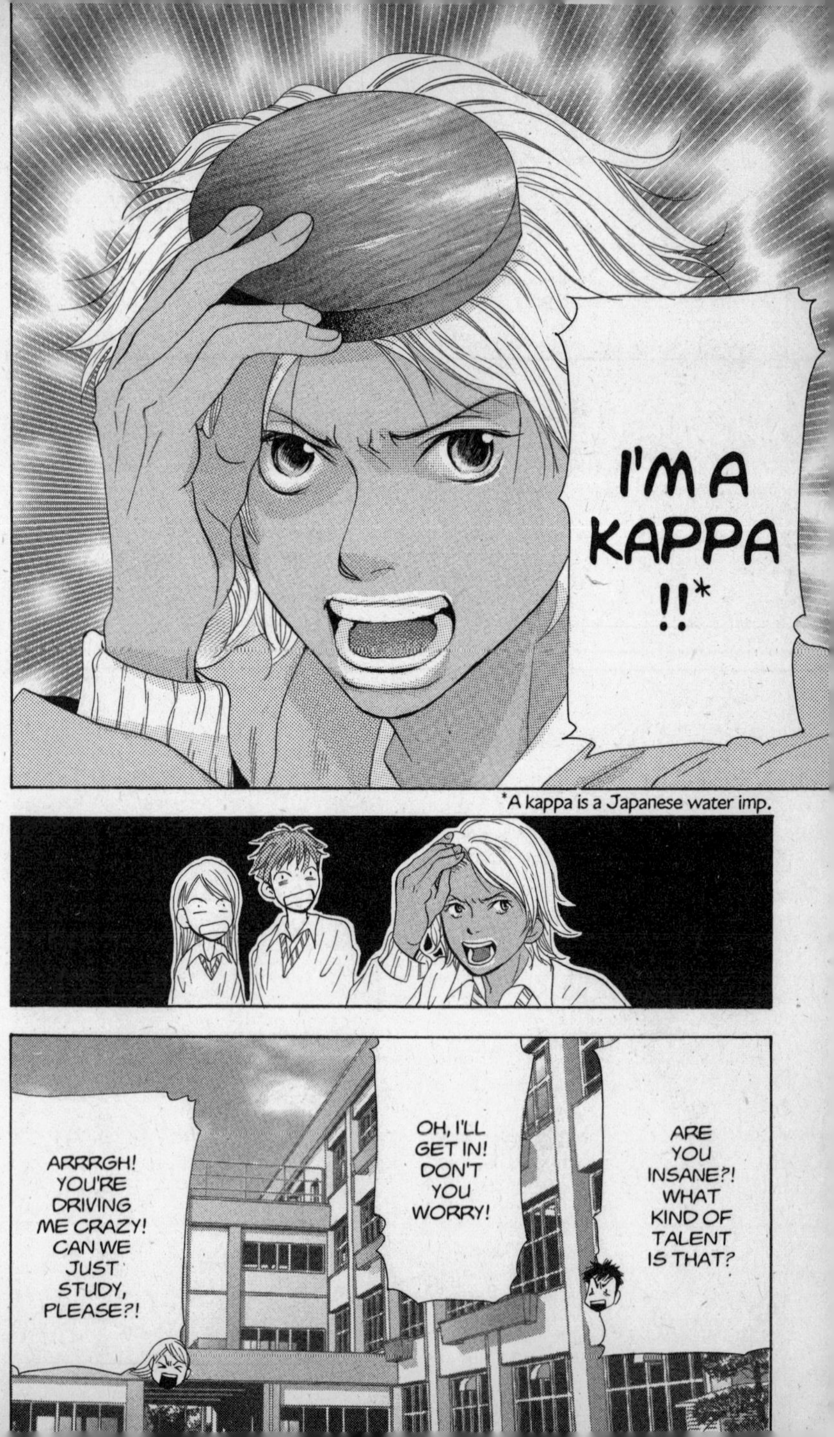
I'M A KAPPA !!*
ARE YOU INSANE?! WHAT KIND OF TALENT IS THAT?
OH, I'LL GET IN! DON'T YOU WORRY!
ARRRGH! YOU'RE DRIVING ME CRAZY! CAN WE JUST STUDY, PLEASE?!

*A kappa is a Japanese water imp.

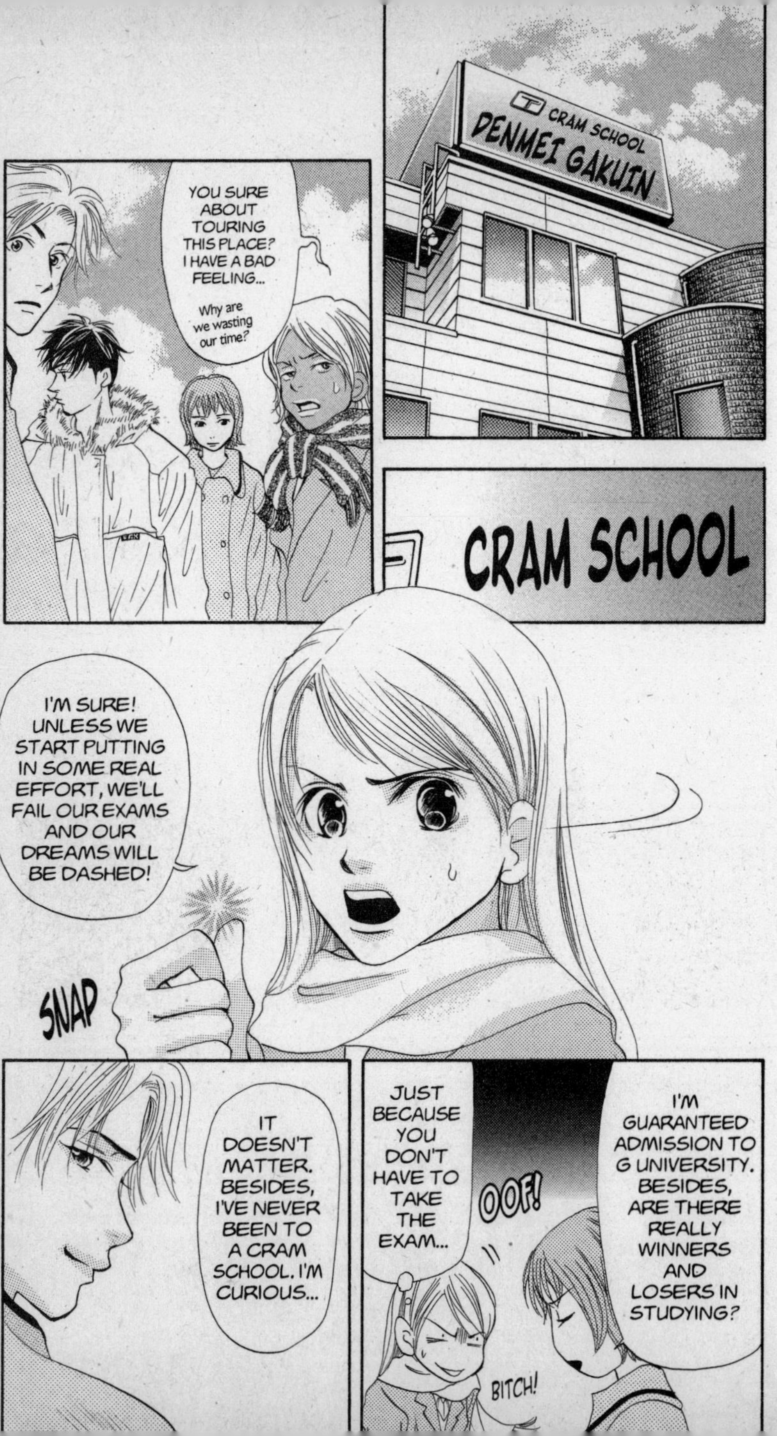
CRAM SCHOOL
DENMEI GAKUIN
CRAM SCHOOL
YOU SURE ABOUT TOURING THIS PLACE? I HAVE A BAD FEELING...
Why are we wasting our time?
I'M SURE! UNLESS WE START PUTTING IN SOME REAL EFFORT, WE'LL FAIL OUR EXAMS AND OUR DREAMS WILL BE DASHED!
SNAP
I'M GUARANTEED ADMISSION TO G UNIVERSITY. BESIDES, ARE THERE REALLY WINNERS AND LOSERS IN STUDYING?
JUST BECAUSE YOU DON'T HAVE TO TAKE THE EXAM...
OOF!
BITCH!
IT DOESN'T MATTER. BESIDES, I'VE NEVER BEEN TO A CRAM SCHOOL. I'M CURIOUS...

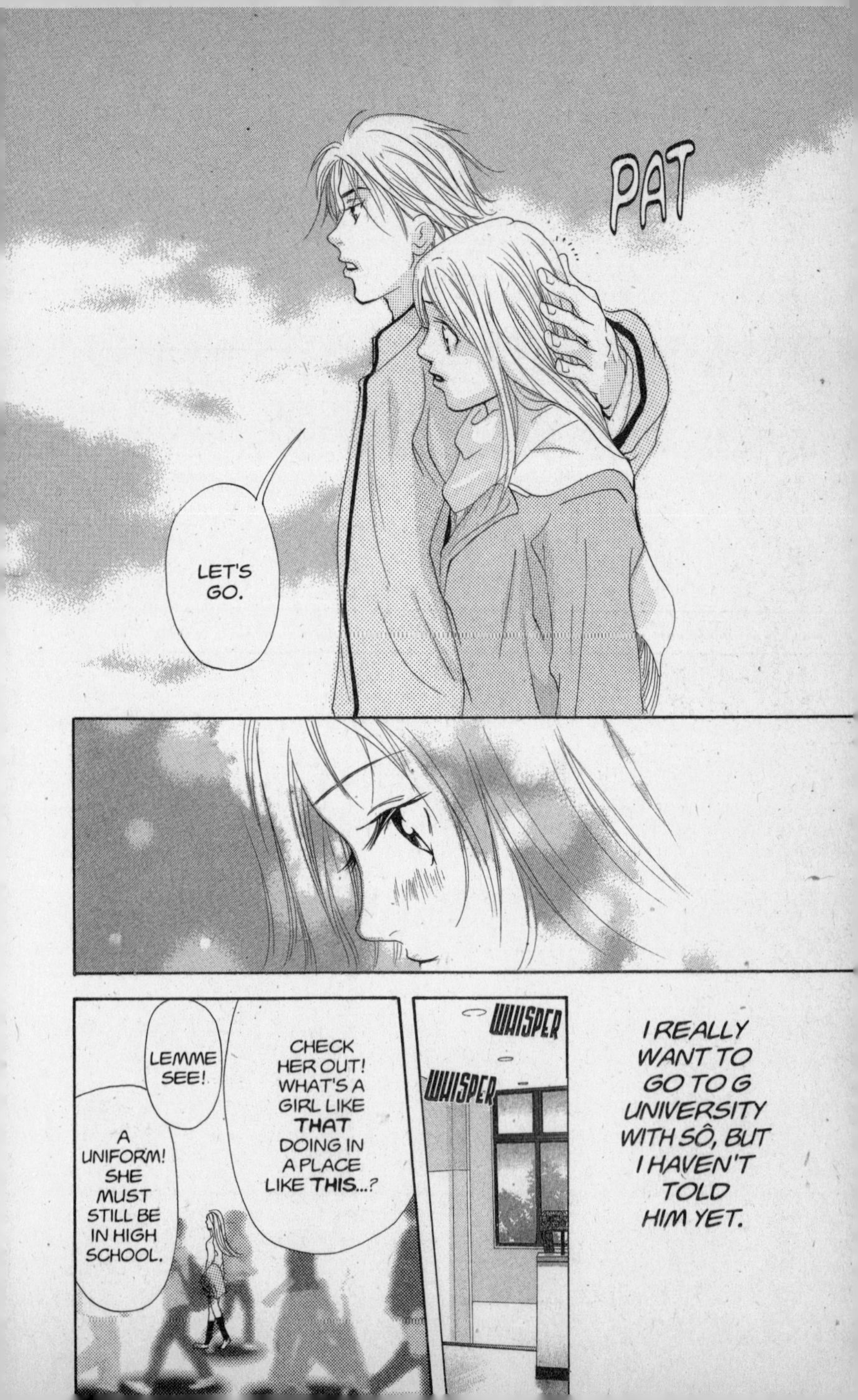
PAT
LET'S GO.
I REALLY WANT TO GO TO G UNIVERSITY WITH SÔ, BUT I HAVEN'T TOLD HIM YET.
WHISPER
WHISPER
CHECK HER OUT! WHAT'S A GIRL LIKE THAT DOING IN A PLACE LIKE THIS...?
LEMME SEE!
A UNIFORM! SHE MUST STILL BE IN HIGH SCHOOL.

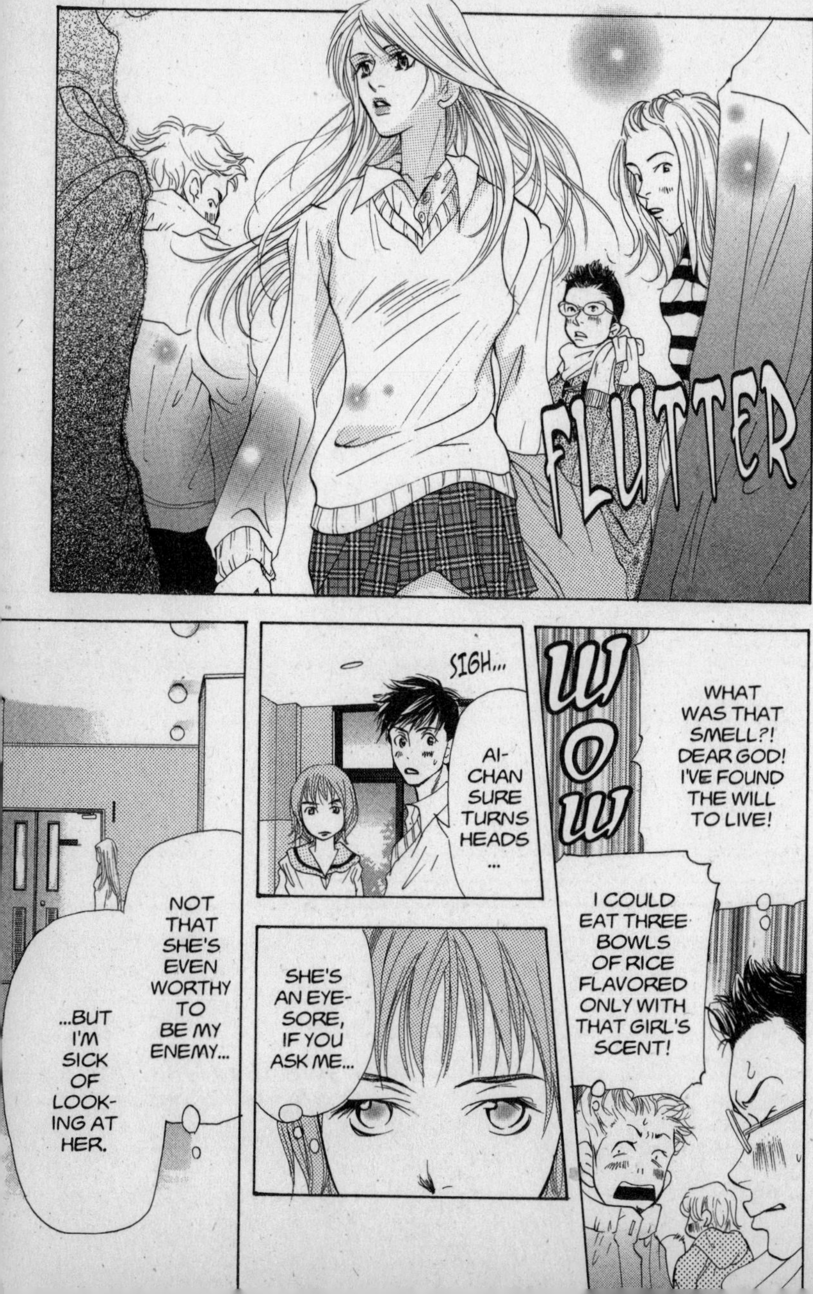
FLUTTER
WOW
WHAT WAS THAT SMELL?! DEAR GOD! I'VE FOUND THE WILL TO LIVE!
I COULD EAT THREE BOWLS OF RICE FLAVORED ONLY WITH THAT GIRL'S SCENT!
SIGH...
AI-CHAN SURE TURNS HEADS...
SHE'S AN EYE-SORE, IF YOU ASK ME...
NOT THAT SHE'S EVEN WORTHY TO BE MY ENEMY...
...BUT I'M SICK OF LOOKING AT HER.

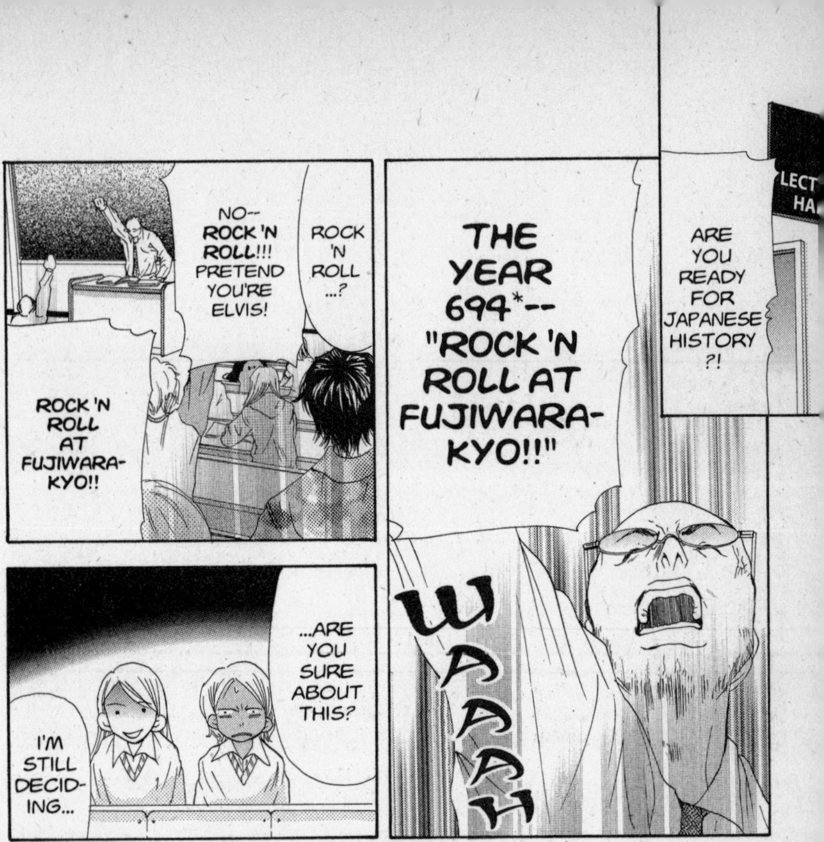
LECT
HA
ARE YOU READY FOR JAPANESE HISTORY?!
THE YEAR 694*-- "ROCK 'N ROLL AT FUJIWARA-KYO!!"
WAAAH
ROCK 'N ROLL ...?
NO-- ROCK 'N ROLL!!! PRETEND YOU'RE ELVIS!
ROCK 'N ROLL AT FUJIWARA-KYO!!
...ARE YOU SURE ABOUT THIS?
I'M STILL DECID-ING...

*In Japanese, "694" sounds sort of similar to "Rock 'n Roll." The teacher is suggesting a mnemonic device

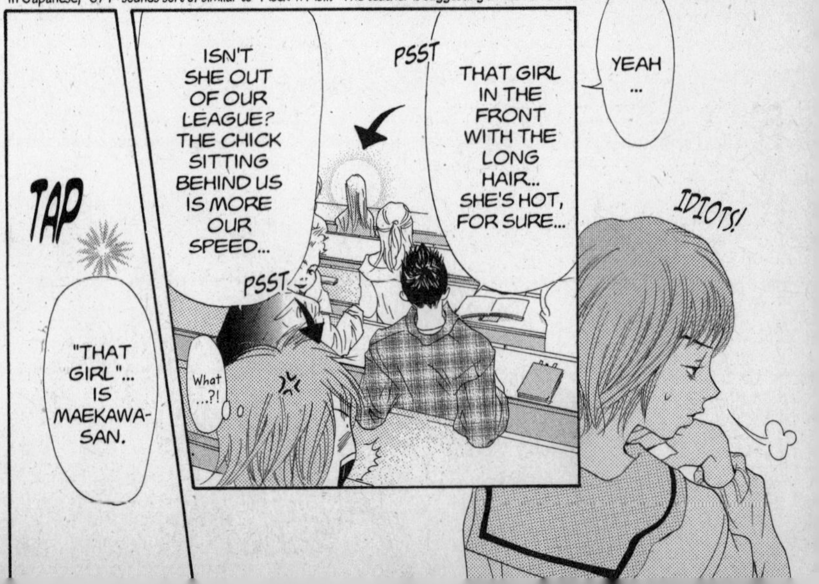
YEAH ...
PSST
THAT GIRL IN THE FRONT WITH THE LONG HAIR... SHE'S HOT, FOR SURE...
ISN'T SHE OUT OF OUR LEAGUE? THE CHICK SITTING BEHIND US IS MORE OUR SPEED...
IDIOTS!
PSST
What ...?!
TAP
"THAT GIRL"... IS MAEKAWA-SAN.

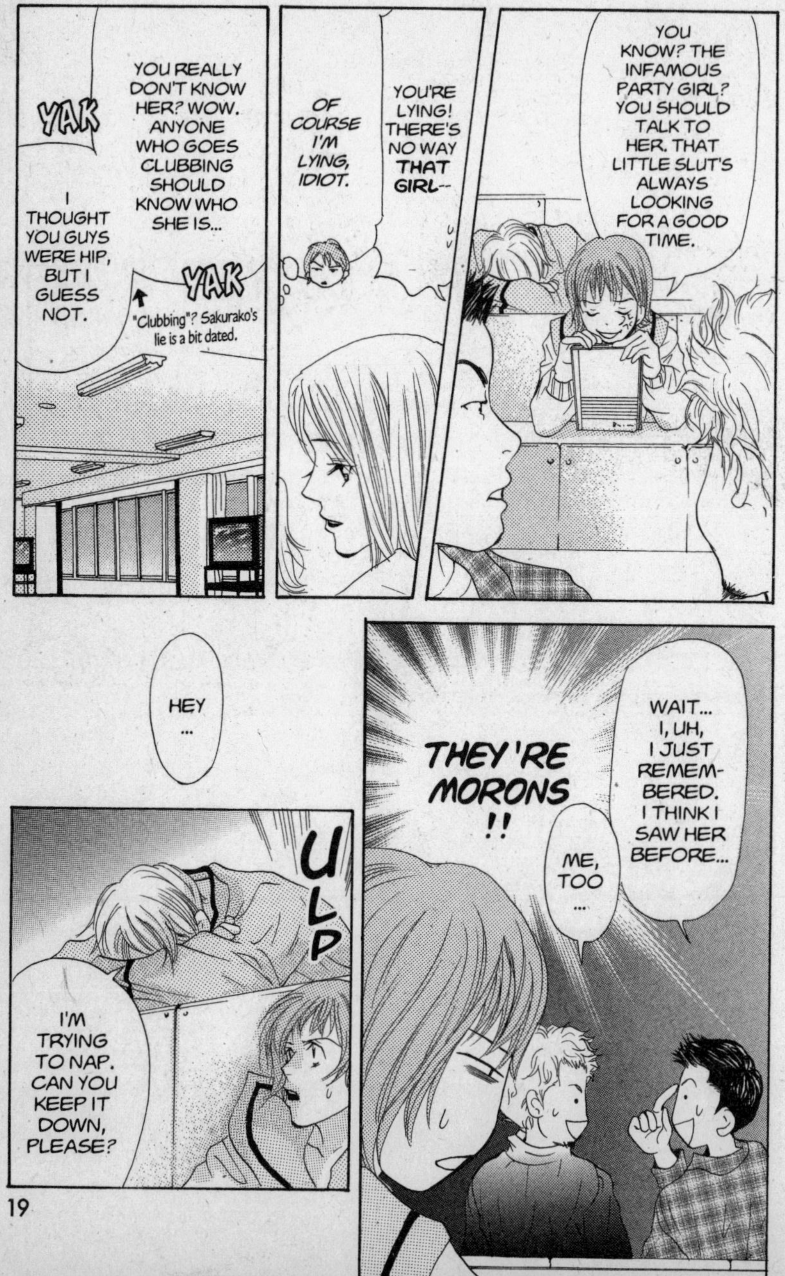
YOU KNOW? THE INFAMOUS PARTY GIRL? YOU SHOULD TALK TO HER. THAT LITTLE SLUT'S ALWAYS LOOKING FOR A GOOD TIME.
YOU'RE LYING! THERE'S NO WAY THAT GIRL--
OF COURSE I'M LYING, IDIOT.
YOU REALLY DON'T KNOW HER? WOW. ANYONE WHO GOES CLUBBING SHOULD KNOW WHO SHE IS...
YAK
I THOUGHT YOU GUYS WERE HIP, BUT I GUESS NOT.
YAK
"Clubbing"? Sakurako's lie is a bit dated.
WAIT... I, UH, I JUST REMEMBERED. I THINK I SAW HER BEFORE...
ME, TOO ...
THEY'RE MORONS !!
HEY ...
ULP
I'M TRYING TO NAP. CAN YOU KEEP IT DOWN, PLEASE?

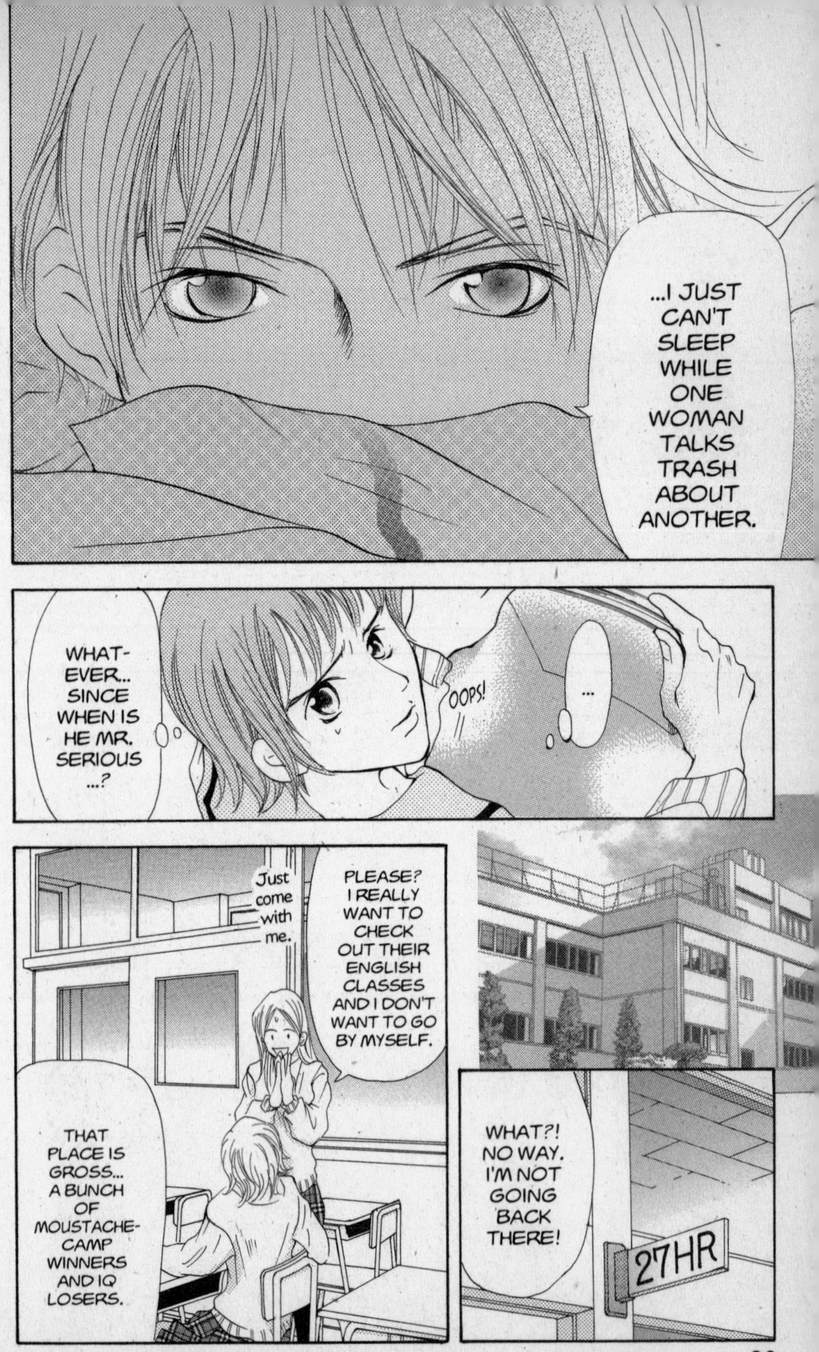
...I JUST CAN'T SLEEP WHILE ONE WOMAN TALKS TRASH ABOUT ANOTHER.
...
OOPS!
WHAT-EVER... SINCE WHEN IS HE MR. SERIOUS ...?
WHAT?! NO WAY. I'M NOT GOING BACK THERE!
27HR
PLEASE? I REALLY WANT TO CHECK OUT THEIR ENGLISH CLASSES AND I DON'T WANT TO GO BY MYSELF.
Just come with me.
THAT PLACE IS GROSS... A BUNCH OF MOUSTACHE-CAMP WINNERS AND IQ LOSERS.

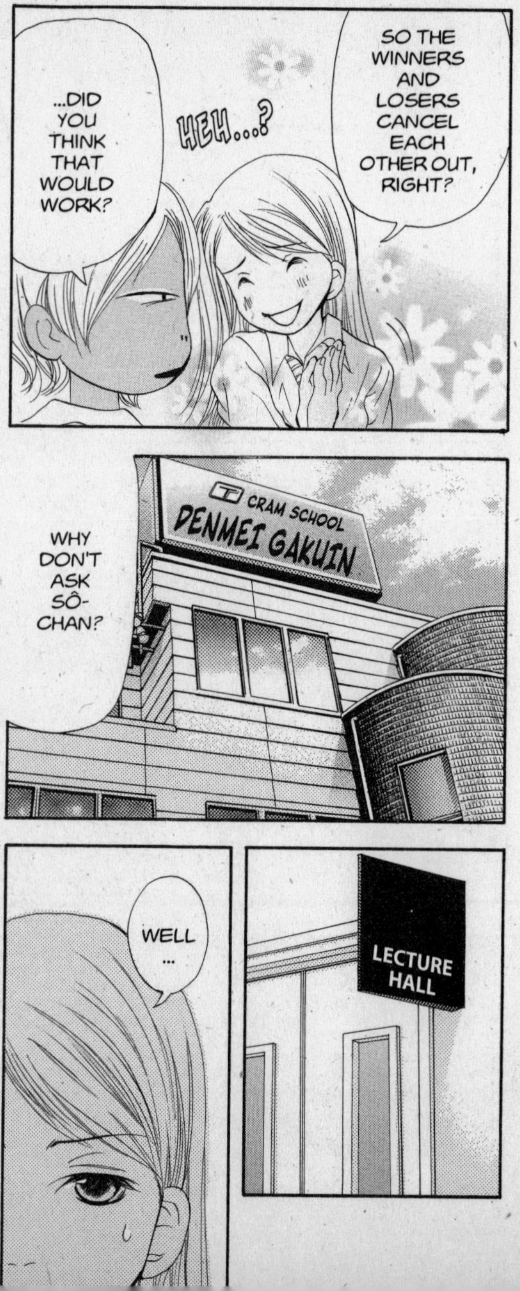
SO THE WINNERS AND LOSERS CANCEL EACH OTHER OUT, RIGHT?
HEH...?
...DID YOU THINK THAT WOULD WORK?
CRAM SCHOOL
DENMEI GAKUIN
WHY DON'T ASK SÔ-CHAN?
LECTURE HALL
WELL ...

Doubt!!
Backstory

Let me take this opportunity to tell you how Doubt!! came to be (in its original format). It all started like this...

(Part 1)

I put together several concepts to pitch to my editor. I actually didn't think "DOUBT!!" was the strongest of the bunch and I kind of hoped it wouldn't get picked...

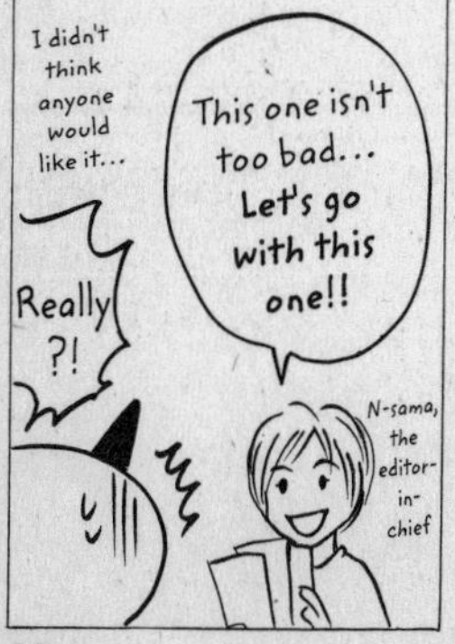
This one isn't too bad... Let's go with this one!!
N-sama, the editor-in-chief
Really ?!
I didn't think anyone would like it...

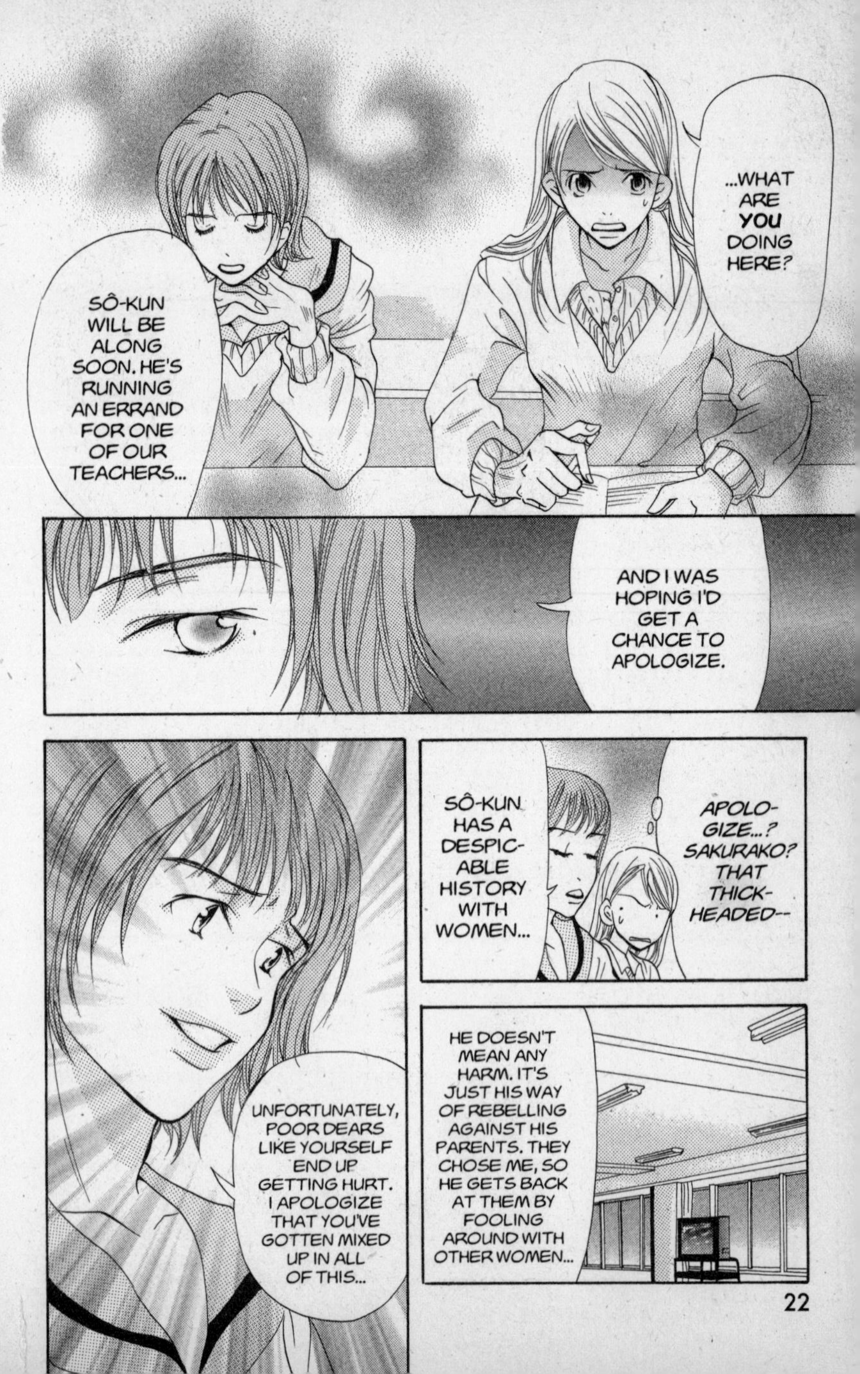

...WHAT ARE **YOU** DOING HERE?
SÔ-KUN WILL BE ALONG SOON. HE'S RUNNING AN ERRAND FOR ONE OF OUR TEACHERS...
AND I WAS HOPING I'D GET A CHANCE TO APOLOGIZE.
APOLOGIZE...? SAKURAKO? THAT THICK-HEADED--
SÔ-KUN HAS A DESPICABLE HISTORY WITH WOMEN...
HE DOESN'T MEAN ANY HARM. IT'S JUST HIS WAY OF REBELLING AGAINST HIS PARENTS. THEY CHOSE ME, SO HE GETS BACK AT THEM BY FOOLING AROUND WITH OTHER WOMEN...
UNFORTUNATELY, POOR DEARS LIKE YOURSELF END UP GETTING HURT. I APOLOGIZE THAT YOU'VE GOTTEN MIXED UP IN ALL OF THIS...

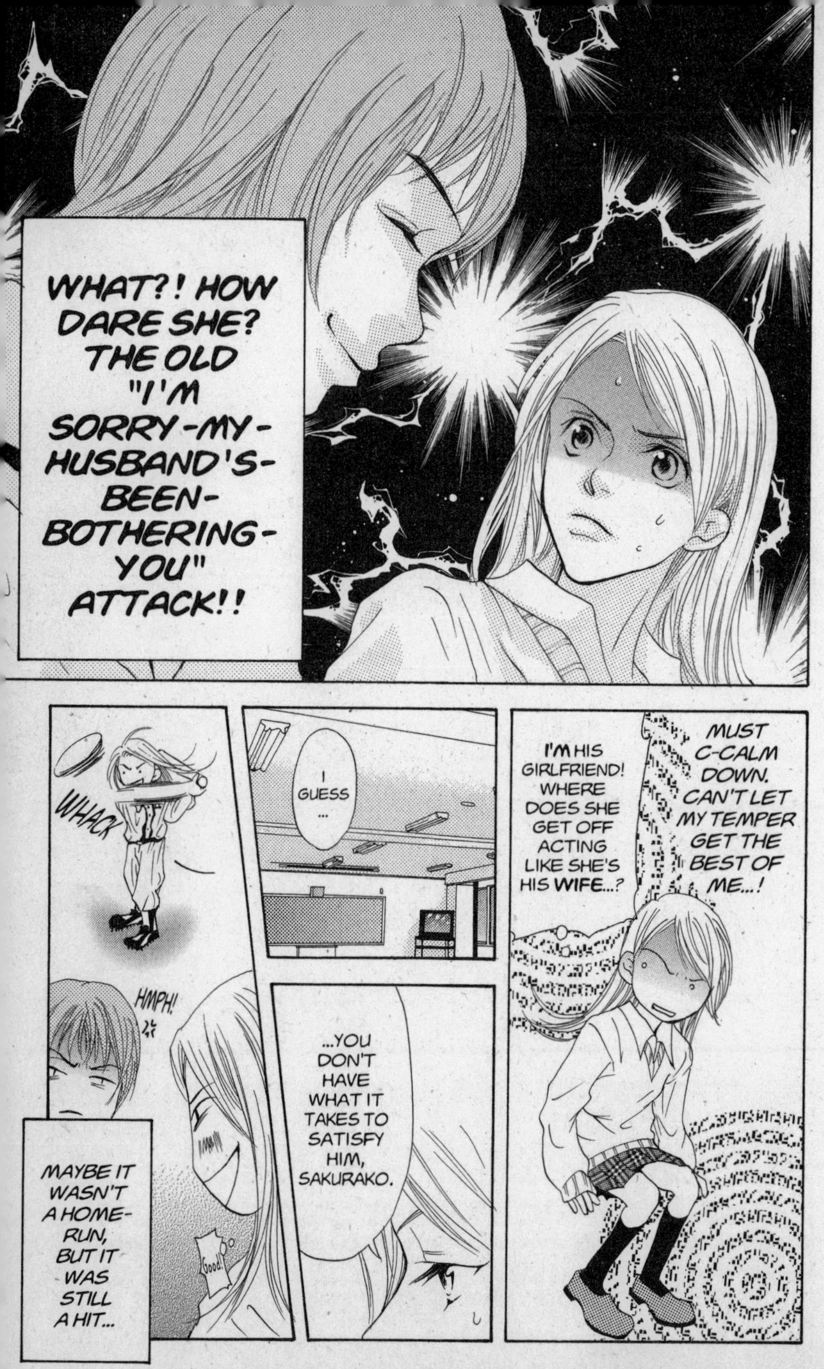
WHAT?! HOW DARE SHE? THE OLD "I'M SORRY-MY-HUSBAND'S-BEEN-BOTHERING-YOU" ATTACK!!
MUST C-CALM DOWN. CAN'T LET MY TEMPER GET THE BEST OF ME...!
I'M HIS GIRLFRIEND! WHERE DOES SHE GET OFF ACTING LIKE SHE'S HIS WIFE...?
I GUESS...
...YOU DON'T HAVE WHAT IT TAKES TO SATISFY HIM, SAKURAKO.
WHACK
HMPH!
Good!
MAYBE IT WASN'T A HOME-RUN, BUT IT WAS STILL A HIT...

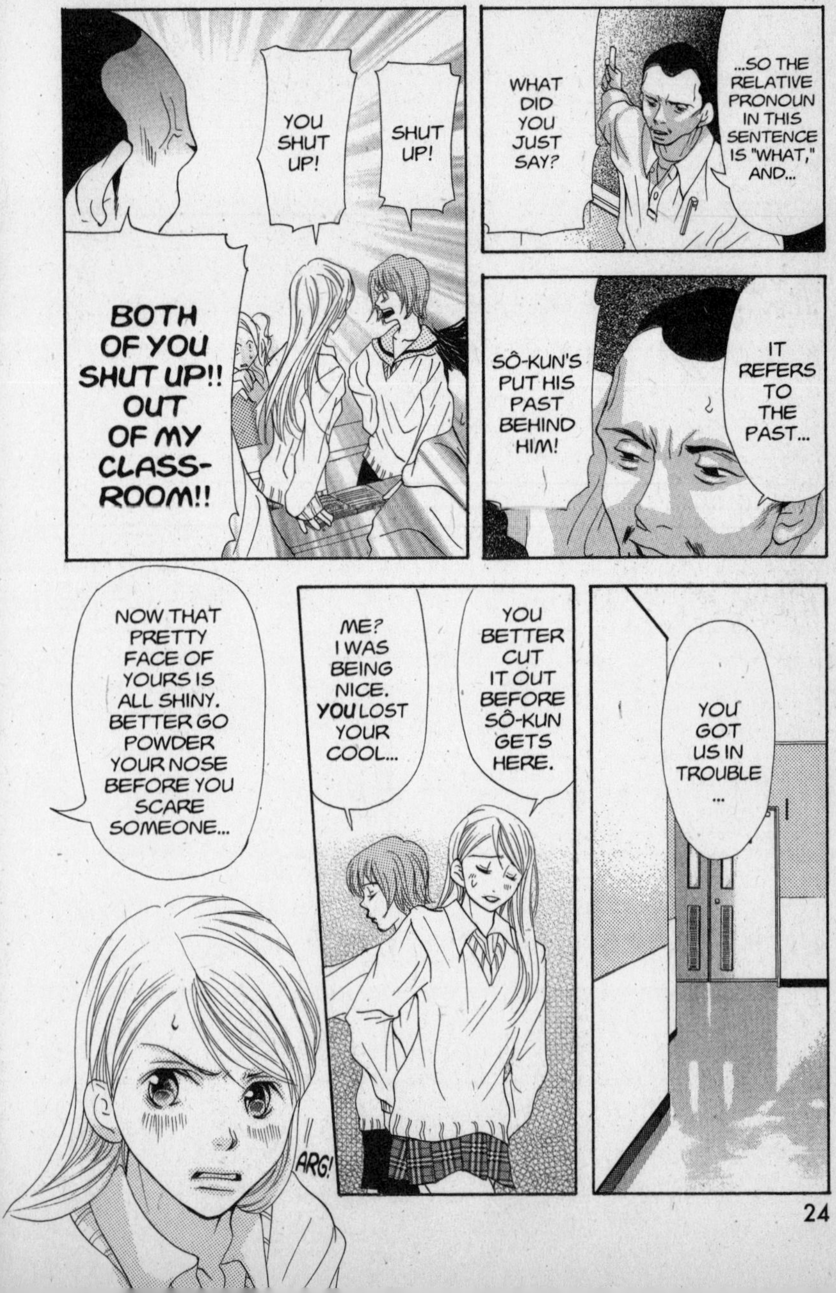
...SO THE RELATIVE PRONOUN IN THIS SENTENCE IS "WHAT," AND...
WHAT DID YOU JUST SAY?
IT REFERS TO THE PAST...
SÔ-KUN'S PUT HIS PAST BEHIND HIM!
SHUT UP!
YOU SHUT UP!
BOTH OF YOU SHUT UP!! OUT OF MY CLASS-ROOM!!
YOU GOT US IN TROUBLE ...
YOU BETTER CUT IT OUT BEFORE SÔ-KUN GETS HERE.
ME? I WAS BEING NICE. **YOU** LOST YOUR COOL...
NOW THAT PRETTY FACE OF YOURS IS ALL SHINY. BETTER GO POWDER YOUR NOSE BEFORE YOU SCARE SOMEONE...
ARG!

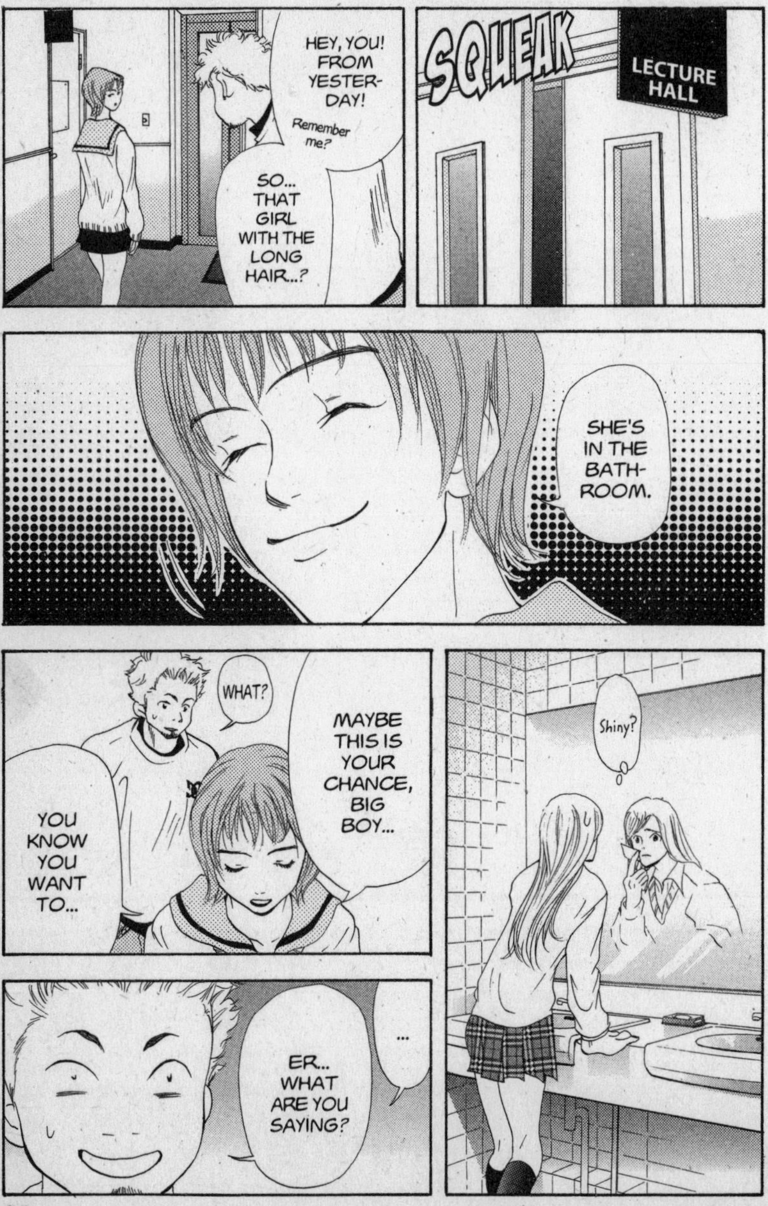
SQUEAK
LECTURE HALL
HEY, YOU! FROM YESTER-DAY!
Remember me?
SO... THAT GIRL WITH THE LONG HAIR...?
SHE'S IN THE BATH-ROOM.
Shiny?
MAYBE THIS IS YOUR CHANCE, BIG BOY...
WHAT?
YOU KNOW YOU WANT TO...
...
ER... WHAT ARE YOU SAYING?

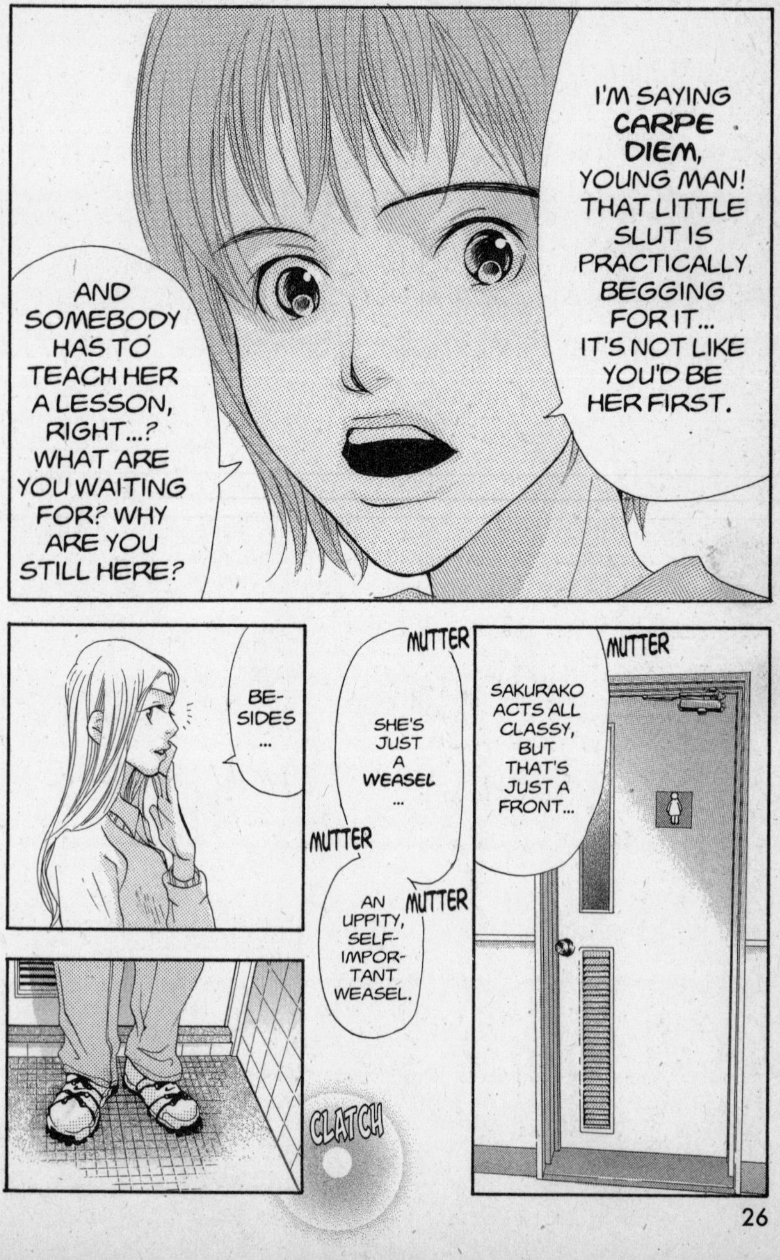
I'M SAYING **CARPE DIEM,** YOUNG MAN! THAT LITTLE SLUT IS PRACTICALLY BEGGING FOR IT... IT'S NOT LIKE YOU'D BE HER FIRST.
AND SOMEBODY HAS TO TEACH HER A LESSON, RIGHT...? WHAT ARE YOU WAITING FOR? WHY ARE YOU STILL HERE?
MUTTER
SAKURAKO ACTS ALL CLASSY, BUT THAT'S JUST A FRONT...
MUTTER
SHE'S JUST A **WEASEL** ...
MUTTER
MUTTER
AN UPPITY, SELF-IMPORTANT WEASEL.
BE-SIDES ...
CLATCH

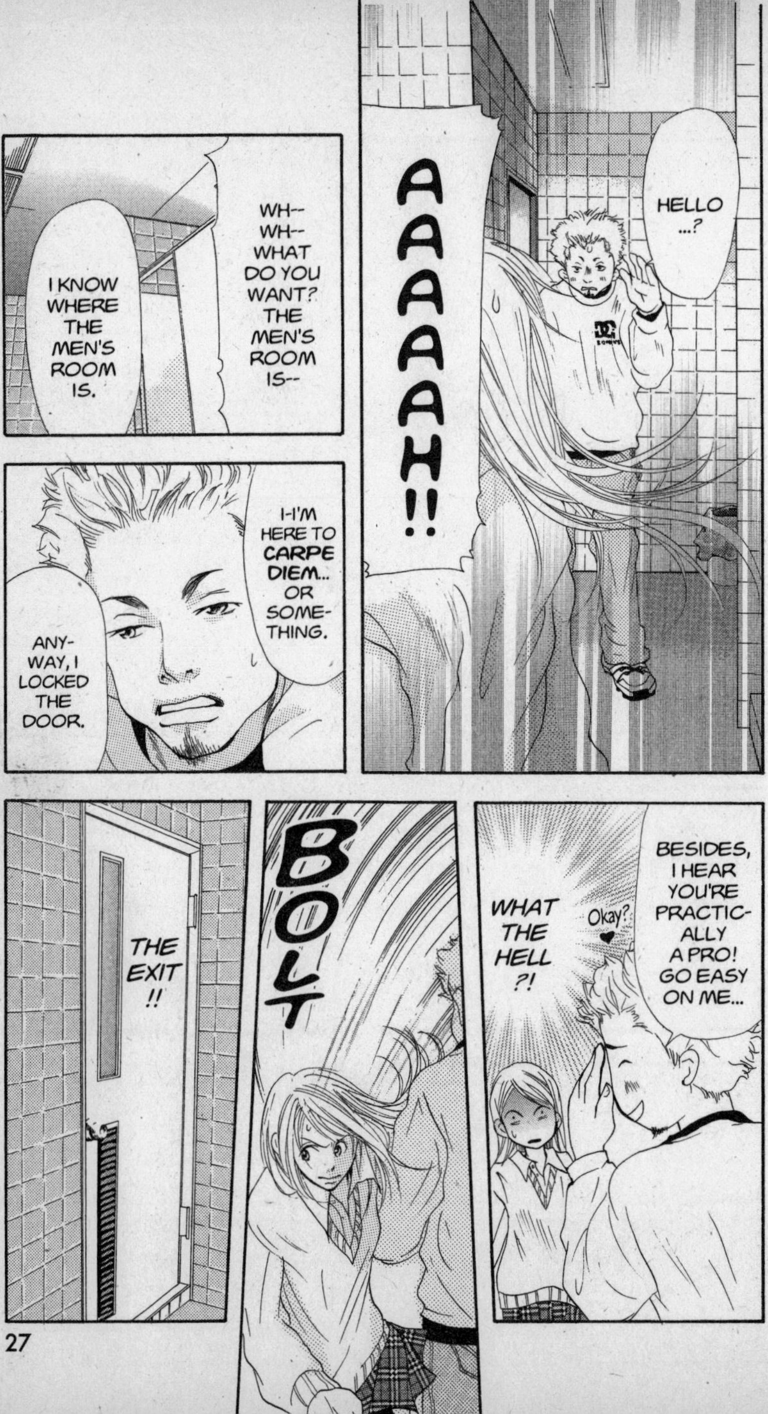
HELLO ...?
AAAAAH!!
WH-- WH-- WHAT DO YOU WANT? THE MEN'S ROOM IS--
I KNOW WHERE THE MEN'S ROOM IS.
I-I'M HERE TO CARPE DIEM... OR SOMETHING.
ANY-WAY, I LOCKED THE DOOR.
BESIDES, I HEAR YOU'RE PRACTIC-ALLY A PRO! GO EASY ON ME...
Okay? ♥
WHAT THE HELL ?!
BOLT
THE EXIT !!

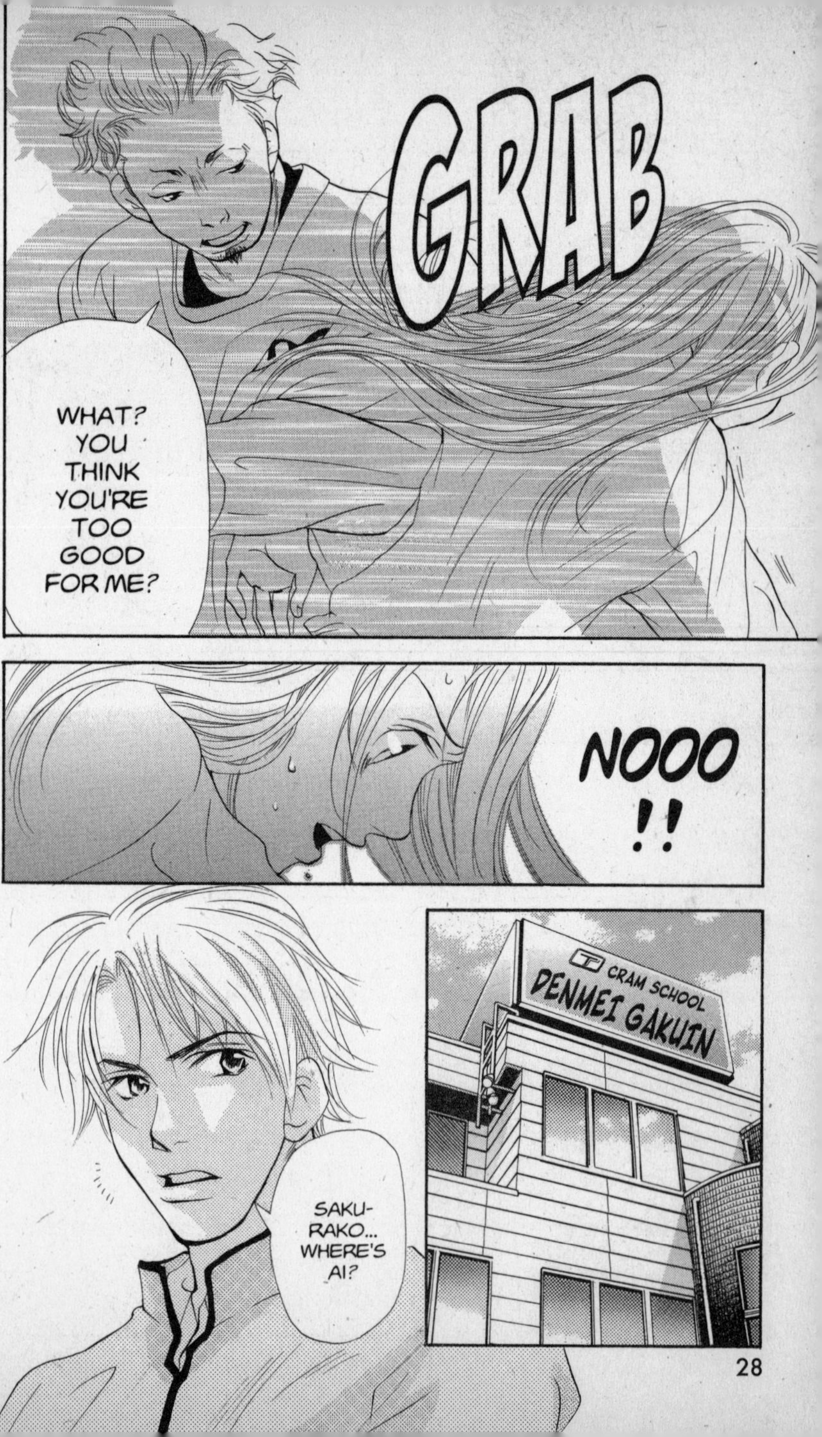
GRAB
WHAT? YOU THINK YOU'RE TOO GOOD FOR ME?
NOOO!!
CRAM SCHOOL DENMEI GAKUIN
SAKU-RAKO... WHERE'S AI?

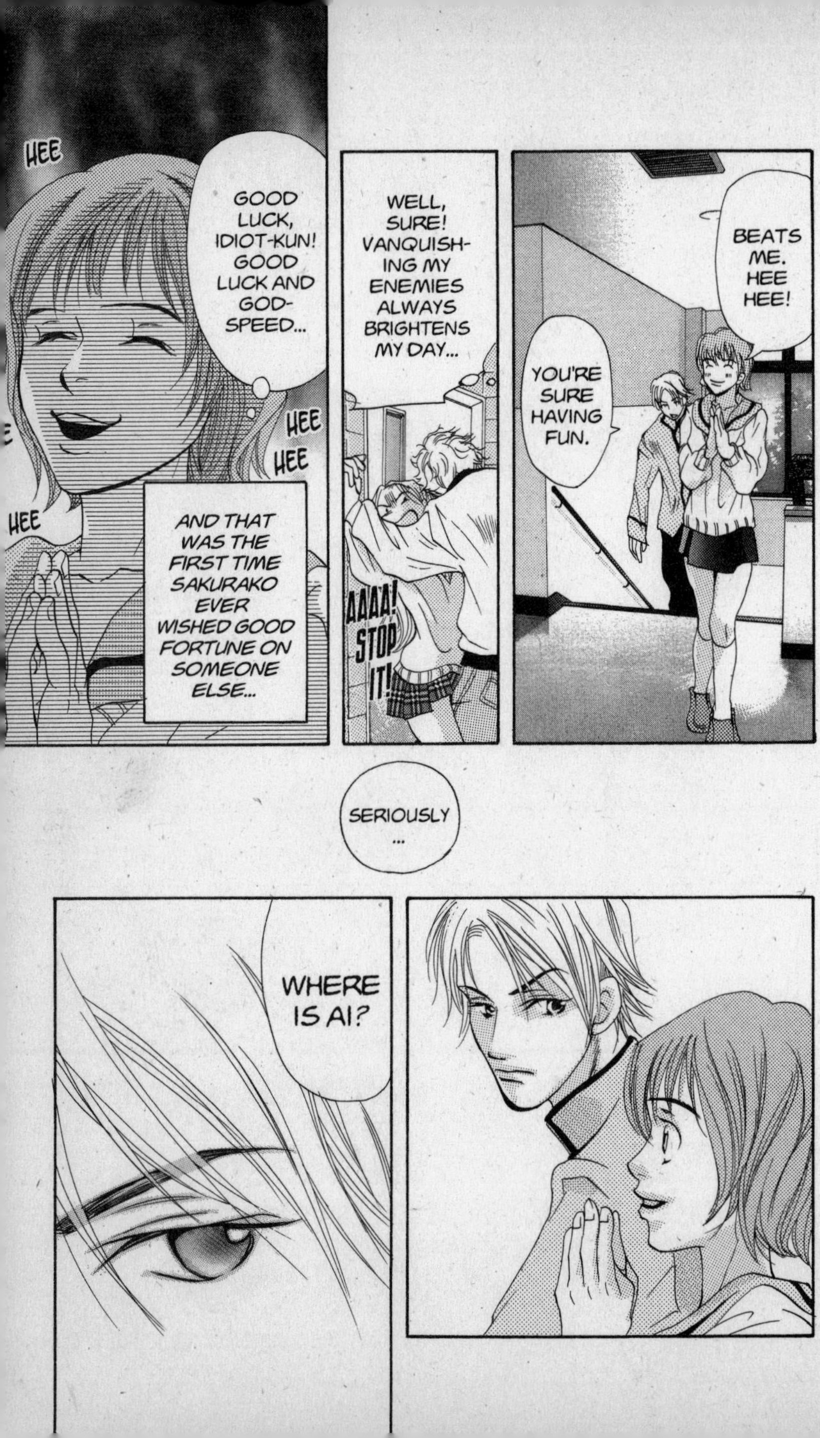

BEATS ME. HEE HEE!
YOU'RE SURE HAVING FUN.
WELL, SURE! VANQUISHING MY ENEMIES ALWAYS BRIGHTENS MY DAY...
AAAA! STOP IT!
HEE
GOOD LUCK, IDIOT-KUN! GOOD LUCK AND GOD-SPEED...
HEE HEE
HEE
AND THAT WAS THE FIRST TIME SAKURAKO EVER WISHED GOOD FORTUNE ON SOMEONE ELSE...
SERIOUSLY...
WHERE IS AI?

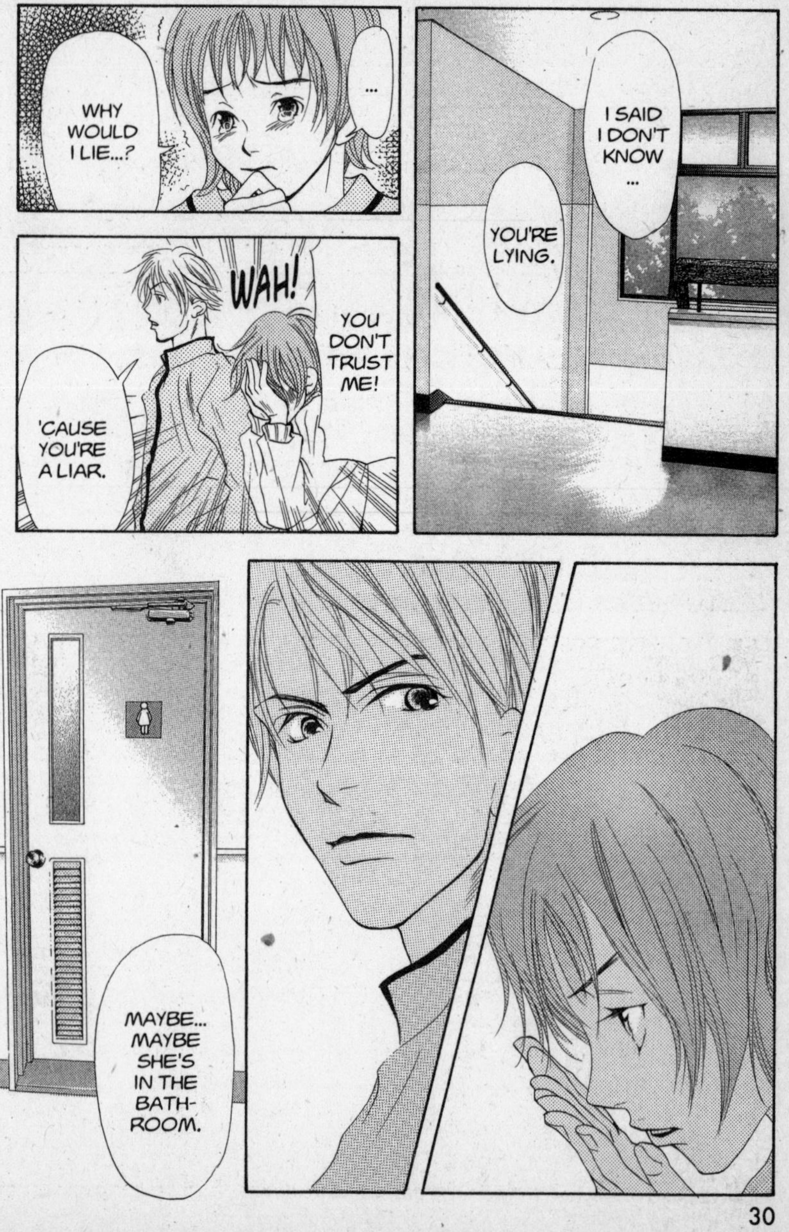
I SAID I DON'T KNOW ...
YOU'RE LYING.
...
WHY WOULD I LIE...?
WAH!
YOU DON'T TRUST ME!
'CAUSE YOU'RE A LIAR.
MAYBE... MAYBE SHE'S IN THE BATH-ROOM.

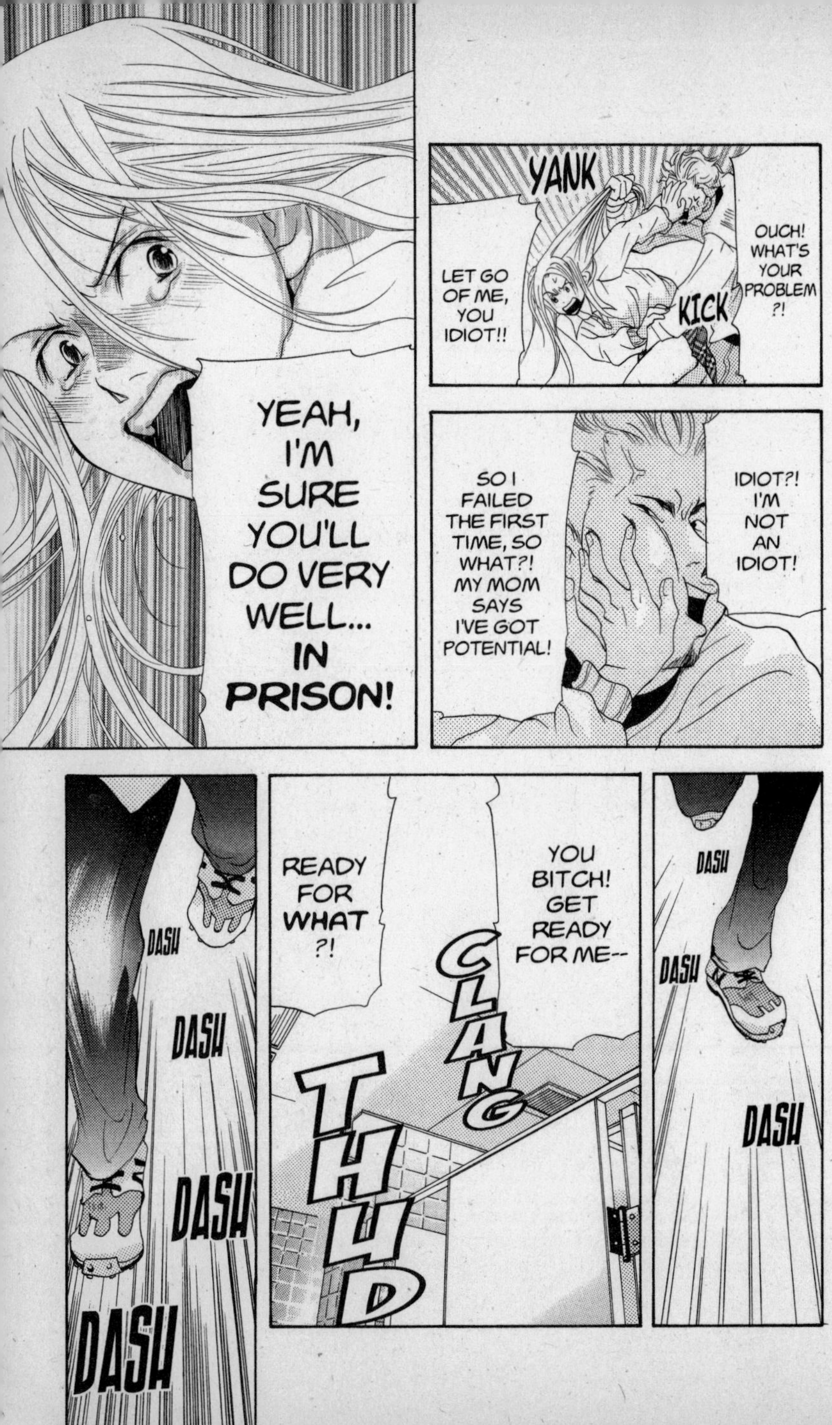
YANK
OUCH! WHAT'S YOUR PROBLEM?!
LET GO OF ME, YOU IDIOT!!
KICK
IDIOT?! I'M NOT AN IDIOT!
SO I FAILED THE FIRST TIME, SO WHAT?! MY MOM SAYS I'VE GOT POTENTIAL!
YEAH, I'M SURE YOU'LL DO VERY WELL... IN PRISON!
DASH
DASH
DASH
YOU BITCH! GET READY FOR ME--
READY FOR WHAT?!
CLANG
THUD
DASH
DASH
DASH
DASH

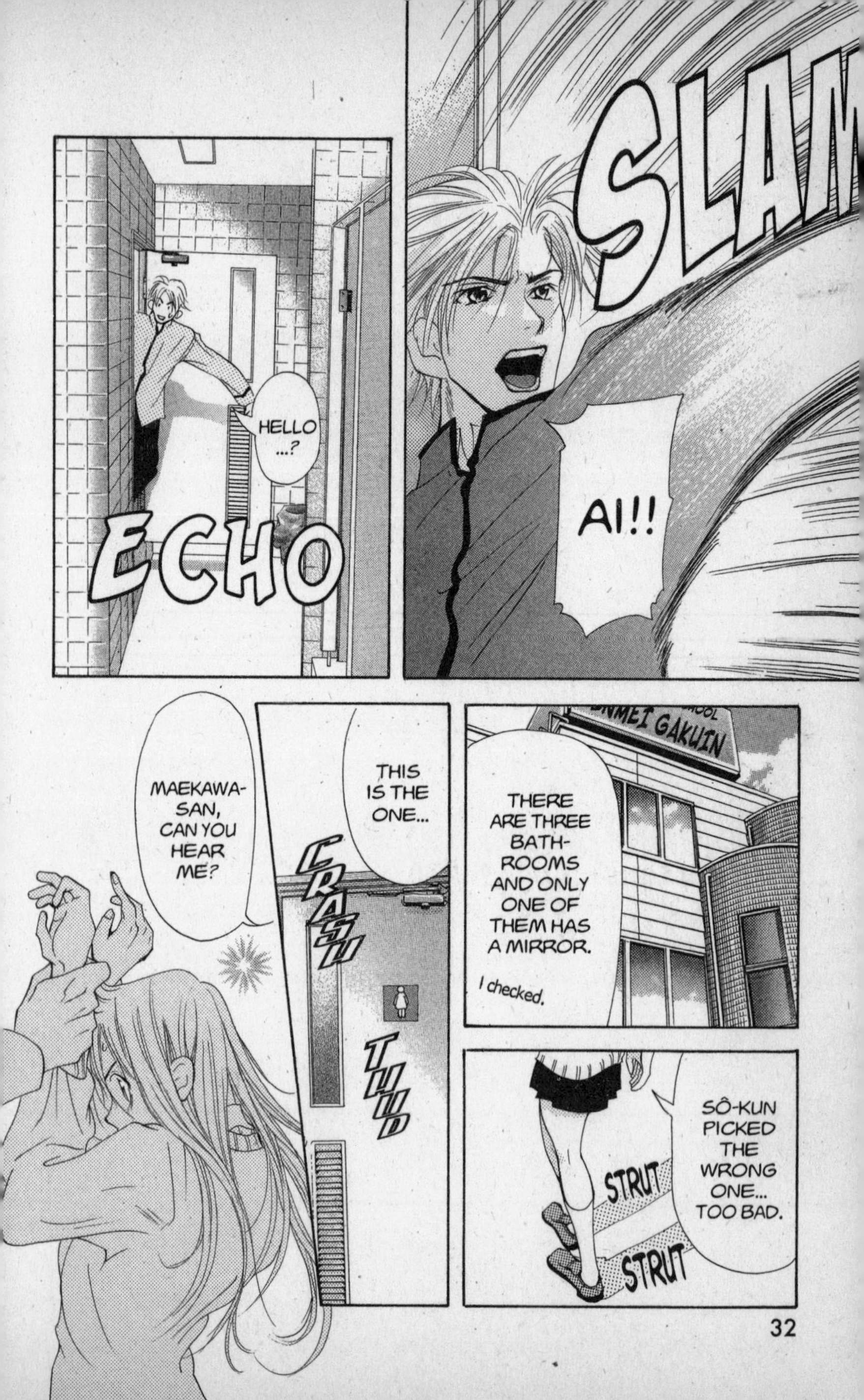
SLAM
AI!!
HELLO ...?
ECHO
THERE ARE THREE BATH-ROOMS AND ONLY ONE OF THEM HAS A MIRROR.
I checked.
SÔ-KUN PICKED THE WRONG ONE... TOO BAD.
STRUT
STRUT
THIS IS THE ONE...
CRASH
THUD
MAEKAWA-SAN, CAN YOU HEAR ME?

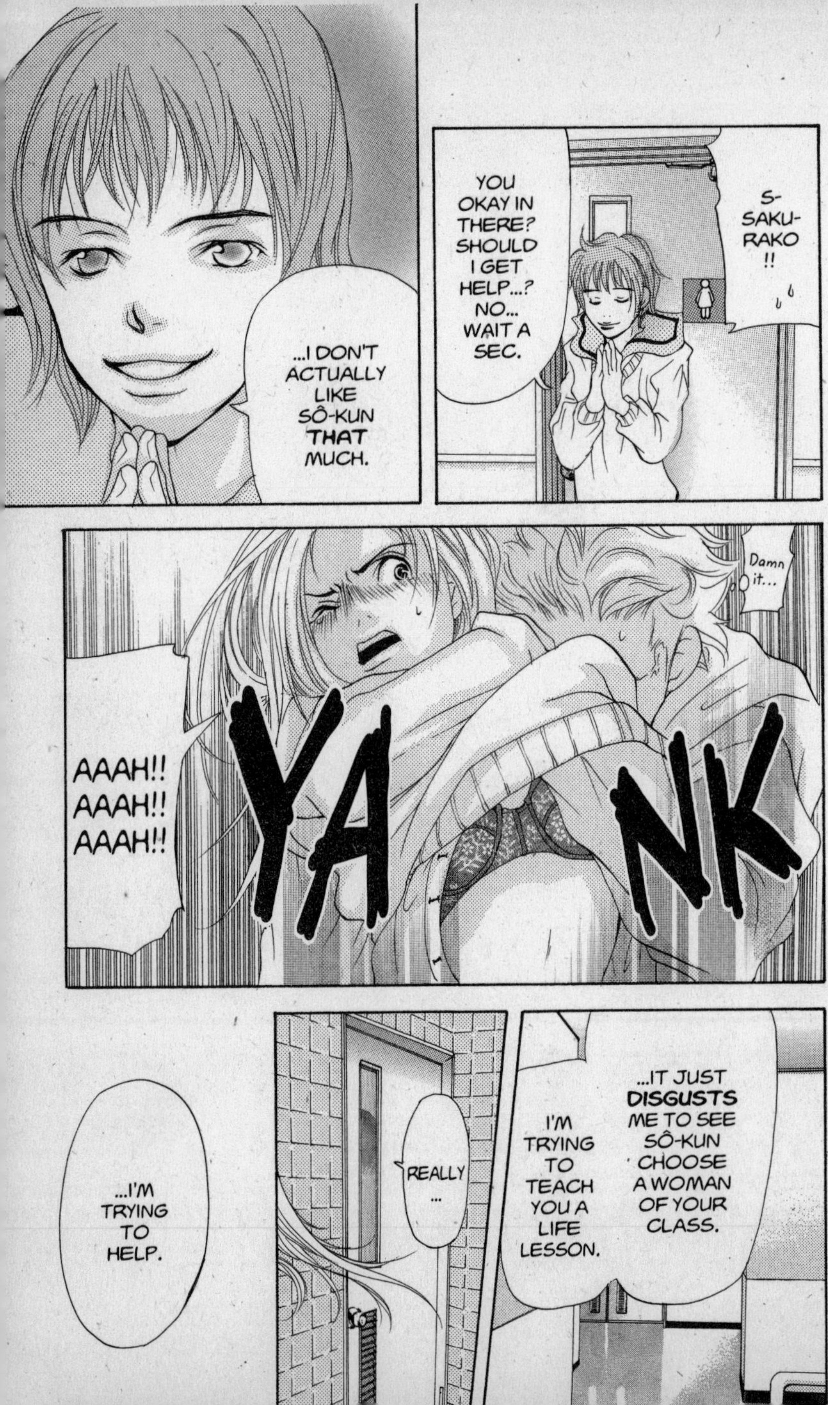
S-SAKURAKO!!
YOU OKAY IN THERE? SHOULD I GET HELP...? NO... WAIT A SEC.
...I DON'T ACTUALLY LIKE SÔ-KUN **THAT** MUCH.
Damn it...
YANK
AAAH!! AAAH!! AAAH!!
...IT JUST **DISGUSTS** ME TO SEE SÔ-KUN CHOOSE A WOMAN OF YOUR CLASS.
I'M TRYING TO TEACH YOU A LIFE LESSON.
REALLY...
...I'M TRYING TO HELP.

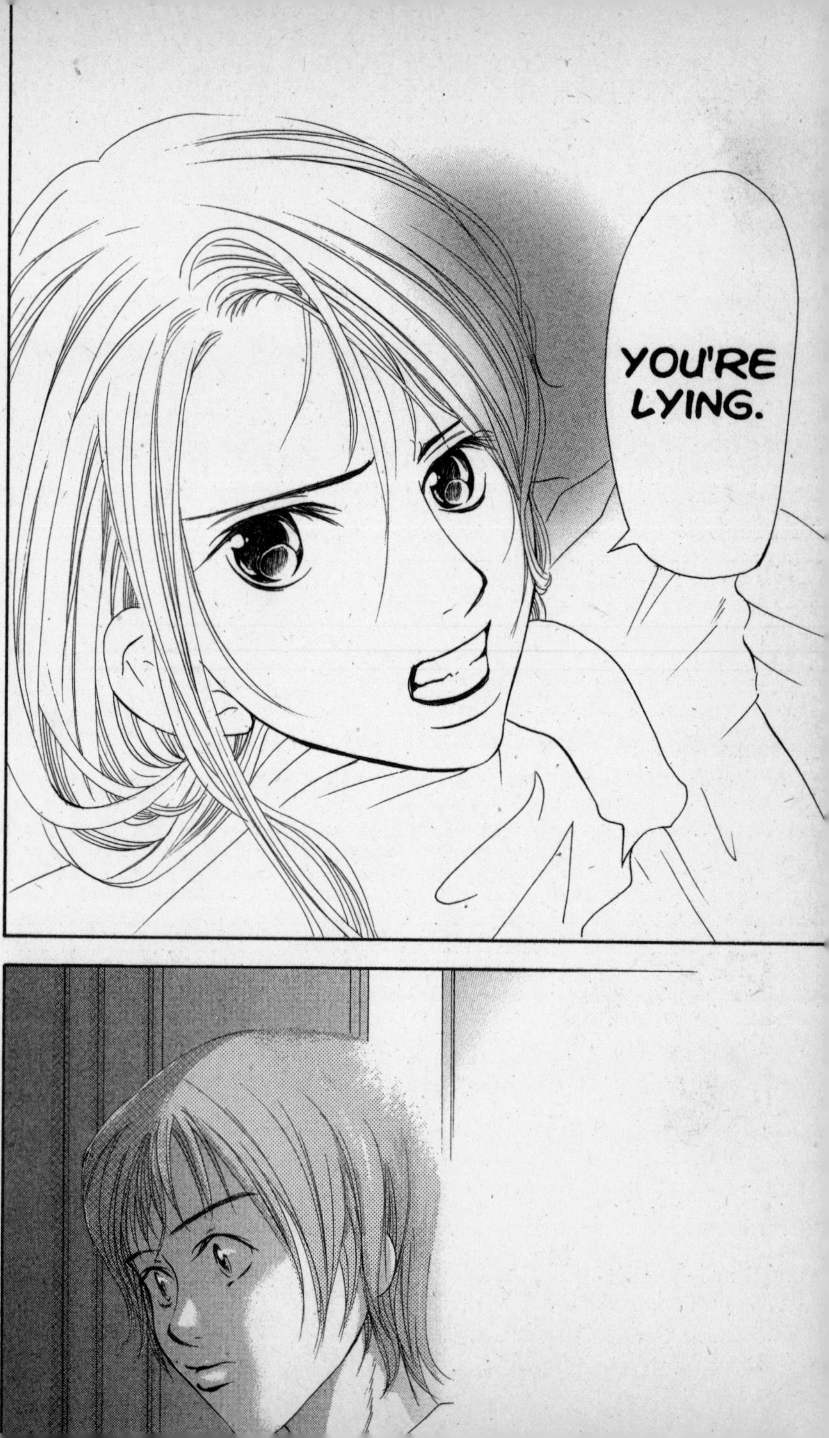
YOU'RE LYING.

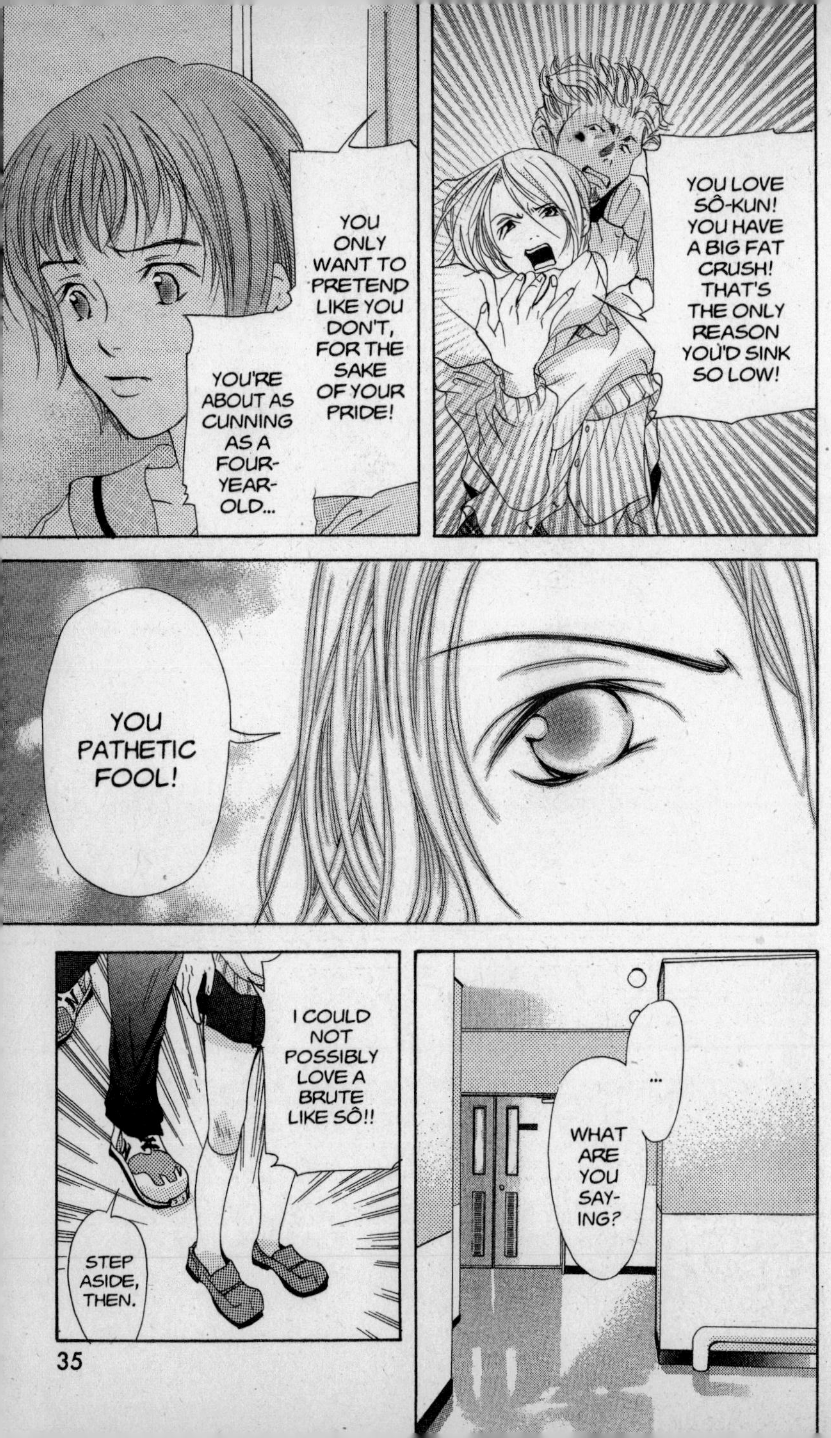
YOU LOVE SÔ-KUN! YOU HAVE A BIG FAT CRUSH! THAT'S THE ONLY REASON YOU'D SINK SO LOW!
YOU ONLY WANT TO PRETEND LIKE YOU DON'T, FOR THE SAKE OF YOUR PRIDE!
YOU'RE ABOUT AS CUNNING AS A FOUR-YEAR-OLD...
YOU PATHETIC FOOL!
...
WHAT ARE YOU SAY-ING?
I COULD NOT POSSIBLY LOVE A BRUTE LIKE SÔ!!
STEP ASIDE, THEN.

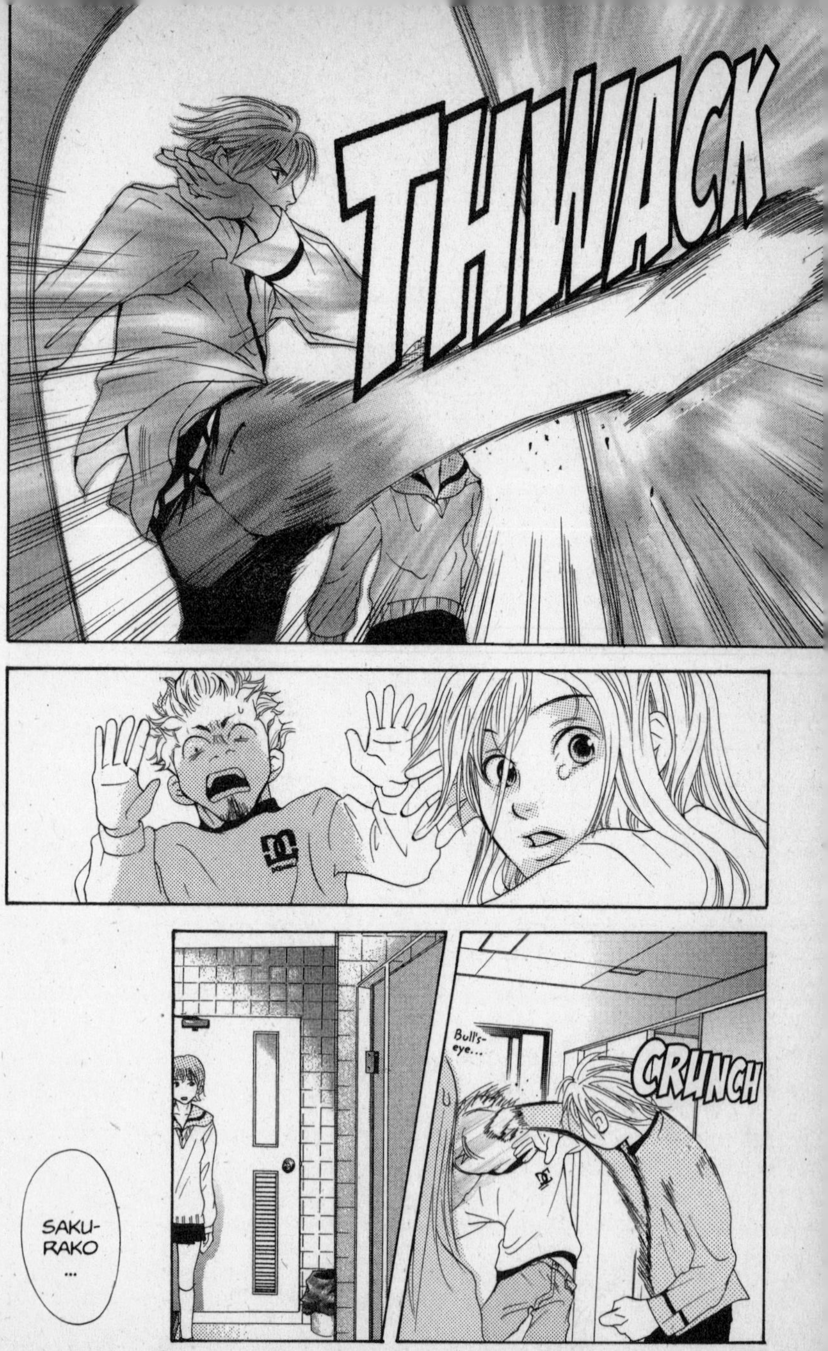
THWACK
CRUNCH
Bull's-eye...
SAKU-RAKO ...

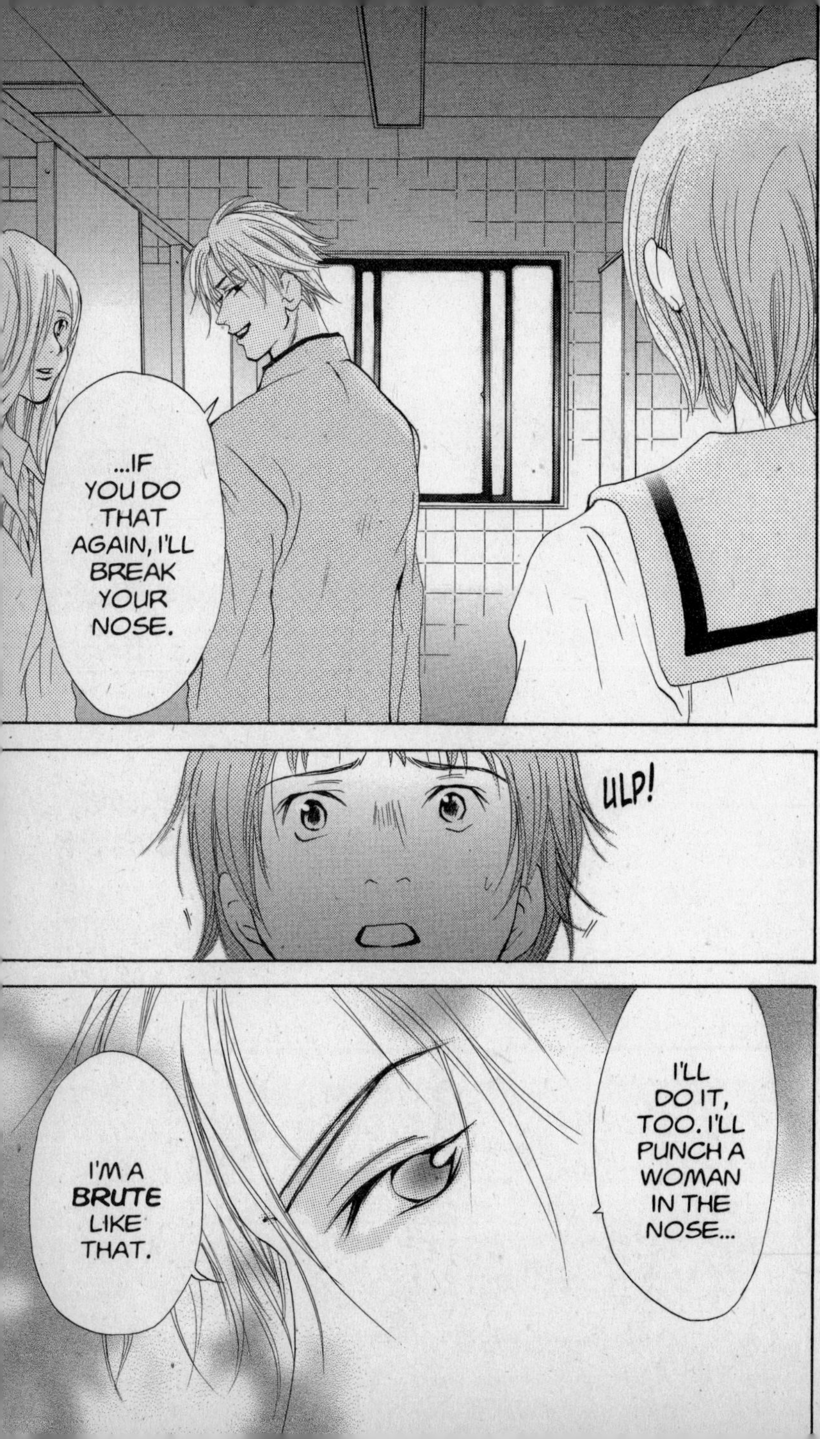
...IF YOU DO THAT AGAIN, I'LL BREAK YOUR NOSE.
ULP!
I'LL DO IT, TOO. I'LL PUNCH A WOMAN IN THE NOSE...
I'M A **BRUTE** LIKE THAT.

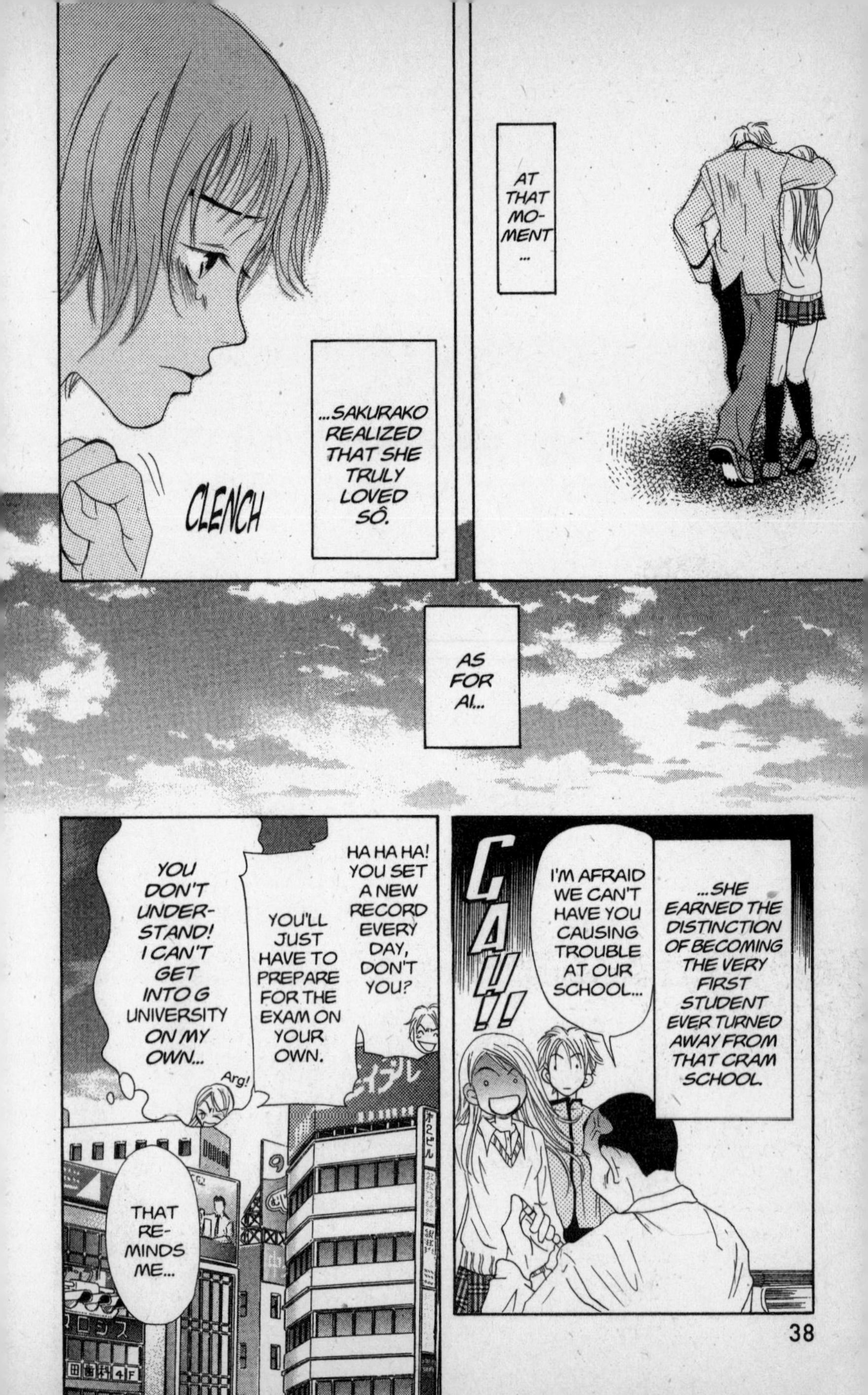
AT THAT MOMENT...
...SAKURAKO REALIZED THAT SHE TRULY LOVED SÔ.
CLENCH
AS FOR AI...
...SHE EARNED THE DISTINCTION OF BECOMING THE VERY FIRST STUDENT EVER TURNED AWAY FROM THAT CRAM SCHOOL.
CAU!!
I'M AFRAID WE CAN'T HAVE YOU CAUSING TROUBLE AT OUR SCHOOL...
HA HA HA! YOU SET A NEW RECORD EVERY DAY, DON'T YOU?
YOU'LL JUST HAVE TO PREPARE FOR THE EXAM ON YOUR OWN.
YOU DON'T UNDERSTAND! I CAN'T GET INTO G UNIVERSITY ON MY OWN...
Arg!
THAT REMINDS ME...

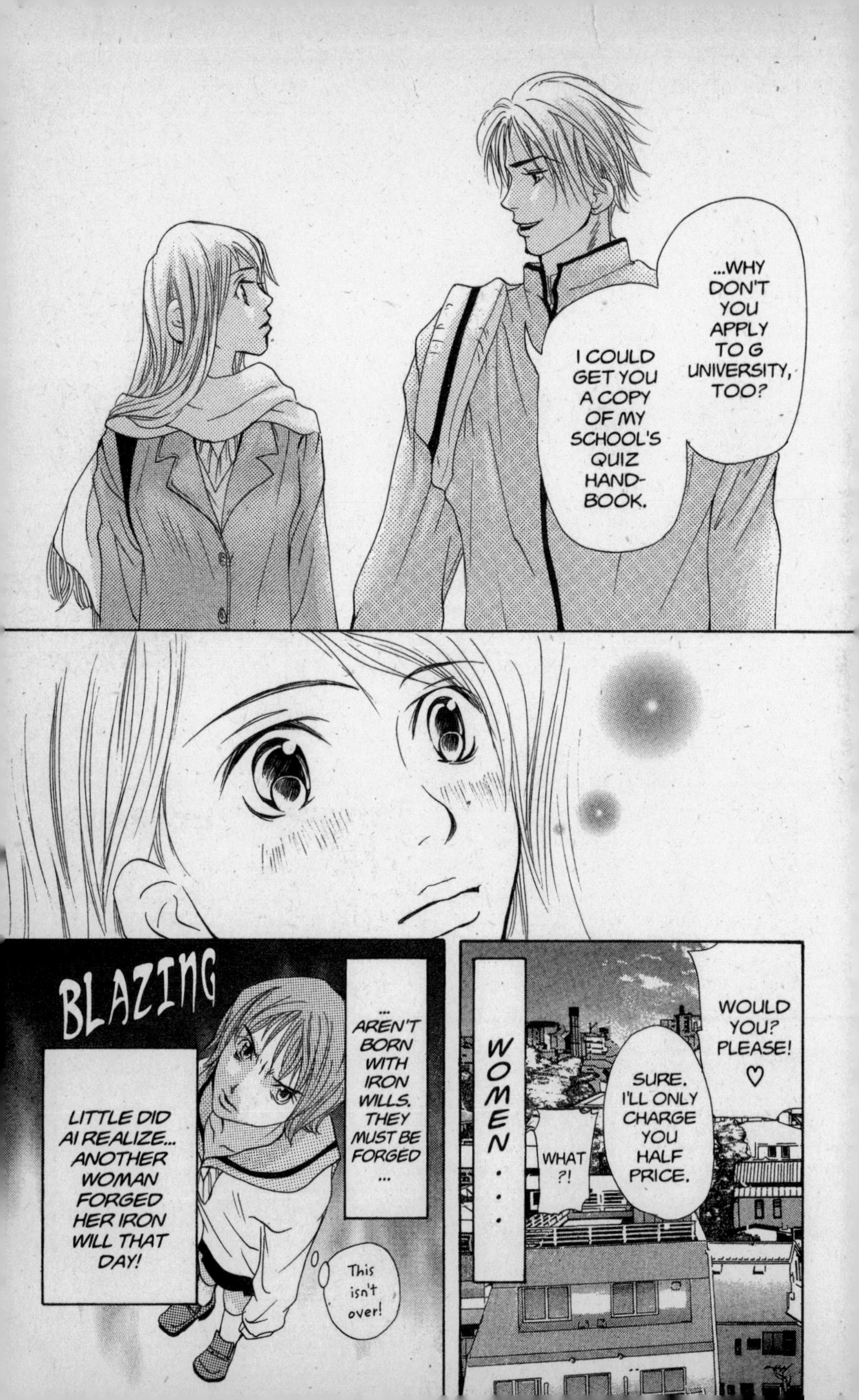
...WHY DON'T YOU APPLY TO G UNIVERSITY, TOO?
I COULD GET YOU A COPY OF MY SCHOOL'S QUIZ HAND-BOOK.
WOULD YOU? PLEASE! ♡
SURE. I'LL ONLY CHARGE YOU HALF PRICE.
WHAT?!
WOMEN...
...AREN'T BORN WITH IRON WILLS. THEY MUST BE FORGED...
BLAZING
LITTLE DID AI REALIZE... ANOTHER WOMAN FORGED HER IRON WILL THAT DAY!
This isn't over!

Chapter 25

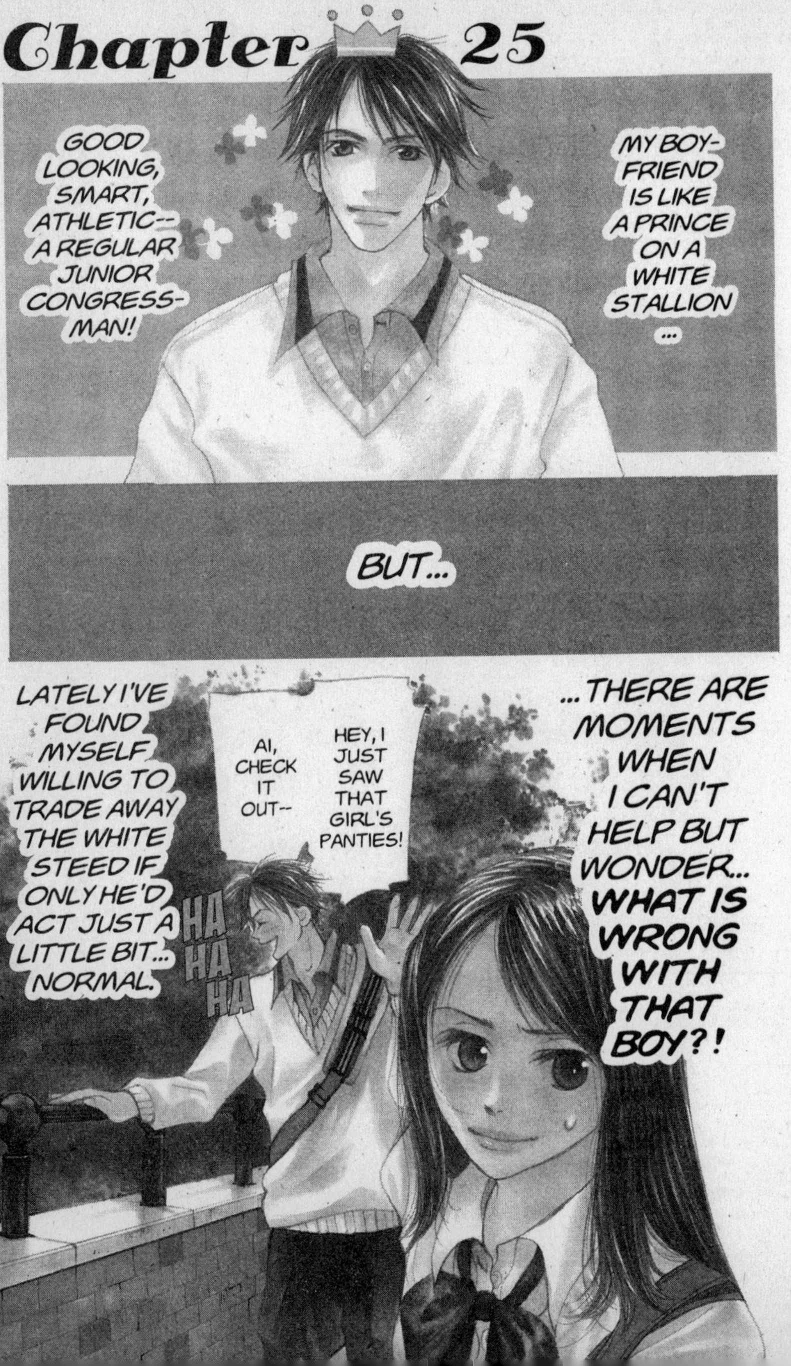
MY BOY-FRIEND IS LIKE A PRINCE ON A WHITE STALLION ...
GOOD LOOKING, SMART, ATHLETIC-- A REGULAR JUNIOR CONGRESS-MAN!
BUT...
...THERE ARE MOMENTS WHEN I CAN'T HELP BUT WONDER... WHAT IS WRONG WITH THAT BOY?!
HEY, I JUST SAW THAT GIRL'S PANTIES!
AI, CHECK IT OUT--
HA HA HA
LATELY I'VE FOUND MYSELF WILLING TO TRADE AWAY THE WHITE STEED IF ONLY HE'D ACT JUST A LITTLE BIT... NORMAL.

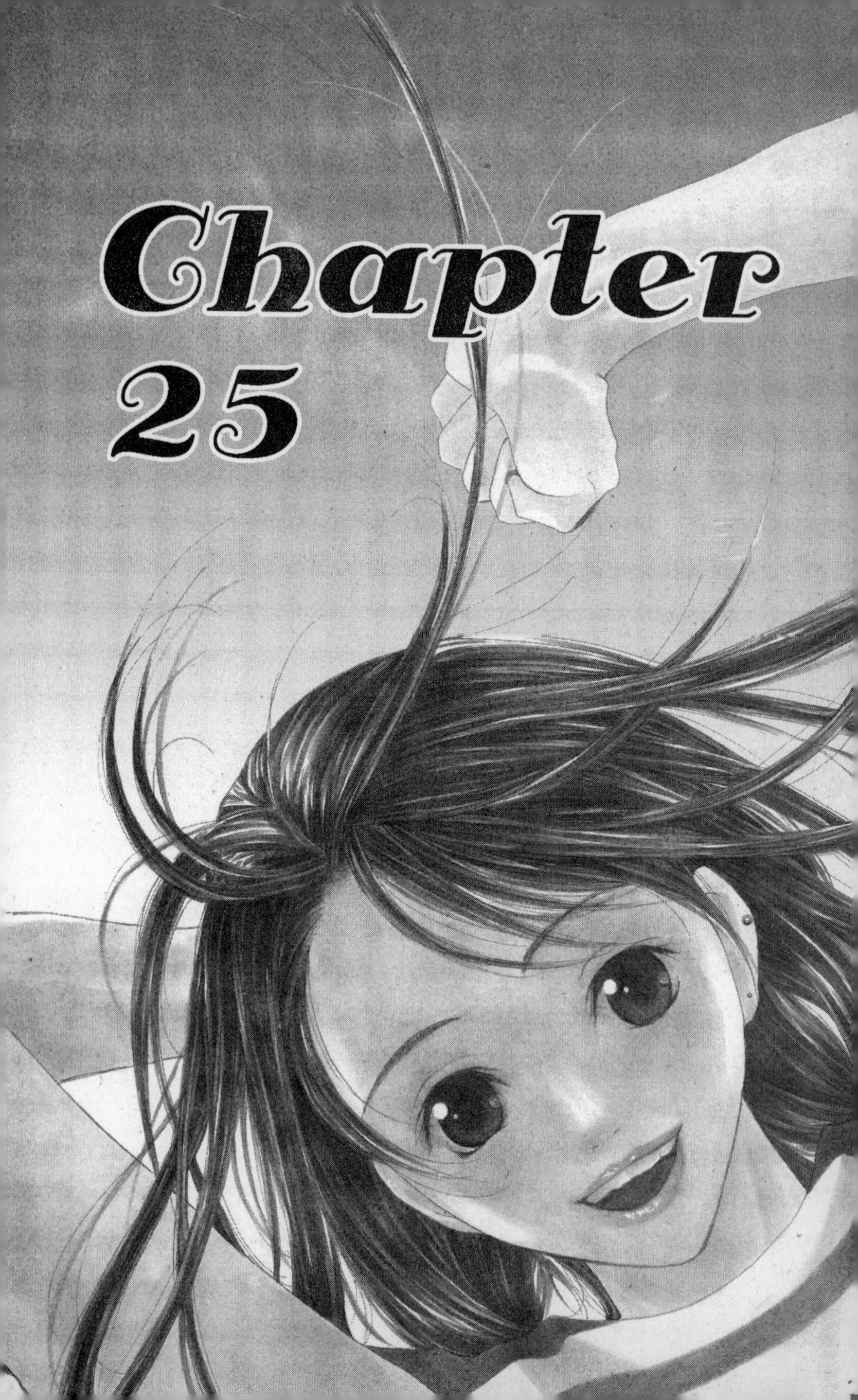
Chapter
25

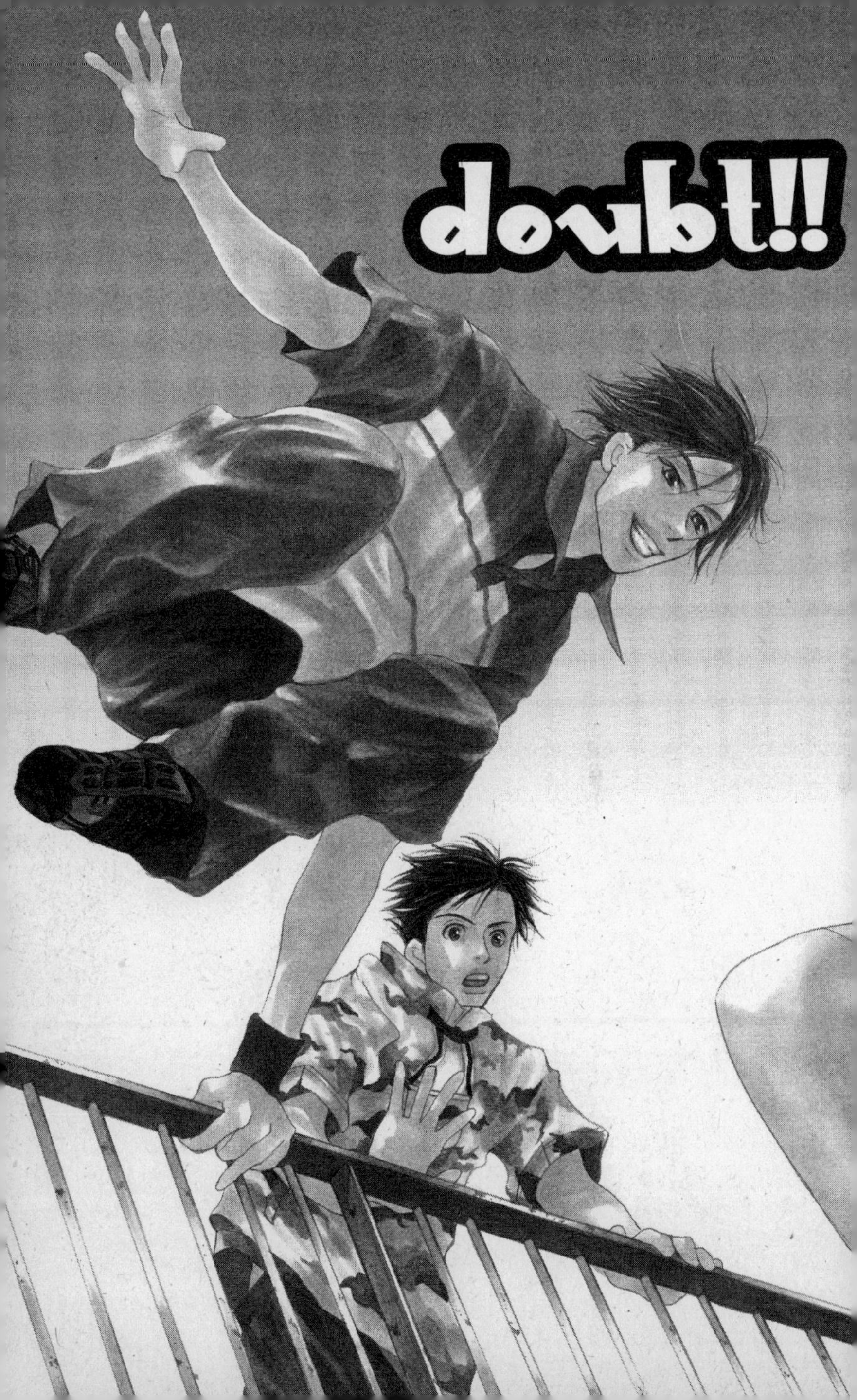
doubt!!

GAZING AT THE MOON...

IT'S CUTE, BUT RABBITS* DON'T SHOW MUCH EMOTION.

SHAKE
SHAKE

*Instead of a "man in the moon," people in Japan see a "rabbit in the moon."

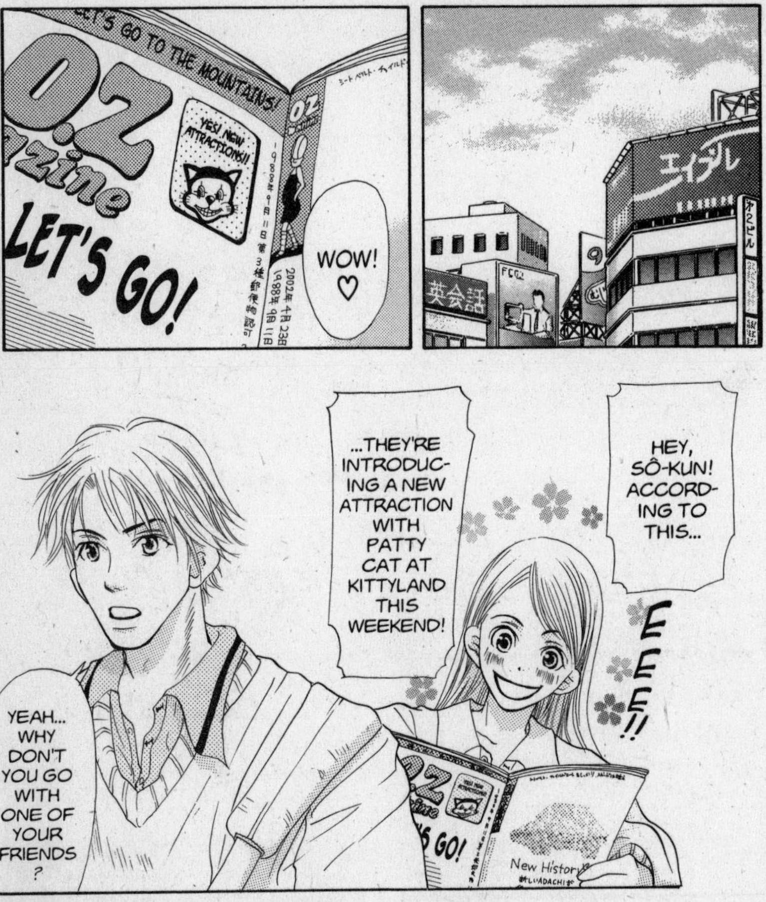
エイブル
英会話
LET'S GO TO THE MOUNTAINS!
O.Z
YES! NEW ATTRACTIONS!!
LET'S GO!
WOW! ♡
HEY, SÔ-KUN! ACCORDING TO THIS...
...THEY'RE INTRODUCING A NEW ATTRACTION WITH PATTY CAT AT KITTYLAND THIS WEEKEND!
EEEE!!
YEAH... WHY DON'T YOU GO WITH ONE OF YOUR FRIENDS?

Yuichiro

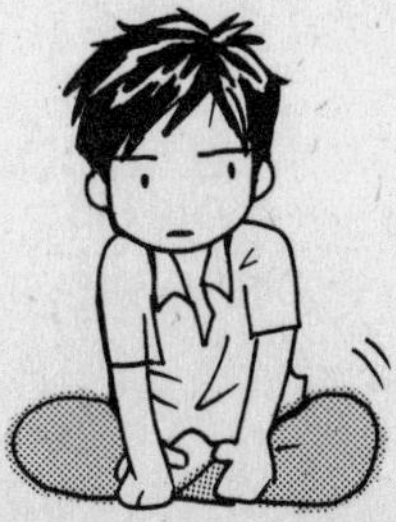

I'd planned a big comeback for him at the end, but I ran out of time and pages... He was very popular--lots of women felt sorry for him.

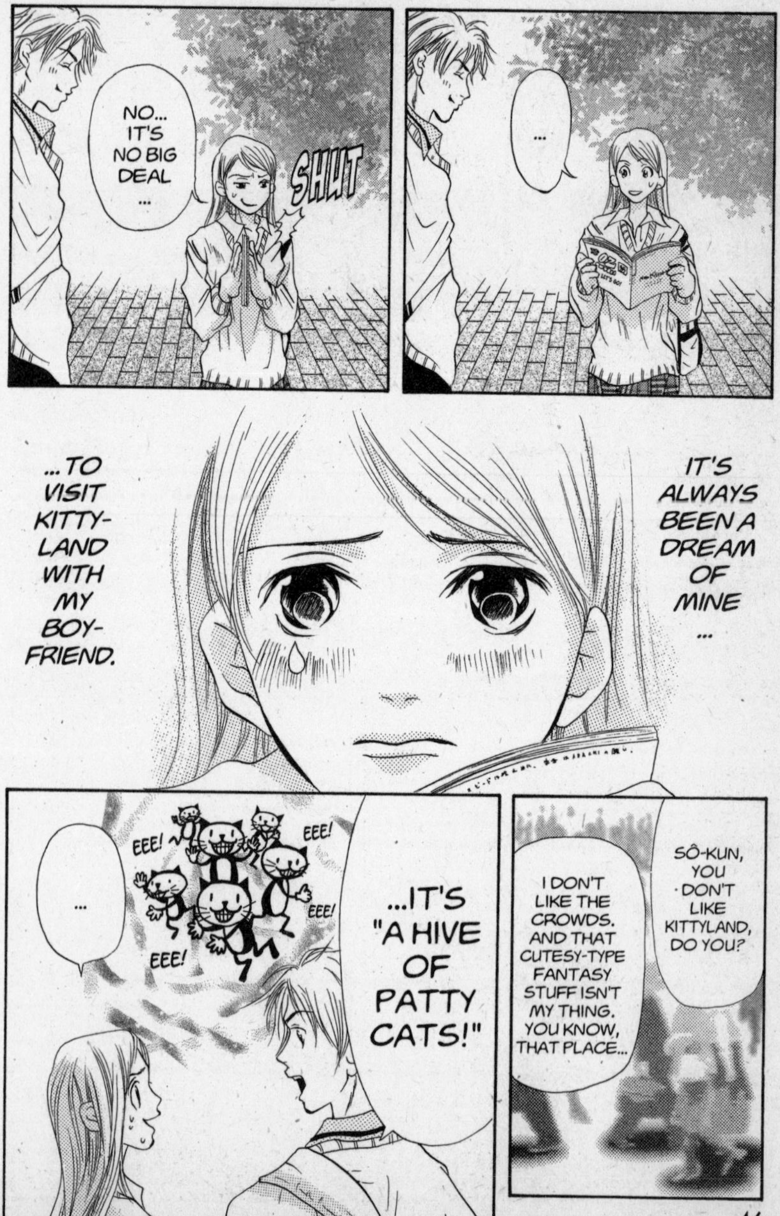
...
NO... IT'S NO BIG DEAL ...
SHUT
IT'S ALWAYS BEEN A DREAM OF MINE ...
...TO VISIT KITTY-LAND WITH MY BOY-FRIEND.
SÔ-KUN, YOU DON'T LIKE KITTYLAND, DO YOU?
I DON'T LIKE THE CROWDS. AND THAT CUTESY-TYPE FANTASY STUFF ISN'T MY THING. YOU KNOW, THAT PLACE...
...IT'S "A HIVE OF PATTY CATS!"
EEE!
EEE!
EEE!
EEE!
...

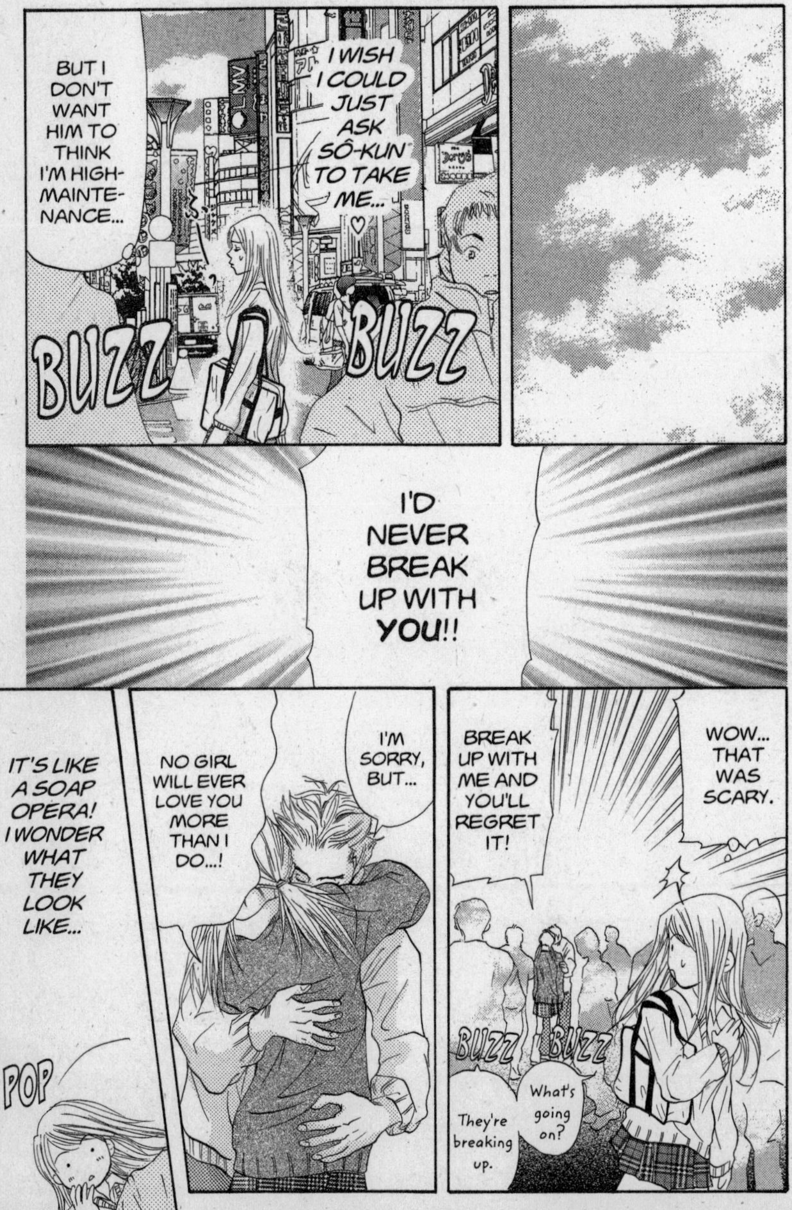
I WISH I COULD JUST ASK SÔ-KUN TO TAKE ME...
BUT I DON'T WANT HIM TO THINK I'M HIGH-MAINTENANCE...
BUZZ
BUZZ
I'D NEVER BREAK UP WITH YOU!!
WOW... THAT WAS SCARY.
BREAK UP WITH ME AND YOU'LL REGRET IT!
BUZZ
BUZZ
What's going on?
They're breaking up.
I'M SORRY, BUT...
NO GIRL WILL EVER LOVE YOU MORE THAN I DO...!
IT'S LIKE A SOAP OPERA! I WONDER WHAT THEY LOOK LIKE...
POP

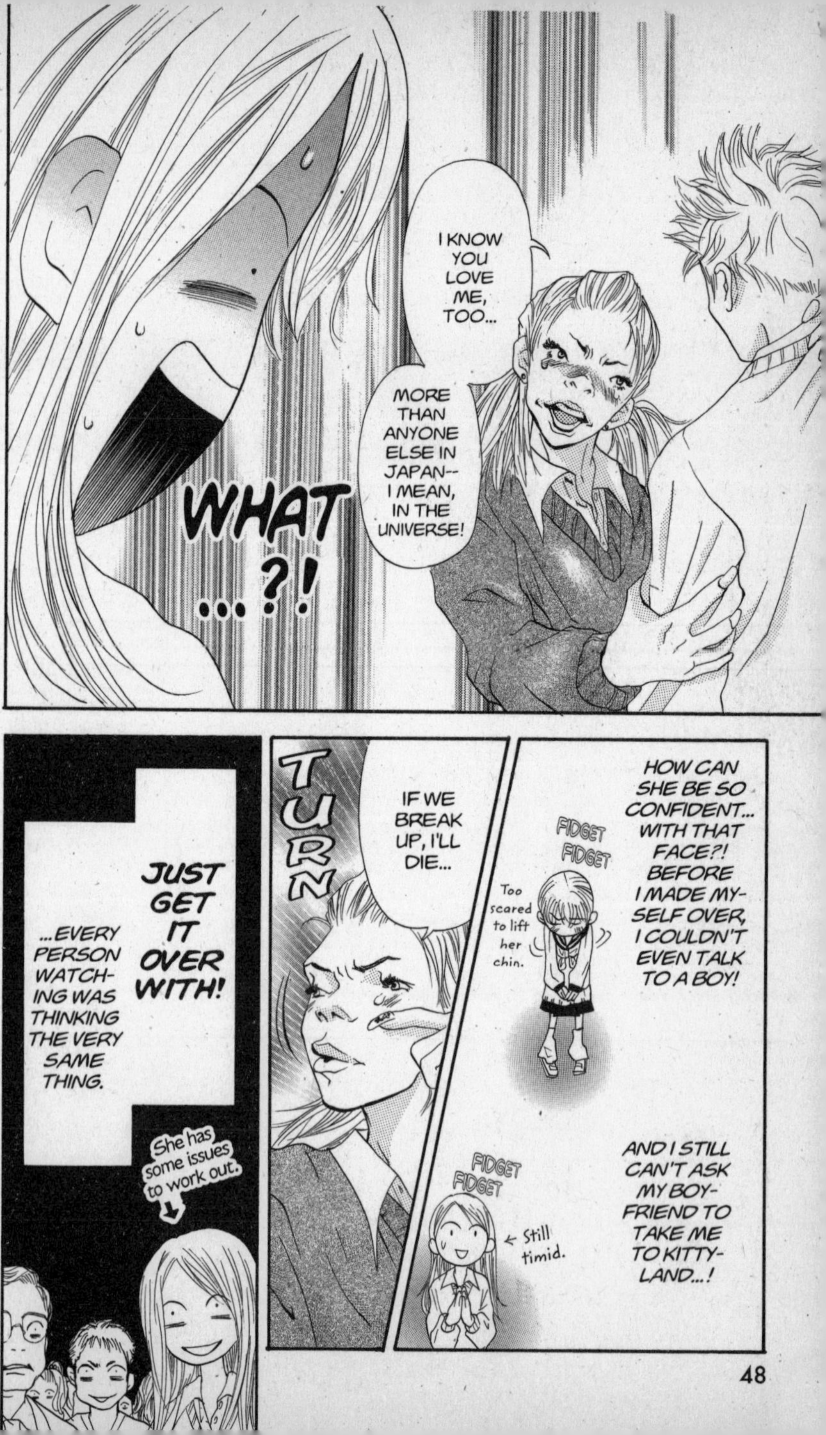
I KNOW YOU LOVE ME, TOO...
MORE THAN ANYONE ELSE IN JAPAN-- I MEAN, IN THE UNIVERSE!
WHAT ...?!
HOW CAN SHE BE SO CONFIDENT... WITH THAT FACE?! BEFORE I MADE MYSELF OVER, I COULDN'T EVEN TALK TO A BOY!
FIDGET FIDGET
Too scared to lift her chin.
AND I STILL CAN'T ASK MY BOYFRIEND TO TAKE ME TO KITTYLAND...!
FIDGET FIDGET
Still timid.
TURN
IF WE BREAK UP, I'LL DIE...
JUST GET IT OVER WITH!
...EVERY PERSON WATCHING WAS THINKING THE VERY SAME THING.
She has some issues to work out.

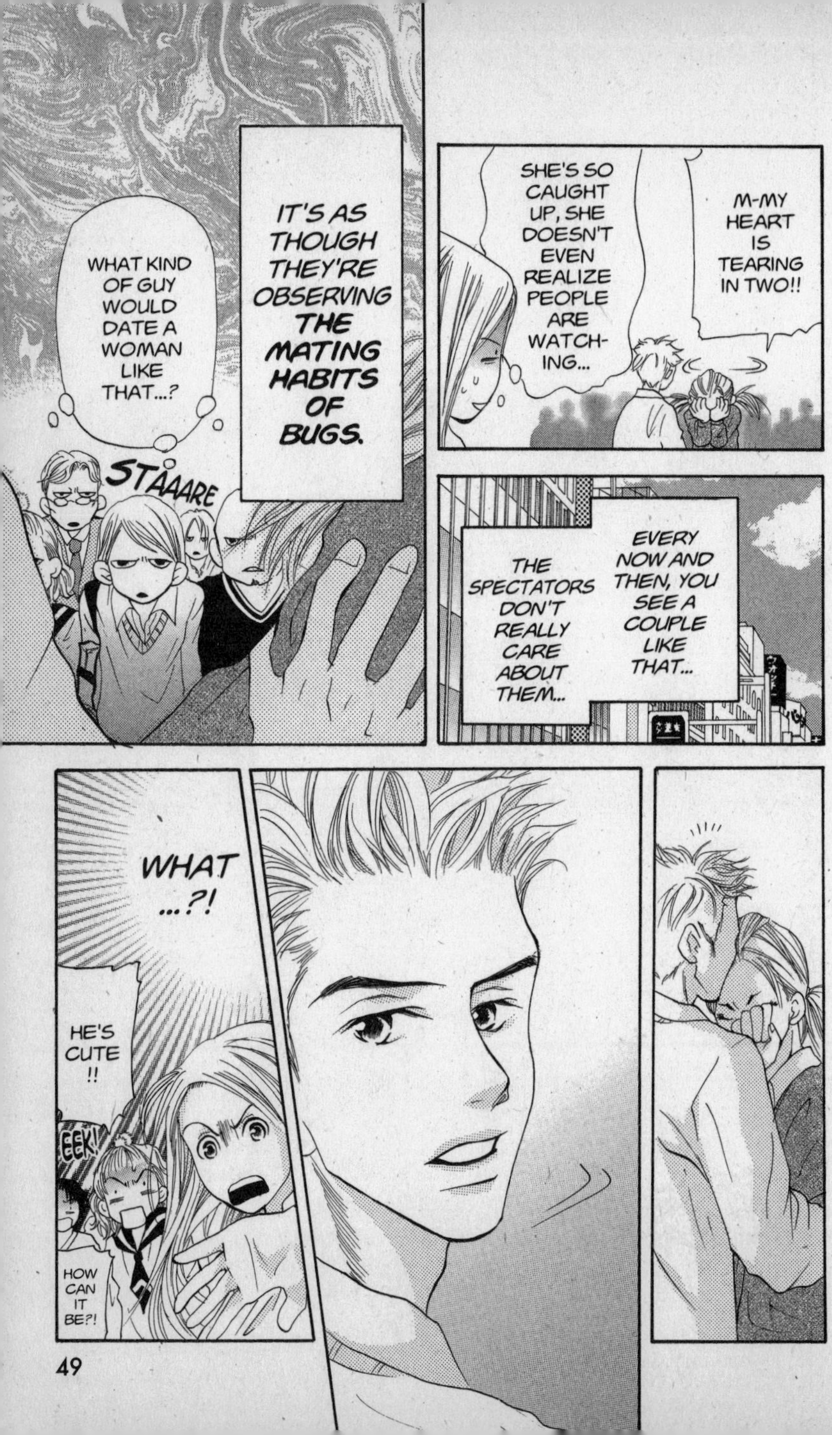
M-MY HEART IS TEARING IN TWO!!
SHE'S SO CAUGHT UP, SHE DOESN'T EVEN REALIZE PEOPLE ARE WATCH-ING...
EVERY NOW AND THEN, YOU SEE A COUPLE LIKE THAT...
THE SPECTATORS DON'T REALLY CARE ABOUT THEM...
IT'S AS THOUGH THEY'RE OBSERVING THE MATING HABITS OF BUGS.
WHAT KIND OF GUY WOULD DATE A WOMAN LIKE THAT...?
STAAARE
WHAT ...?!
HE'S CUTE !!
EEK!
HOW CAN IT BE?!

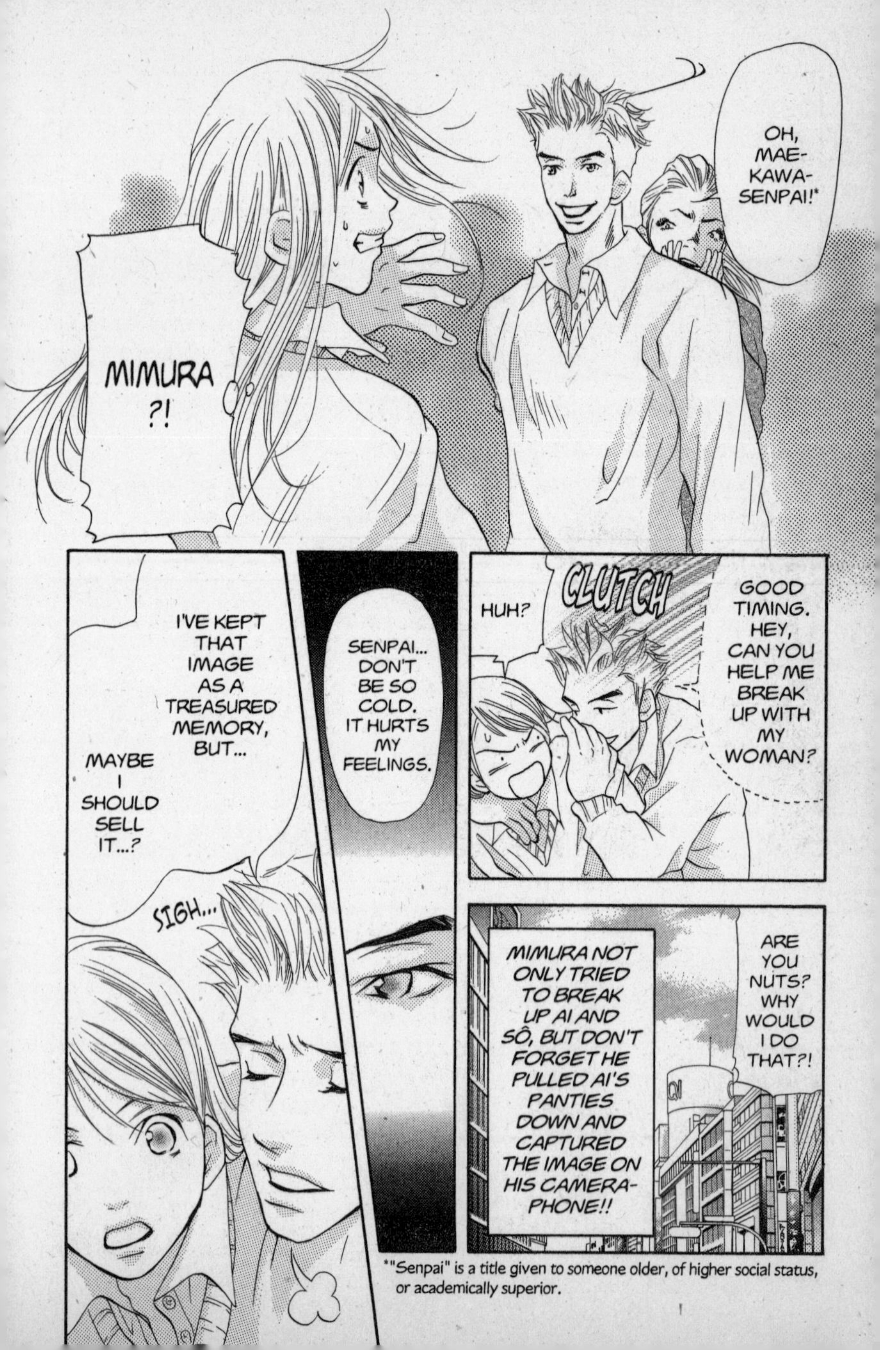
OH, MAE-KAWA-SENPAI!*
MIMURA ?!
GOOD TIMING. HEY, CAN YOU HELP ME BREAK UP WITH MY WOMAN?
CLUTCH
HUH?
ARE YOU NUTS? WHY WOULD I DO THAT?!
MIMURA NOT ONLY TRIED TO BREAK UP AI AND SÔ, BUT DON'T FORGET HE PULLED AI'S PANTIES DOWN AND CAPTURED THE IMAGE ON HIS CAMERA-PHONE!!
SENPAI... DON'T BE SO COLD. IT HURTS MY FEELINGS.
I'VE KEPT THAT IMAGE AS A TREASURED MEMORY, BUT...
MAYBE I SHOULD SELL IT...?
SIGH...

*"Senpai" is a title given to someone older, of higher social status, or academically superior.

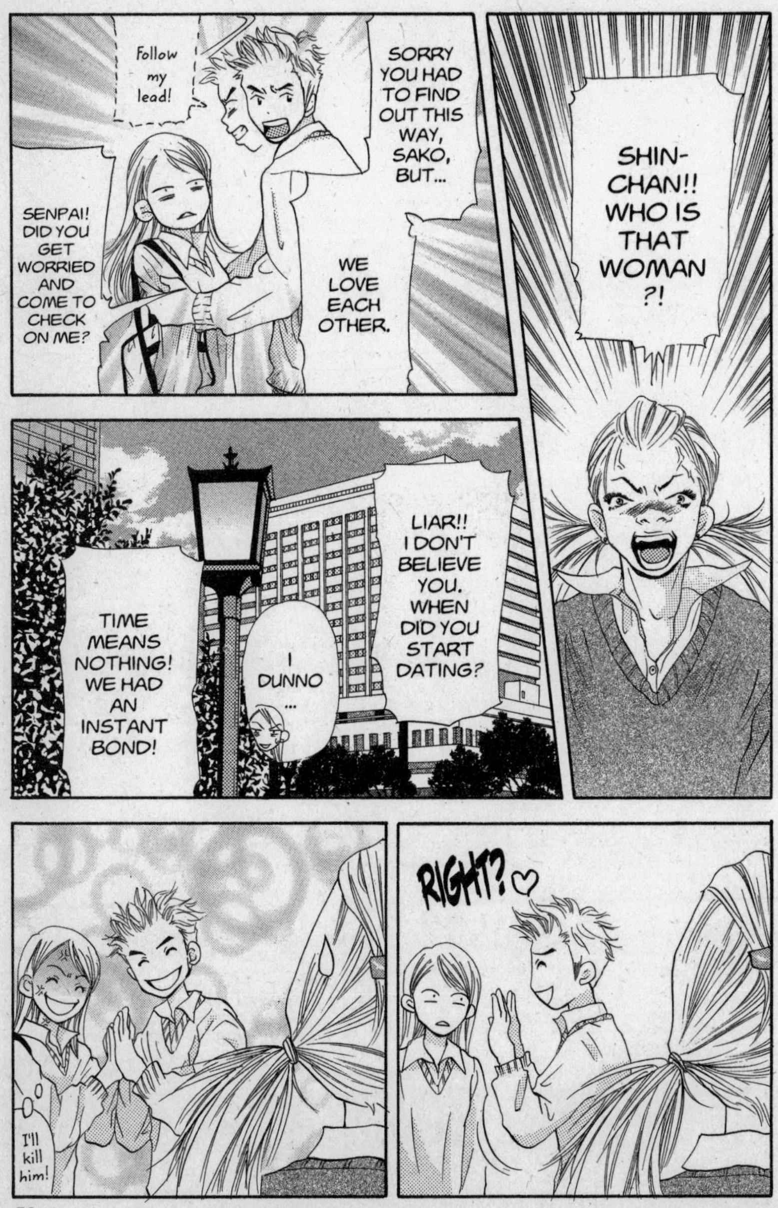

SHIN-CHAN!! WHO IS THAT WOMAN ?!
SORRY YOU HAD TO FIND OUT THIS WAY, SAKO, BUT...
Follow my lead!
WE LOVE EACH OTHER.
SENPAI! DID YOU GET WORRIED AND COME TO CHECK ON ME?
LIAR!! I DON'T BELIEVE YOU. WHEN DID YOU START DATING?
I DUNNO ...
TIME MEANS NOTHING! WE HAD AN INSTANT BOND!
RIGHT? ♡
I'll kill him!

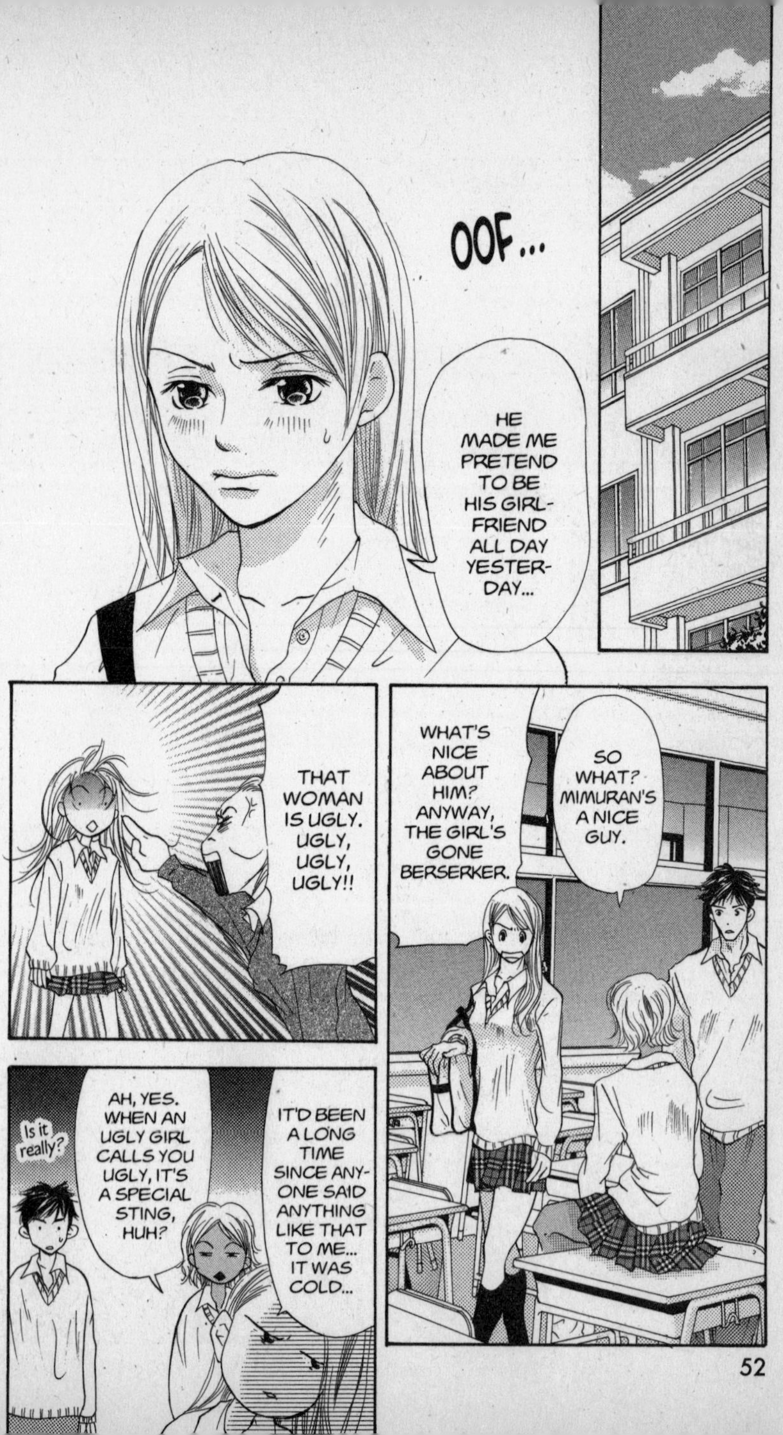
OOF...
HE MADE ME PRETEND TO BE HIS GIRL-FRIEND ALL DAY YESTER-DAY...
SO WHAT? MIMURAN'S A NICE GUY.
WHAT'S NICE ABOUT HIM? ANYWAY, THE GIRL'S GONE BERSERKER.
THAT WOMAN IS UGLY. UGLY, UGLY, UGLY!!
IT'D BEEN A LONG TIME SINCE ANY-ONE SAID ANYTHING LIKE THAT TO ME... IT WAS COLD...
AH, YES. WHEN AN UGLY GIRL CALLS YOU UGLY, IT'S A SPECIAL STING, HUH?
Is it really?

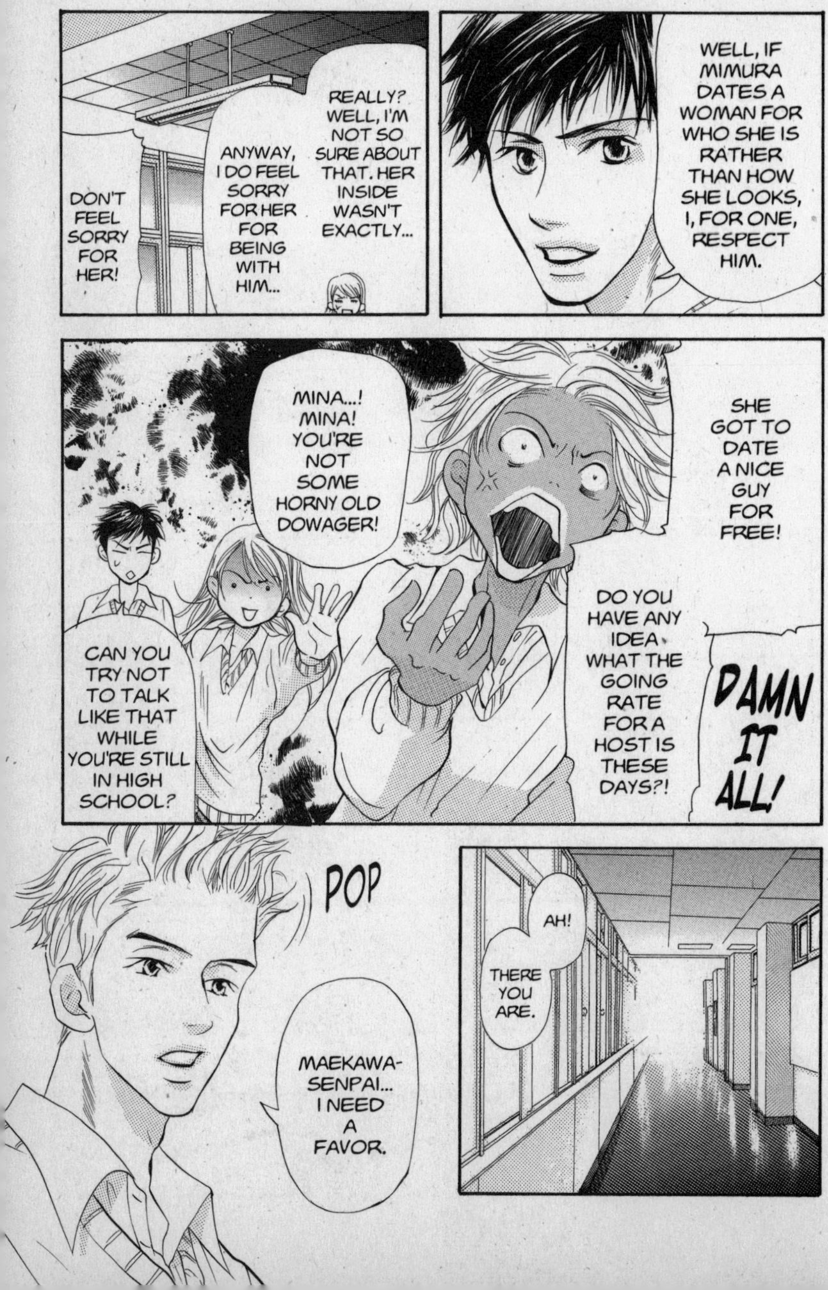
WELL, IF MIMURA DATES A WOMAN FOR WHO SHE IS RATHER THAN HOW SHE LOOKS, I, FOR ONE, RESPECT HIM.
REALLY? WELL, I'M NOT SO SURE ABOUT THAT. HER INSIDE WASN'T EXACTLY...
ANYWAY, I DO FEEL SORRY FOR HER FOR BEING WITH HIM...
DON'T FEEL SORRY FOR HER!
SHE GOT TO DATE A NICE GUY FOR FREE!
DAMN IT ALL!
DO YOU HAVE ANY IDEA WHAT THE GOING RATE FOR A HOST IS THESE DAYS?!
MINA...! MINA! YOU'RE NOT SOME HORNY OLD DOWAGER!
CAN YOU TRY NOT TO TALK LIKE THAT WHILE YOU'RE STILL IN HIGH SCHOOL?
AH!
THERE YOU ARE.
POP
MAEKAWA-SENPAI... I NEED A FAVOR.

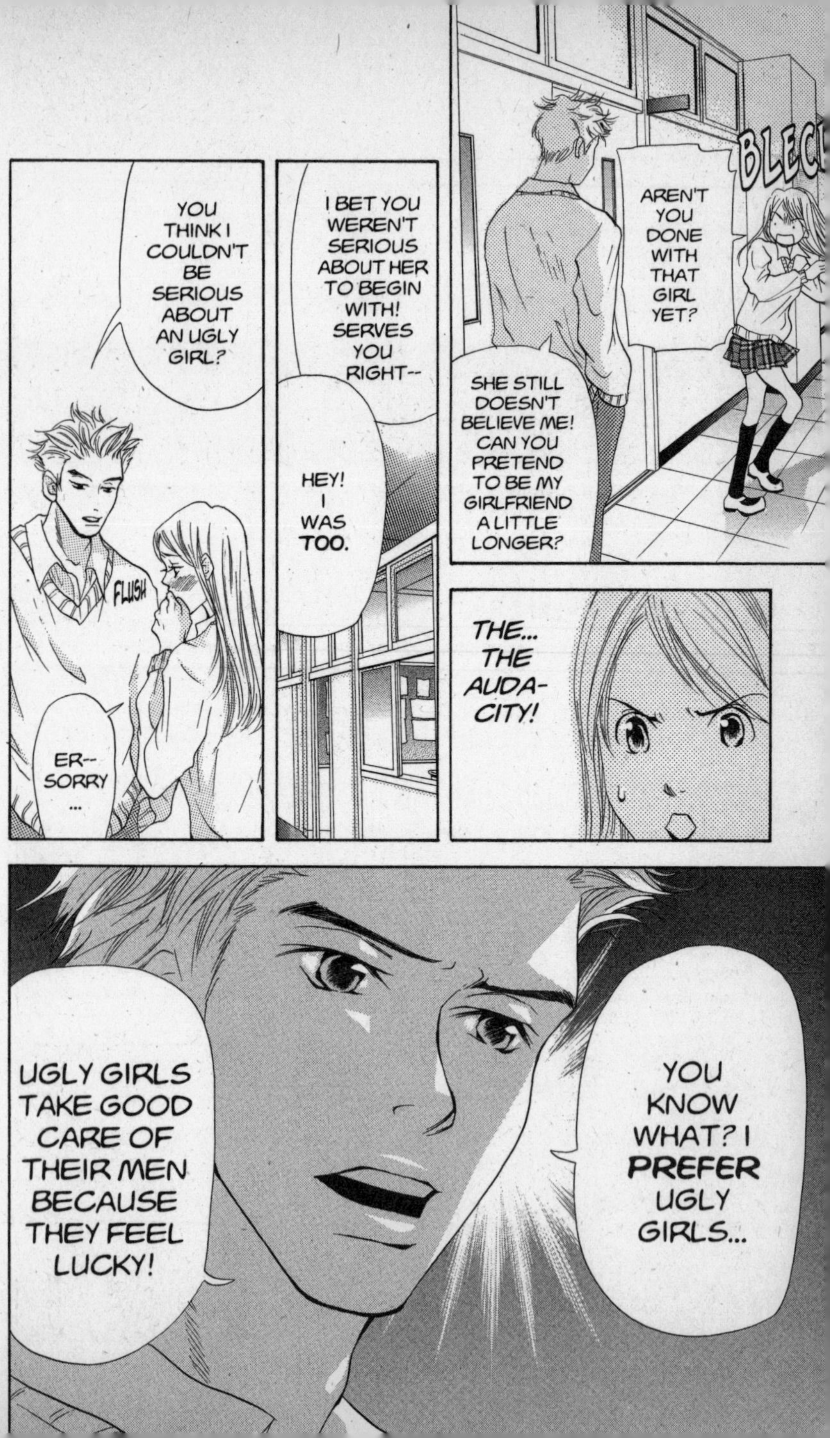
BLEC
AREN'T YOU DONE WITH THAT GIRL YET?
SHE STILL DOESN'T BELIEVE ME! CAN YOU PRETEND TO BE MY GIRLFRIEND A LITTLE LONGER?
THE... THE AUDACITY!
I BET YOU WEREN'T SERIOUS ABOUT HER TO BEGIN WITH! SERVES YOU RIGHT--
HEY! I WAS **TOO.**
YOU THINK I COULDN'T BE SERIOUS ABOUT AN UGLY GIRL?
FLUSH
ER-- SORRY ...
YOU KNOW WHAT? I **PREFER** UGLY GIRLS...
UGLY GIRLS TAKE GOOD CARE OF THEIR MEN BECAUSE THEY FEEL LUCKY!

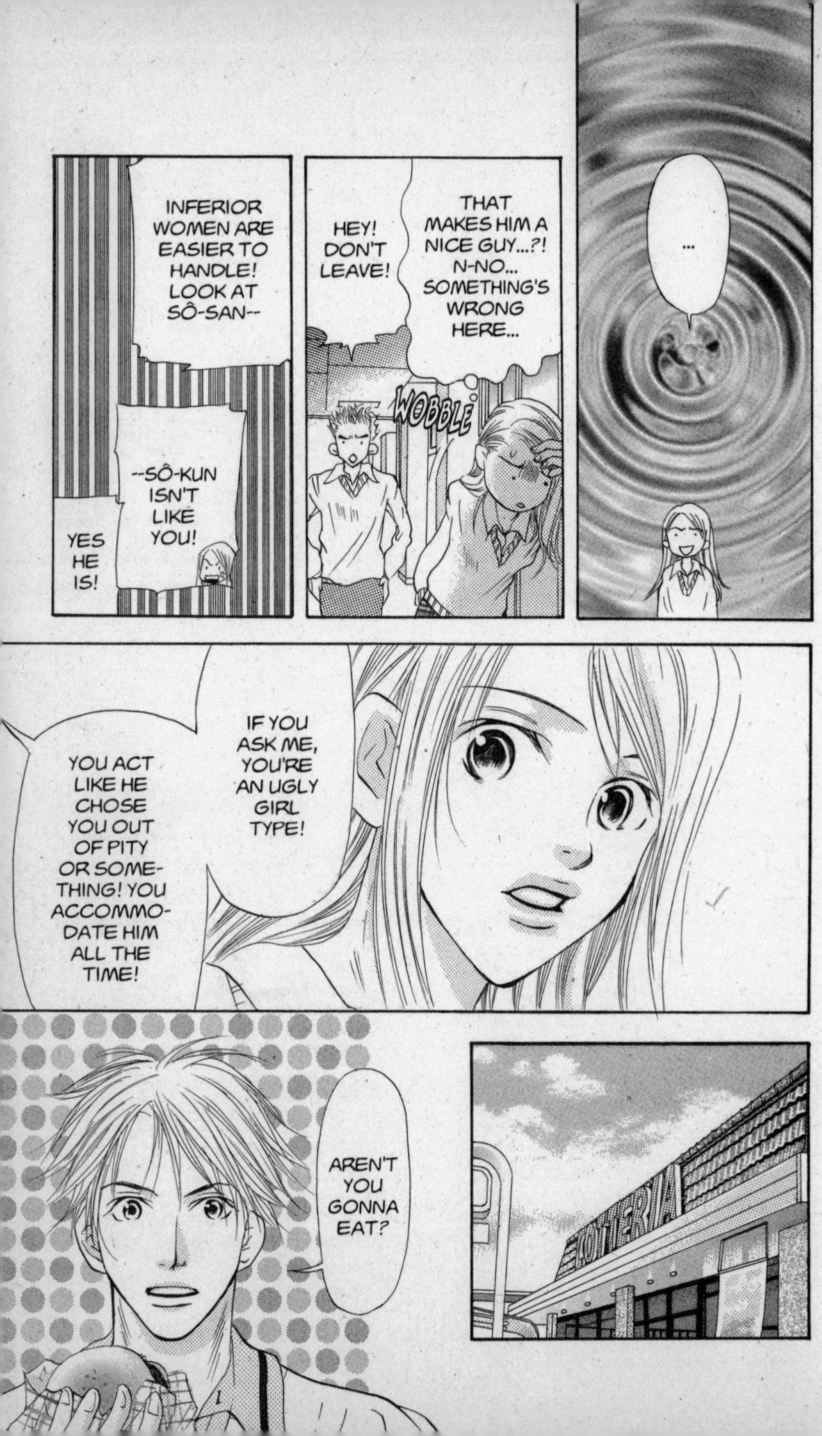
...
THAT MAKES HIM A NICE GUY...?! N-NO... SOMETHING'S WRONG HERE...
HEY! DON'T LEAVE!
WOBBLE
INFERIOR WOMEN ARE EASIER TO HANDLE! LOOK AT SÔ-SAN--
--SÔ-KUN ISN'T LIKE YOU!
YES HE IS!
IF YOU ASK ME, YOU'RE AN UGLY GIRL TYPE!
YOU ACT LIKE HE CHOSE YOU OUT OF PITY OR SOMETHING! YOU ACCOMMODATE HIM ALL THE TIME!
AREN'T YOU GONNA EAT?

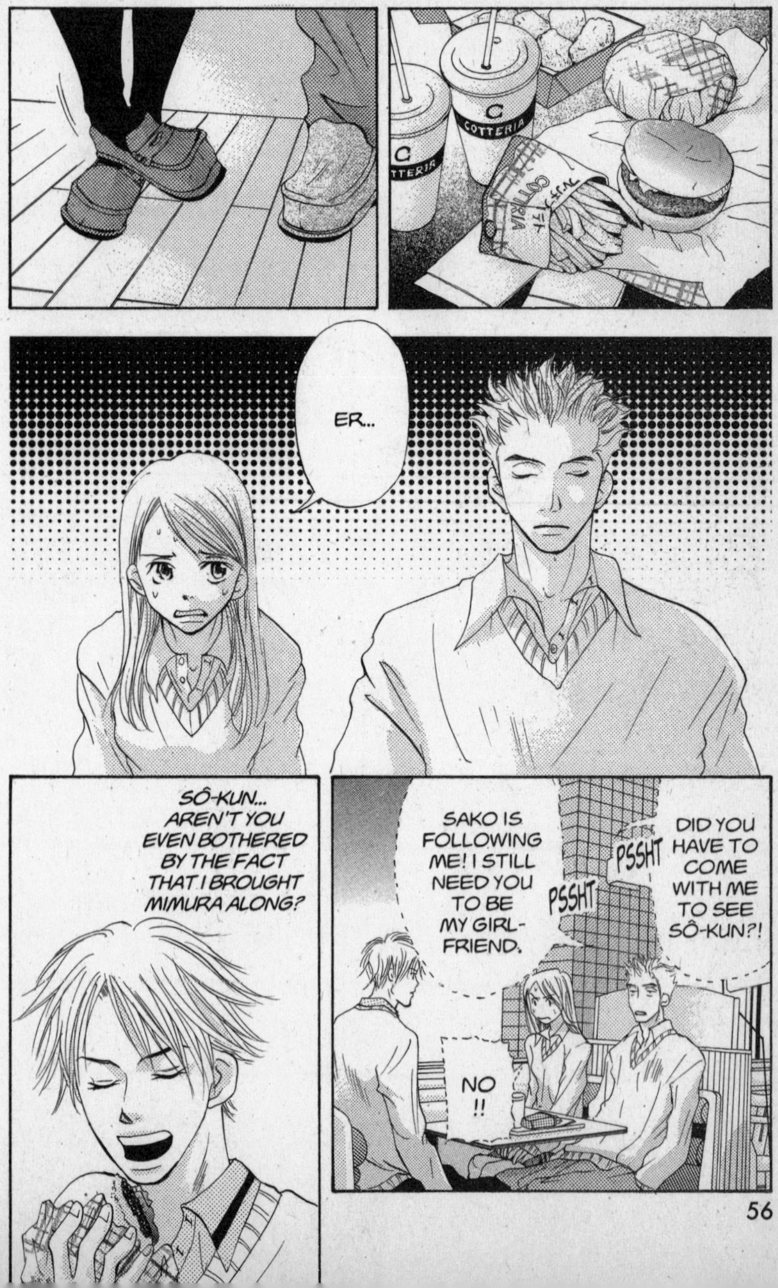
C
COTTERIA
COTTERIA
ER...
DID YOU HAVE TO COME WITH ME TO SEE SÔ-KUN?!
PSSHT
PSSHT
SAKO IS FOLLOWING ME! I STILL NEED YOU TO BE MY GIRL-FRIEND.
NO !!
SÔ-KUN... AREN'T YOU EVEN BOTHERED BY THE FACT THAT I BROUGHT MIMURA ALONG?

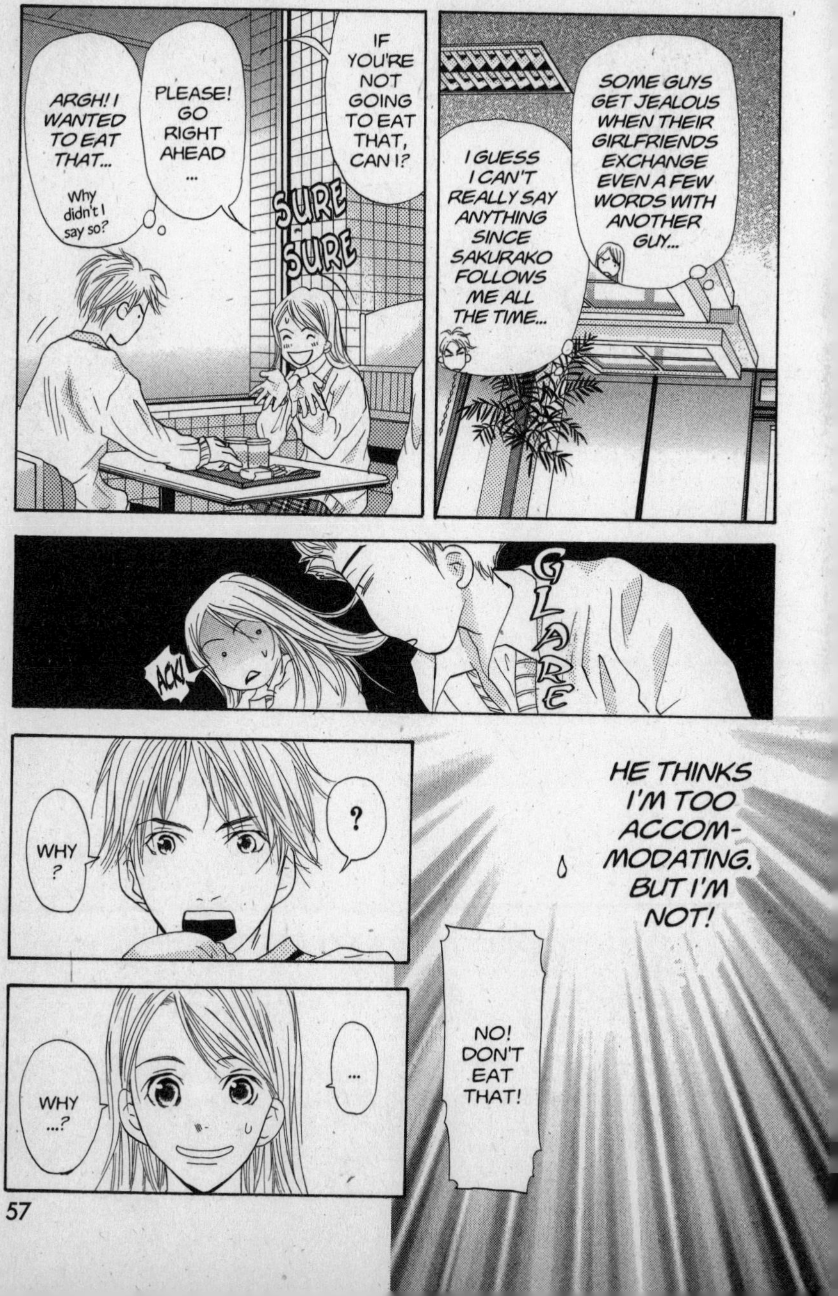
SOME GUYS GET JEALOUS WHEN THEIR GIRLFRIENDS EXCHANGE EVEN A FEW WORDS WITH ANOTHER GUY...
I GUESS I CAN'T REALLY SAY ANYTHING SINCE SAKURAKO FOLLOWS ME ALL THE TIME...
IF YOU'RE NOT GOING TO EAT THAT, CAN I?
SURE SURE
PLEASE! GO RIGHT AHEAD ...
ARGH! I WANTED TO EAT THAT...
Why didn't I say so?
GLARE
ACK!
HE THINKS I'M TOO ACCOM-MODATING. BUT I'M NOT!
NO! DON'T EAT THAT!
?
WHY ?
...
WHY ...?

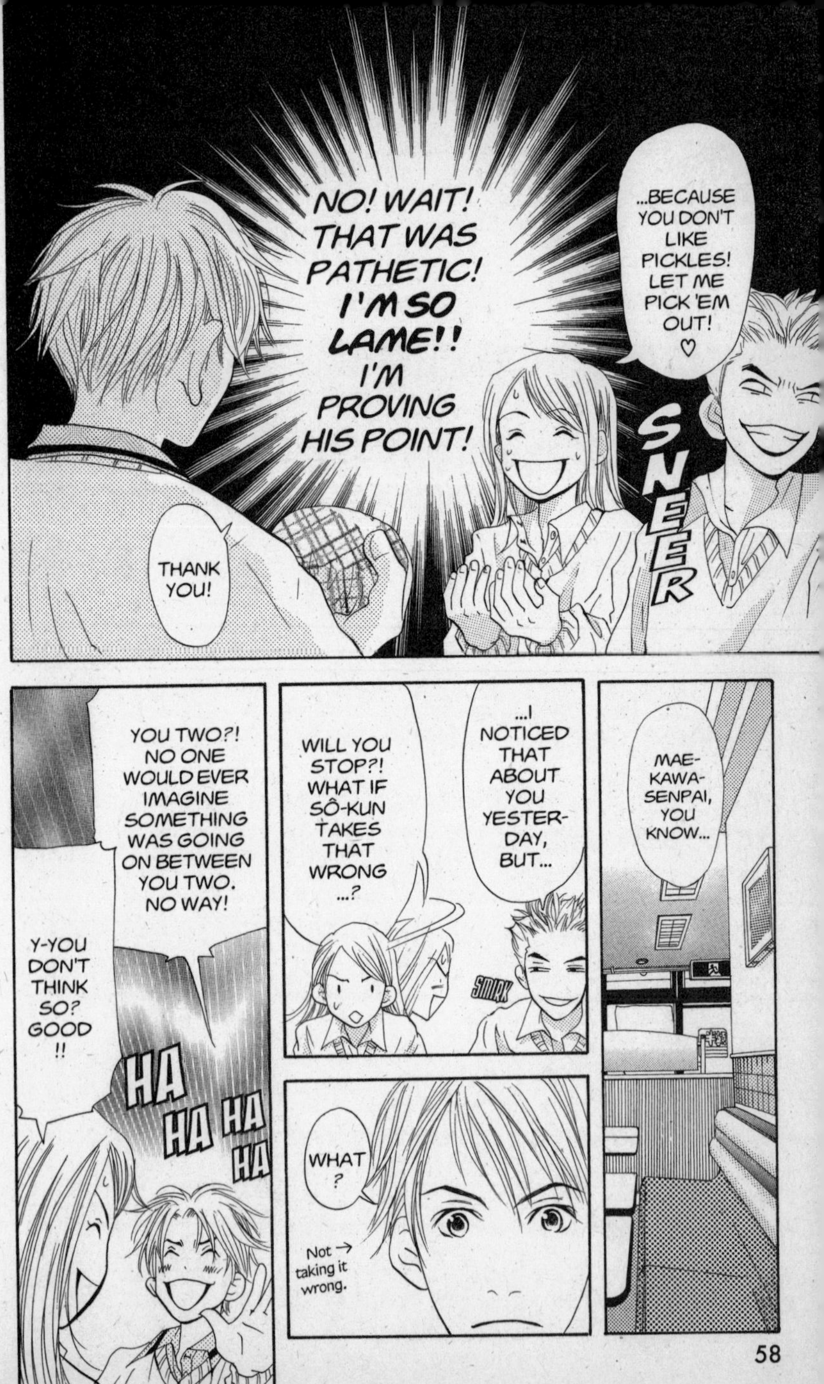
...BECAUSE YOU DON'T LIKE PICKLES! LET ME PICK 'EM OUT! ♡
NO! WAIT! THAT WAS PATHETIC! I'M SO LAME!! I'M PROVING HIS POINT!
SNEER
THANK YOU!
MAE-KAWA-SENPAI, YOU KNOW...
...I NOTICED THAT ABOUT YOU YESTER-DAY, BUT...
WILL YOU STOP?! WHAT IF SÔ-KUN TAKES THAT WRONG ...?
SMIRK
WHAT ?
Not → taking it wrong.
YOU TWO?! NO ONE WOULD EVER IMAGINE SOMETHING WAS GOING ON BETWEEN YOU TWO. NO WAY!
Y-YOU DON'T THINK SO? GOOD !!
HA HA HA HA

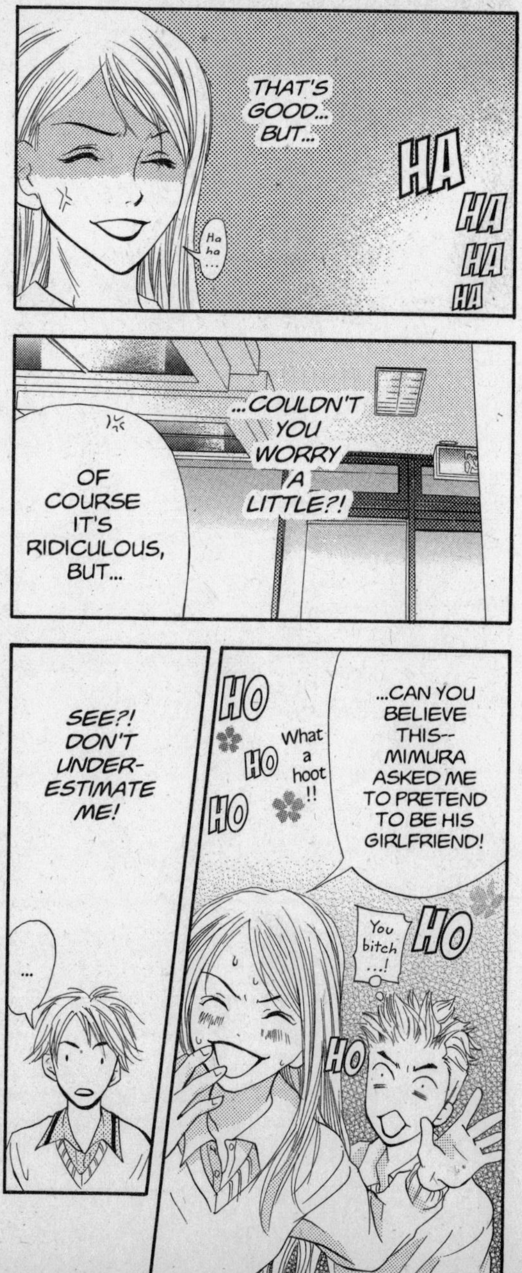
THAT'S GOOD... BUT...
HA HA HA HA
Ha ha...
...COULDN'T YOU WORRY A LITTLE?!
OF COURSE IT'S RIDICULOUS, BUT...
...CAN YOU BELIEVE THIS-- MIMURA ASKED ME TO PRETEND TO BE HIS GIRLFRIEND!
HO HO HO
What a hoot!!
You bitch...!
HO
HO
SEE?! DON'T UNDER-ESTIMATE ME!
...

Doubt!! Backstory

Part 2

I have trouble saying the names of my characters out loud. It makes me feel dizzy. Whenever I have no choice but to refer to them...

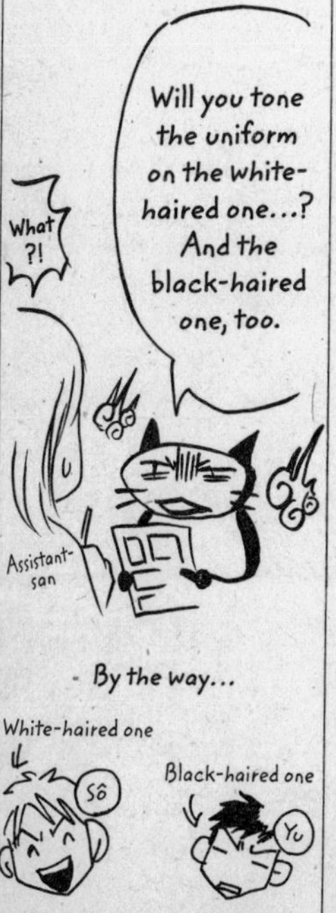
Will you tone the uniform on the white-haired one...? And the black-haired one, too.
What?!
Assistant-san
- By the way...
White-haired one
Sô
Black-haired one
Yu

the long-haired one, the dark-skinned one, the one with long eyelashes, etc...

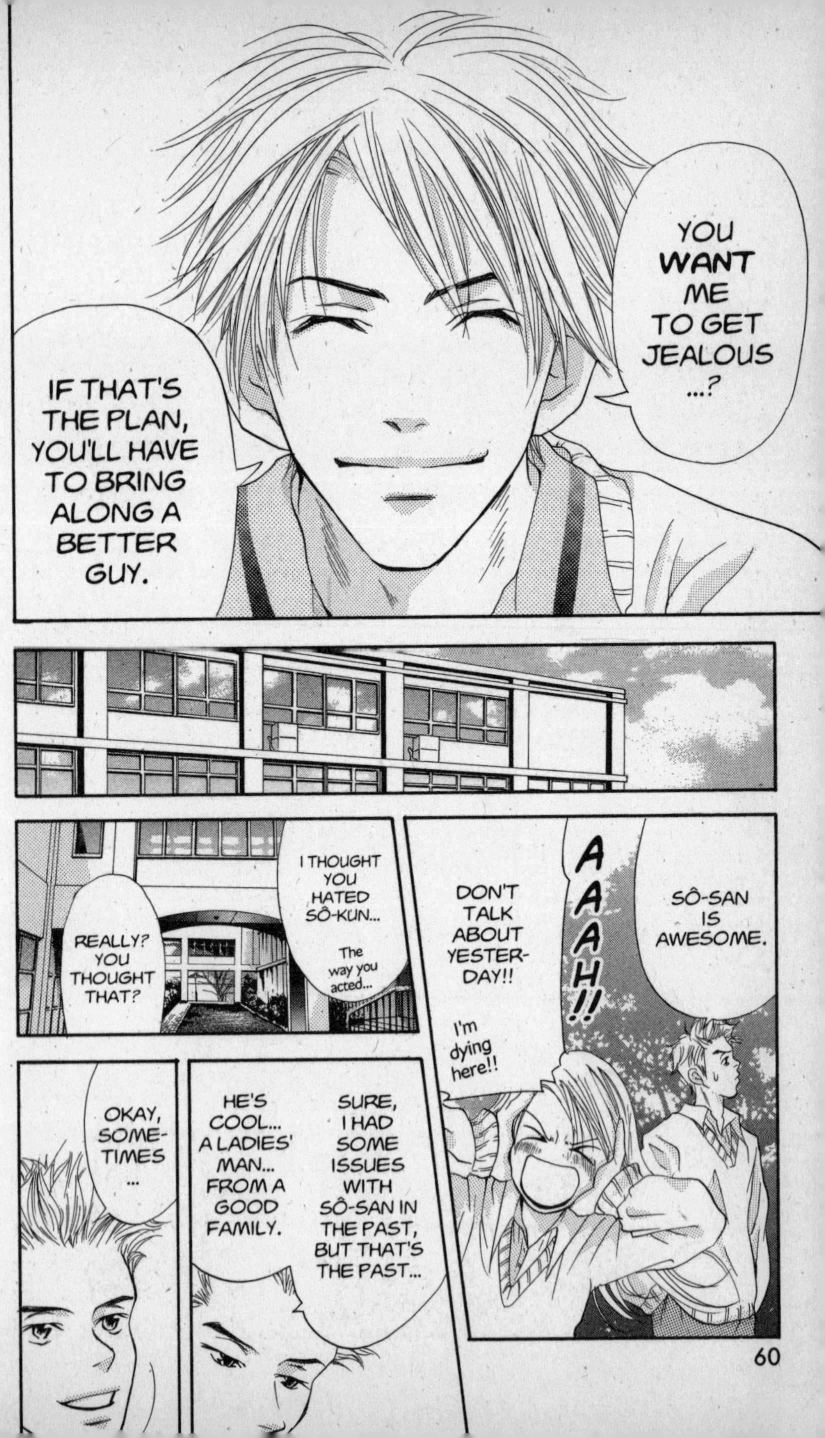
YOU **WANT** ME TO GET JEALOUS ...?
IF THAT'S THE PLAN, YOU'LL HAVE TO BRING ALONG A BETTER GUY.
SÔ-SAN IS AWESOME.
AAAAH!!
DON'T TALK ABOUT YESTER-DAY!!
I'm dying here!!
I THOUGHT YOU HATED SÔ-KUN...
The way you acted...
REALLY? YOU THOUGHT THAT?
SURE, I HAD SOME ISSUES WITH SÔ-SAN IN THE PAST, BUT THAT'S THE PAST...
HE'S COOL... A LADIES' MAN... FROM A GOOD FAMILY.
OKAY, SOME-TIMES ...

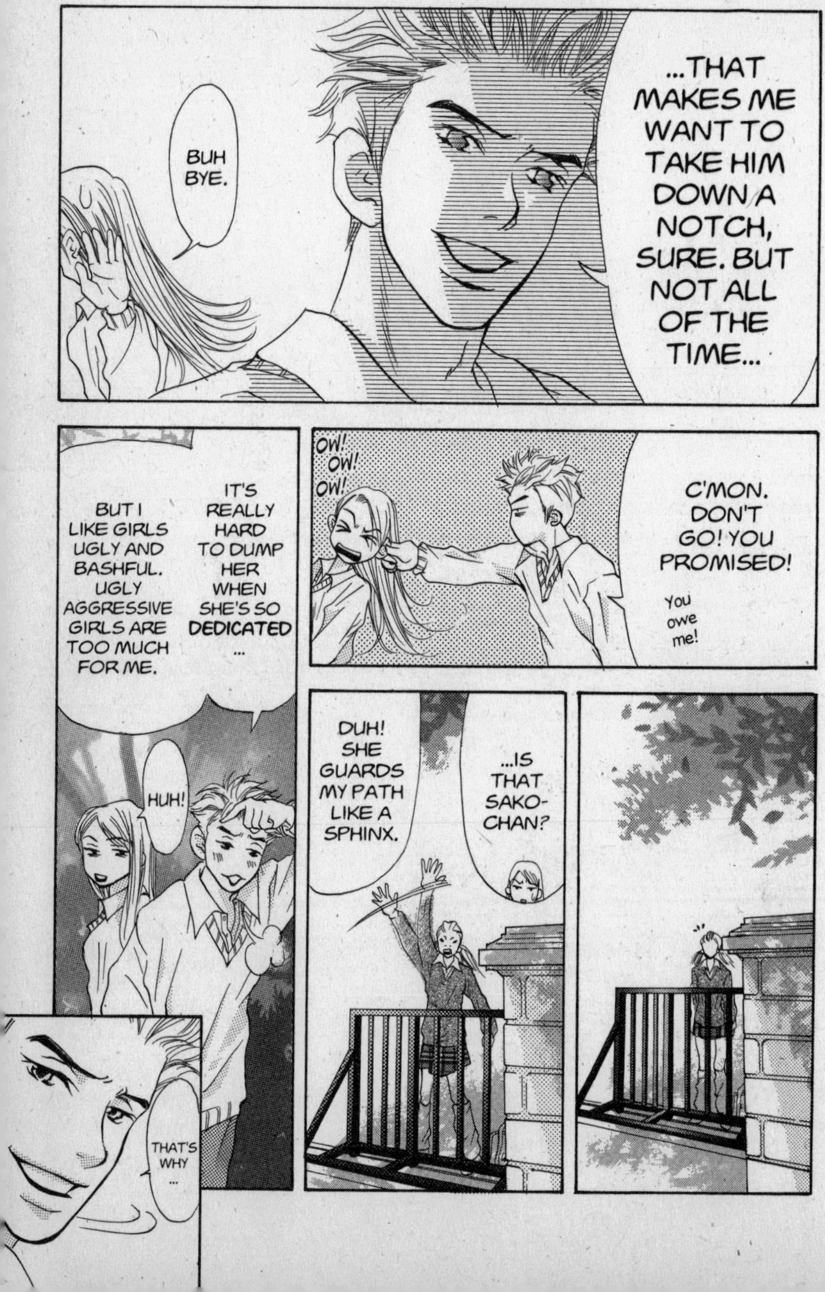
...THAT MAKES ME WANT TO TAKE HIM DOWN A NOTCH, SURE. BUT NOT ALL OF THE TIME...
BUH BYE.
C'MON. DON'T GO! YOU PROMISED!
You owe me!
OW! OW! OW!
...IS THAT SAKO-CHAN?
DUH! SHE GUARDS MY PATH LIKE A SPHINX.
IT'S REALLY HARD TO DUMP HER WHEN SHE'S SO DEDICATED ...
BUT I LIKE GIRLS UGLY AND BASHFUL. UGLY AGGRESSIVE GIRLS ARE TOO MUCH FOR ME.
HUH!
THAT'S WHY ...

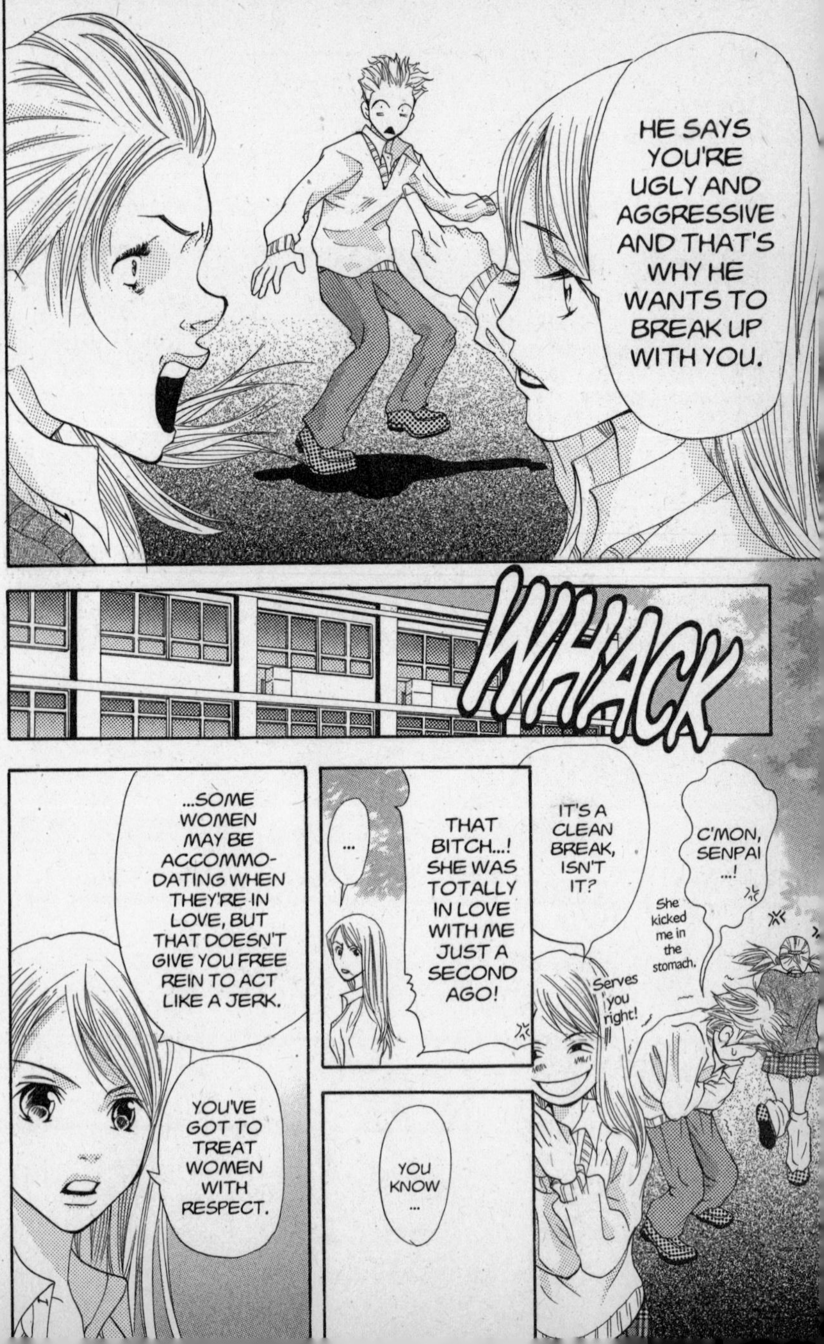
HE SAYS YOU'RE UGLY AND AGGRESSIVE AND THAT'S WHY HE WANTS TO BREAK UP WITH YOU.
WHACK
C'MON, SENPAI ...!
She kicked me in the stomach.
IT'S A CLEAN BREAK, ISN'T IT?
Serves you right!
THAT BITCH...! SHE WAS TOTALLY IN LOVE WITH ME JUST A SECOND AGO!
...
YOU KNOW ...
...SOME WOMEN MAY BE ACCOMMO-DATING WHEN THEY'RE IN LOVE, BUT THAT DOESN'T GIVE YOU FREE REIN TO ACT LIKE A JERK.
YOU'VE GOT TO TREAT WOMEN WITH RESPECT.

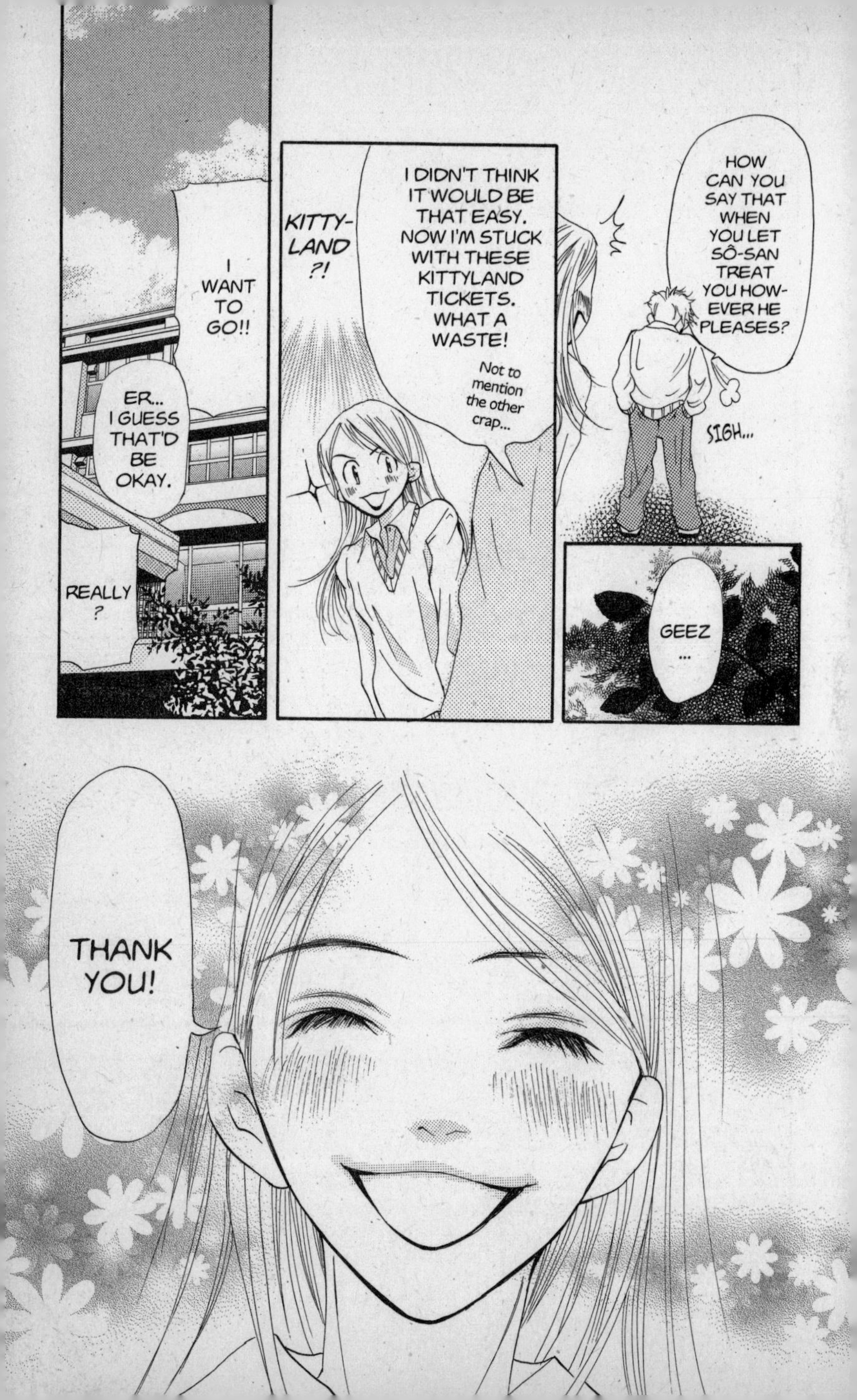
HOW CAN YOU SAY THAT WHEN YOU LET SÔ-SAN TREAT YOU HOW-EVER HE PLEASES?
SIGH...
GEEZ ...
I DIDN'T THINK IT WOULD BE THAT EASY. NOW I'M STUCK WITH THESE KITTYLAND TICKETS. WHAT A WASTE!
KITTY-LAND ?!
Not to mention the other crap...
I WANT TO GO!!
ER... I GUESS THAT'D BE OKAY.
REALLY ?
THANK YOU!

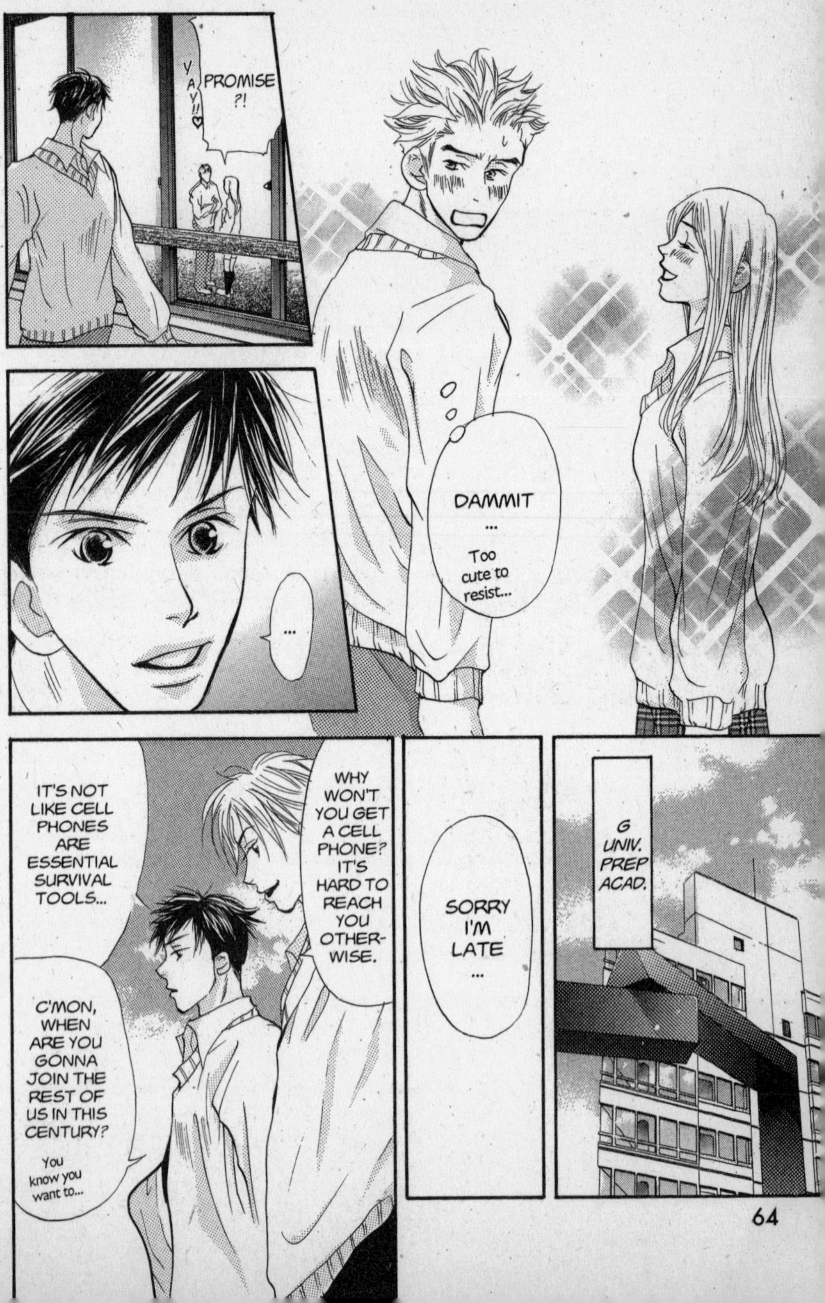
DAMMIT ... Too cute to resist...
YAY!!♡
PROMISE ?!
...
G UNIV. PREP ACAD.
SORRY I'M LATE ...
WHY WON'T YOU GET A CELL PHONE? IT'S HARD TO REACH YOU OTHER-WISE.
IT'S NOT LIKE CELL PHONES ARE ESSENTIAL SURVIVAL TOOLS...
C'MON, WHEN ARE YOU GONNA JOIN THE REST OF US IN THIS CENTURY?
You know you want to...

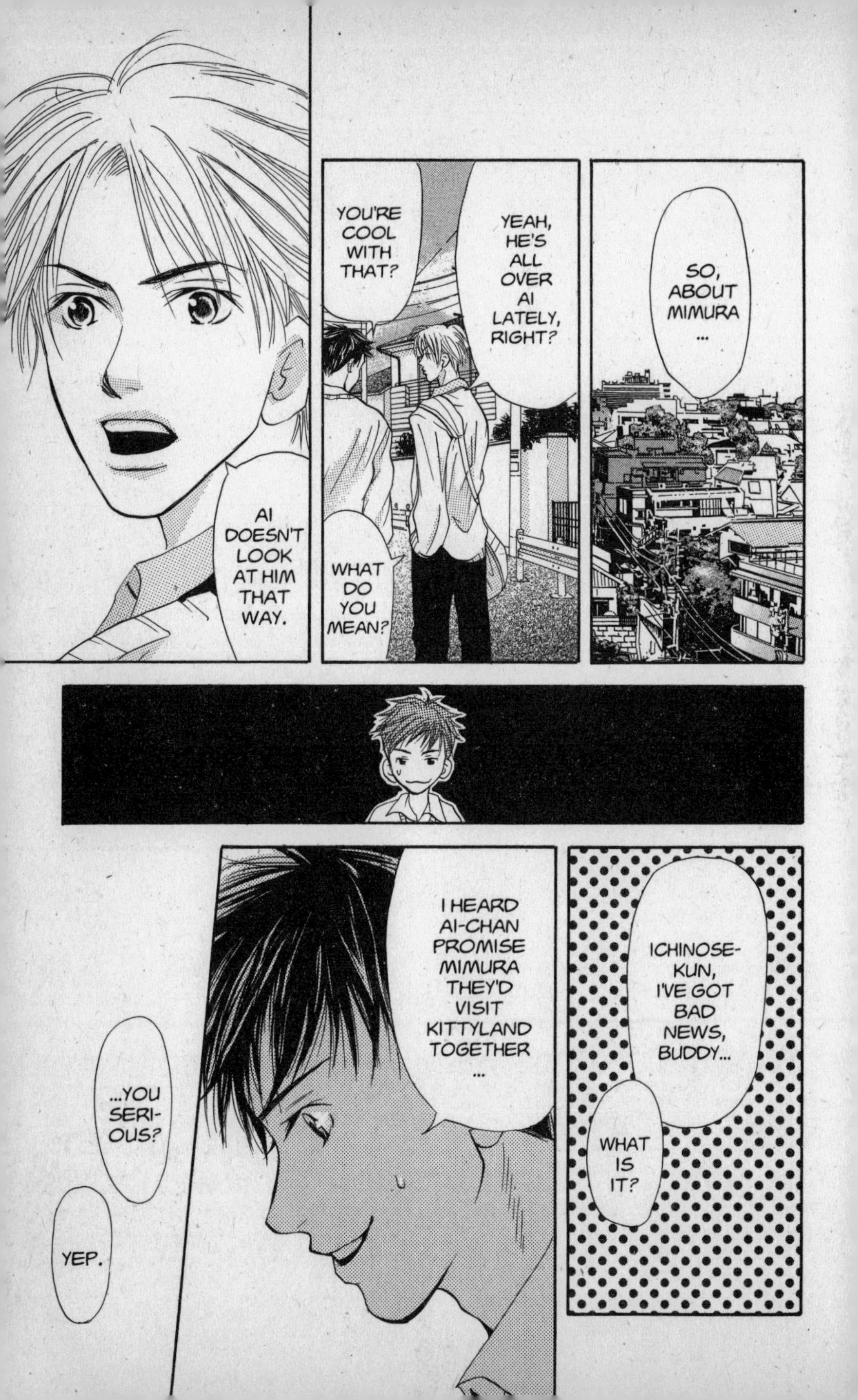
SO, ABOUT MIMURA ...
YEAH, HE'S ALL OVER AI LATELY, RIGHT?
YOU'RE COOL WITH THAT?
WHAT DO YOU MEAN?
AI DOESN'T LOOK AT HIM THAT WAY.
ICHINOSE-KUN, I'VE GOT BAD NEWS, BUDDY...
WHAT IS IT?
I HEARD AI-CHAN PROMISE MIMURA THEY'D VISIT KITTYLAND TOGETHER ...
...YOU SERIOUS?
YEP.

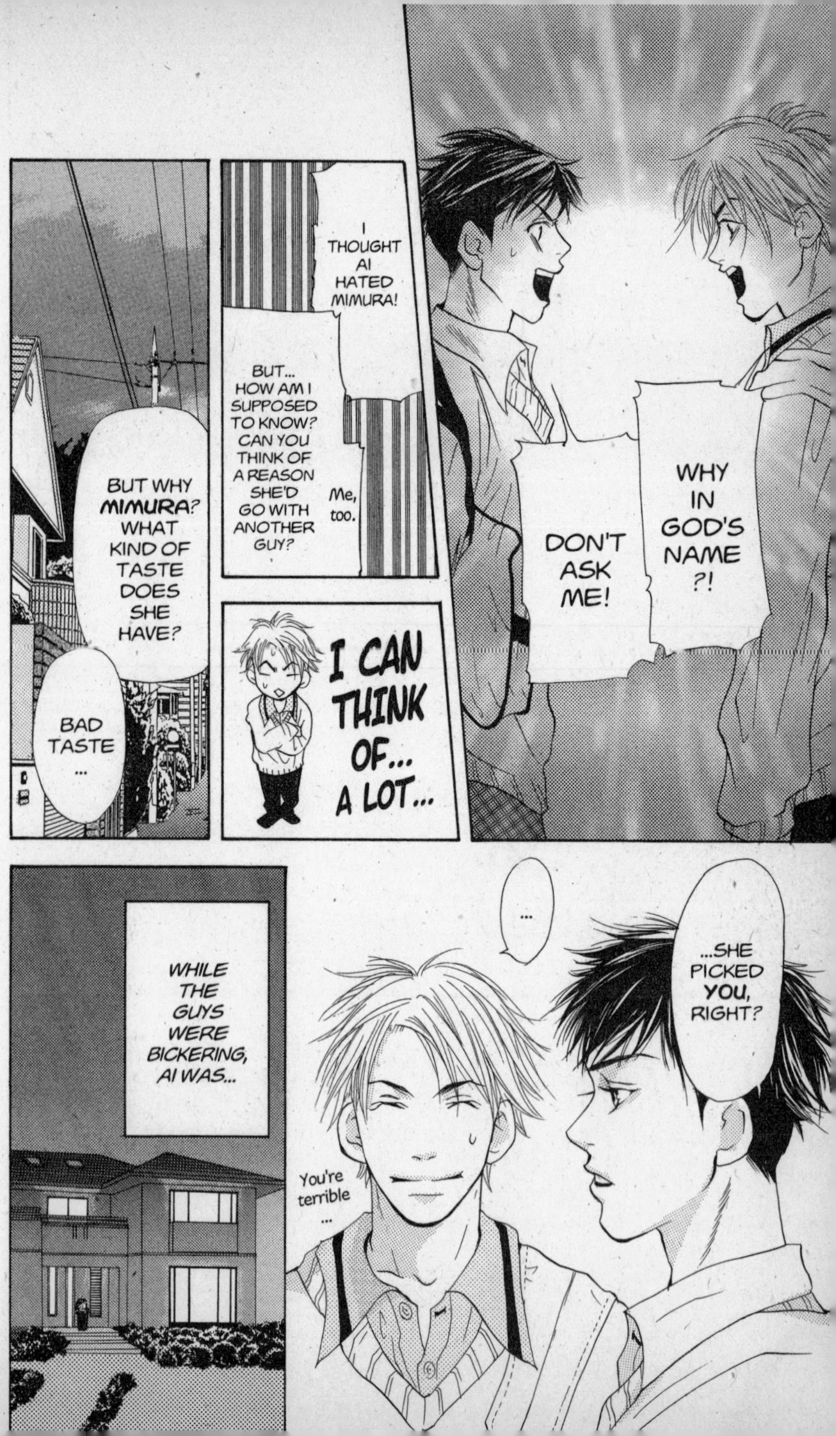
WHY IN GOD'S NAME?!
DON'T ASK ME!
I THOUGHT AI HATED MIMURA!
BUT... HOW AM I SUPPOSED TO KNOW? CAN YOU THINK OF A REASON SHE'D GO WITH ANOTHER GUY?
Me, too.
I CAN THINK OF... A LOT...
BUT WHY MIMURA? WHAT KIND OF TASTE DOES SHE HAVE?
BAD TASTE ...
...SHE PICKED YOU, RIGHT?
...
You're terrible ...
WHILE THE GUYS WERE BICKERING, AI WAS...

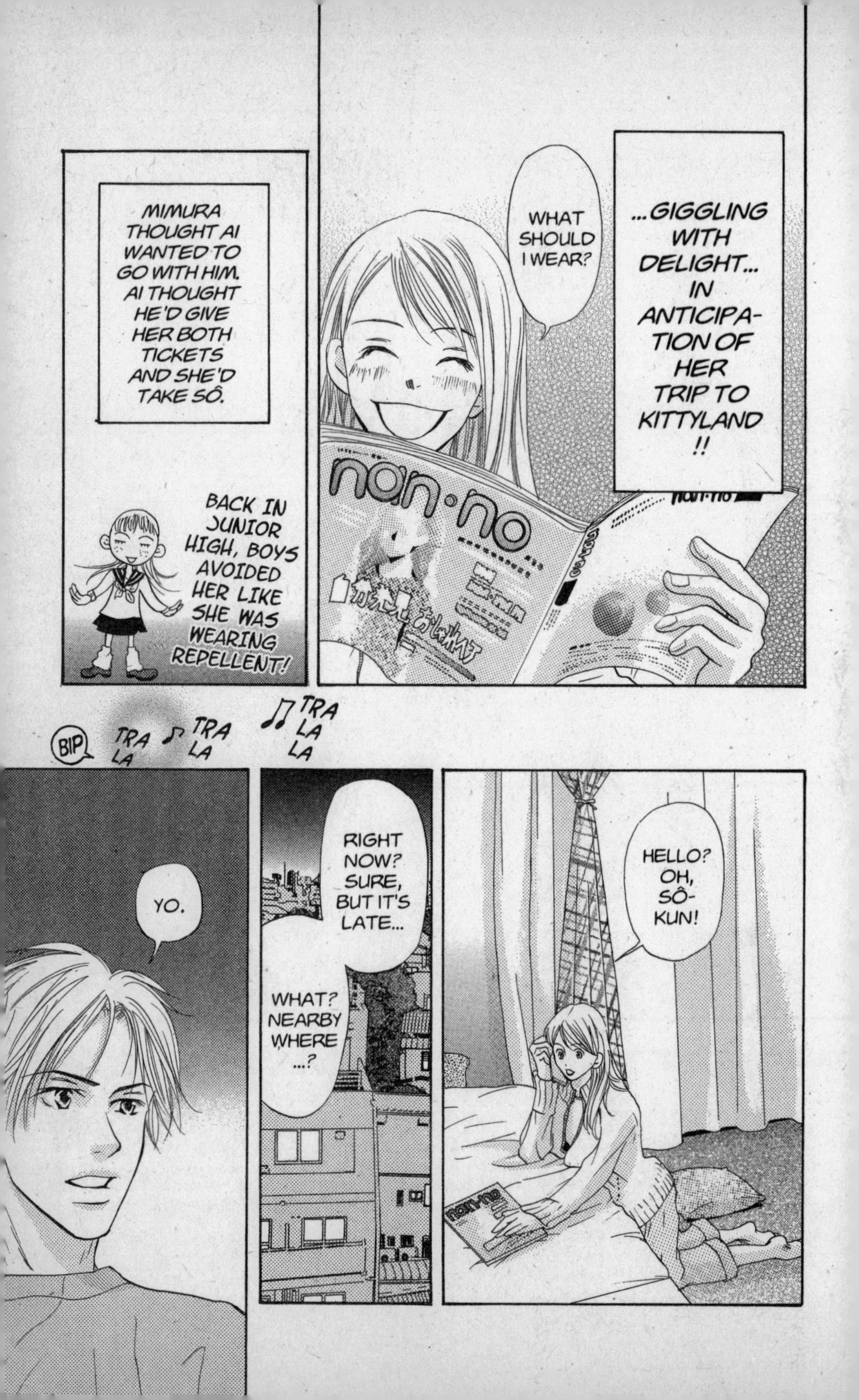
...GIGGLING WITH DELIGHT... IN ANTICIPATION OF HER TRIP TO KITTYLAND !!
WHAT SHOULD I WEAR?
MIMURA THOUGHT AI WANTED TO GO WITH HIM. AI THOUGHT HE'D GIVE HER BOTH TICKETS AND SHE'D TAKE SÔ.
BACK IN JUNIOR HIGH, BOYS AVOIDED HER LIKE SHE WAS WEARING REPELLENT!
TRA LA LA
TRA LA
TRA LA
BIP
HELLO? OH, SÔ-KUN!
RIGHT NOW? SURE, BUT IT'S LATE...
WHAT? NEARBY WHERE ...?
YO.

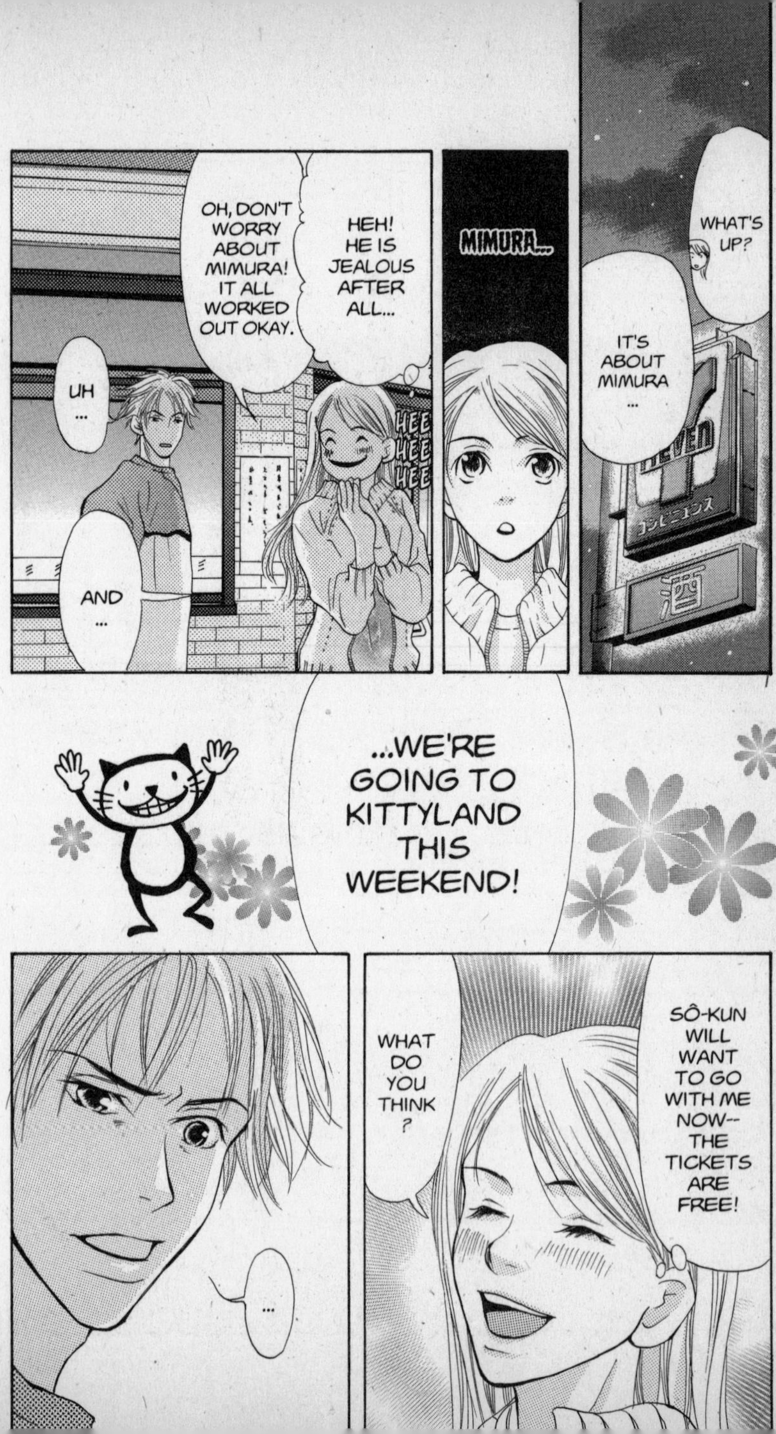
WHAT'S UP?
IT'S ABOUT MIMURA...
MIMURA...
HEH! HE IS JEALOUS AFTER ALL...
HEE HEE HEE
OH, DON'T WORRY ABOUT MIMURA! IT ALL WORKED OUT OKAY.
UH...
AND...
...WE'RE GOING TO KITTYLAND THIS WEEKEND!
SÔ-KUN WILL WANT TO GO WITH ME NOW-- THE TICKETS ARE FREE!
WHAT DO YOU THINK?
...

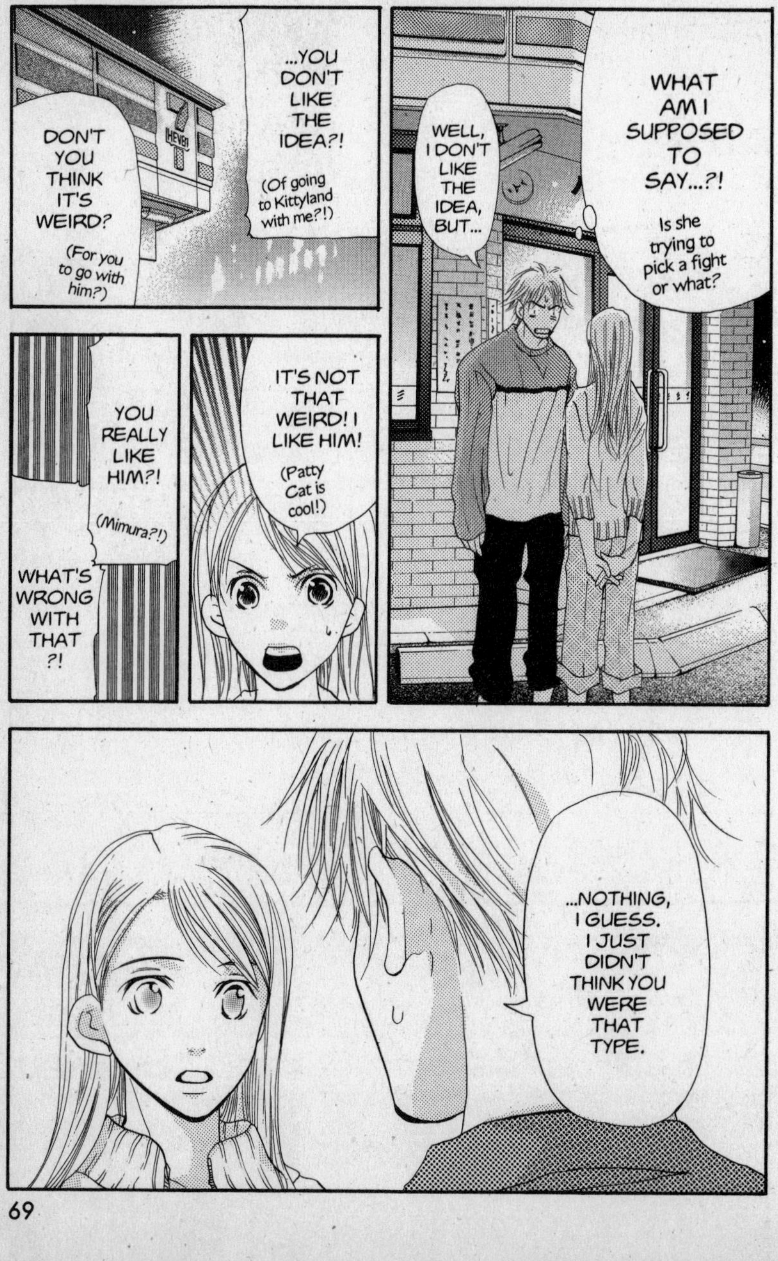
WHAT AM I SUPPOSED TO SAY...?!
Is she trying to pick a fight or what?
WELL, I DON'T LIKE THE IDEA, BUT...
...YOU DON'T LIKE THE IDEA?!
(Of going to Kittyland with me?!)
DON'T YOU THINK IT'S WEIRD?
(For you to go with him?)
IT'S NOT THAT WEIRD! I LIKE HIM!
(Patty Cat is cool!)
YOU REALLY LIKE HIM?!
(Mimura?!)
WHAT'S WRONG WITH THAT?!
...NOTHING, I GUESS. I JUST DIDN'T THINK YOU WERE THAT TYPE.

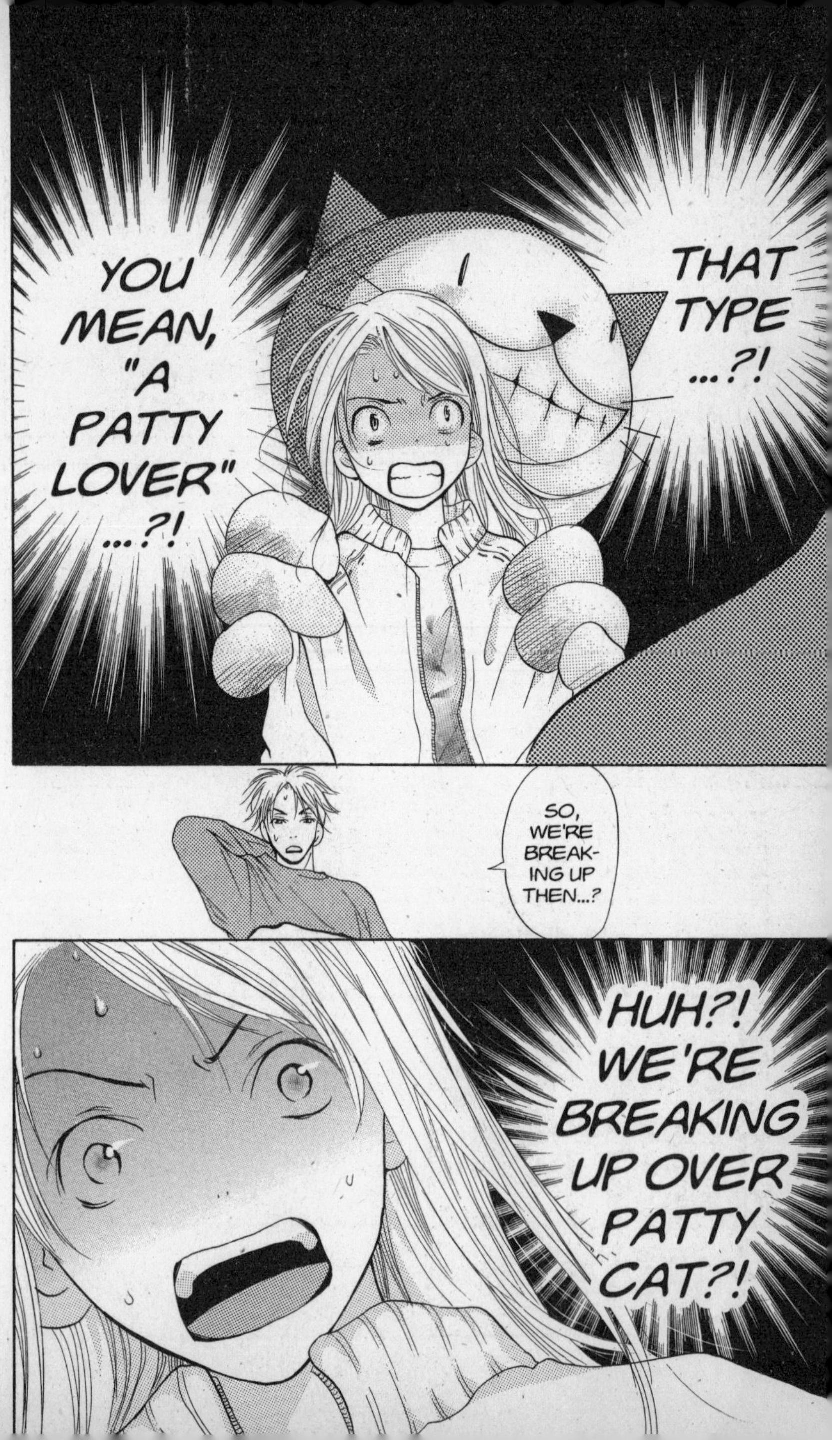
THAT TYPE ...?!
YOU MEAN, "A PATTY LOVER" ...?!
SO, WE'RE BREAKING UP THEN...?
HUH?! WE'RE BREAKING UP OVER PATTY CAT?!

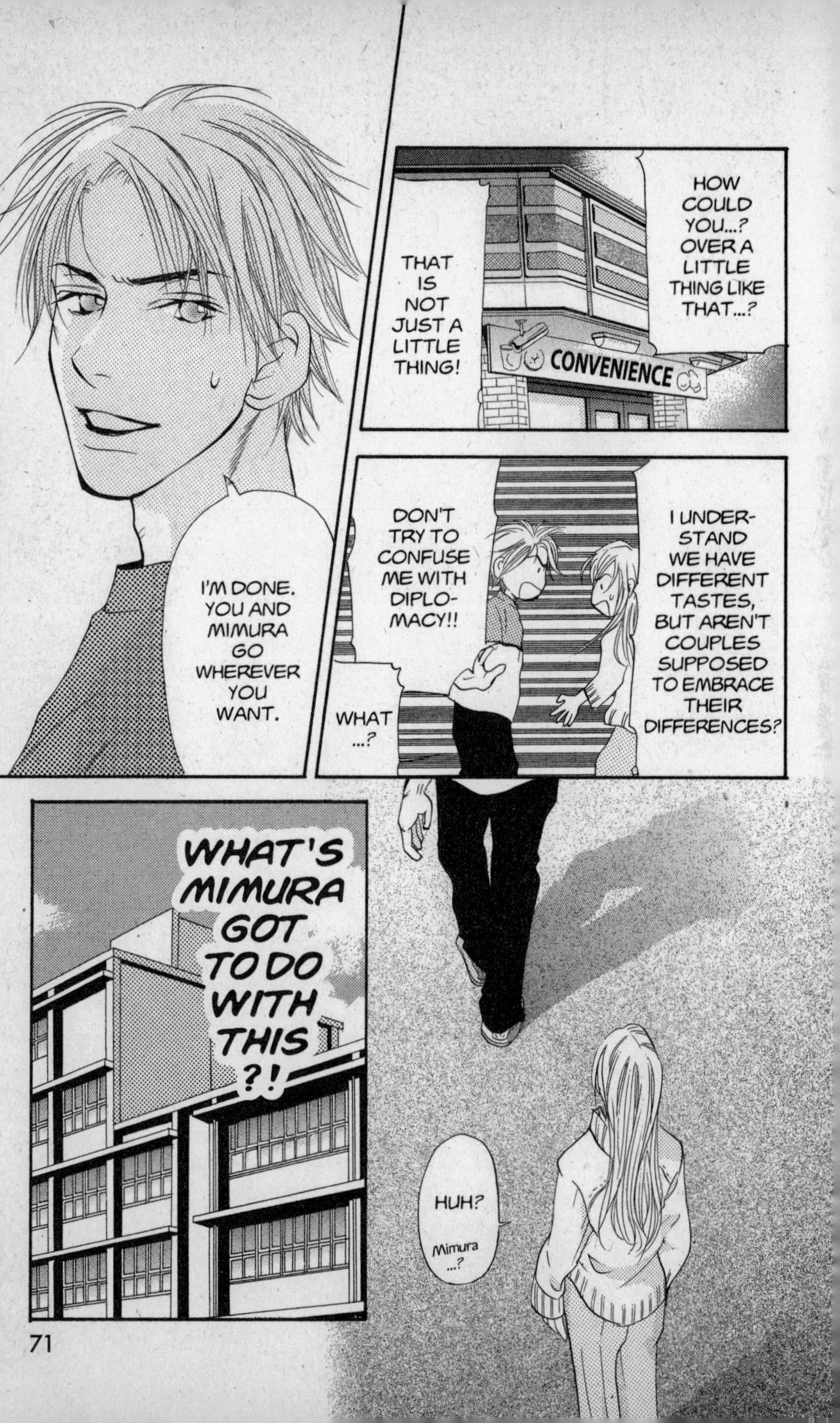
HOW COULD YOU...? OVER A LITTLE THING LIKE THAT...?
CONVENIENCE
THAT IS NOT JUST A LITTLE THING!
I UNDERSTAND WE HAVE DIFFERENT TASTES, BUT AREN'T COUPLES SUPPOSED TO EMBRACE THEIR DIFFERENCES?
DON'T TRY TO CONFUSE ME WITH DIPLOMACY!!
WHAT ...?
I'M DONE. YOU AND MIMURA GO WHEREVER YOU WANT.
HUH?
Mimura ...?
WHAT'S MIMURA GOT TO DO WITH THIS?!

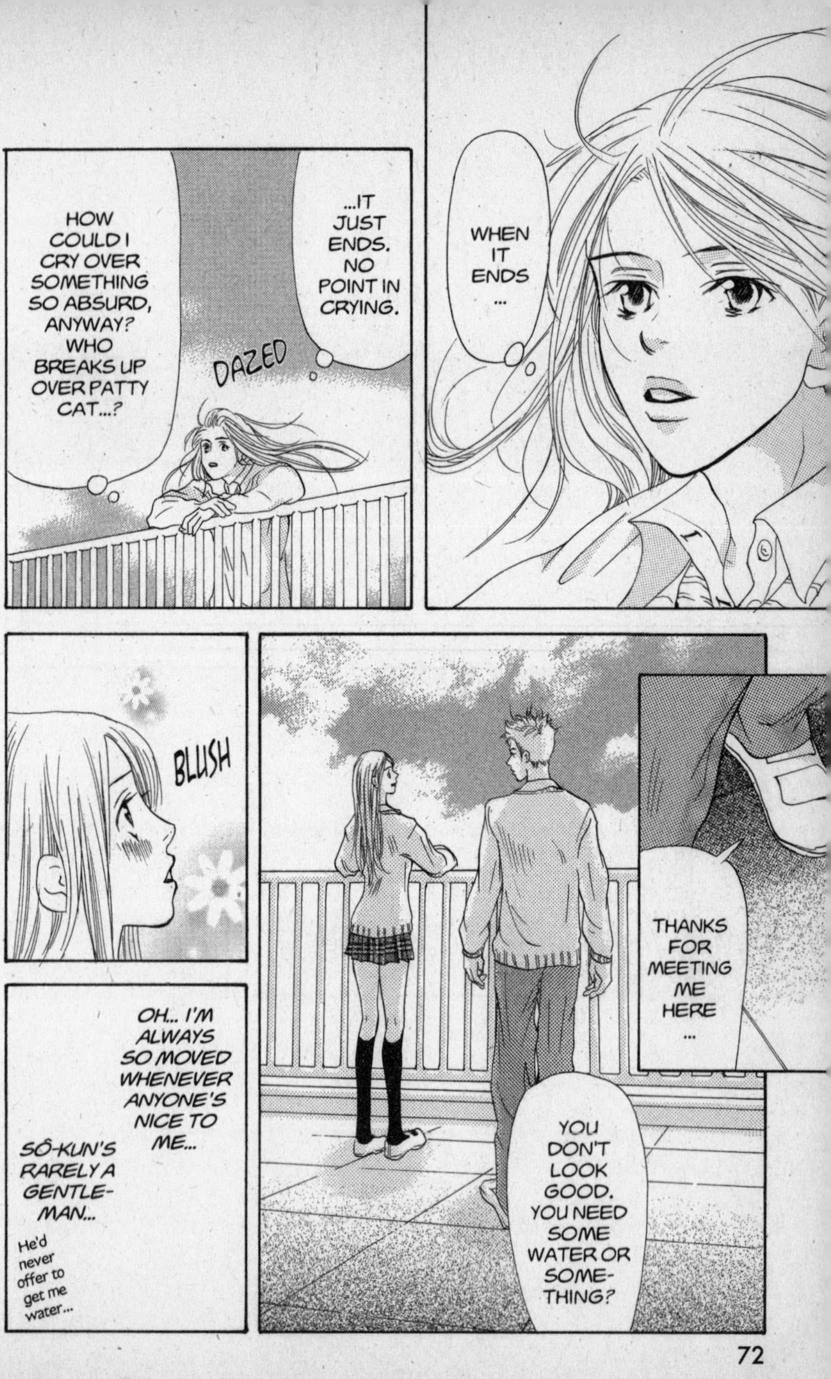
WHEN IT ENDS ...
...IT JUST ENDS. NO POINT IN CRYING.
HOW COULD I CRY OVER SOMETHING SO ABSURD, ANYWAY? WHO BREAKS UP OVER PATTY CAT...?
DAZED
THANKS FOR MEETING ME HERE ...
YOU DON'T LOOK GOOD. YOU NEED SOME WATER OR SOME-THING?
BLUSH
OH... I'M ALWAYS SO MOVED WHENEVER ANYONE'S NICE TO ME...
SÔ-KUN'S RARELY A GENTLE-MAN...
He'd never offer to get me water...

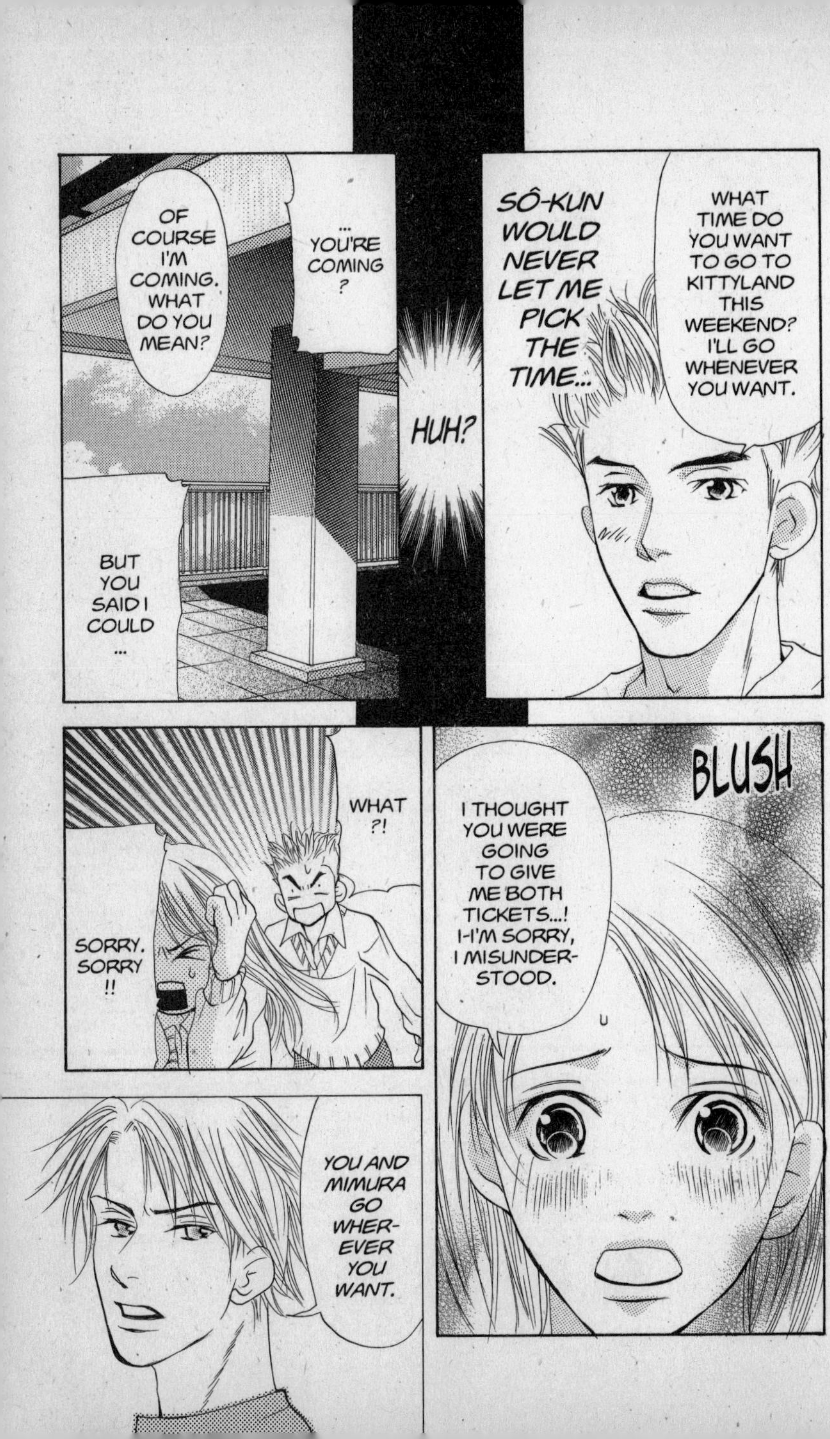
WHAT TIME DO YOU WANT TO GO TO KITTYLAND THIS WEEKEND? I'LL GO WHENEVER YOU WANT.
SÔ-KUN WOULD NEVER LET ME PICK THE TIME...
HUH?
... YOU'RE COMING?
OF COURSE I'M COMING. WHAT DO YOU MEAN?
BUT YOU SAID I COULD ...
BLUSH
I THOUGHT YOU WERE GOING TO GIVE ME BOTH TICKETS...! I-I'M SORRY, I MISUNDERSTOOD.
WHAT ?!
SORRY. SORRY !!
YOU AND MIMURA GO WHEREVER YOU WANT.

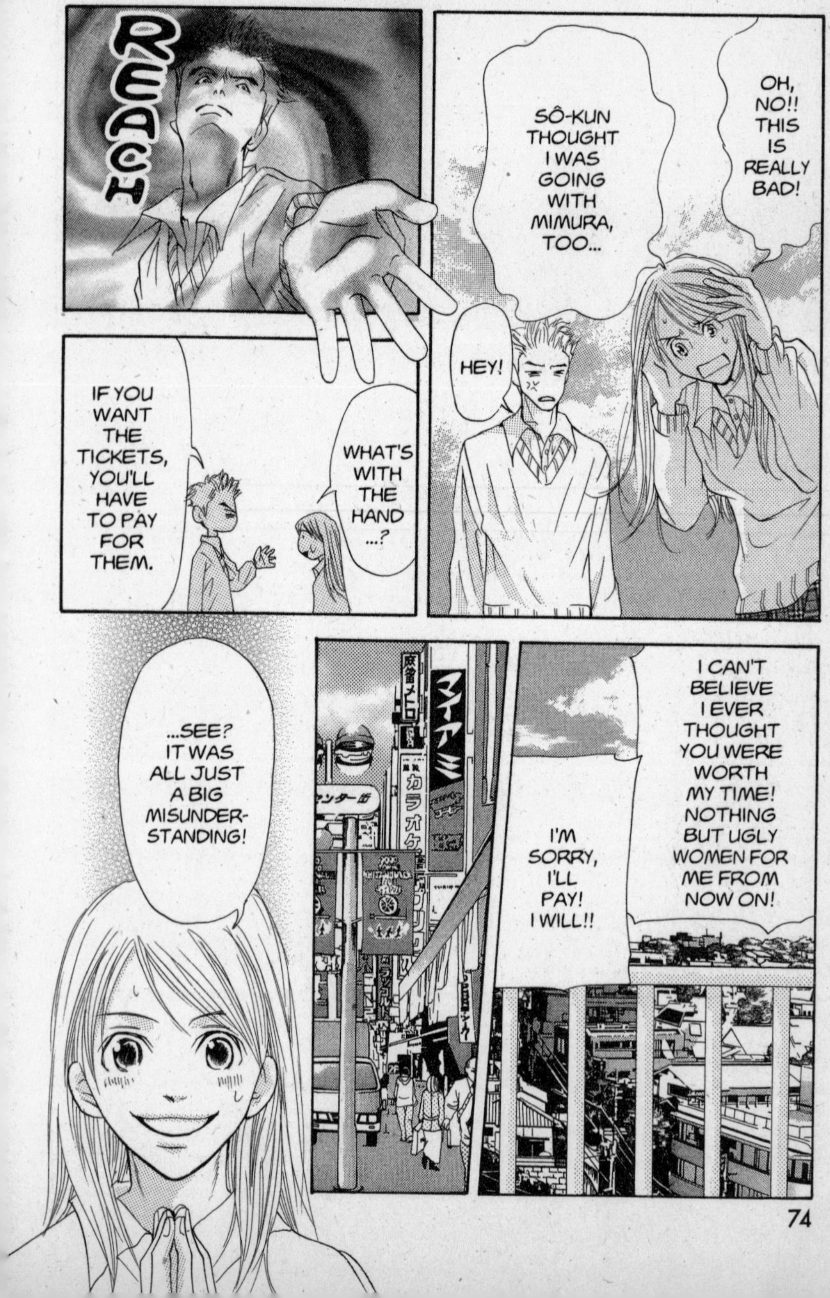
OH, NO!! THIS IS REALLY BAD!
SÔ-KUN THOUGHT I WAS GOING WITH MIMURA, TOO...
HEY!
REACH
WHAT'S WITH THE HAND ...?
IF YOU WANT THE TICKETS, YOU'LL HAVE TO PAY FOR THEM.
I CAN'T BELIEVE I EVER THOUGHT YOU WERE WORTH MY TIME! NOTHING BUT UGLY WOMEN FOR ME FROM NOW ON!
I'M SORRY, I'LL PAY! I WILL!!
...SEE? IT WAS ALL JUST A BIG MISUNDER-STANDING!

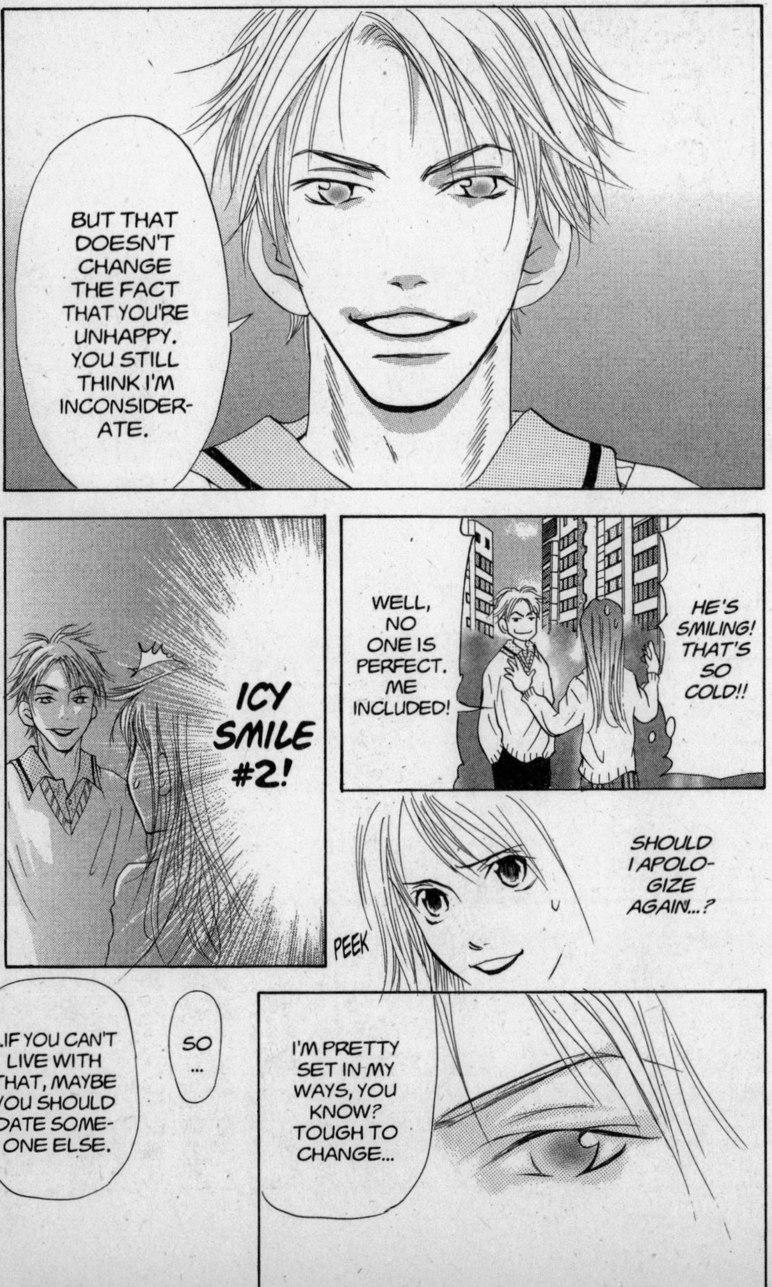
BUT THAT DOESN'T CHANGE THE FACT THAT YOU'RE UNHAPPY. YOU STILL THINK I'M INCONSIDER-ATE.
HE'S SMILING! THAT'S SO COLD!!
WELL, NO ONE IS PERFECT. ME INCLUDED!
SHOULD I APOLO-GIZE AGAIN...?
PEEK
ICY SMILE #2!
I'M PRETTY SET IN MY WAYS, YOU KNOW? TOUGH TO CHANGE...
SO ...
...IF YOU CAN'T LIVE WITH THAT, MAYBE YOU SHOULD DATE SOME-ONE ELSE.

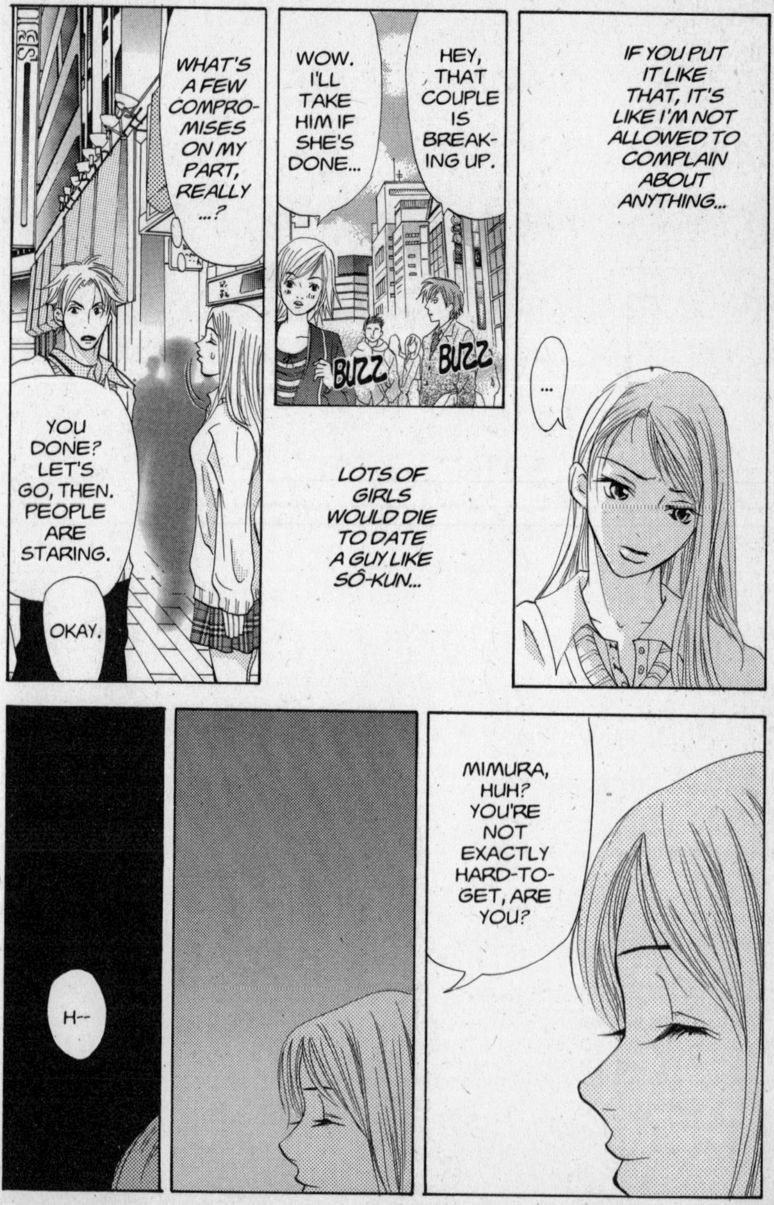
IF YOU PUT IT LIKE THAT, IT'S LIKE I'M NOT ALLOWED TO COMPLAIN ABOUT ANYTHING...
...
HEY, THAT COUPLE IS BREAKING UP.
WOW. I'LL TAKE HIM IF SHE'S DONE...
BUZZ
BUZZ
LOTS OF GIRLS WOULD DIE TO DATE A GUY LIKE SÔ-KUN...
WHAT'S A FEW COMPROMISES ON MY PART, REALLY ...?
YOU DONE? LET'S GO, THEN. PEOPLE ARE STARING.
OKAY.
MIMURA, HUH? YOU'RE NOT EXACTLY HARD-TO-GET, ARE YOU?
H--

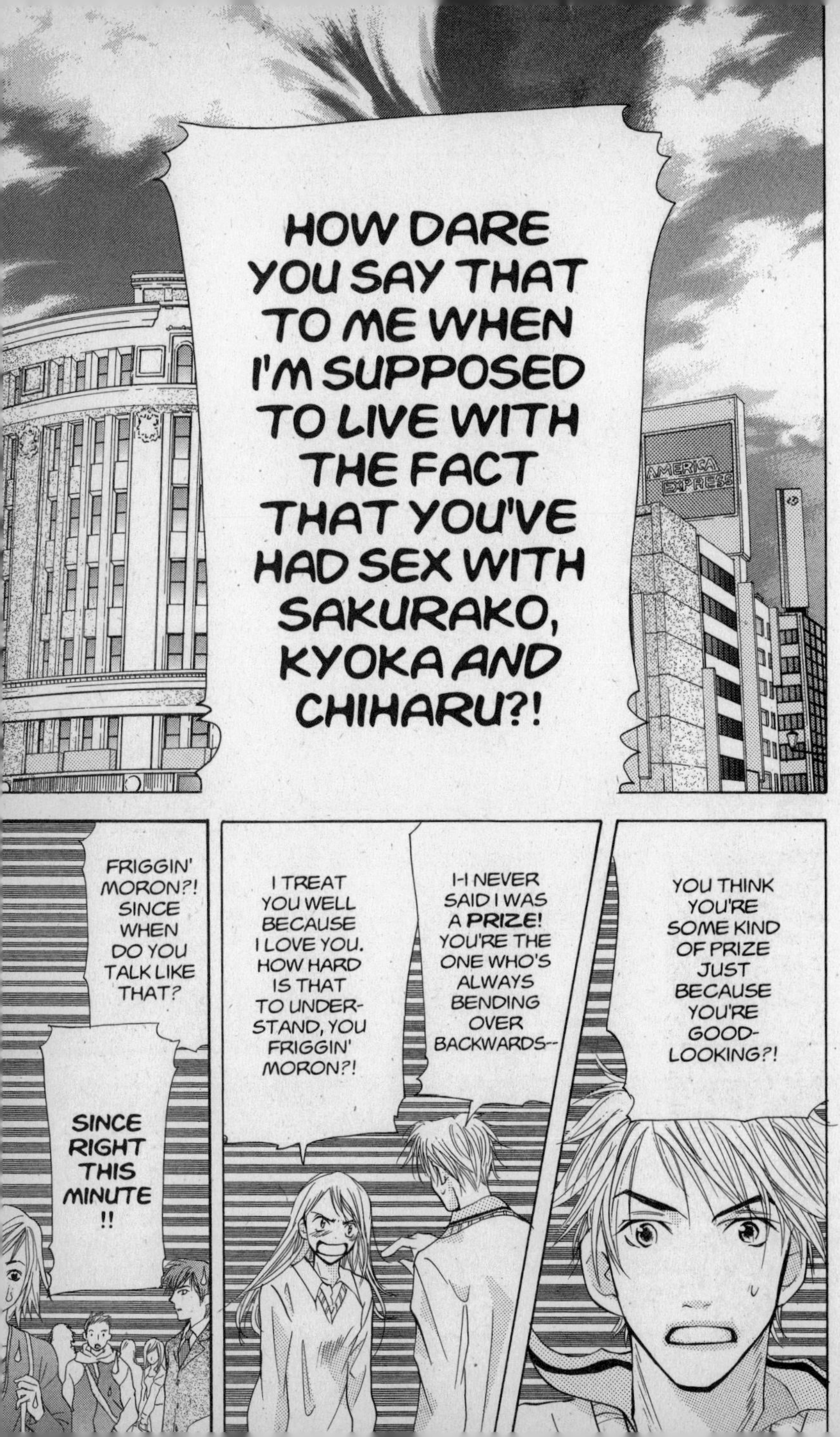
HOW DARE YOU SAY THAT TO ME WHEN I'M SUPPOSED TO LIVE WITH THE FACT THAT YOU'VE HAD SEX WITH SAKURAKO, KYOKA AND CHIHARU?!
AMERICA EXPRESS
YOU THINK YOU'RE SOME KIND OF PRIZE JUST BECAUSE YOU'RE GOOD-LOOKING?!
I-I NEVER SAID I WAS A **PRIZE**! YOU'RE THE ONE WHO'S ALWAYS BENDING OVER BACKWARDS--
I TREAT YOU WELL BECAUSE I LOVE YOU. HOW HARD IS THAT TO UNDER-STAND, YOU FRIGGIN' MORON?!
FRIGGIN' MORON?! SINCE WHEN DO YOU TALK LIKE THAT?
SINCE RIGHT THIS MINUTE!!

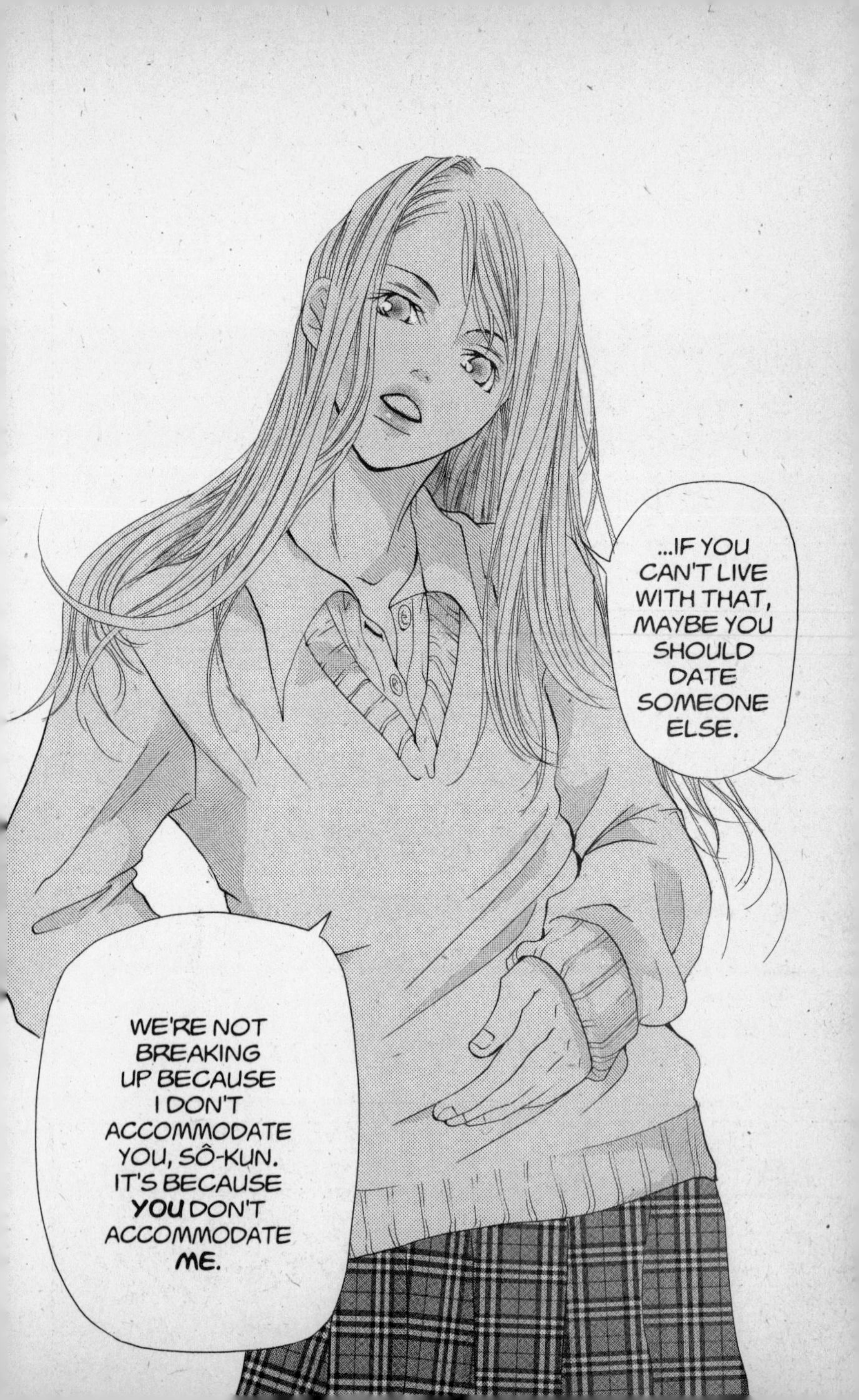
...IF YOU CAN'T LIVE WITH THAT, MAYBE YOU SHOULD DATE SOMEONE ELSE.
WE'RE NOT BREAKING UP BECAUSE I DON'T ACCOMMODATE YOU, SÔ-KUN. IT'S BECAUSE **YOU** DON'T ACCOMMODATE **ME**.

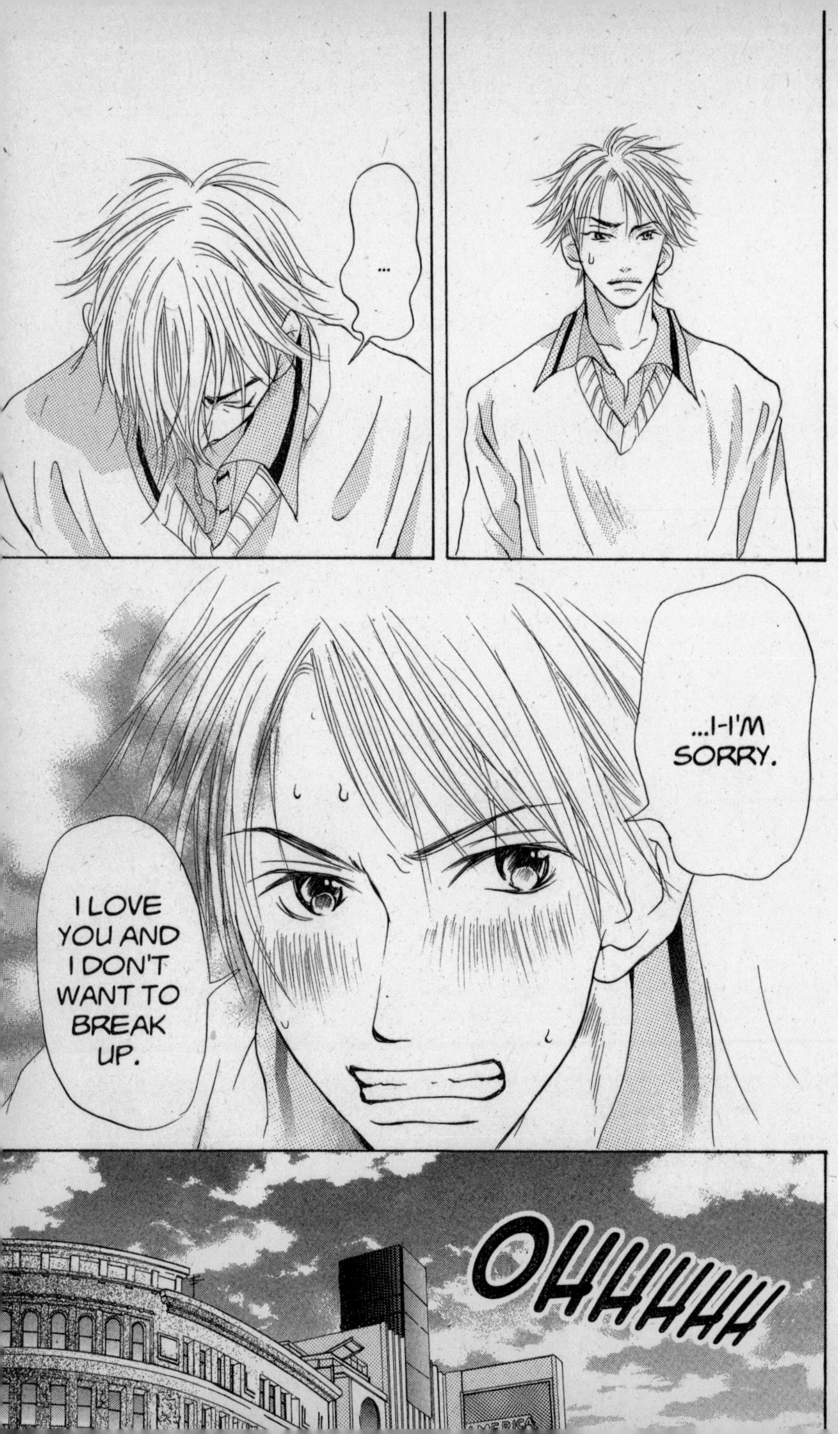
...
...I-I'M SORRY.
I LOVE YOU AND I DON'T WANT TO BREAK UP.
OHHHHH

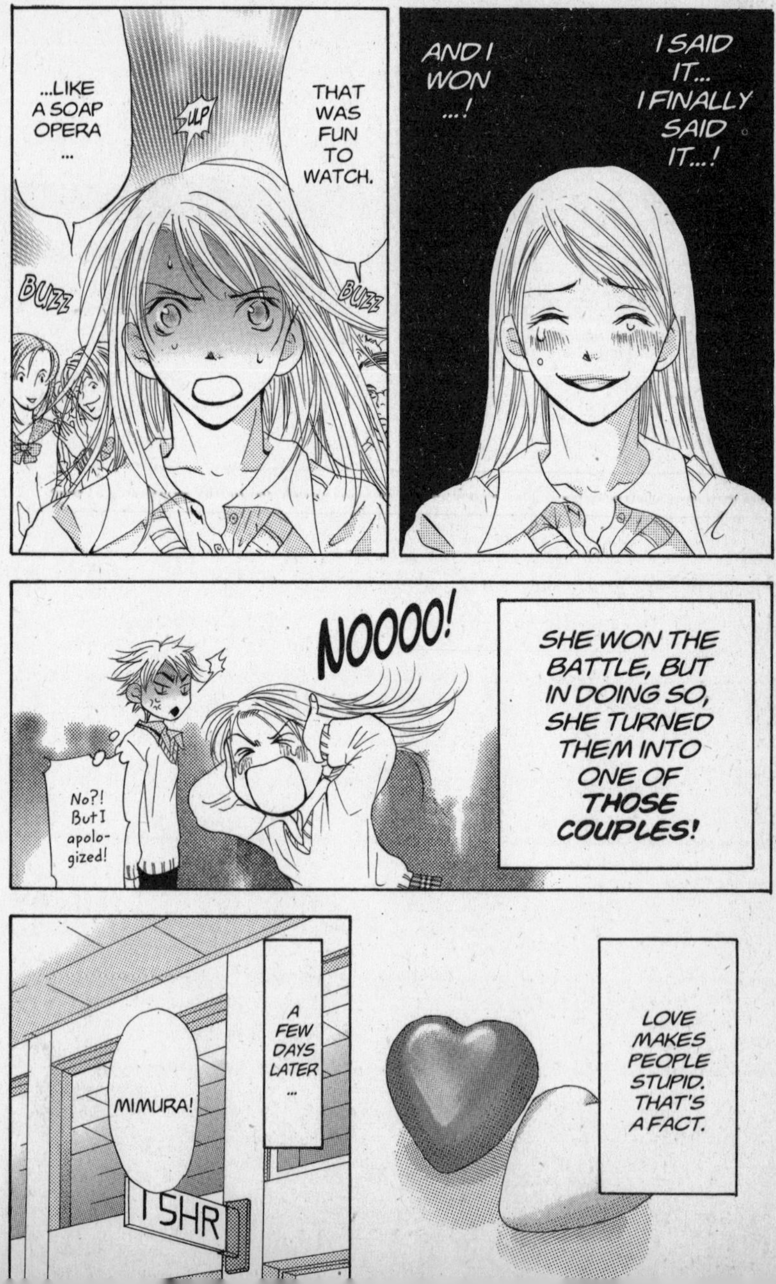
I SAID IT... I FINALLY SAID IT...!
AND I WON ...!
THAT WAS FUN TO WATCH.
ULP
...LIKE A SOAP OPERA ...
BUZZ
BUZZ
SHE WON THE BATTLE, BUT IN DOING SO, SHE TURNED THEM INTO ONE OF THOSE COUPLES!
NOOOO!
No?! But I apologized!
LOVE MAKES PEOPLE STUPID. THAT'S A FACT.
A FEW DAYS LATER ...
MIMURA!
1 5HR

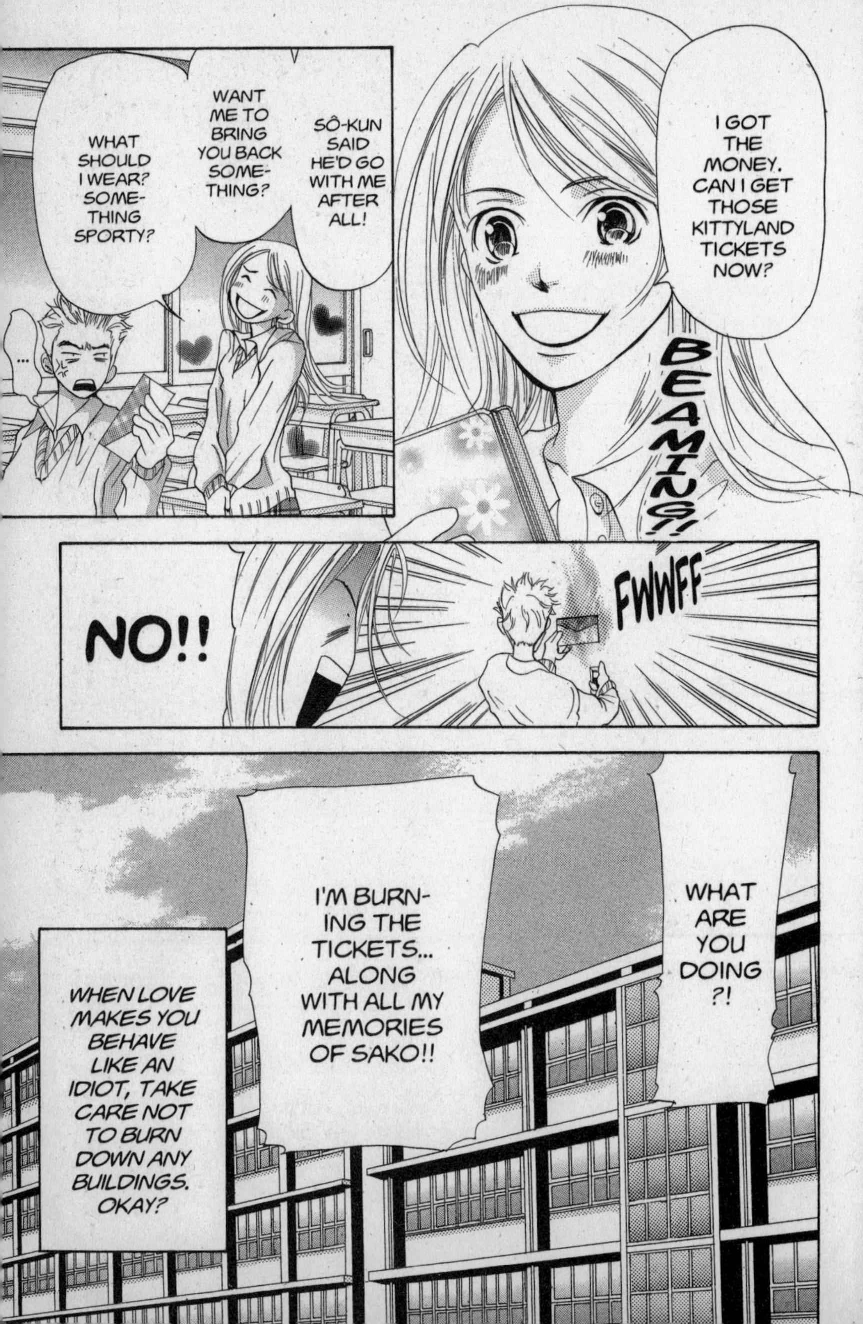
I GOT THE MONEY. CAN I GET THOSE KITTYLAND TICKETS NOW?
BEAMING!!
SÔ-KUN SAID HE'D GO WITH ME AFTER ALL!
WANT ME TO BRING YOU BACK SOME-THING?
WHAT SHOULD I WEAR? SOME-THING SPORTY?
...
FWWFF
NO!!
WHAT ARE YOU DOING ?!
I'M BURN-ING THE TICKETS... ALONG WITH ALL MY MEMORIES OF SAKO!!
WHEN LOVE MAKES YOU BEHAVE LIKE AN IDIOT, TAKE CARE NOT TO BURN DOWN ANY BUILDINGS. OKAY?

Dearest Readers of DOUBT!!

At this point, the series moved from "Bessatsu Shôjo Comics" to "Betsucomi," which forced me to change the tone and direction a little. It's best to read the remaining chapters in one sitting.

There were so many things that I didn't get a chance to do before the series was cancelled. The only reason I was even able to bring it to a conclusion was because you all showed your support. All joking aside (which is unusual for me), I want to express my heartfelt appreciation.

Thank you so much!

Izumi

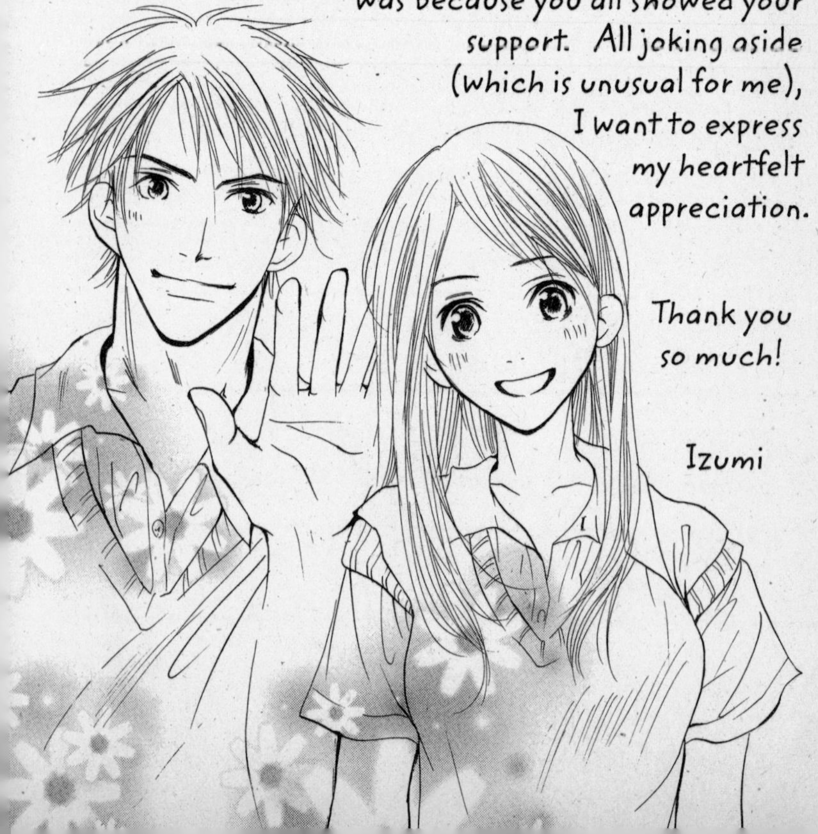

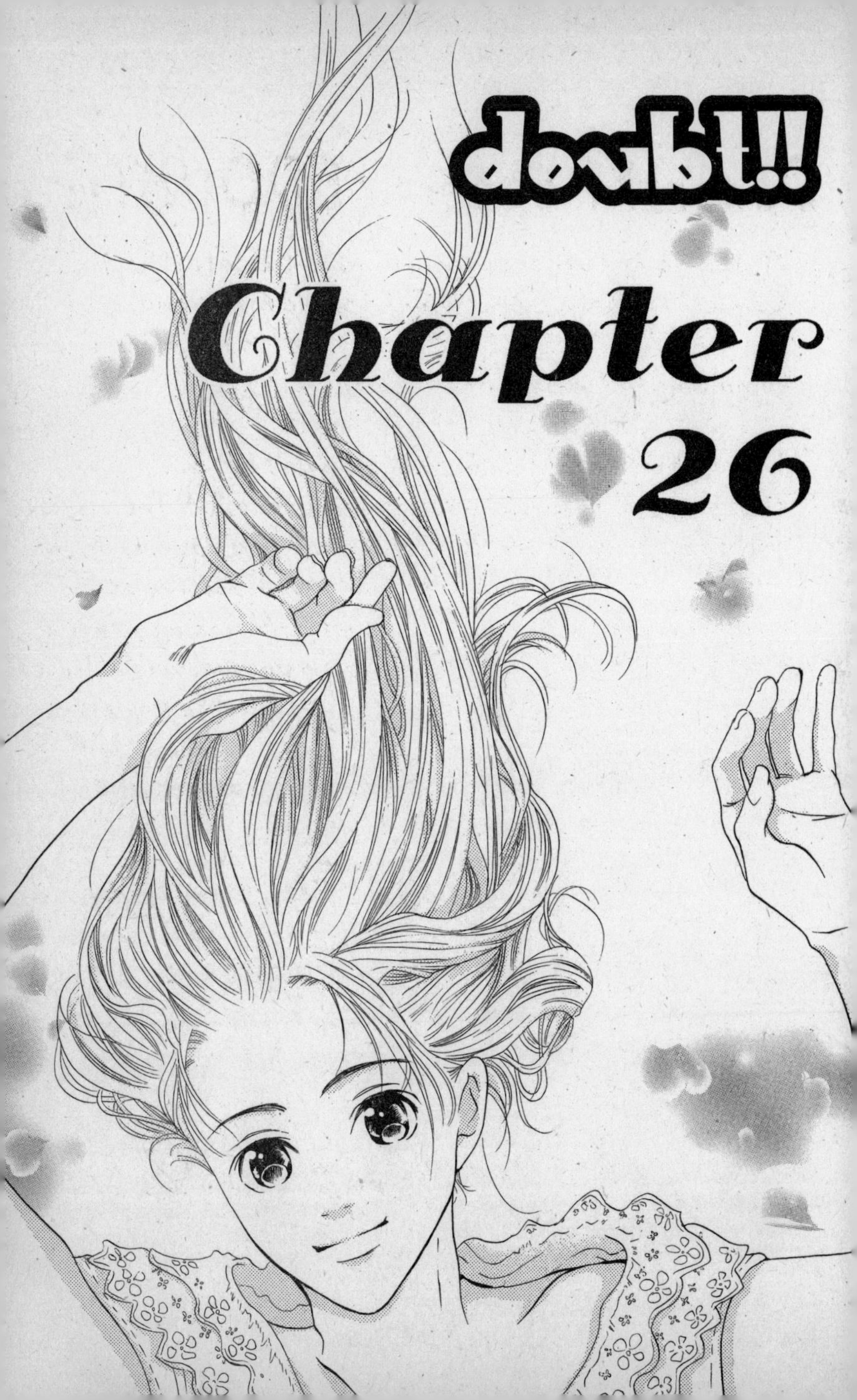
doubt!!
Chapter 26

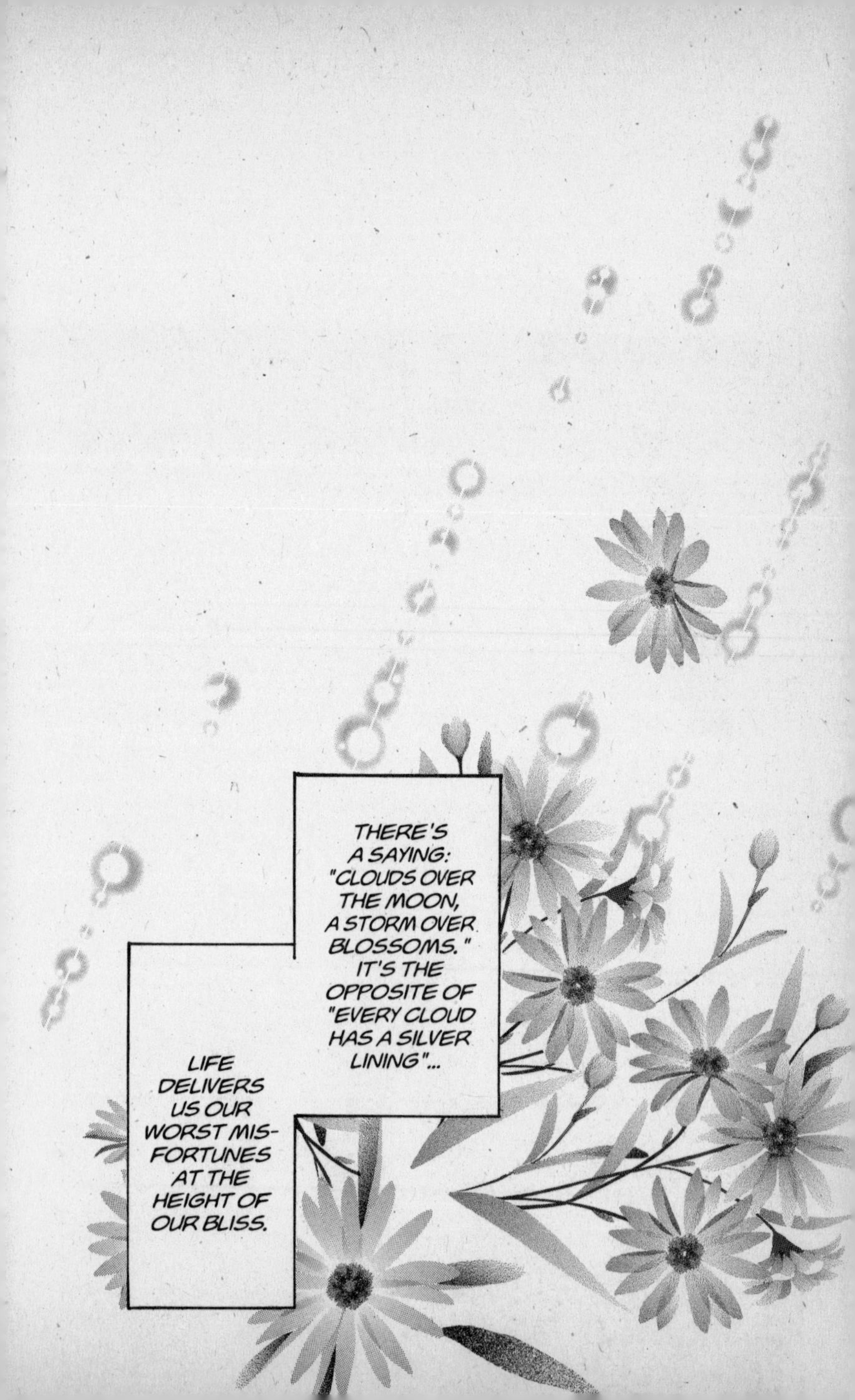
THERE'S A SAYING: "CLOUDS OVER THE MOON, A STORM OVER BLOSSOMS." IT'S THE OPPOSITE OF "EVERY CLOUD HAS A SILVER LINING"...
LIFE DELIVERS US OUR WORST MIS-FORTUNES AT THE HEIGHT OF OUR BLISS.

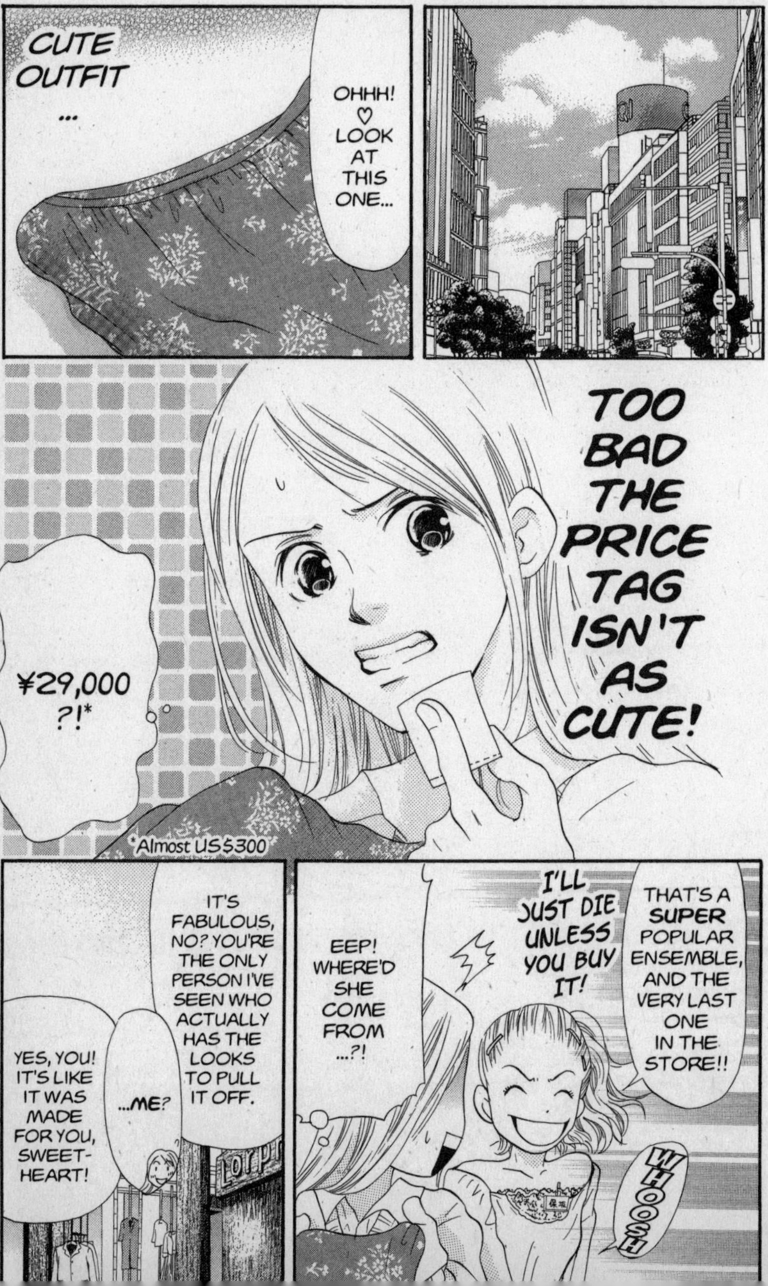

OHHH! ♡ LOOK AT THIS ONE...
CUTE OUTFIT ...
TOO BAD THE PRICE TAG ISN'T AS CUTE!
¥29,000 ?!*
*Almost US$300
THAT'S A SUPER POPULAR ENSEMBLE, AND THE VERY LAST ONE IN THE STORE!!
I'LL JUST DIE UNLESS YOU BUY IT!
EEP! WHERE'D SHE COME FROM ...?!
WHOOSH
IT'S FABULOUS, NO? YOU'RE THE ONLY PERSON I'VE SEEN WHO ACTUALLY HAS THE LOOKS TO PULL IT OFF.
...ME?
YES, YOU! IT'S LIKE IT WAS MADE FOR YOU, SWEET-HEART!

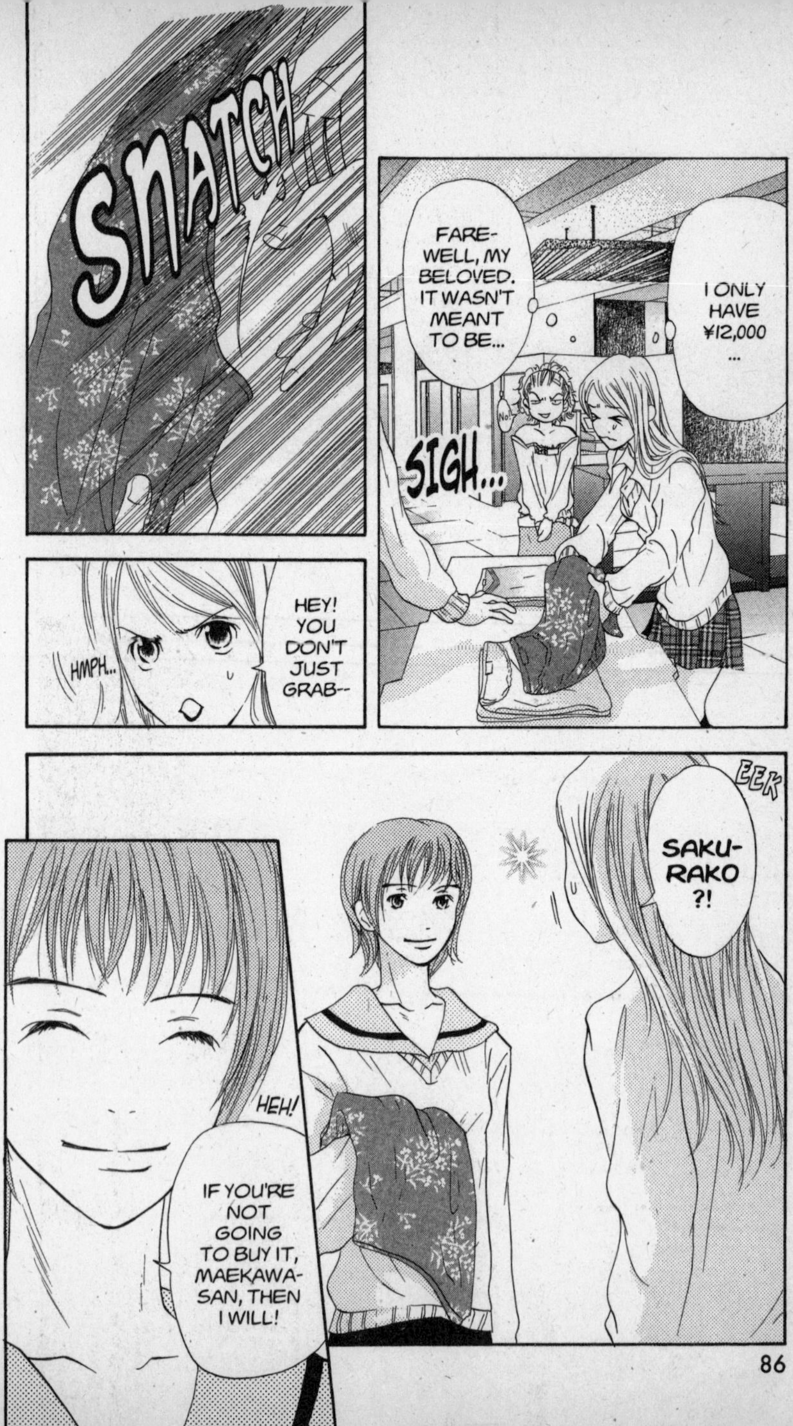
I ONLY HAVE ¥12,000 ...
FARE-WELL, MY BELOVED. IT WASN'T MEANT TO BE...
No!
SIGH...
SNATCH
HEY! YOU DON'T JUST GRAB--
HMPH...
EEK
SAKU-RAKO ?!
HEH!
IF YOU'RE NOT GOING TO BUY IT, MAEKAWA-SAN, THEN I WILL!

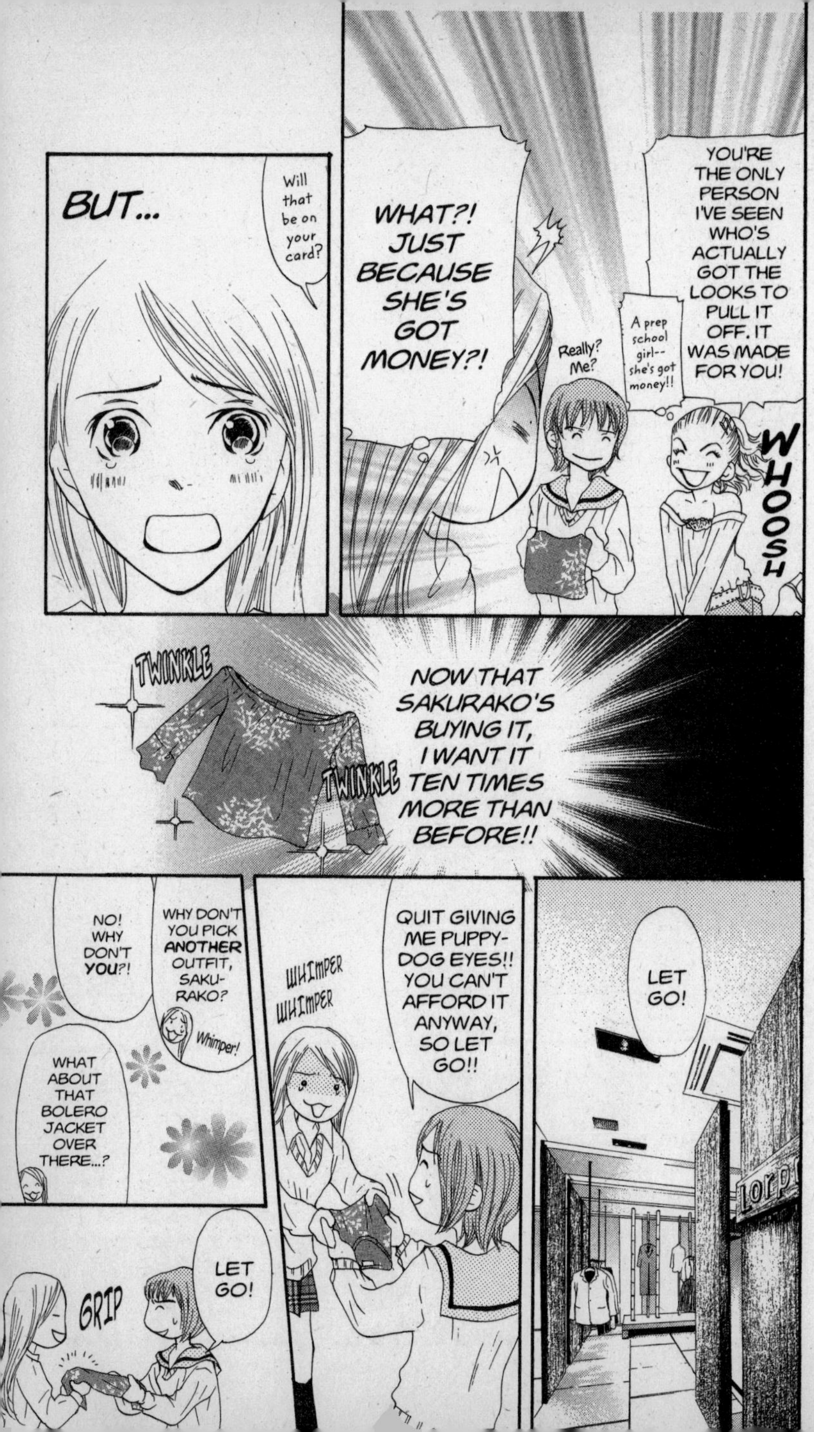

YOU'RE THE ONLY PERSON I'VE SEEN WHO'S ACTUALLY GOT THE LOOKS TO PULL IT OFF. IT WAS MADE FOR YOU!
A prep school girl-- she's got money!!
Really? Me?
WHOOSH
WHAT?! JUST BECAUSE SHE'S GOT MONEY?!
Will that be on your card?
BUT...
NOW THAT SAKURAKO'S BUYING IT, I WANT IT TEN TIMES MORE THAN BEFORE!!
TWINKLE
TWINKLE
LET GO!
QUIT GIVING ME PUPPY-DOG EYES!! YOU CAN'T AFFORD IT ANYWAY, SO LET GO!!
WHIMPER WHIMPER
WHY DON'T YOU PICK ANOTHER OUTFIT, SAKU-RAKO?
Whimper!
NO! WHY DON'T YOU?!
WHAT ABOUT THAT BOLERO JACKET OVER THERE...?
LET GO!
GRIP

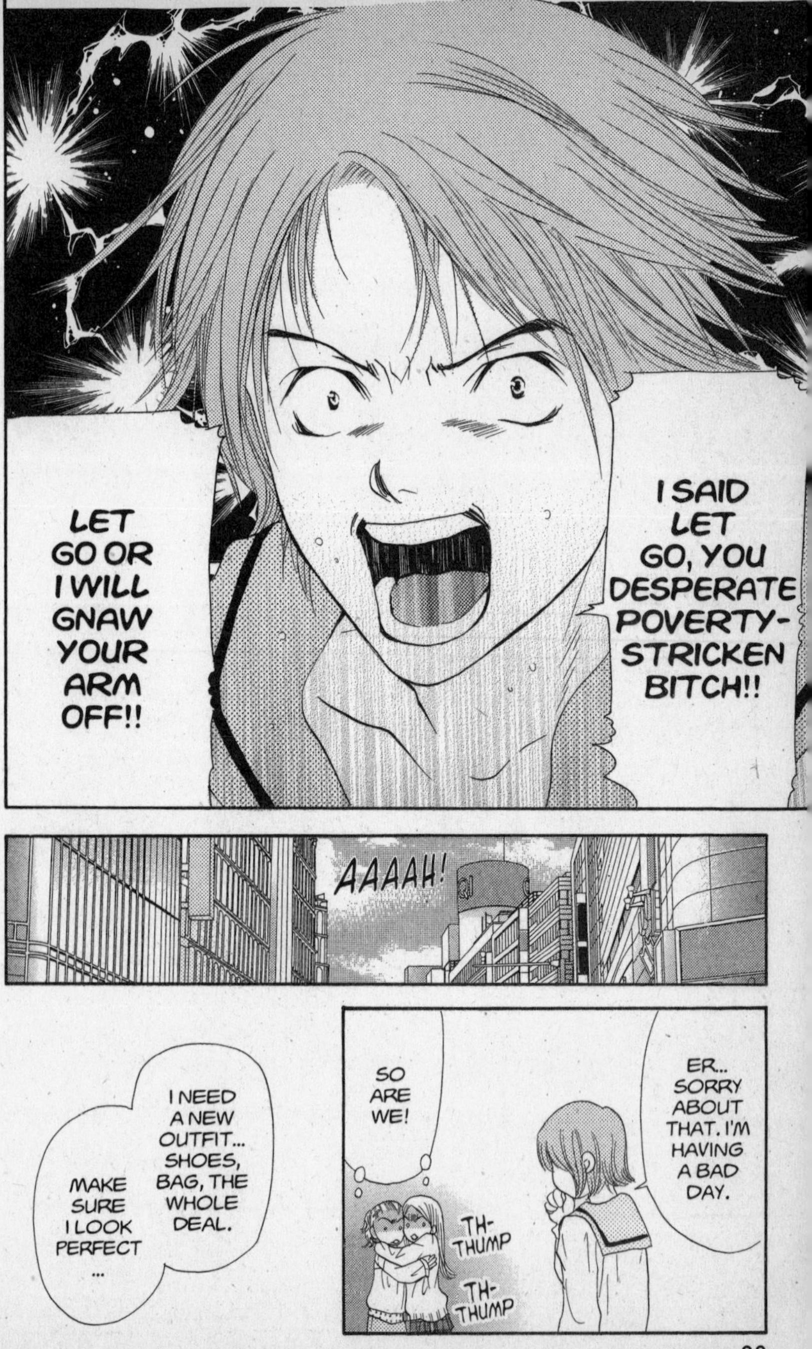
I SAID LET GO, YOU DESPERATE POVERTY-STRICKEN BITCH!!
LET GO OR I WILL GNAW YOUR ARM OFF!!
AAAAH!
ER... SORRY ABOUT THAT. I'M HAVING A BAD DAY.
SO ARE WE!
TH-THUMP
TH-THUMP
I NEED A NEW OUTFIT... SHOES, BAG, THE WHOLE DEAL.
MAKE SURE I LOOK PERFECT...

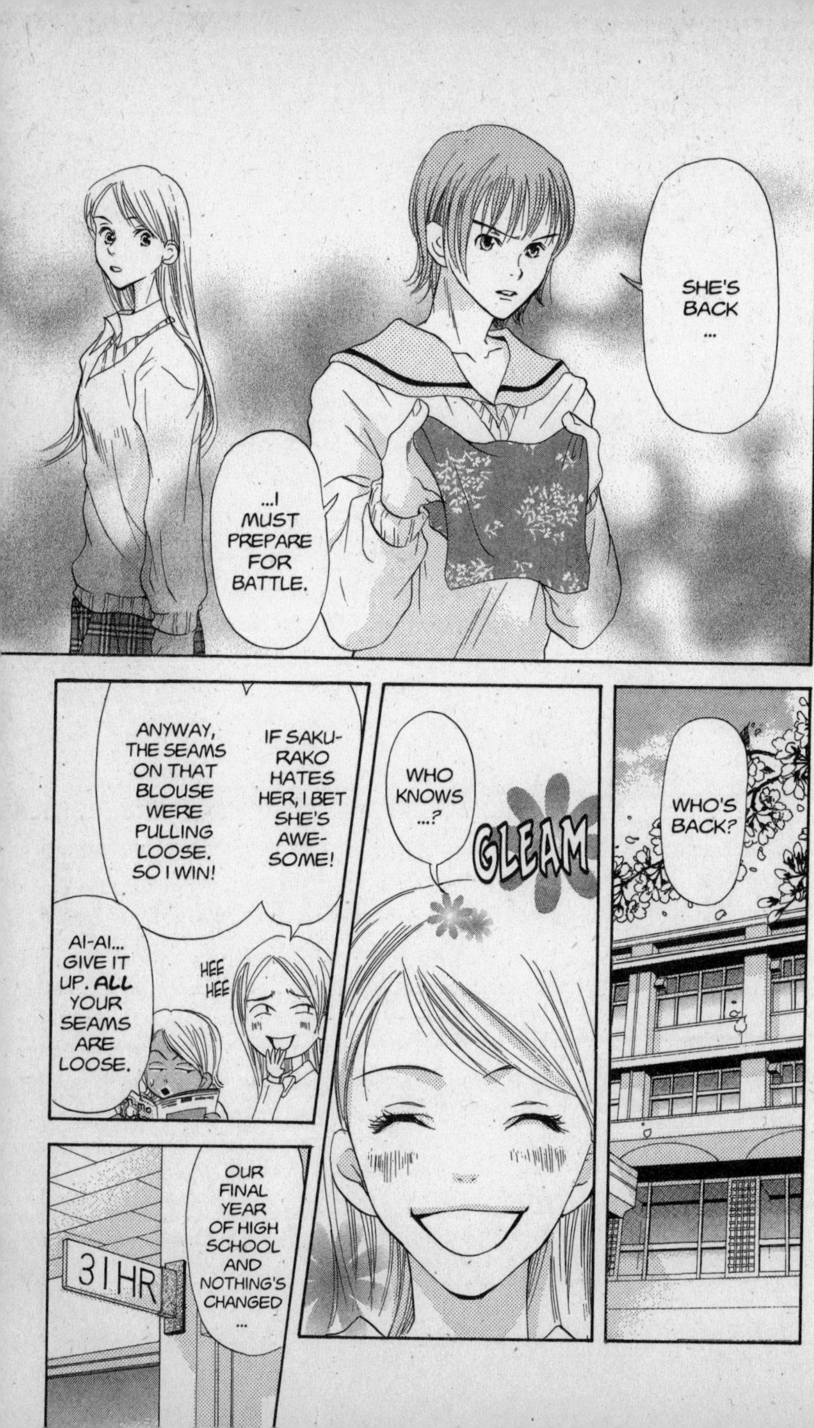
SHE'S BACK ...
...I MUST PREPARE FOR BATTLE.
WHO'S BACK?
WHO KNOWS ...?
GLEAM
IF SAKU-RAKO HATES HER, I BET SHE'S AWE-SOME!
ANYWAY, THE SEAMS ON THAT BLOUSE WERE PULLING LOOSE. SO I WIN!
HEE HEE
AI-AI... GIVE IT UP. ALL YOUR SEAMS ARE LOOSE.
31 HR
OUR FINAL YEAR OF HIGH SCHOOL AND NOTHING'S CHANGED ...

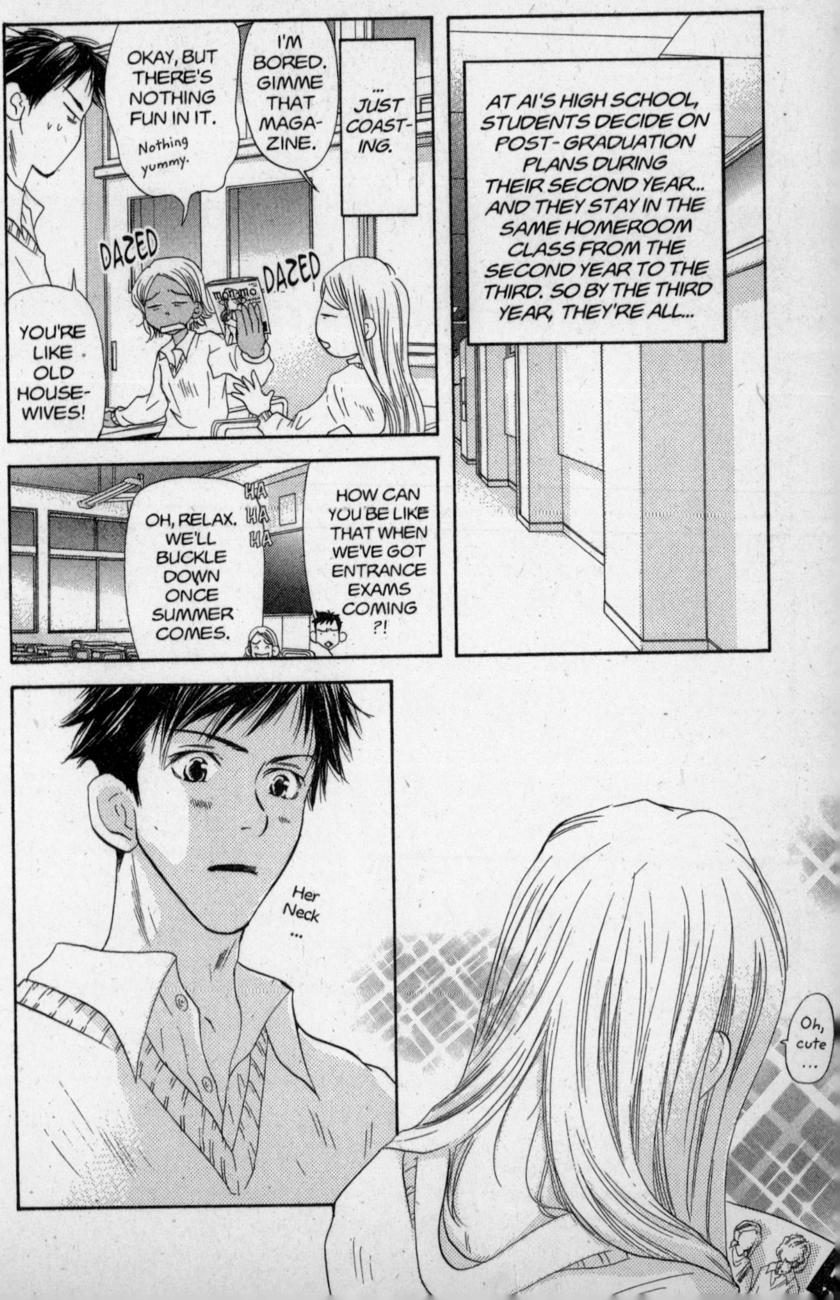
AT AI'S HIGH SCHOOL, STUDENTS DECIDE ON POST-GRADUATION PLANS DURING THEIR SECOND YEAR... AND THEY STAY IN THE SAME HOMEROOM CLASS FROM THE SECOND YEAR TO THE THIRD. SO BY THE THIRD YEAR, THEY'RE ALL...
... JUST COAST-ING.
I'M BORED. GIMME THAT MAGA-ZINE.
OKAY, BUT THERE'S NOTHING FUN IN IT.
Nothing yummy.
DAZED
DAZED
YOU'RE LIKE OLD HOUSE-WIVES!
HOW CAN YOU BE LIKE THAT WHEN WE'VE GOT ENTRANCE EXAMS COMING ?!
HA HA HA
OH, RELAX. WE'LL BUCKLE DOWN ONCE SUMMER COMES.
Oh, cute ...
Her Neck ...

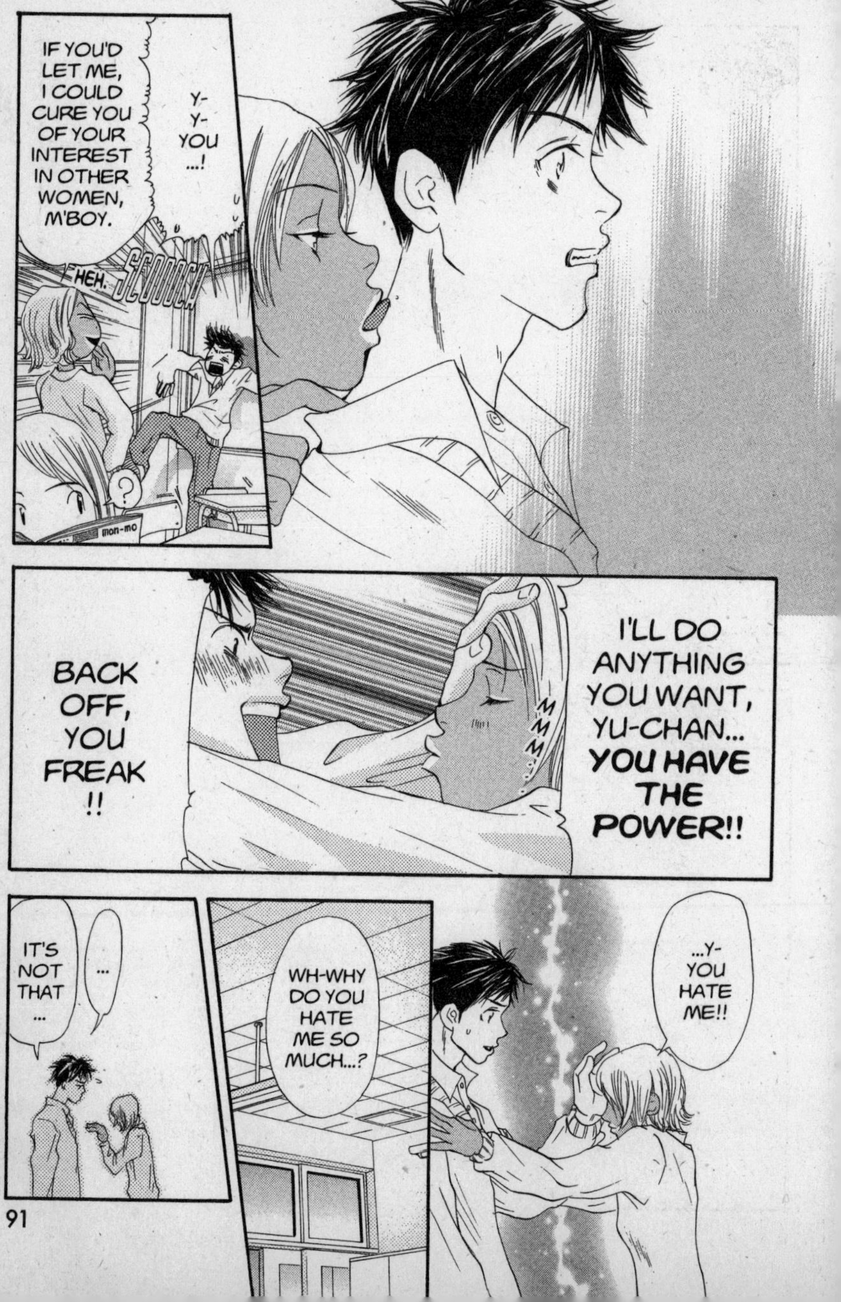
Y-Y-YOU ...!
IF YOU'D LET ME, I COULD CURE YOU OF YOUR INTEREST IN OTHER WOMEN, M'BOY.
HEH.
SCOOOCH
mon-mo
I'LL DO ANYTHING YOU WANT, YU-CHAN... YOU HAVE THE POWER!!
MMM...
BACK OFF, YOU FREAK !!
...Y-YOU HATE ME!!
WH-WHY DO YOU HATE ME SO MUCH...?
...
IT'S NOT THAT ...

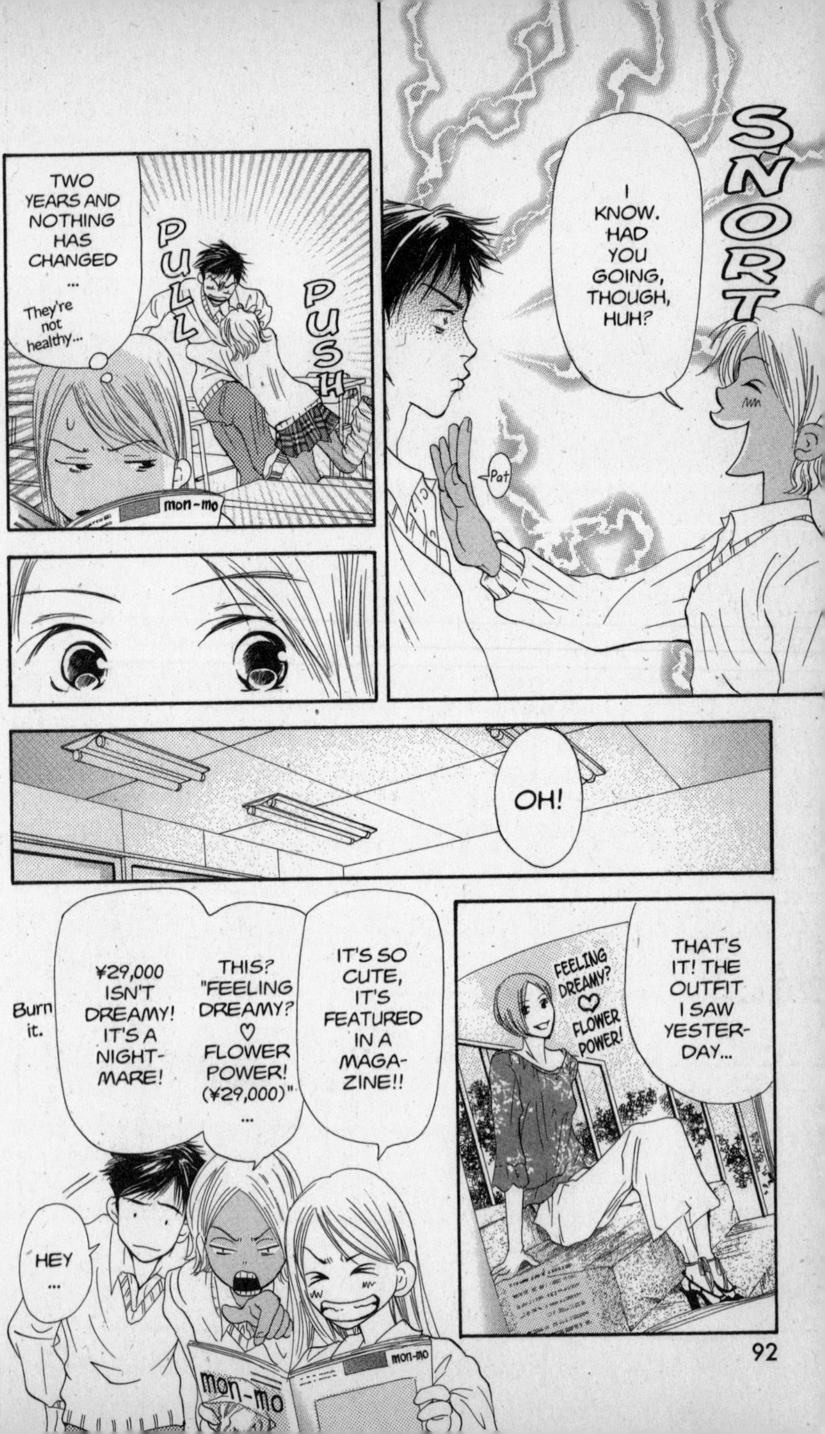
SNORT
I KNOW. HAD YOU GOING, THOUGH, HUH?
Pat
TWO YEARS AND NOTHING HAS CHANGED ...
They're not healthy...
PULL
PUSH
mon-mo
OH!
THAT'S IT! THE OUTFIT I SAW YESTER-DAY...
FEELING DREAMY? ♡ FLOWER POWER!
IT'S SO CUTE, IT'S FEATURED IN A MAGA-ZINE!!
THIS? "FEELING DREAMY? ♡ FLOWER POWER! (¥29,000)" ...
¥29,000 ISN'T DREAMY! IT'S A NIGHT-MARE!
Burn it.
HEY ...
mon-mo
mon-mo

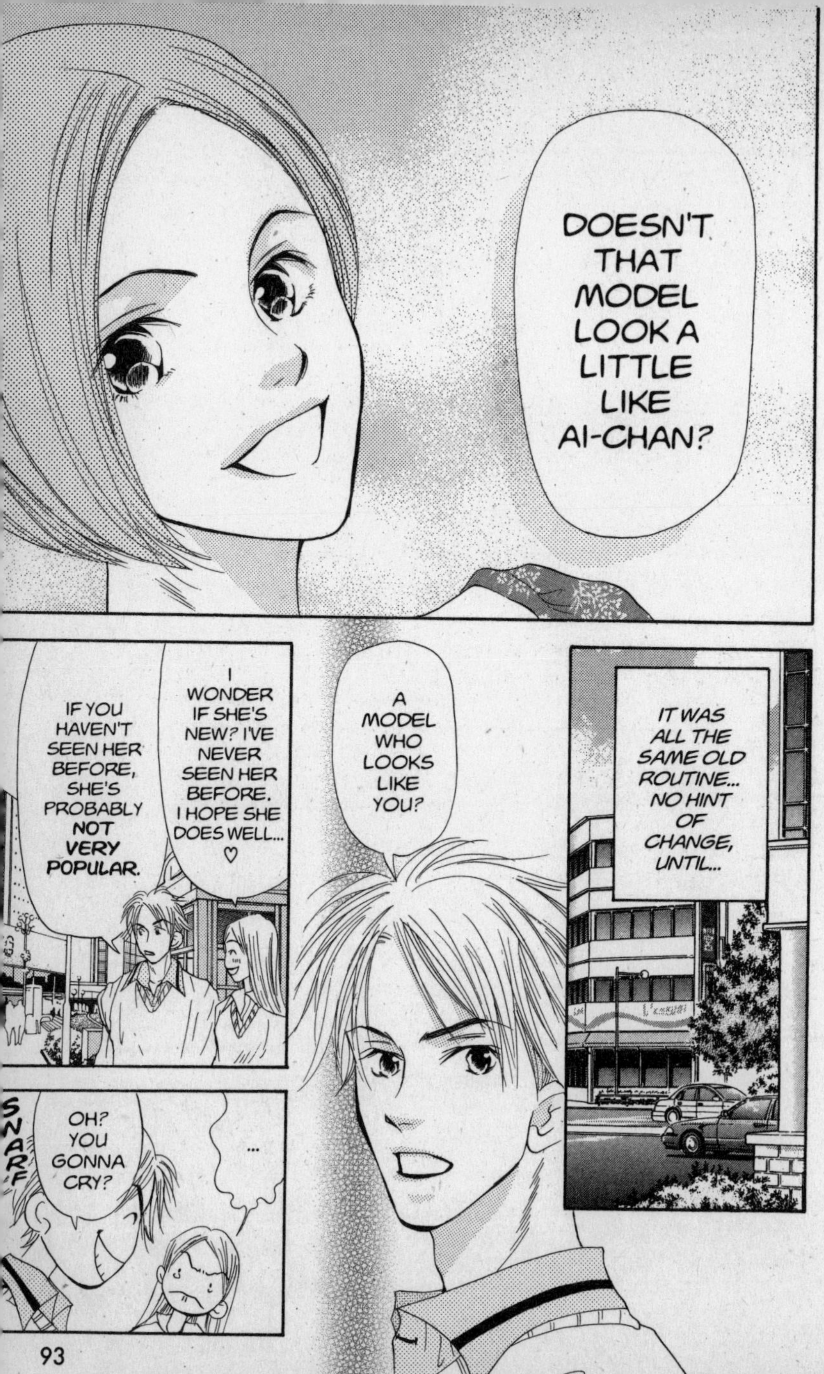
DOESN'T THAT MODEL LOOK A LITTLE LIKE AI-CHAN?
IT WAS ALL THE SAME OLD ROUTINE... NO HINT OF CHANGE, UNTIL...
A MODEL WHO LOOKS LIKE YOU?
I WONDER IF SHE'S NEW? I'VE NEVER SEEN HER BEFORE. I HOPE SHE DOES WELL... ♡
IF YOU HAVEN'T SEEN HER BEFORE, SHE'S PROBABLY **NOT VERY POPULAR.**
...
OH? YOU GONNA CRY?
SNARF

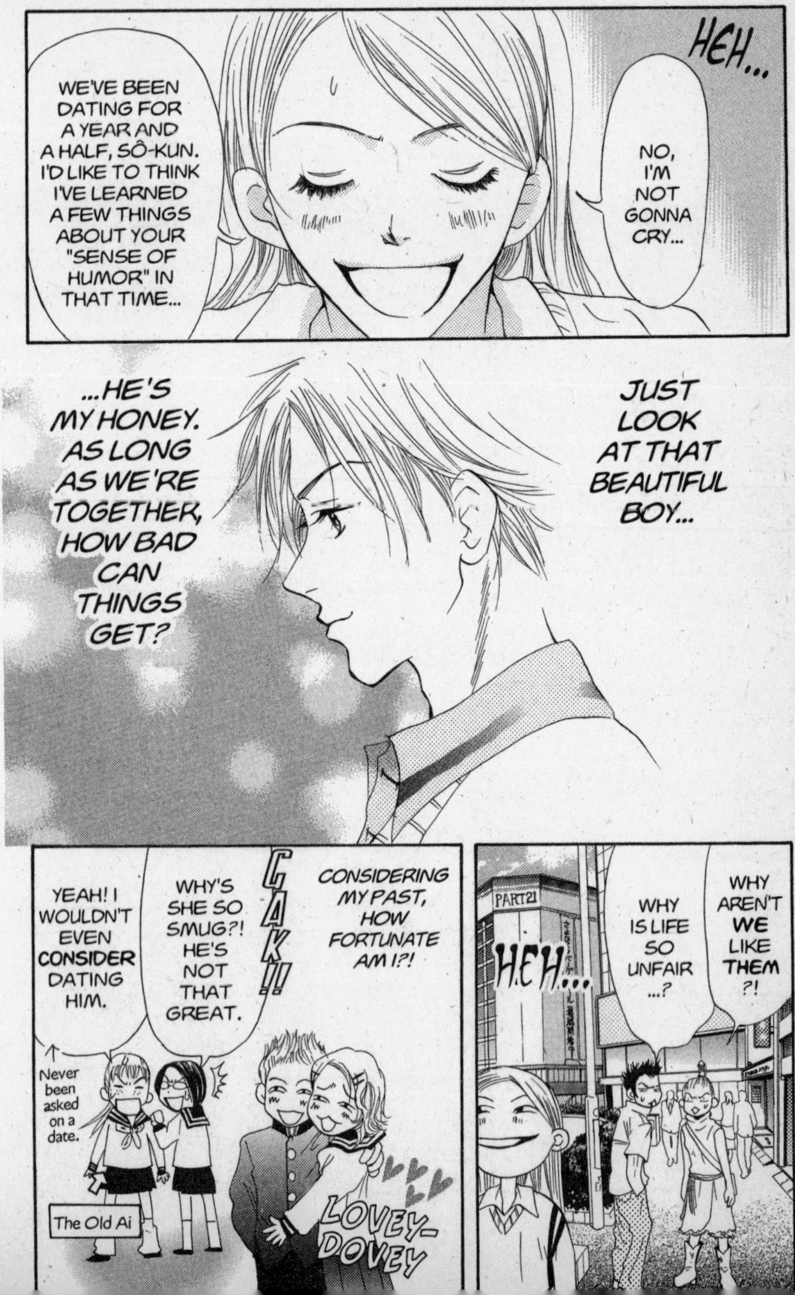
HEH...
NO, I'M NOT GONNA CRY...
WE'VE BEEN DATING FOR A YEAR AND A HALF, SÔ-KUN. I'D LIKE TO THINK I'VE LEARNED A FEW THINGS ABOUT YOUR "SENSE OF HUMOR" IN THAT TIME...
JUST LOOK AT THAT BEAUTIFUL BOY...
...HE'S MY HONEY. AS LONG AS WE'RE TOGETHER, HOW BAD CAN THINGS GET?
PART21
WHY AREN'T WE LIKE THEM?!
WHY IS LIFE SO UNFAIR ...?
HEH...
CONSIDERING MY PAST, HOW FORTUNATE AM I?!
GAK!!
WHY'S SHE SO SMUG?! HE'S NOT THAT GREAT.
YEAH! I WOULDN'T EVEN CONSIDER DATING HIM.
Never been asked on a date.
LOVEY-DOVEY
The Old Ai

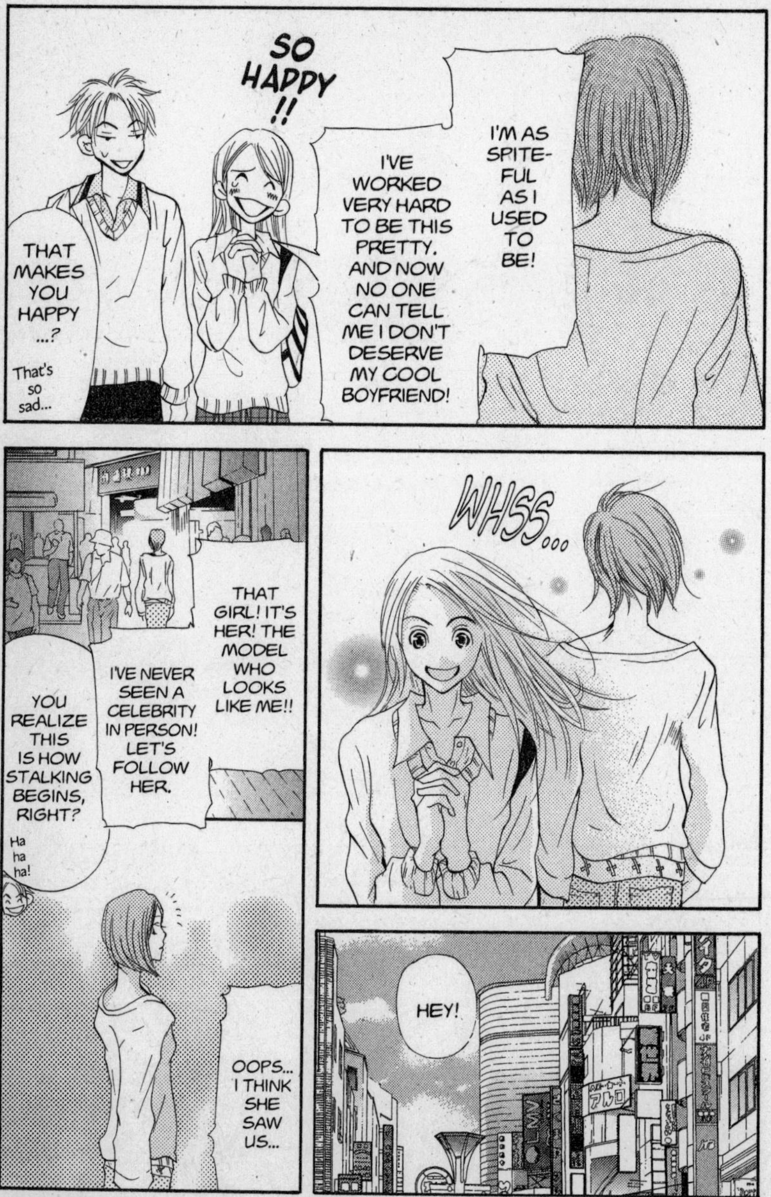
I'M AS SPITEFUL AS I USED TO BE!
I'VE WORKED VERY HARD TO BE THIS PRETTY. AND NOW NO ONE CAN TELL ME I DON'T DESERVE MY COOL BOYFRIEND!
SO HAPPY !!
THAT MAKES YOU HAPPY ...?
That's so sad...
WHSS...
THAT GIRL! IT'S HER! THE MODEL WHO LOOKS LIKE ME!!
I'VE NEVER SEEN A CELEBRITY IN PERSON! LET'S FOLLOW HER.
YOU REALIZE THIS IS HOW STALKING BEGINS, RIGHT?
Ha ha ha!
HEY!
OOPS... I THINK SHE SAW US...

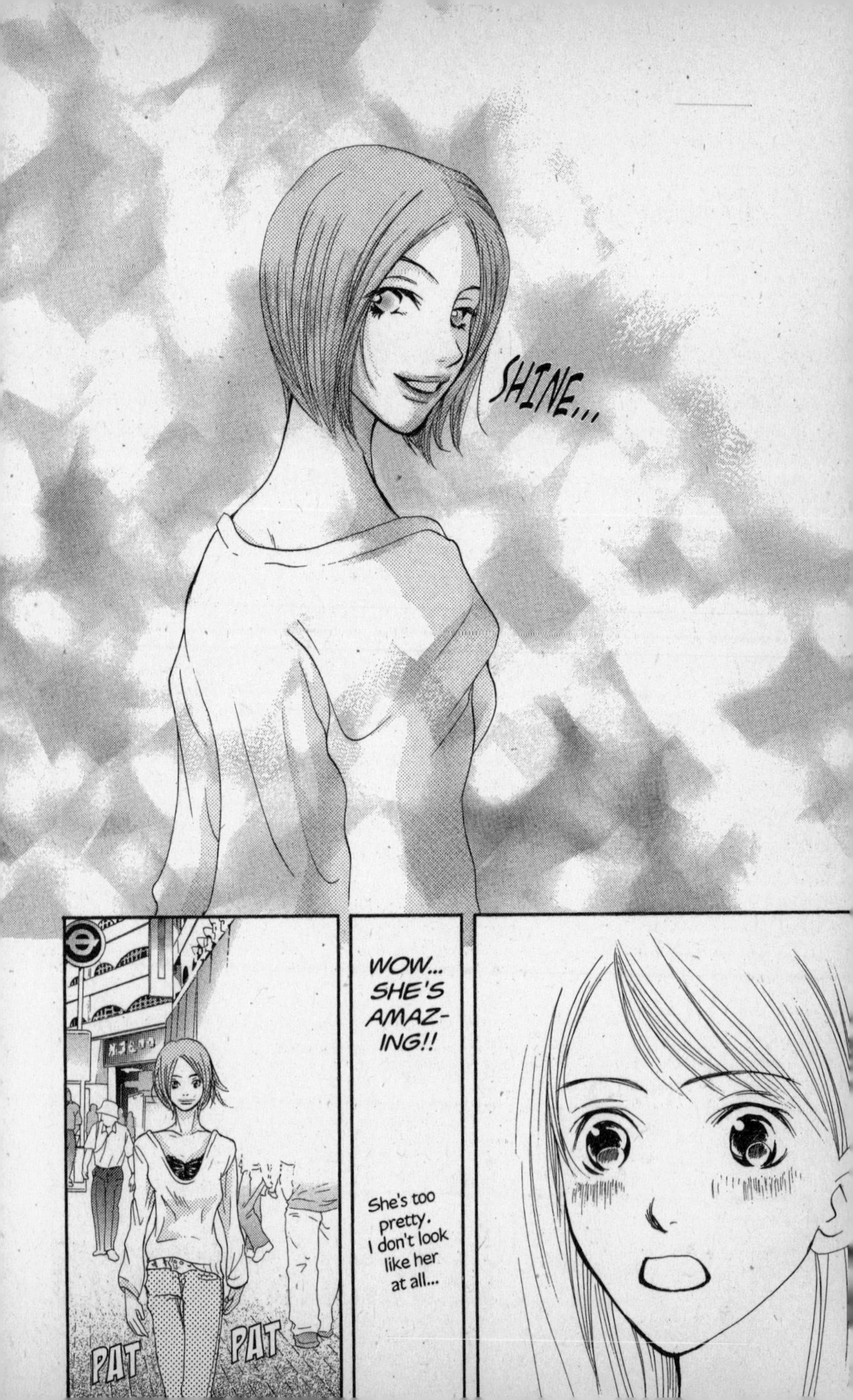
SHINE...
WOW... SHE'S AMAZING!!
She's too pretty. I don't look like her at all...
PAT
PAT

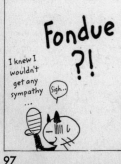

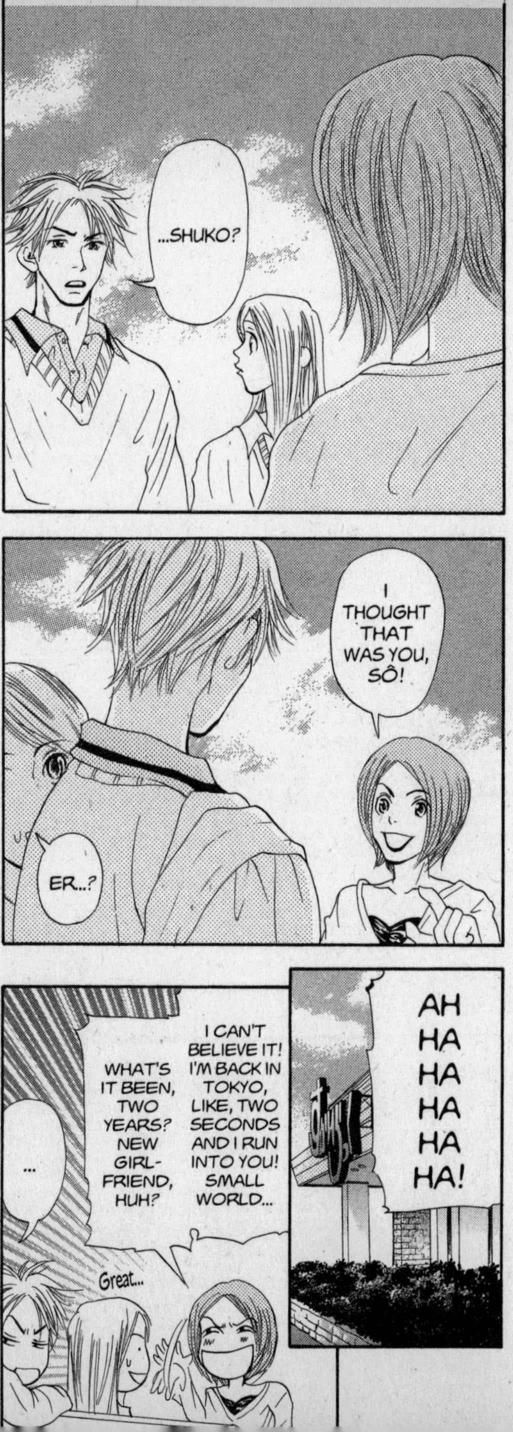
...SHUKO?
I THOUGHT THAT WAS YOU, SÔ!
ER...?
AH HA HA HA HA HA!
I CAN'T BELIEVE IT! I'M BACK IN TOKYO, LIKE, TWO SECONDS AND I RUN INTO YOU! SMALL WORLD...
WHAT'S IT BEEN, TWO YEARS? NEW GIRL-FRIEND, HUH?
...
Great...

Doubt!! Backstory

Part 3

Even while working on a series, I have to keep living my life, you know? Living involves eating, which requires cooking, and while I was cooking, I accidentally submerged my hand in a vat of boiling cheese (long story)... Can you say, "Human Fondue"?!

I burned my right hand so bad it was too painful to grip a pen. I didn't want to tell anyone, though, so I managed to complete the draft by resting my hand in icy water baths.

Fondue ?!

I knew I wouldn't get any sympathy ...

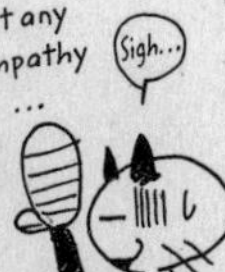
Sigh...

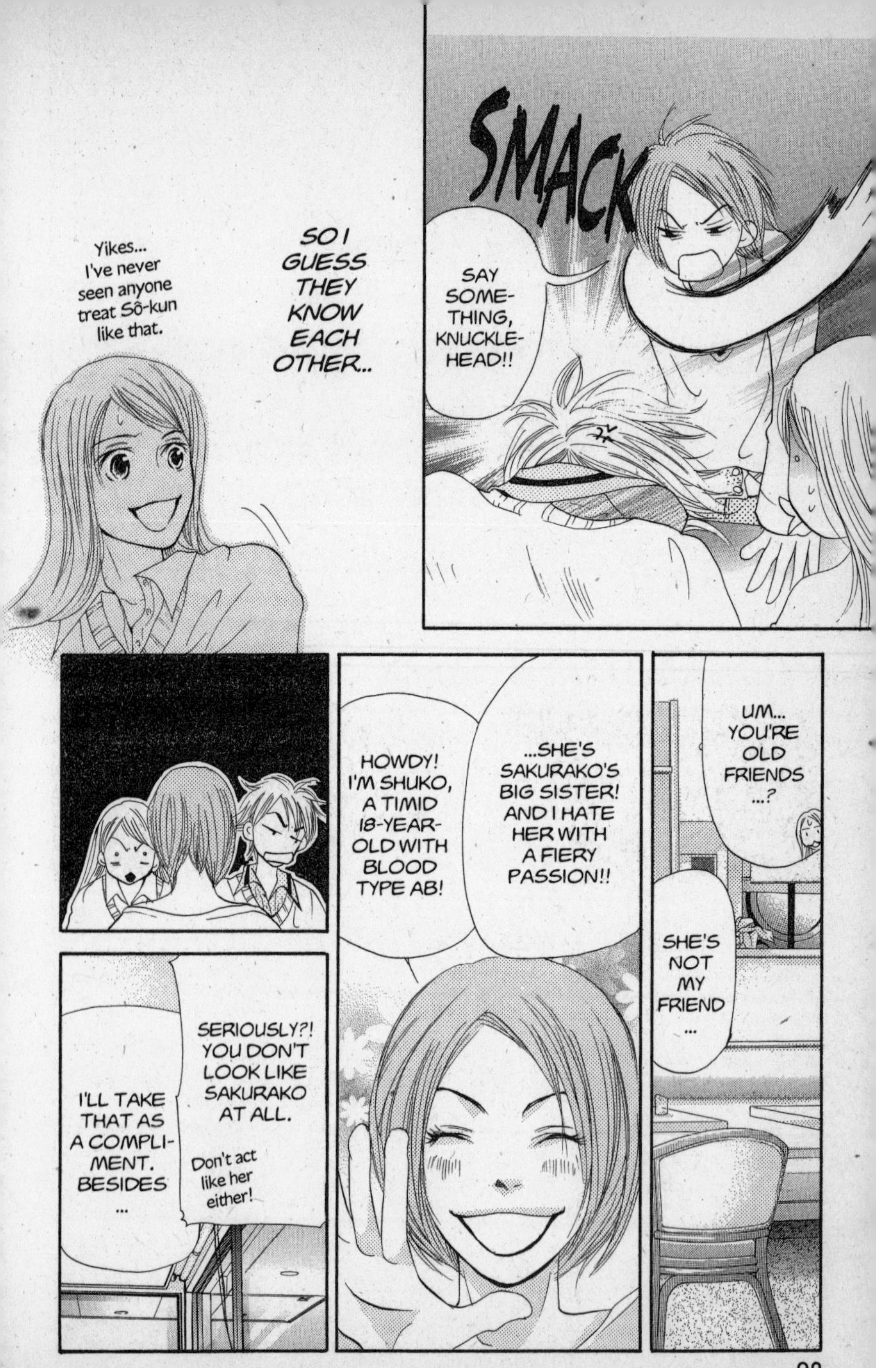
SMACK
SAY SOME-THING, KNUCKLE-HEAD!!
SO I GUESS THEY KNOW EACH OTHER...
Yikes... I've never seen anyone treat Sô-kun like that.
UM... YOU'RE OLD FRIENDS ...?
SHE'S NOT MY FRIEND ...
...SHE'S SAKURAKO'S BIG SISTER! AND I HATE HER WITH A FIERY PASSION!!
HOWDY! I'M SHUKO, A TIMID 18-YEAR-OLD WITH BLOOD TYPE AB!
SERIOUSLY?! YOU DON'T LOOK LIKE SAKURAKO AT ALL.
Don't act like her either!
I'LL TAKE THAT AS A COMPLI-MENT. BESIDES ...

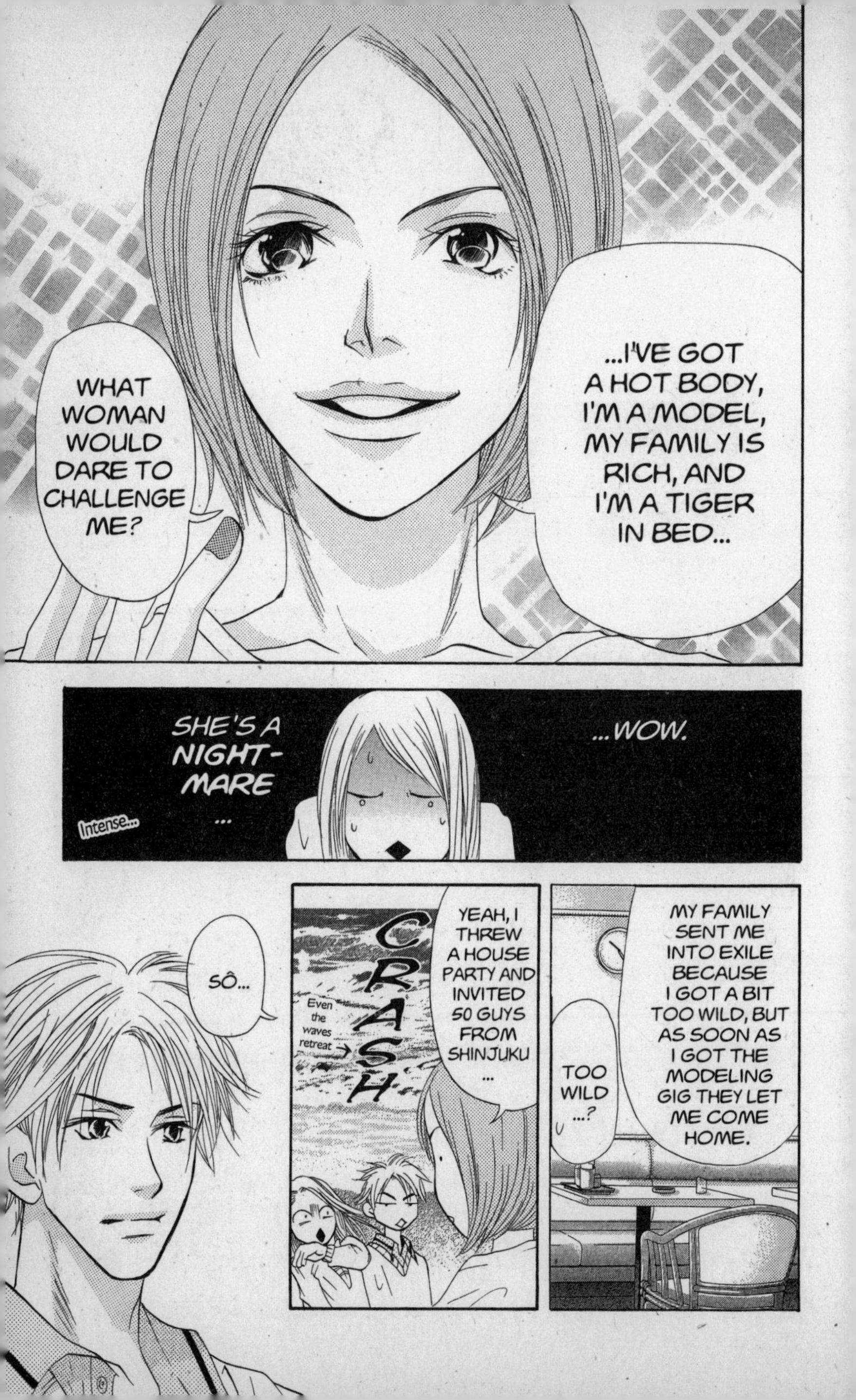
...I'VE GOT A HOT BODY, I'M A MODEL, MY FAMILY IS RICH, AND I'M A TIGER IN BED...
WHAT WOMAN WOULD DARE TO CHALLENGE ME?
...WOW.
SHE'S A NIGHT-MARE ...
Intense...
MY FAMILY SENT ME INTO EXILE BECAUSE I GOT A BIT TOO WILD, BUT AS SOON AS I GOT THE MODELING GIG THEY LET ME COME HOME.
TOO WILD ...?
YEAH, I THREW A HOUSE PARTY AND INVITED 50 GUYS FROM SHINJUKU ...
CRASH
Even the waves retreat
SÔ...

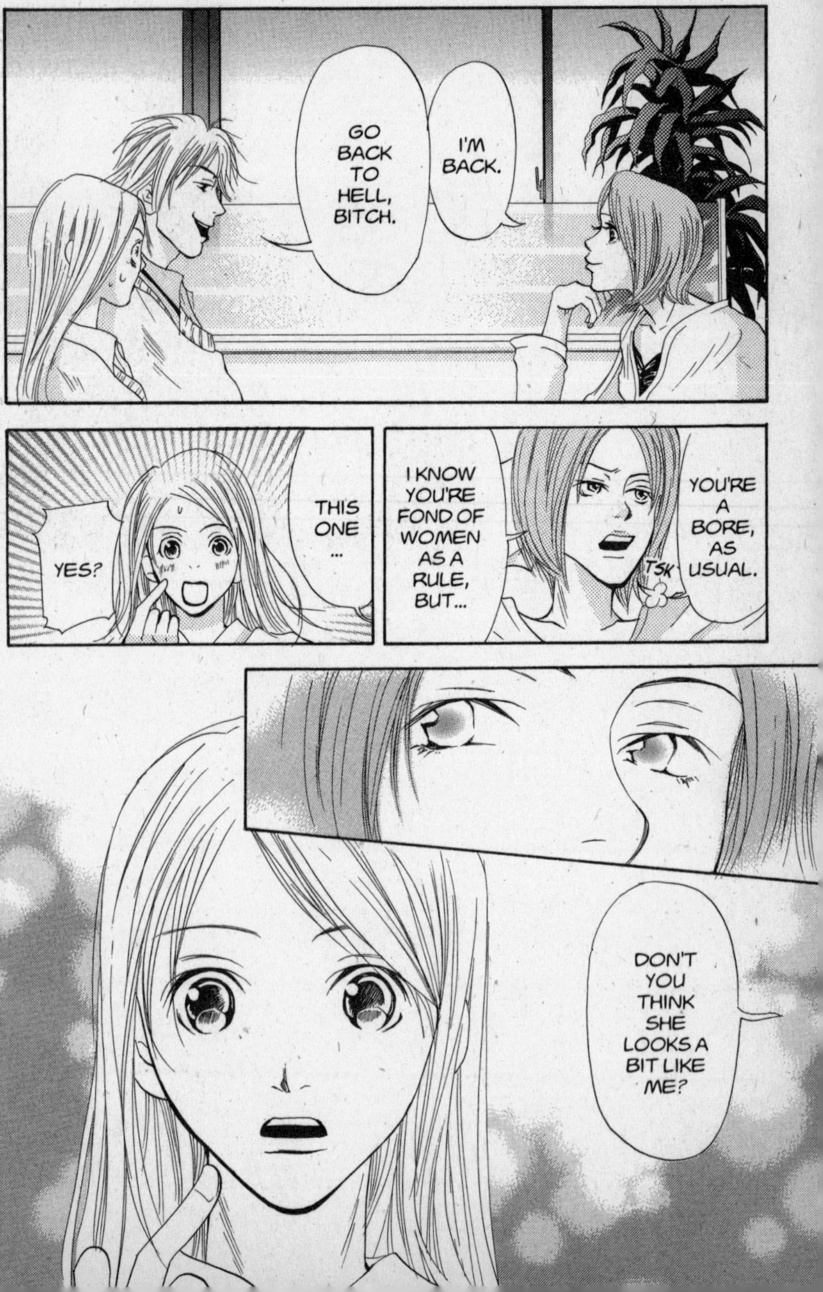
I'M BACK.
GO BACK TO HELL, BITCH.
YOU'RE A BORE, AS USUAL.
TSK
I KNOW YOU'RE FOND OF WOMEN AS A RULE, BUT...
THIS ONE ...
YES?
DON'T YOU THINK SHE LOOKS A BIT LIKE ME?

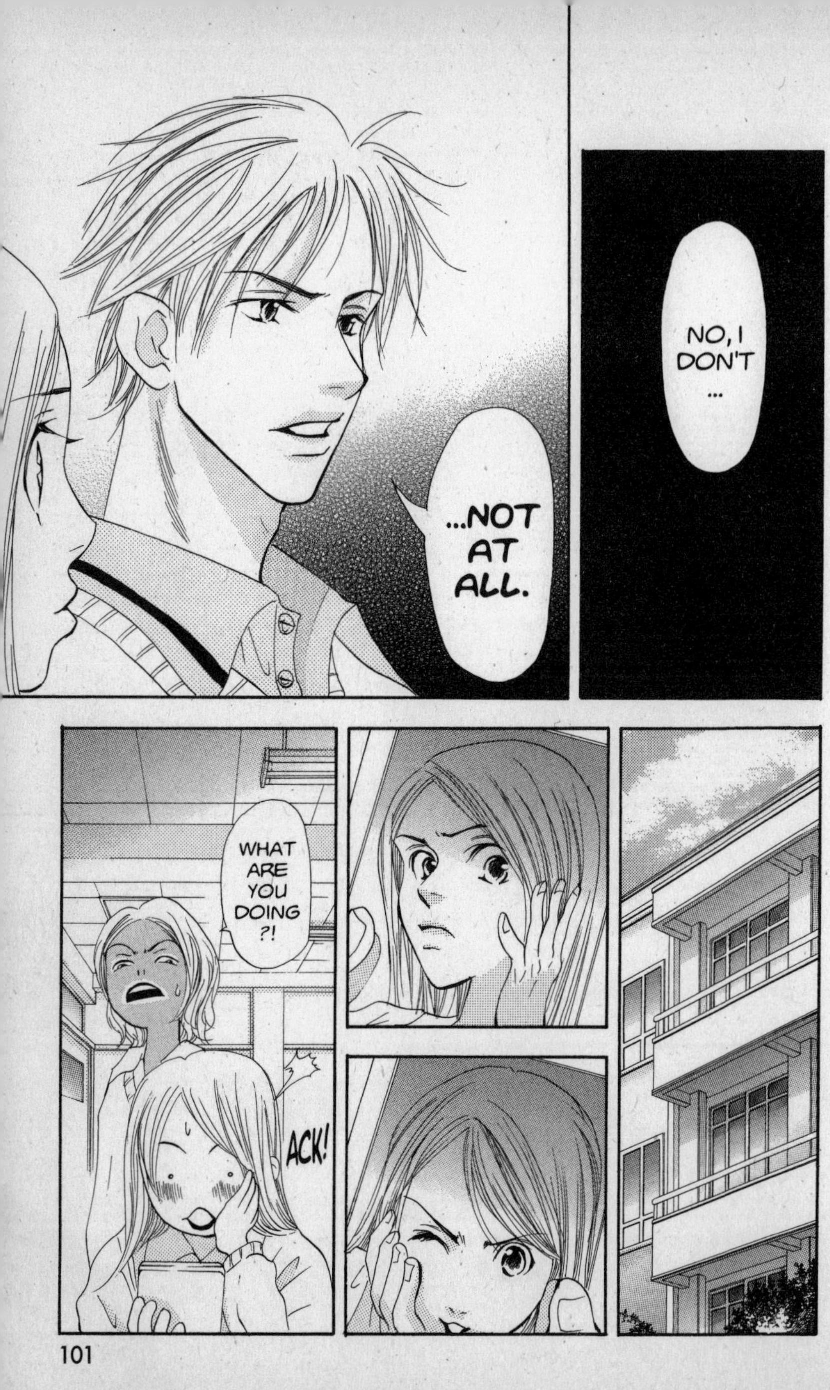
NO, I DON'T ...
...NOT AT ALL.
WHAT ARE YOU DOING ?!
ACK!

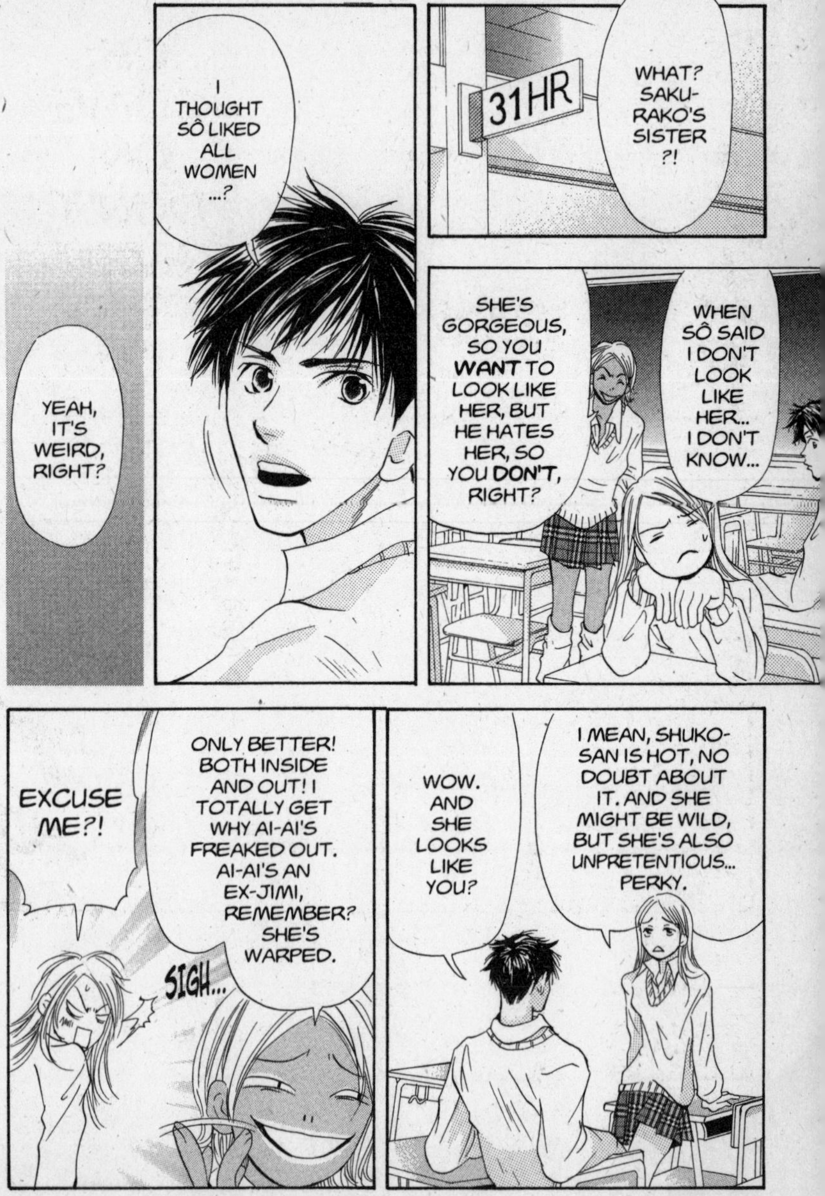

31HR
WHAT? SAKU-RAKO'S SISTER ?!
WHEN SÔ SAID I DON'T LOOK LIKE HER... I DON'T KNOW...
SHE'S GORGEOUS, SO YOU **WANT** TO LOOK LIKE HER, BUT HE HATES HER, SO YOU **DON'T**, RIGHT?
I THOUGHT SÔ LIKED ALL WOMEN ...?
YEAH, IT'S WEIRD, RIGHT?
I MEAN, SHUKO-SAN IS HOT, NO DOUBT ABOUT IT. AND SHE MIGHT BE WILD, BUT SHE'S ALSO UNPRETENTIOUS... PERKY.
WOW. AND SHE LOOKS LIKE YOU?
ONLY BETTER! BOTH INSIDE AND OUT! I TOTALLY GET WHY AI-AI'S FREAKED OUT. AI-AI'S AN EX-JIMI, REMEMBER? SHE'S WARPED.
SIGH...
EXCUSE ME?!

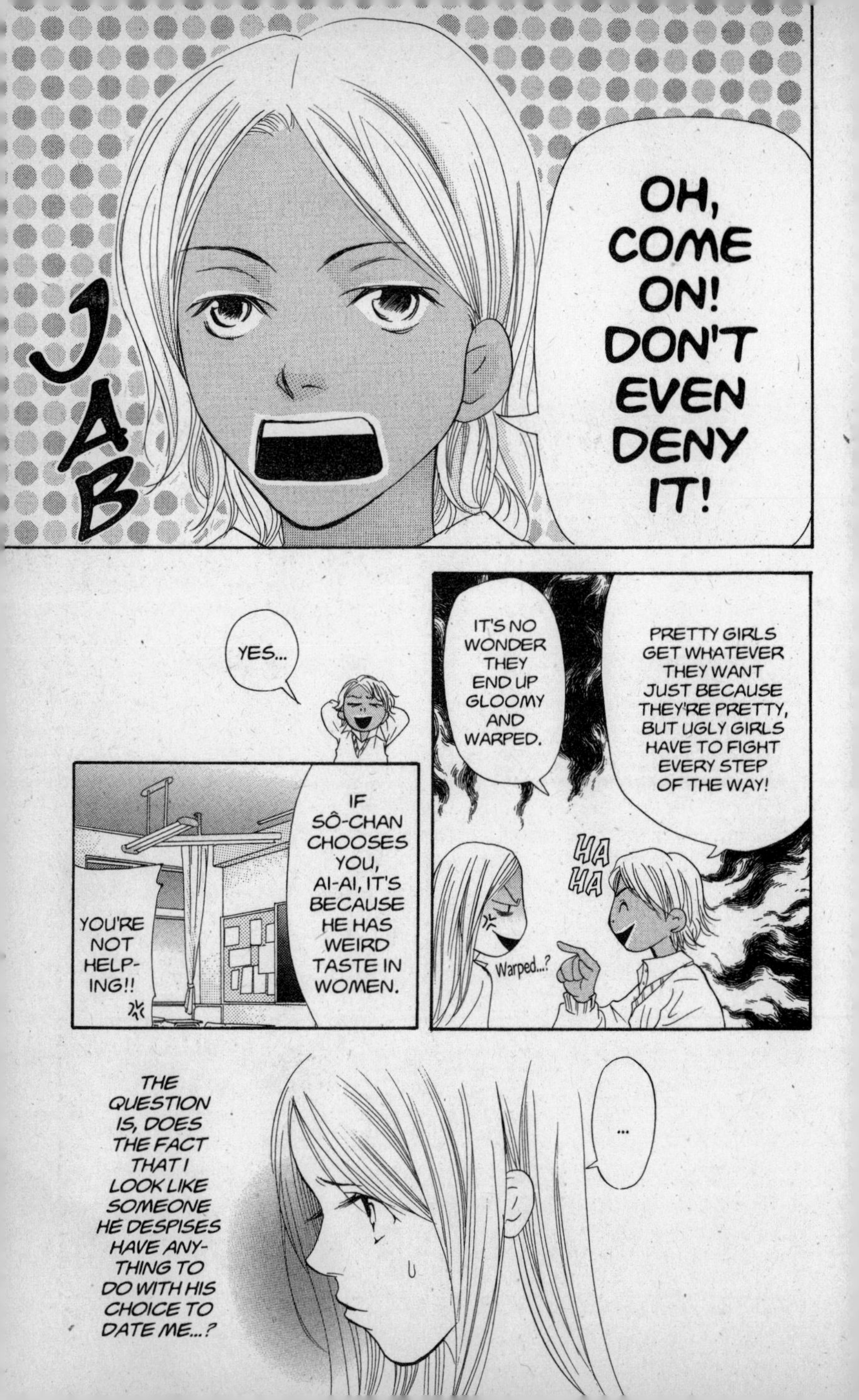
OH, COME ON! DON'T EVEN DENY IT!
JAB
PRETTY GIRLS GET WHATEVER THEY WANT JUST BECAUSE THEY'RE PRETTY, BUT UGLY GIRLS HAVE TO FIGHT EVERY STEP OF THE WAY!
IT'S NO WONDER THEY END UP GLOOMY AND WARPED.
HA HA
Warped...?
YES...
IF SÔ-CHAN CHOOSES YOU, AI-AI, IT'S BECAUSE HE HAS WEIRD TASTE IN WOMEN.
YOU'RE NOT HELPING!!
...
THE QUESTION IS, DOES THE FACT THAT I LOOK LIKE SOMEONE HE DESPISES HAVE ANYTHING TO DO WITH HIS CHOICE TO DATE ME...?

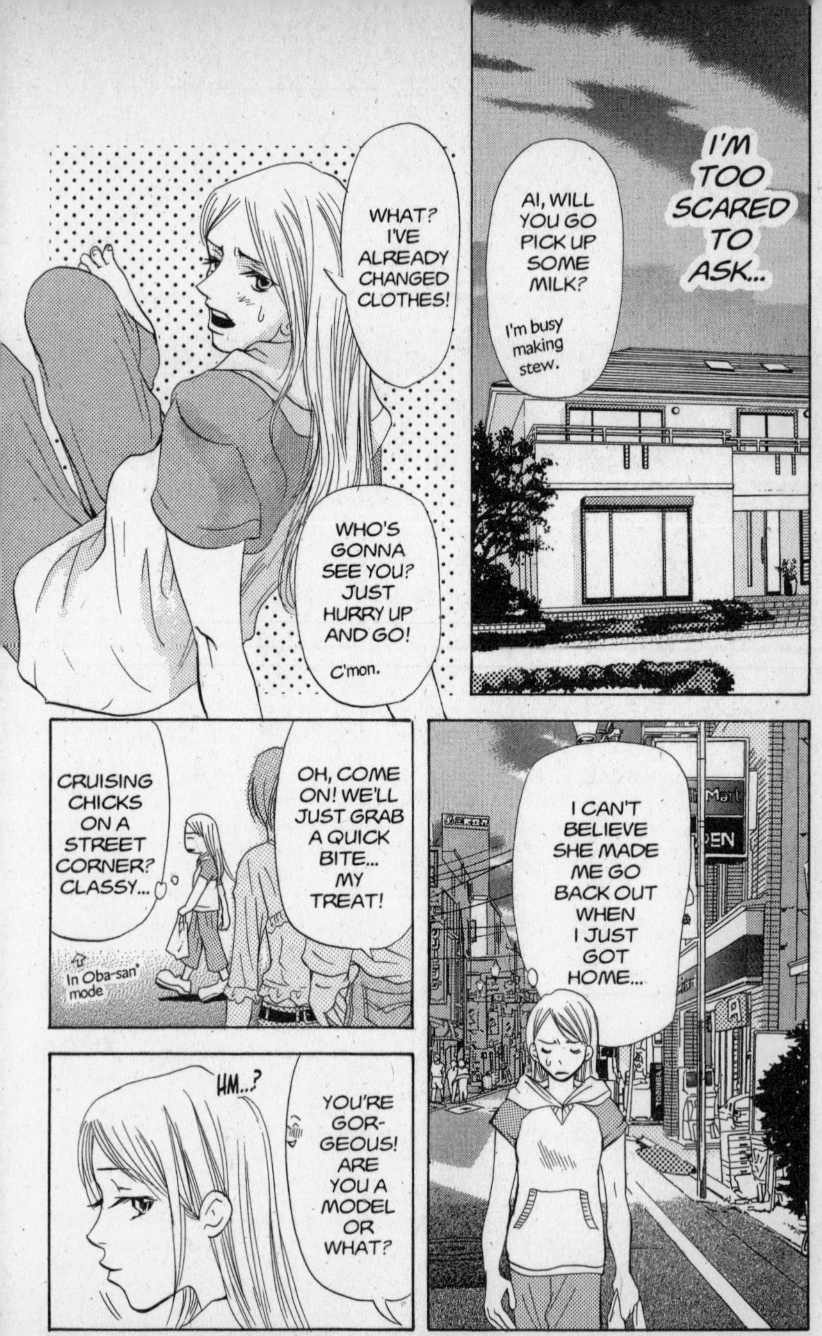
I'M TOO SCARED TO ASK...
AI, WILL YOU GO PICK UP SOME MILK?
I'm busy making stew.
WHAT? I'VE ALREADY CHANGED CLOTHES!
WHO'S GONNA SEE YOU? JUST HURRY UP AND GO!
C'mon.
I CAN'T BELIEVE SHE MADE ME GO BACK OUT WHEN I JUST GOT HOME...
OH, COME ON! WE'LL JUST GRAB A QUICK BITE... MY TREAT!
CRUISING CHICKS ON A STREET CORNER? CLASSY...
In Oba-san* mode
YOU'RE GOR-GEOUS! ARE YOU A MODEL OR WHAT?
HM..?

*"Oba-san" means something like "Auntie," but can be used to address any older woman. In this context, it's more like "Old Maid."

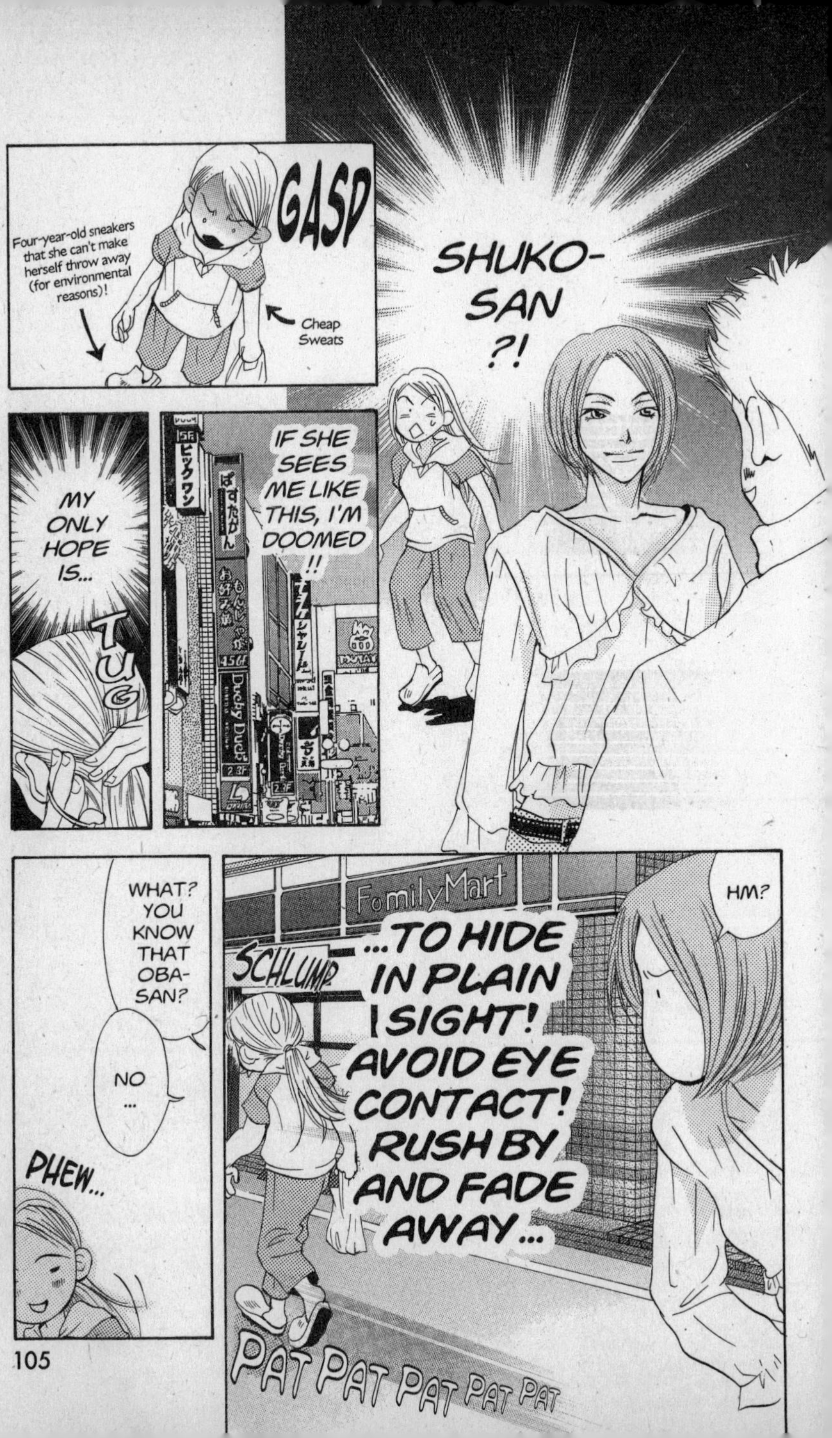
SHUKO-SAN ?!
GASP
Four-year-old sneakers that she can't make herself throw away (for environmental reasons)!
Cheap Sweats
IF SHE SEES ME LIKE THIS, I'M DOOMED !!
MY ONLY HOPE IS...
TUG
HM?
...TO HIDE IN PLAIN SIGHT! AVOID EYE CONTACT! RUSH BY AND FADE AWAY...
FamilyMart
SCHLUMP
PAT PAT PAT PAT PAT
WHAT? YOU KNOW THAT OBA-SAN?
NO ...
PHEW...

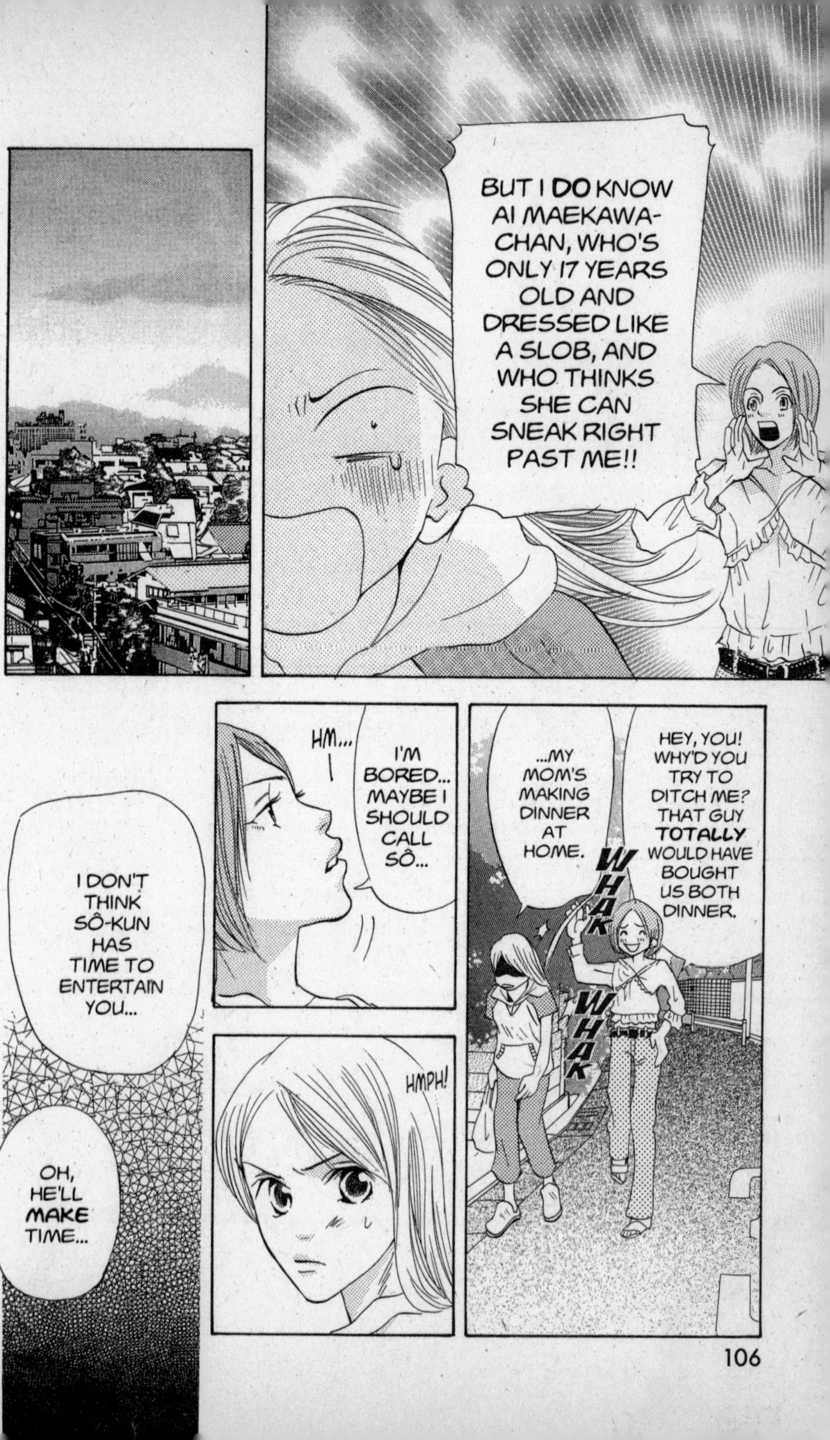
BUT I DO KNOW AI MAEKAWA-CHAN, WHO'S ONLY 17 YEARS OLD AND DRESSED LIKE A SLOB, AND WHO THINKS SHE CAN SNEAK RIGHT PAST ME!!
HEY, YOU! WHY'D YOU TRY TO DITCH ME? THAT GUY TOTALLY WOULD HAVE BOUGHT US BOTH DINNER.
...MY MOM'S MAKING DINNER AT HOME.
WHAK
WHAK
I'M BORED... MAYBE I SHOULD CALL SÔ...
HM... !
HMPH!
I DON'T THINK SÔ-KUN HAS TIME TO ENTERTAIN YOU...
OH, HE'LL MAKE TIME...

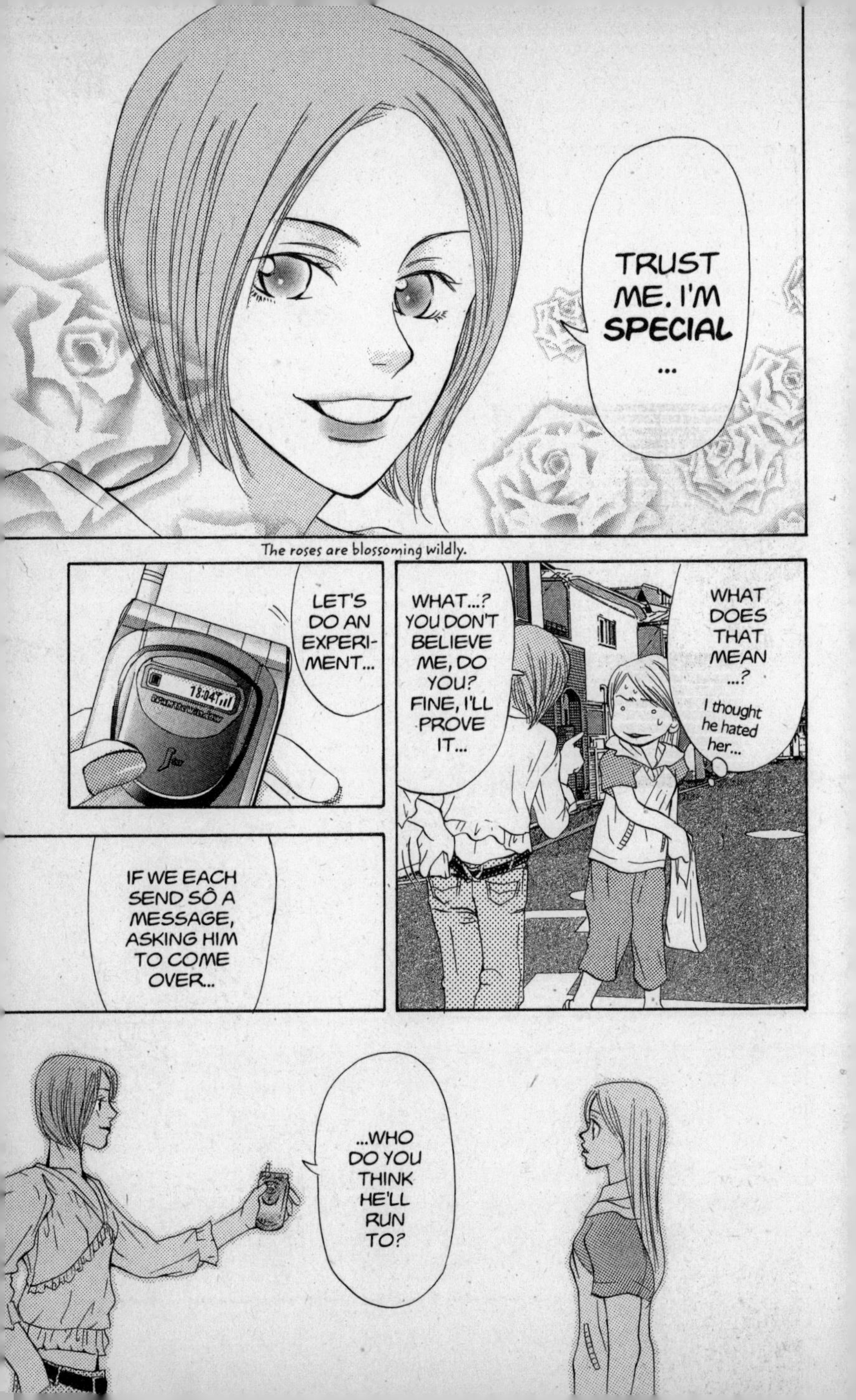
TRUST ME. I'M SPECIAL ...
The roses are blossoming wildly.
WHAT DOES THAT MEAN ...?
I thought he hated her...
WHAT...? YOU DON'T BELIEVE ME, DO YOU? FINE, I'LL PROVE IT...
LET'S DO AN EXPERIMENT...
IF WE EACH SEND SÔ A MESSAGE, ASKING HIM TO COME OVER...
...WHO DO YOU THINK HE'LL RUN TO?

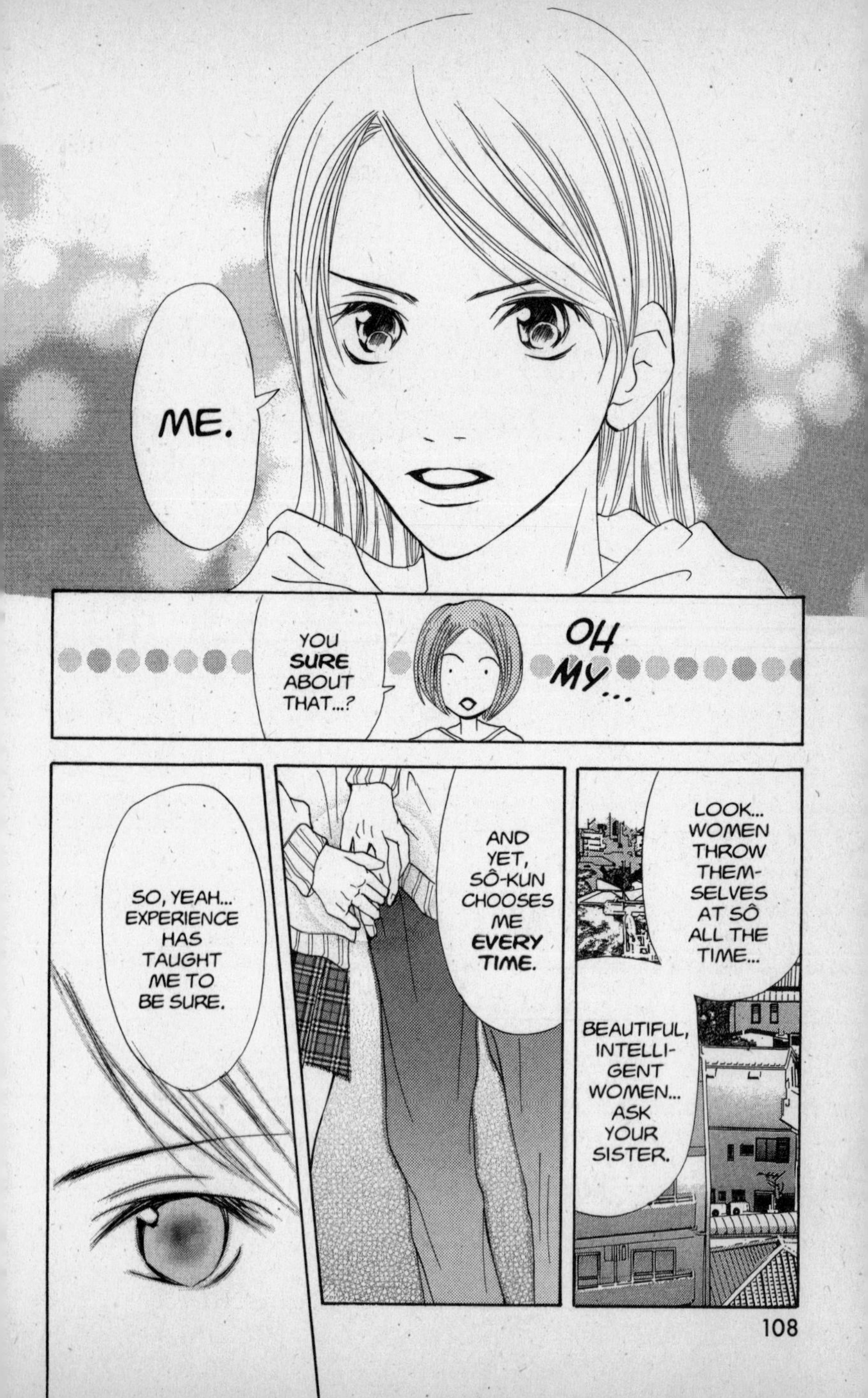
ME.
OH MY...
YOU SURE ABOUT THAT...?
LOOK... WOMEN THROW THEM-SELVES AT SÔ ALL THE TIME...
BEAUTIFUL, INTELLI-GENT WOMEN... ASK YOUR SISTER.
AND YET, SÔ-KUN CHOOSES ME EVERY TIME.
SO, YEAH... EXPERIENCE HAS TAUGHT ME TO BE SURE.

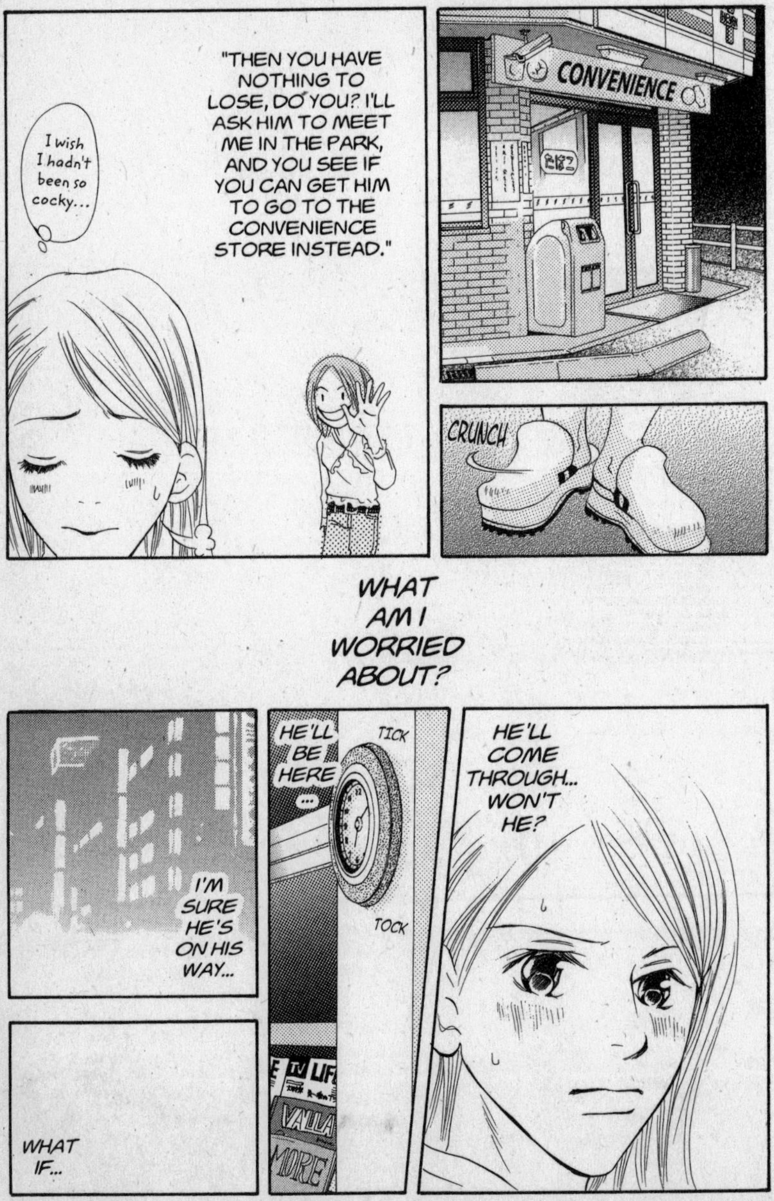
CONVENIENCE
CRUNCH
"THEN YOU HAVE NOTHING TO LOSE, DO YOU? I'LL ASK HIM TO MEET ME IN THE PARK, AND YOU SEE IF YOU CAN GET HIM TO GO TO THE CONVENIENCE STORE INSTEAD."
I wish I hadn't been so cocky...
WHAT AM I WORRIED ABOUT?
HE'LL COME THROUGH... WON'T HE?
HE'LL BE HERE ...
TICK
TOCK
MORE
I'M SURE HE'S ON HIS WAY...
WHAT IF...

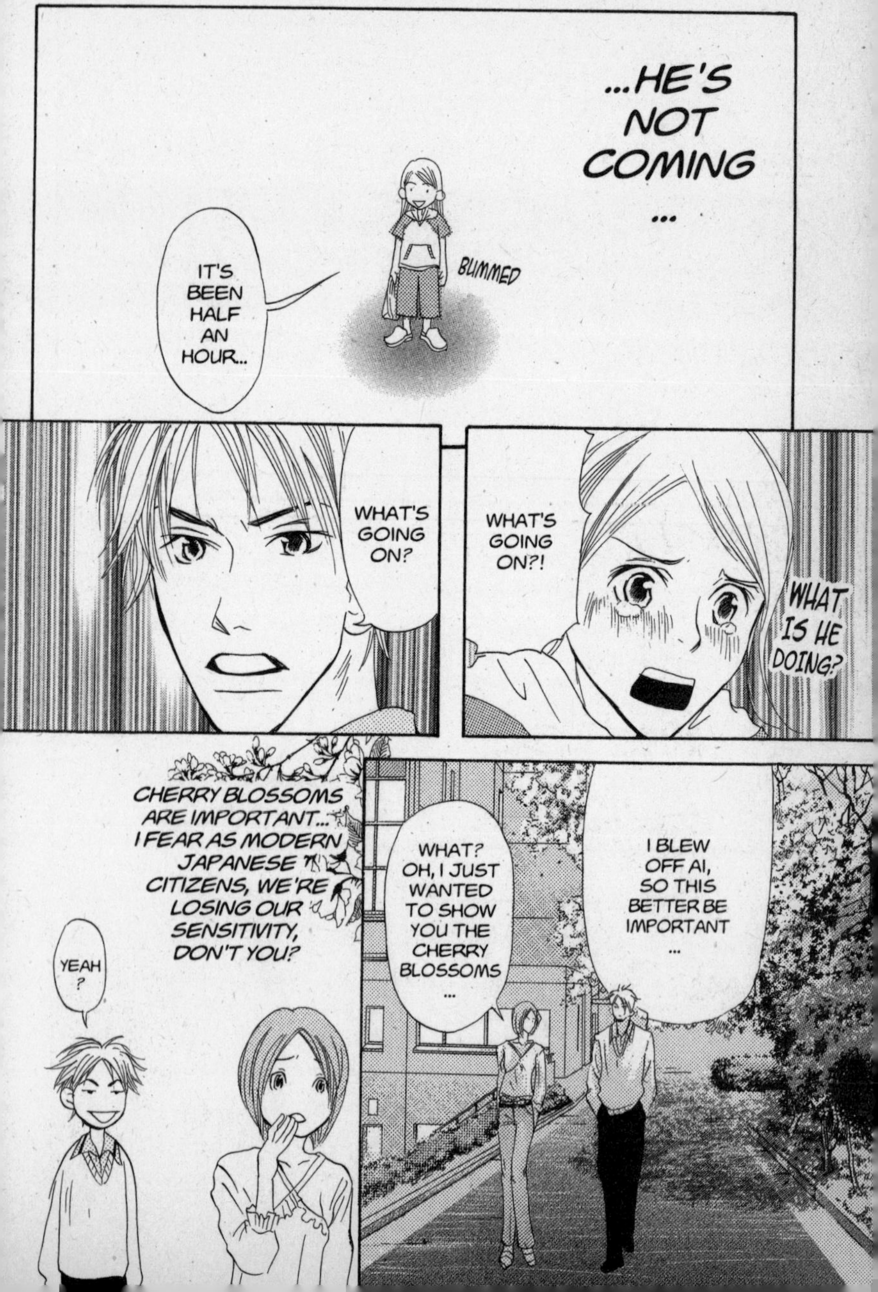
...HE'S NOT COMING ...
BUMMED
IT'S BEEN HALF AN HOUR...
WHAT'S GOING ON?!
WHAT IS HE DOING?
WHAT'S GOING ON?
I BLEW OFF AI, SO THIS BETTER BE IMPORTANT ...
WHAT? OH, I JUST WANTED TO SHOW YOU THE CHERRY BLOSSOMS ...
CHERRY BLOSSOMS ARE IMPORTANT... I FEAR AS MODERN JAPANESE CITIZENS, WE'RE LOSING OUR SENSITIVITY, DON'T YOU?
YEAH ?

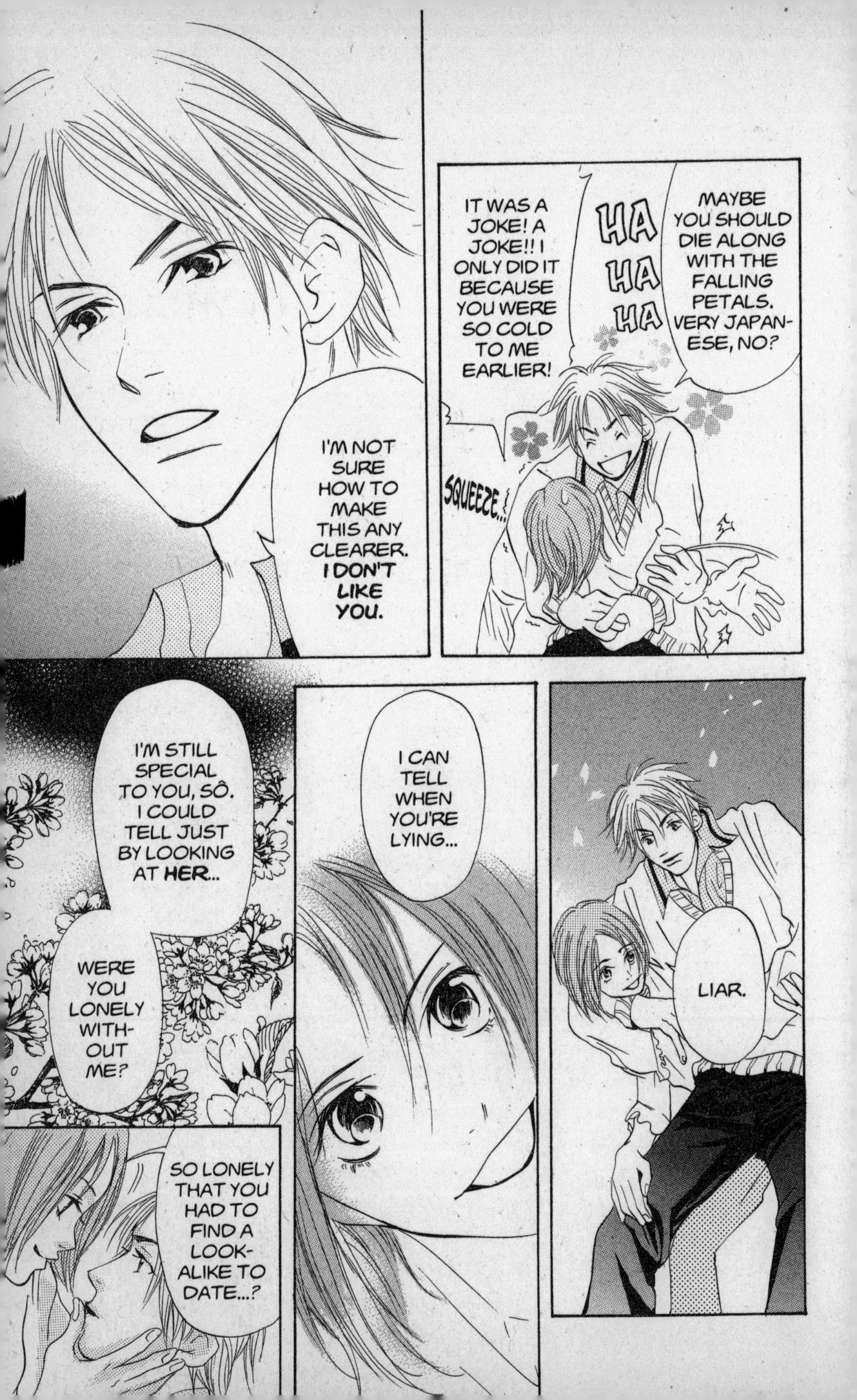
MAYBE YOU SHOULD DIE ALONG WITH THE FALLING PETALS. VERY JAPANESE, NO?
HA HA HA
IT WAS A JOKE! A JOKE!! I ONLY DID IT BECAUSE YOU WERE SO COLD TO ME EARLIER!
SQUEEZE...
I'M NOT SURE HOW TO MAKE THIS ANY CLEARER. **I DON'T LIKE YOU.**
LIAR.
I CAN TELL WHEN YOU'RE LYING...
I'M STILL SPECIAL TO YOU, SÔ. I COULD TELL JUST BY LOOKING AT **HER**...
WERE YOU LONELY WITHOUT ME?
SO LONELY THAT YOU HAD TO FIND A LOOK-ALIKE TO DATE...?

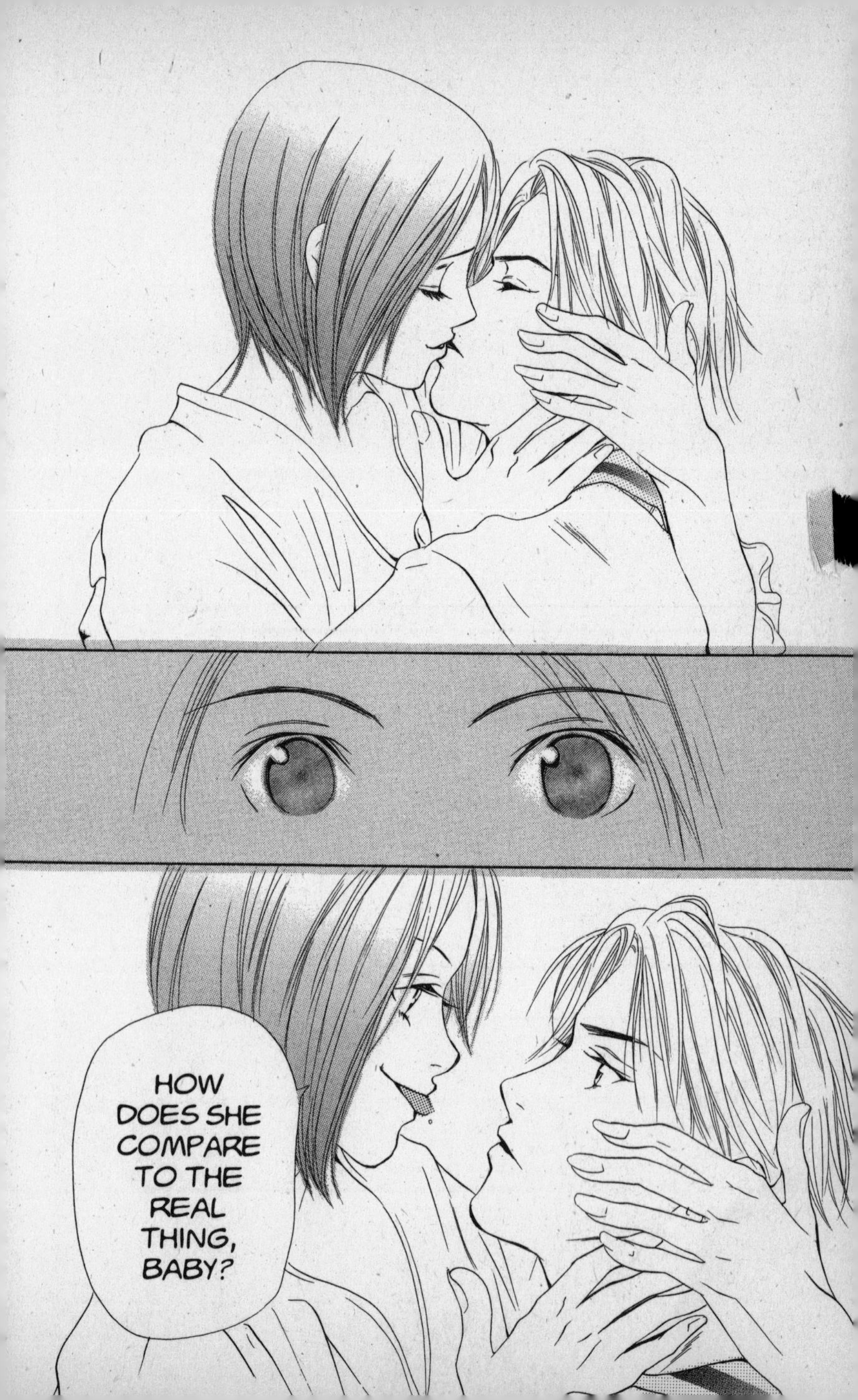
HOW DOES SHE COMPARE TO THE REAL THING, BABY?

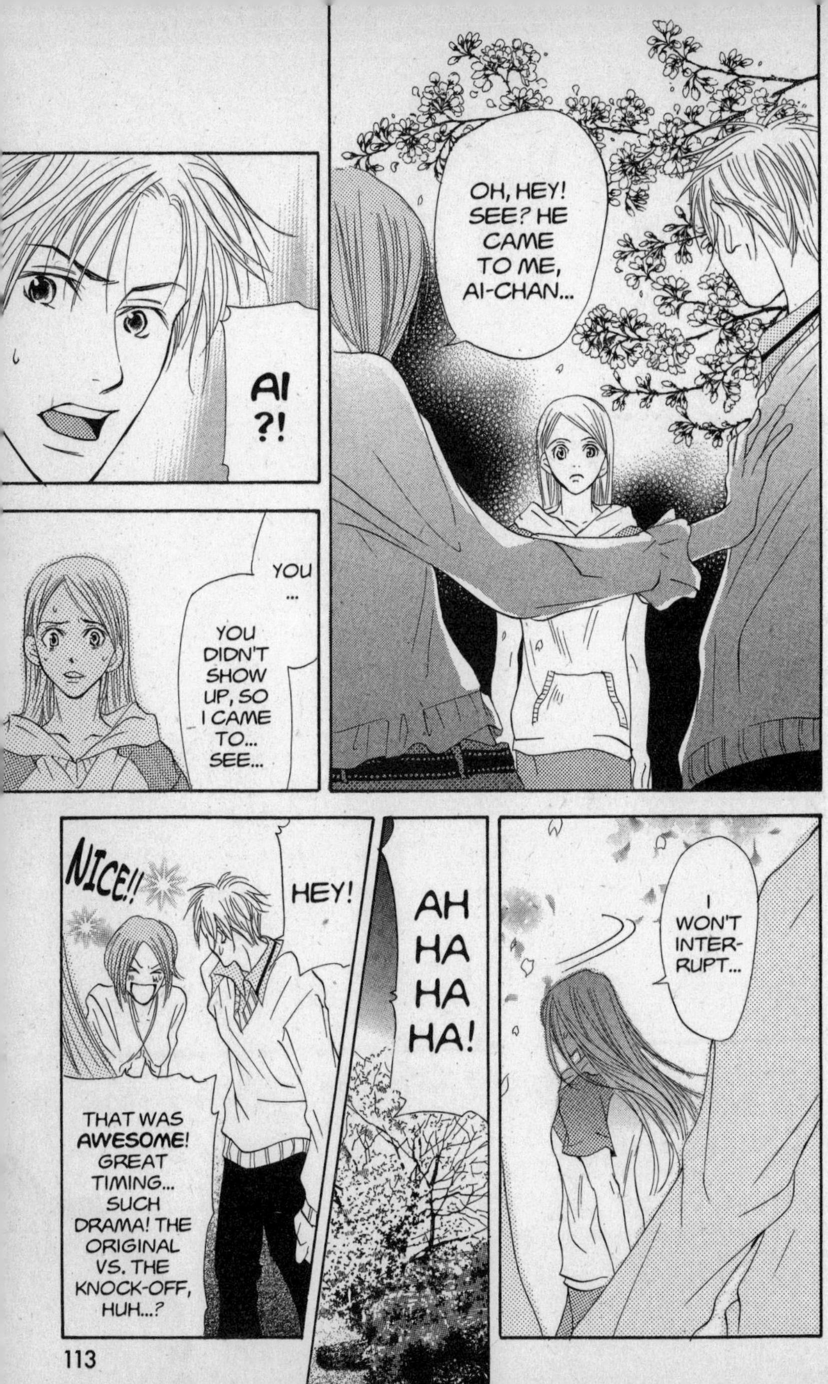
OH, HEY! SEE? HE CAME TO ME, AI-CHAN...
AI ?!
YOU ...
YOU DIDN'T SHOW UP, SO I CAME TO... SEE...
I WON'T INTER-RUPT...
AH HA HA HA!
HEY!
NICE!!
THAT WAS AWESOME! GREAT TIMING... SUCH DRAMA! THE ORIGINAL VS. THE KNOCK-OFF, HUH...?

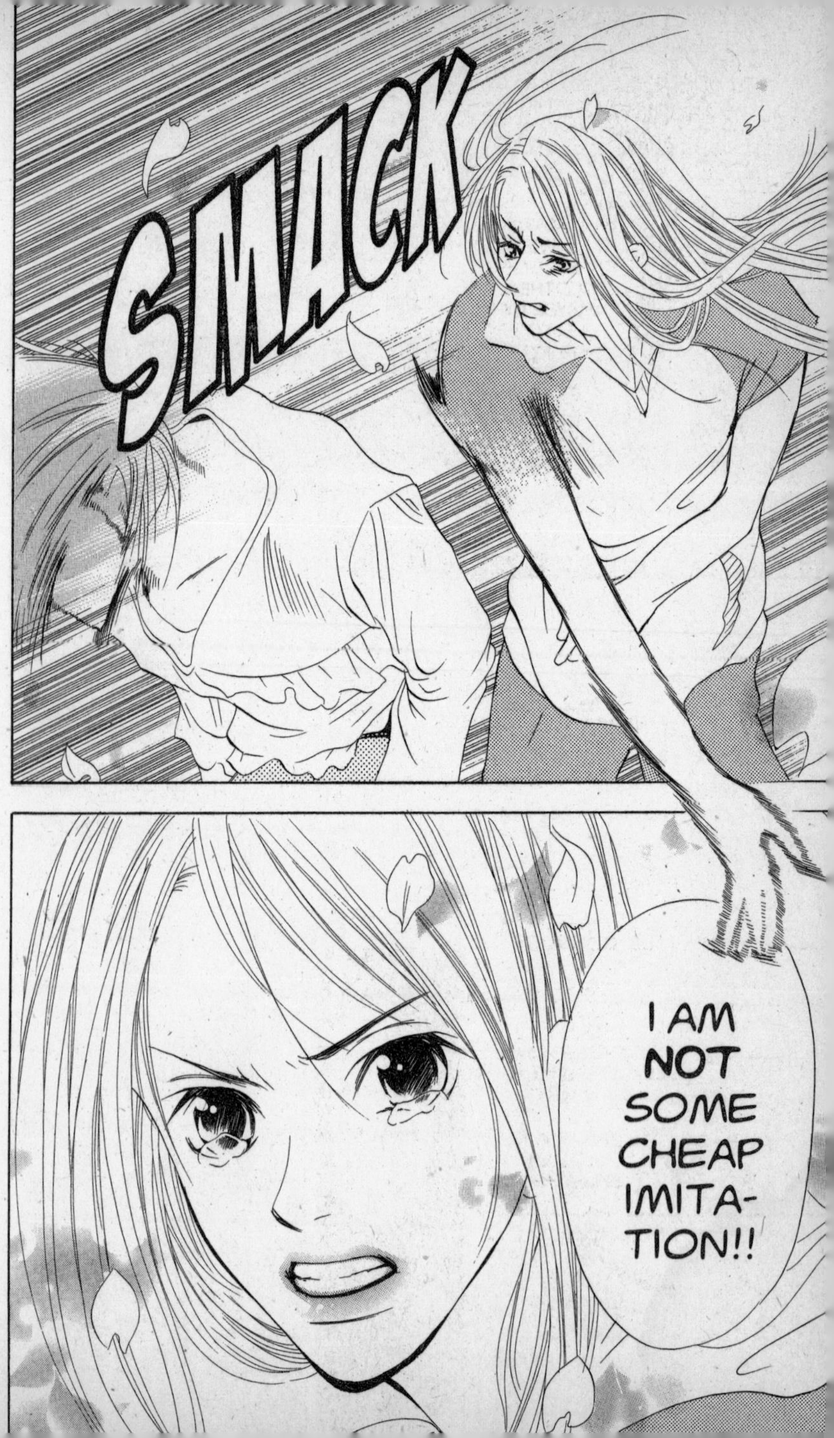
SMACK
I AM NOT SOME CHEAP IMITA-TION!!

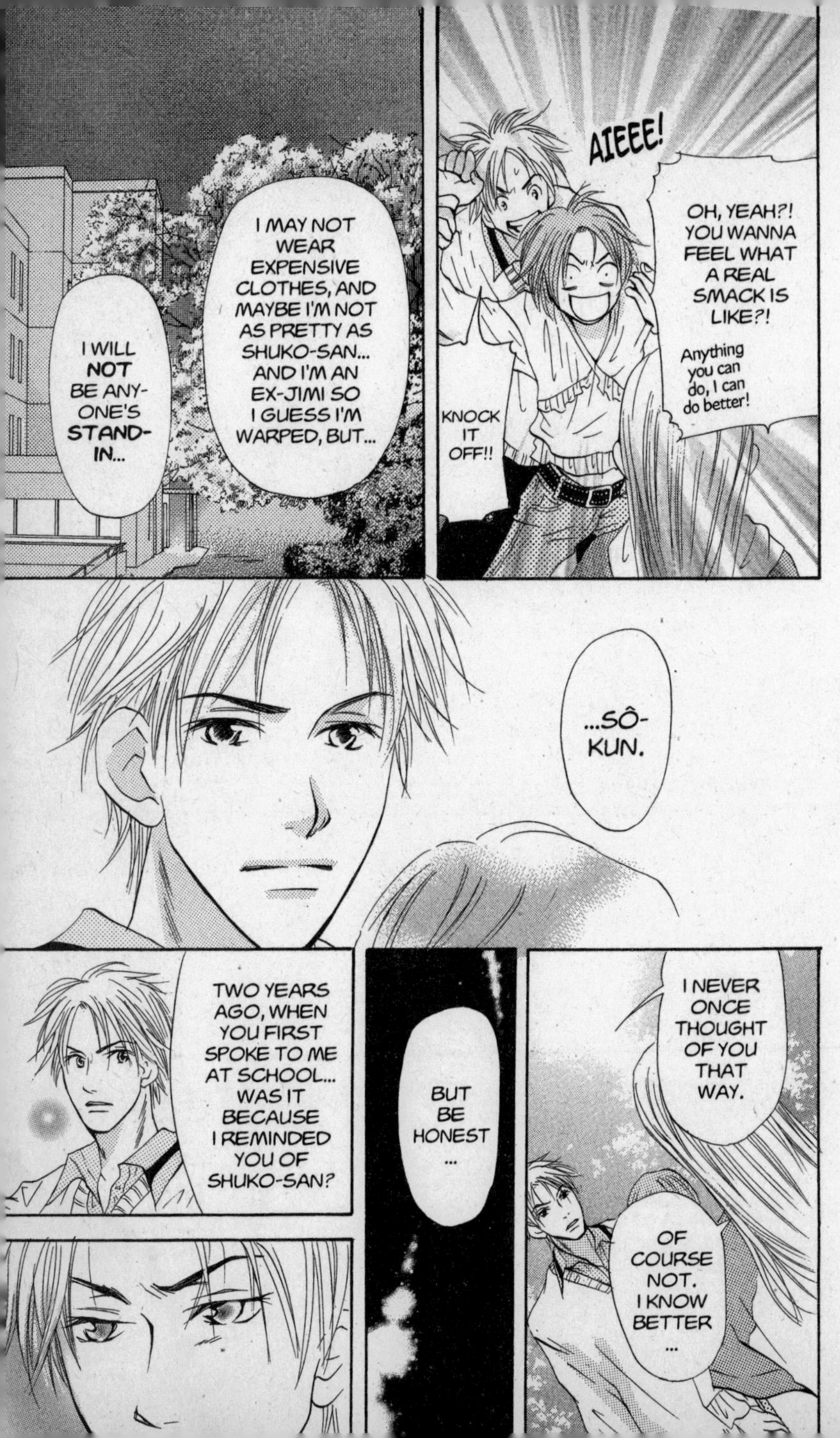
AIEEE!
OH, YEAH?! YOU WANNA FEEL WHAT A REAL SMACK IS LIKE?!
Anything you can do, I can do better!
KNOCK IT OFF!!
I MAY NOT WEAR EXPENSIVE CLOTHES, AND MAYBE I'M NOT AS PRETTY AS SHUKO-SAN... AND I'M AN EX-JIMI SO I GUESS I'M WARPED, BUT...
I WILL NOT BE ANY-ONE'S STAND-IN...
...SÔ-KUN.
I NEVER ONCE THOUGHT OF YOU THAT WAY.
OF COURSE NOT. I KNOW BETTER...
BUT BE HONEST...
TWO YEARS AGO, WHEN YOU FIRST SPOKE TO ME AT SCHOOL... WAS IT BECAUSE I REMINDED YOU OF SHUKO-SAN?

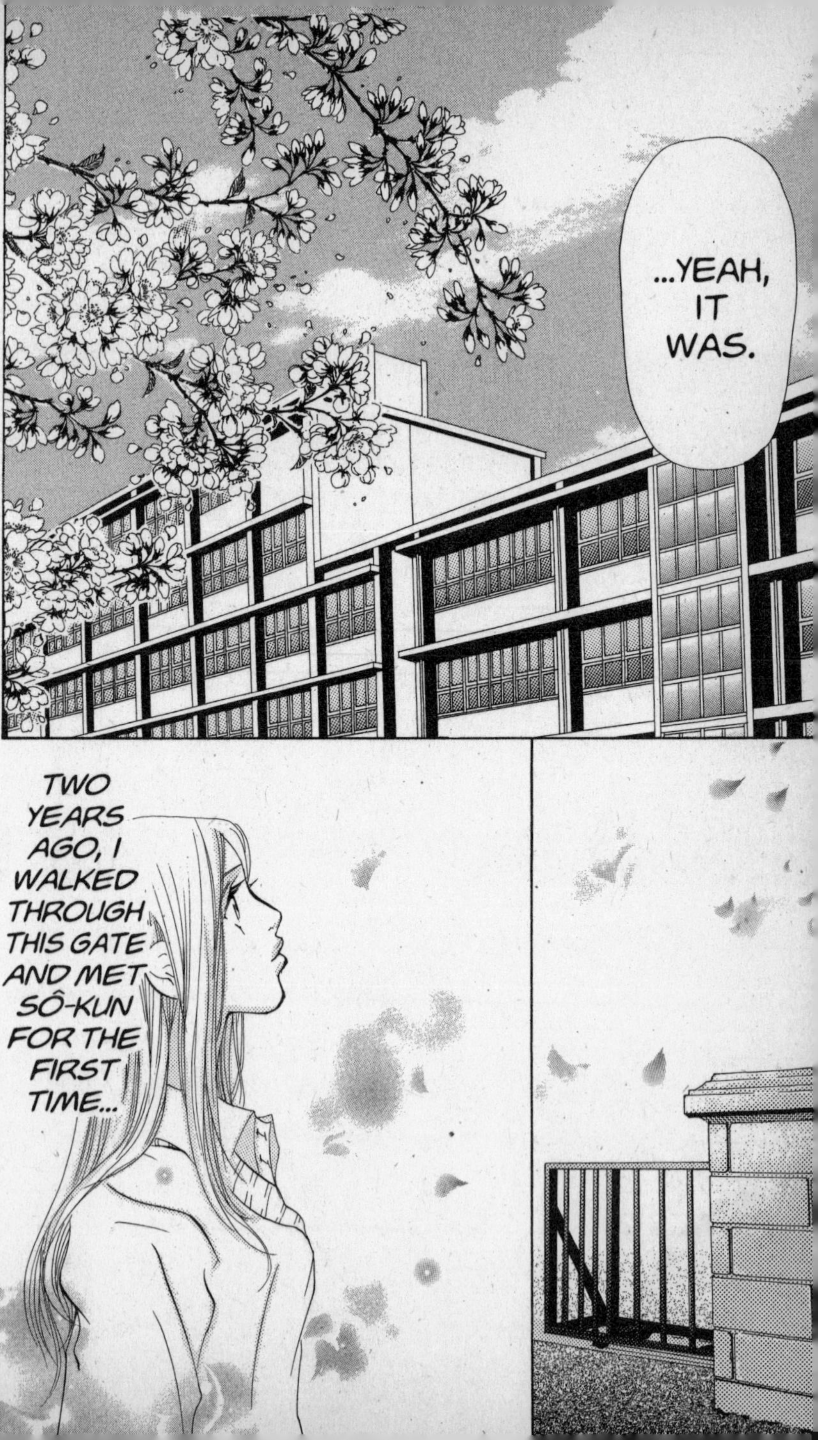
...YEAH, IT WAS.
TWO YEARS AGO, I WALKED THROUGH THIS GATE AND MET SÔ-KUN FOR THE FIRST TIME...

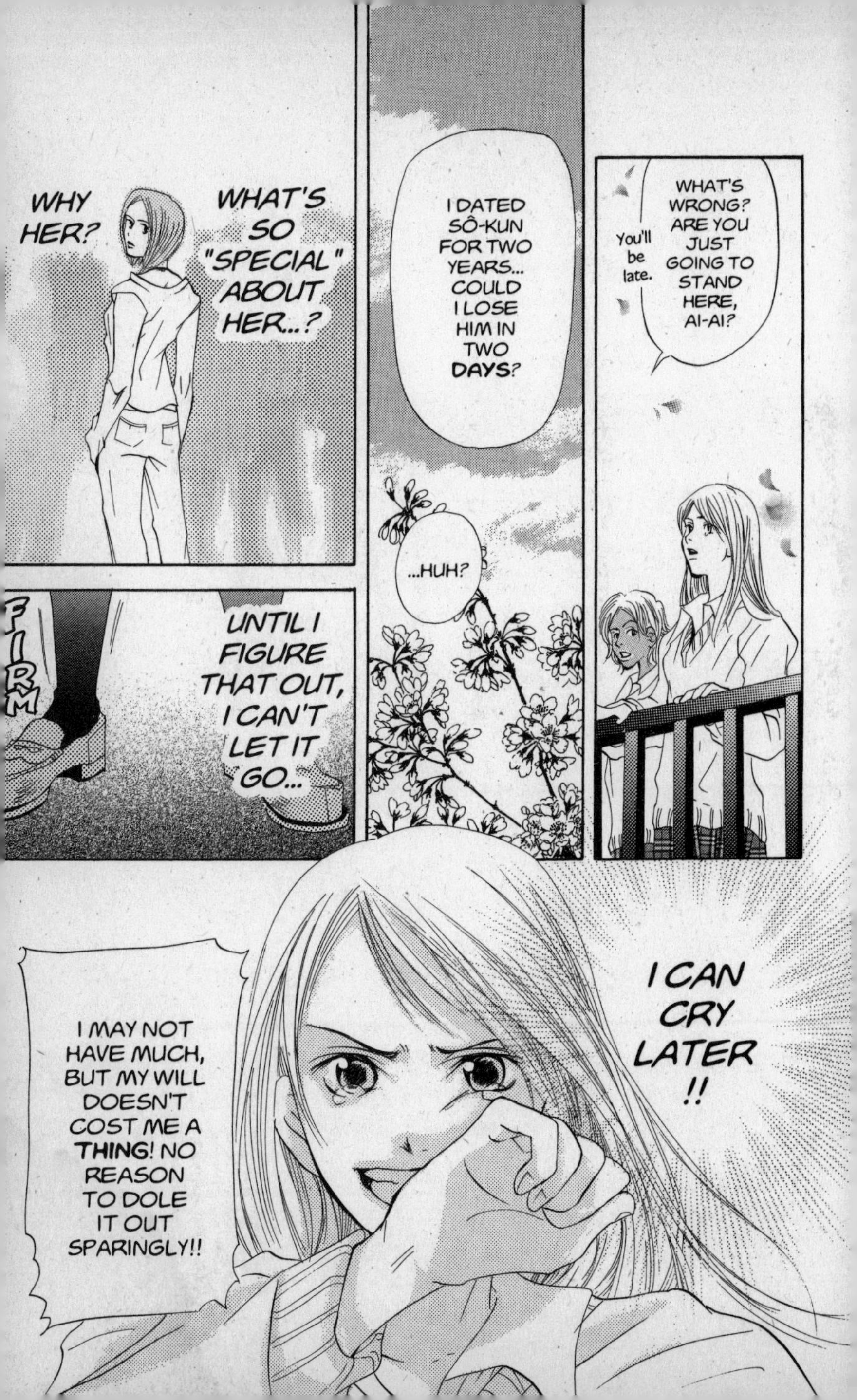
WHAT'S WRONG? ARE YOU JUST GOING TO STAND HERE, AI-AI?
You'll be late.
I DATED SÔ-KUN FOR TWO YEARS... COULD I LOSE HIM IN TWO DAYS?
...HUH?
WHAT'S SO "SPECIAL" ABOUT HER...?
WHY HER?
UNTIL I FIGURE THAT OUT, I CAN'T LET IT GO...
FIRM
I CAN CRY LATER!!
I MAY NOT HAVE MUCH, BUT MY WILL DOESN'T COST ME A THING! NO REASON TO DOLE IT OUT SPARINGLY!!

Thank you for buying the tankobon!!

You're a sweetheart for buying the book when you could
have read the story at the magazine stand for free!!
You're wonderful. Sincerely. I mean that. In return for
your generosity, let me tell you a little about this tankobon,
so that you feel like you got your money's worth.
First: the art is better. Look, this is how the art appeared...

(1) In the magazine.

(2) In the tankobon
(Her chin is cleaned up, see?)

So much **better, right?!** Between the publication of the magazine
and the time when the book goes to print, we have a chance to go in
and make changes and clean images up for the sake of aesthetics.
That's why you'll often see normal-looking bodies in the anthologies
that look like they got a dose of **steroids** in the tankobon. (That's a
trade secret, so SHHH!) What?! You'd prefer the magazine then?
Wait just a second, dear reader!! This tankobon also has more original
pages, and I've revised some of the dialogue from the serialized version.
It's so much better!! (Am I the only one who sees that...?) Please
continue to purchase the tankobon volumes!!
(I'm begging you with my heart and soul...)

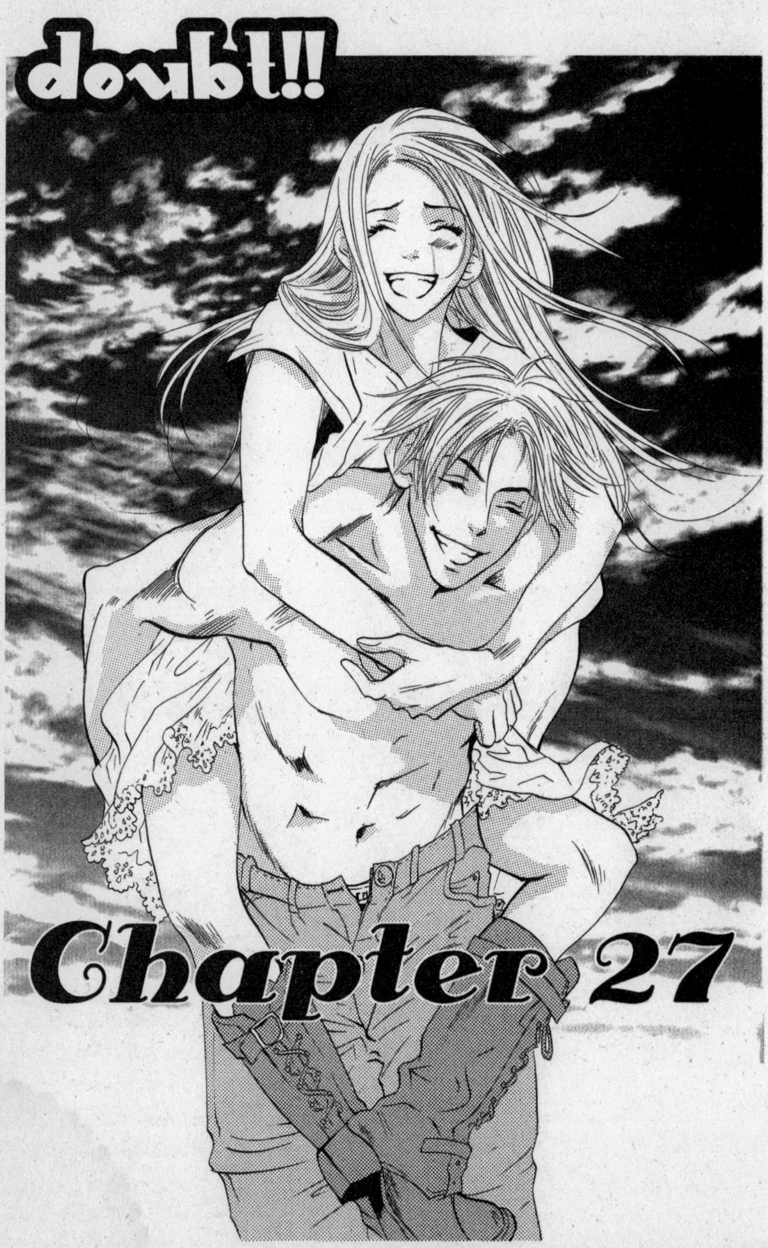
doubt!!
Chapter 27

❀ Sô ❀

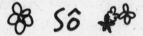

*What a pain he was to work with…!
Very stubborn! Oh, well. You can't control
men like him, no matter how hard you try.
Maybe that belief of mine was
unconsciously reflected in the story…?*

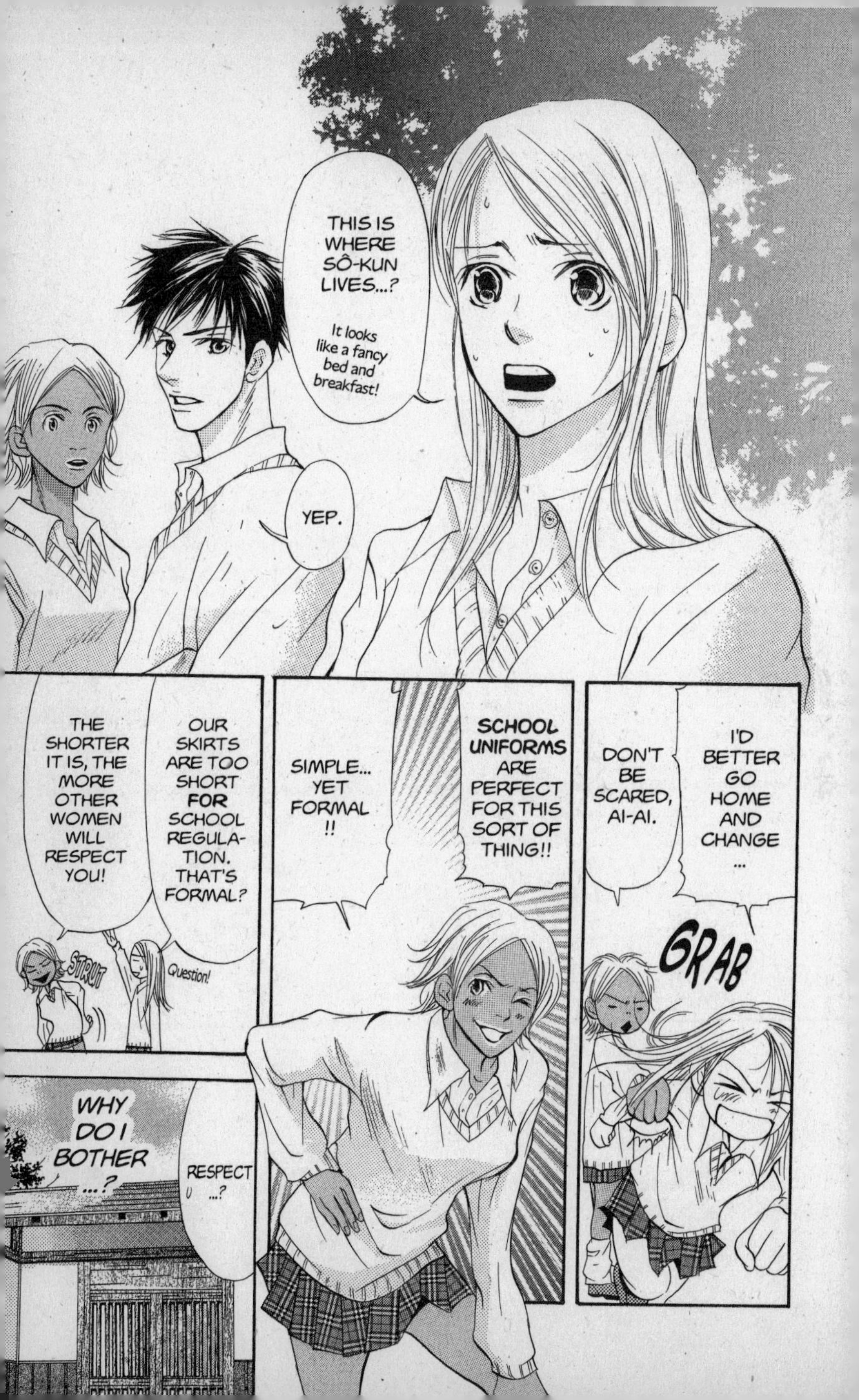
THIS IS WHERE SÔ-KUN LIVES...?
It looks like a fancy bed and breakfast!
YEP.
I'D BETTER GO HOME AND CHANGE ...
DON'T BE SCARED, AI-AI.
GRAB
SCHOOL UNIFORMS ARE PERFECT FOR THIS SORT OF THING!!
SIMPLE... YET FORMAL !!
OUR SKIRTS ARE TOO SHORT FOR SCHOOL REGULATION. THAT'S FORMAL?
Question!
THE SHORTER IT IS, THE MORE OTHER WOMEN WILL RESPECT YOU!
STRUT
RESPECT ...?
WHY DO I BOTHER ...?

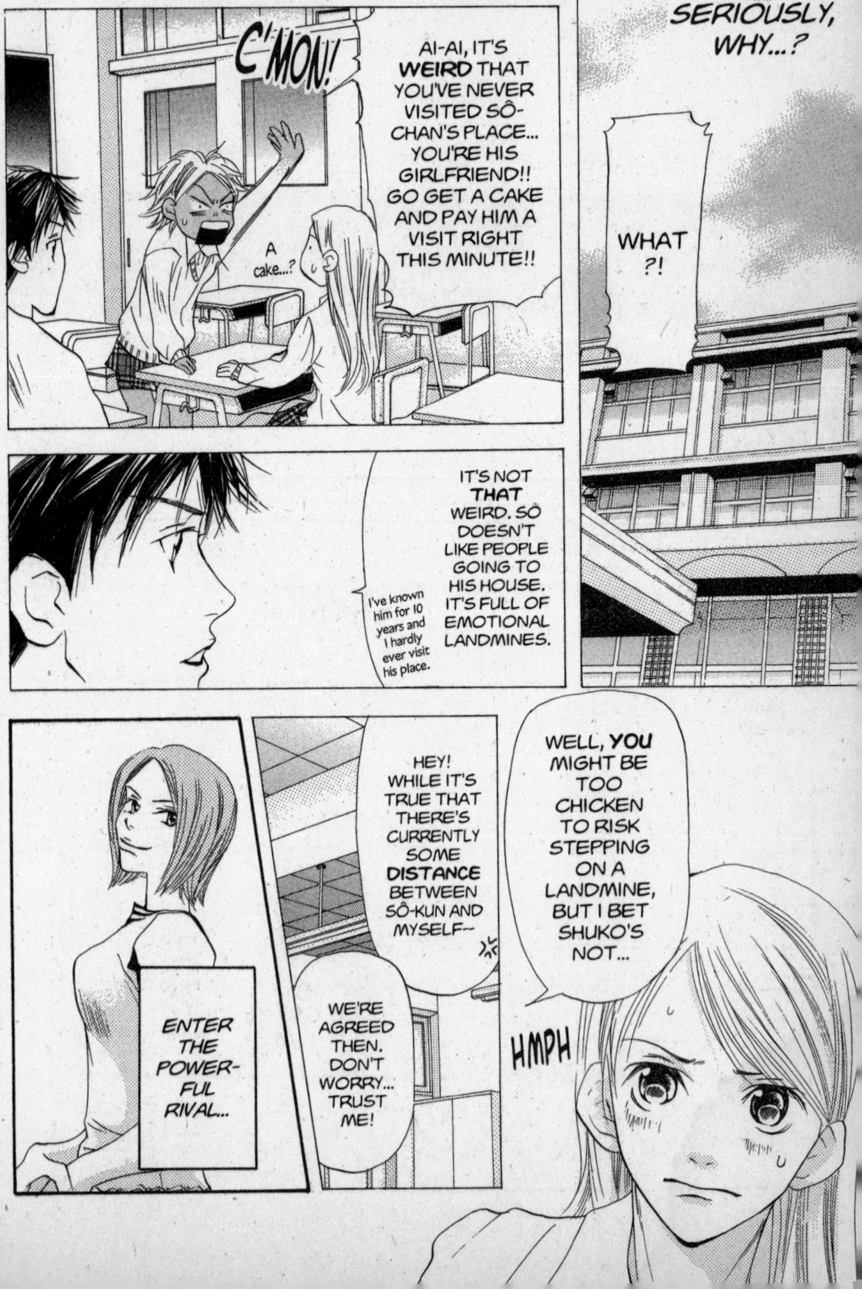
SERIOUSLY, WHY...?
WHAT ?!
AI-AI, IT'S WEIRD THAT YOU'VE NEVER VISITED SÔ-CHAN'S PLACE... YOU'RE HIS GIRLFRIEND!! GO GET A CAKE AND PAY HIM A VISIT RIGHT THIS MINUTE!!
C'MON!
A cake...?
IT'S NOT THAT WEIRD. SO DOESN'T LIKE PEOPLE GOING TO HIS HOUSE. IT'S FULL OF EMOTIONAL LANDMINES.
I've known him for 10 years and I hardly ever visit his place.
WELL, YOU MIGHT BE TOO CHICKEN TO RISK STEPPING ON A LANDMINE, BUT I BET SHUKO'S NOT...
HMPH
HEY! WHILE IT'S TRUE THAT THERE'S CURRENTLY SOME DISTANCE BETWEEN SÔ-KUN AND MYSELF--
WE'RE AGREED THEN. DON'T WORRY... TRUST ME!
ENTER THE POWER-FUL RIVAL...

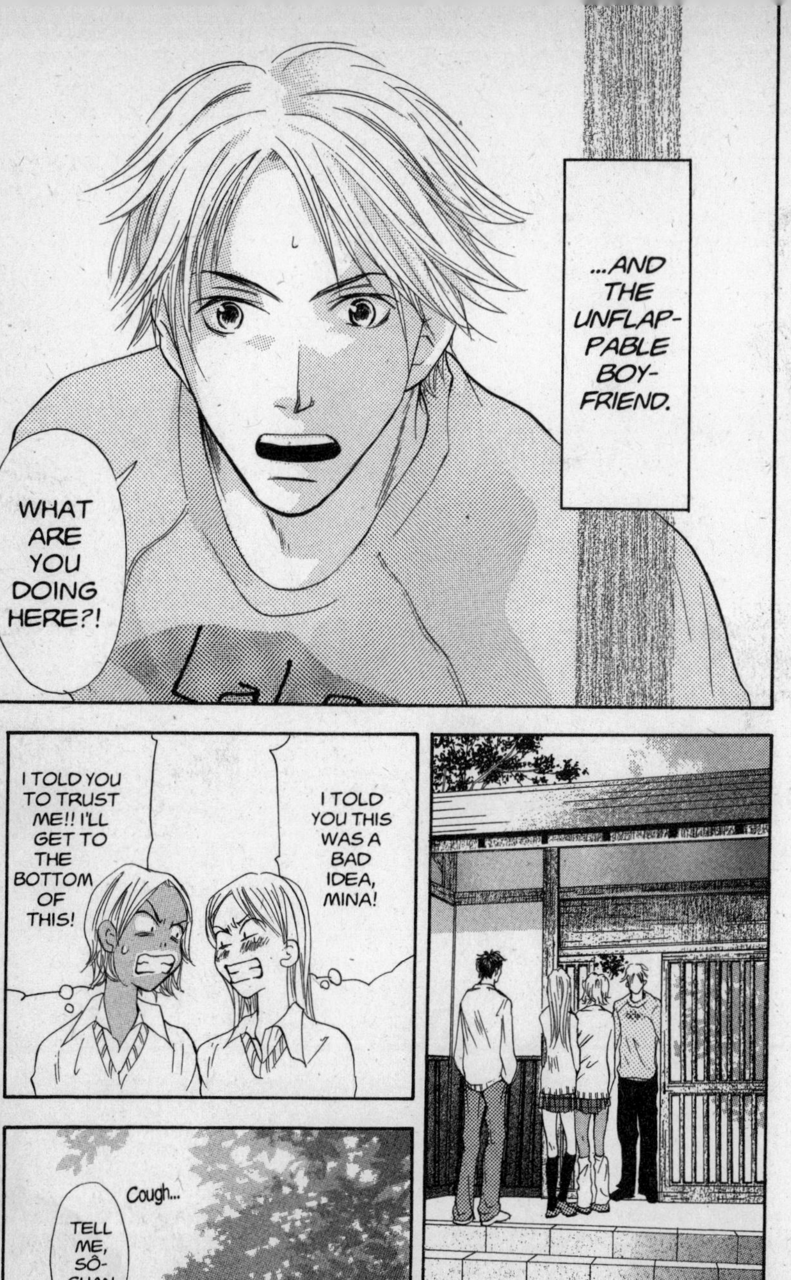
...AND THE UNFLAPPABLE BOYFRIEND.
WHAT ARE YOU DOING HERE?!
I TOLD YOU THIS WAS A BAD IDEA, MINA!
I TOLD YOU TO TRUST ME!! I'LL GET TO THE BOTTOM OF THIS!
Cough...
TELL ME, SÔ-CHAN ...

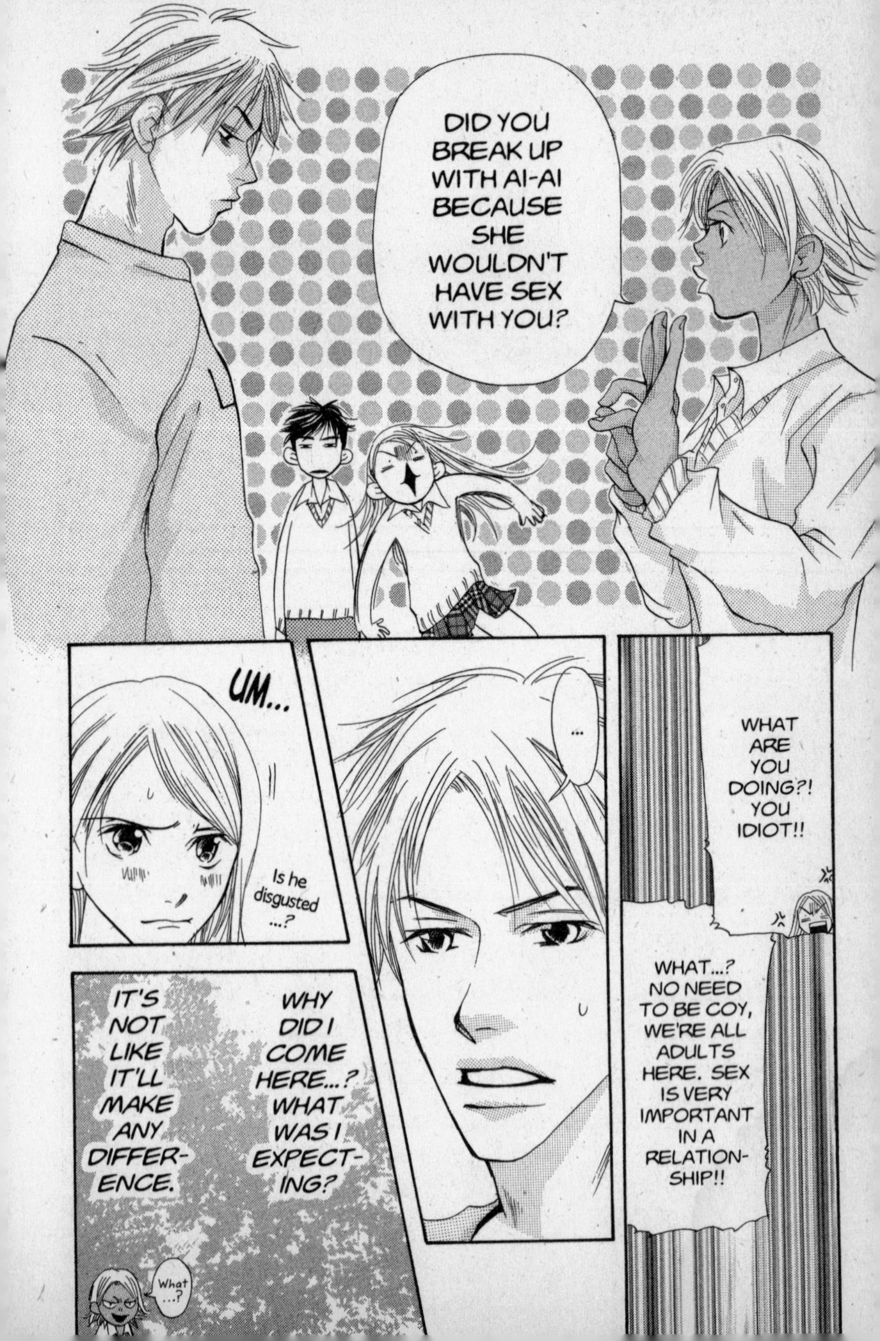
DID YOU BREAK UP WITH AI-AI BECAUSE SHE WOULDN'T HAVE SEX WITH YOU?
WHAT ARE YOU DOING?! YOU IDIOT!!
WHAT...? NO NEED TO BE COY, WE'RE ALL ADULTS HERE. SEX IS VERY IMPORTANT IN A RELATION-SHIP!!
...
UM...
Is he disgusted ...?
WHY DID I COME HERE...? WHAT WAS I EXPECT-ING?
IT'S NOT LIKE IT'LL MAKE ANY DIFFER-ENCE.
What ...?

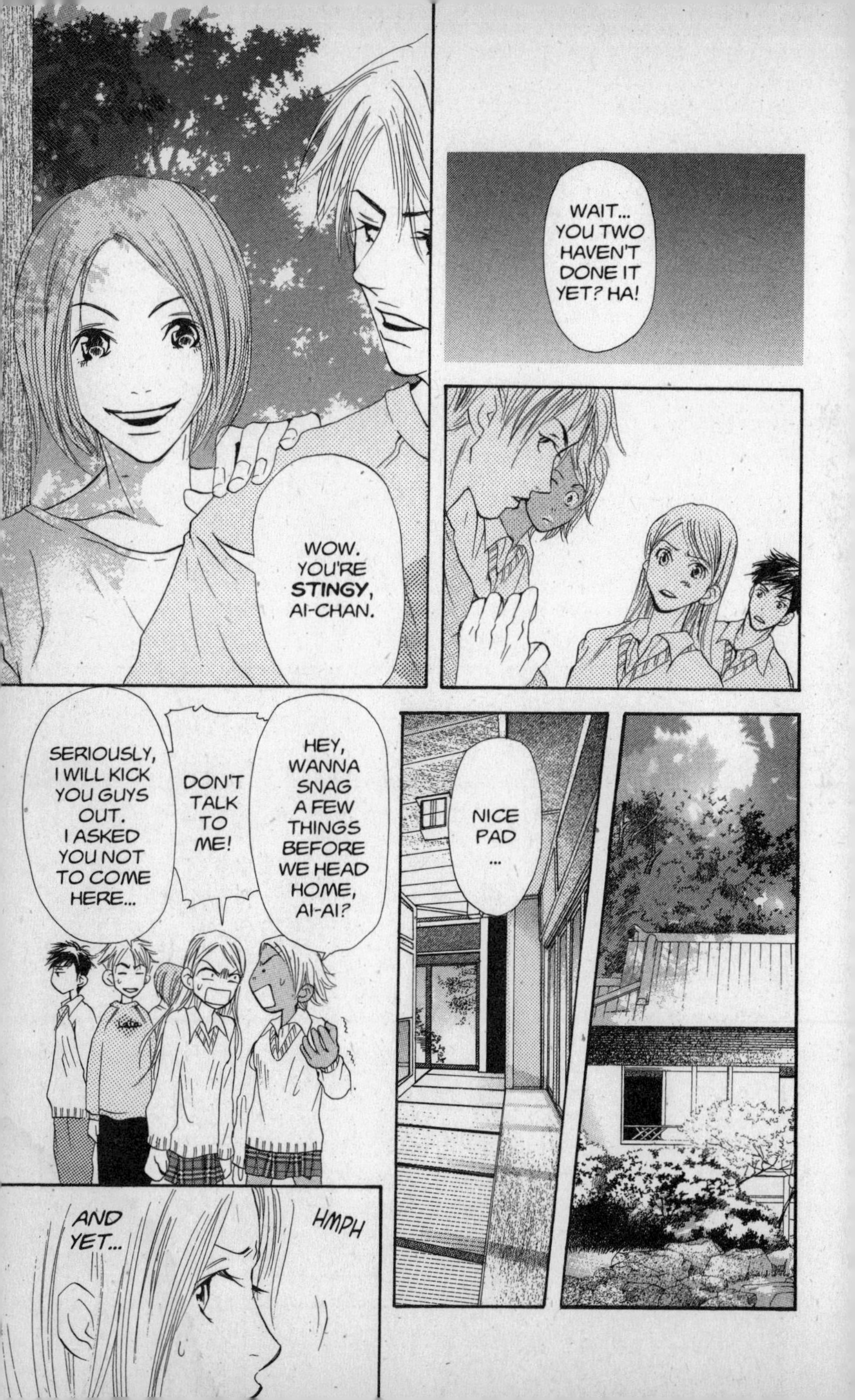
WAIT... YOU TWO HAVEN'T DONE IT YET? HA!
WOW. YOU'RE **STINGY**, AI-CHAN.
NICE PAD ...
HEY, WANNA SNAG A FEW THINGS BEFORE WE HEAD HOME, AI-AI?
DON'T TALK TO ME!
SERIOUSLY, I WILL KICK YOU GUYS OUT. I ASKED YOU NOT TO COME HERE...
HMPH
AND YET...

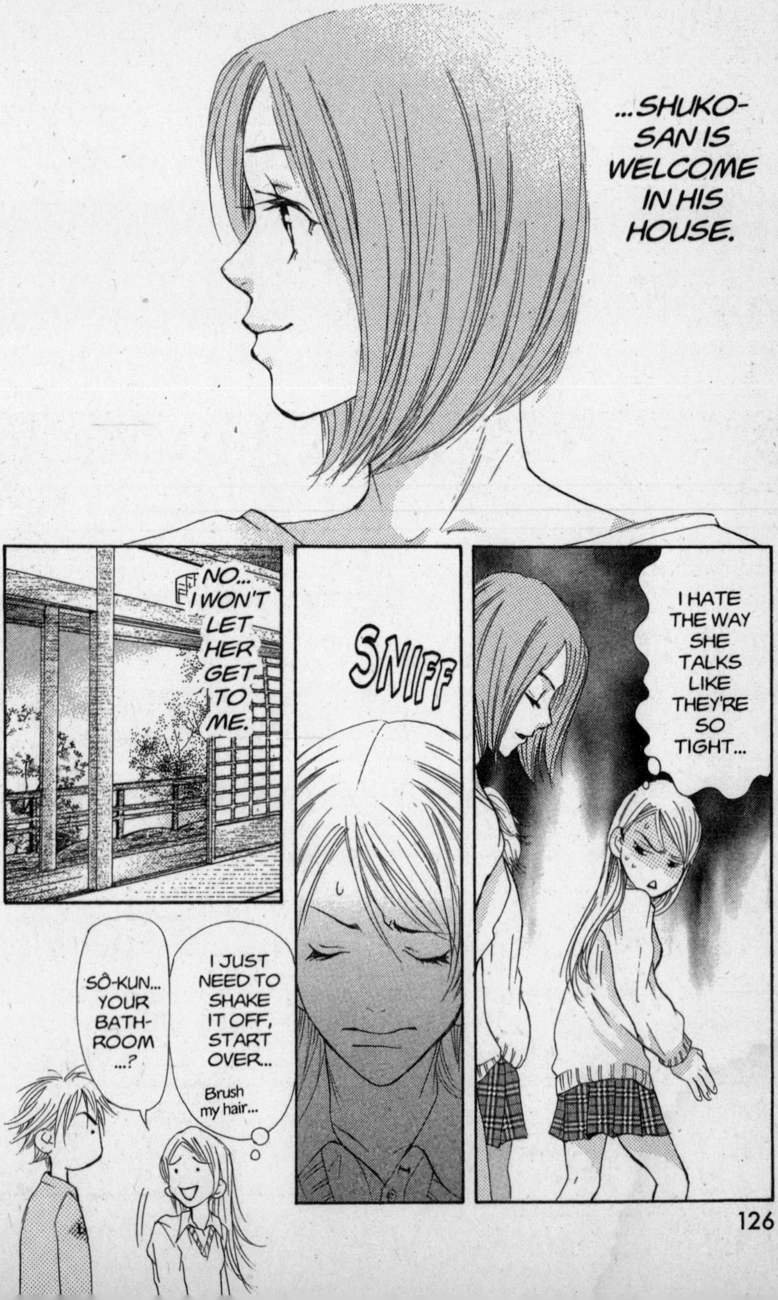
...SHUKO-SAN IS WELCOME IN HIS HOUSE.
I HATE THE WAY SHE TALKS LIKE THEY'RE SO TIGHT...
SNIFF
NO... I WON'T LET HER GET TO ME.
I JUST NEED TO SHAKE IT OFF, START OVER...
Brush my hair...
SÔ-KUN... YOUR BATHROOM...?

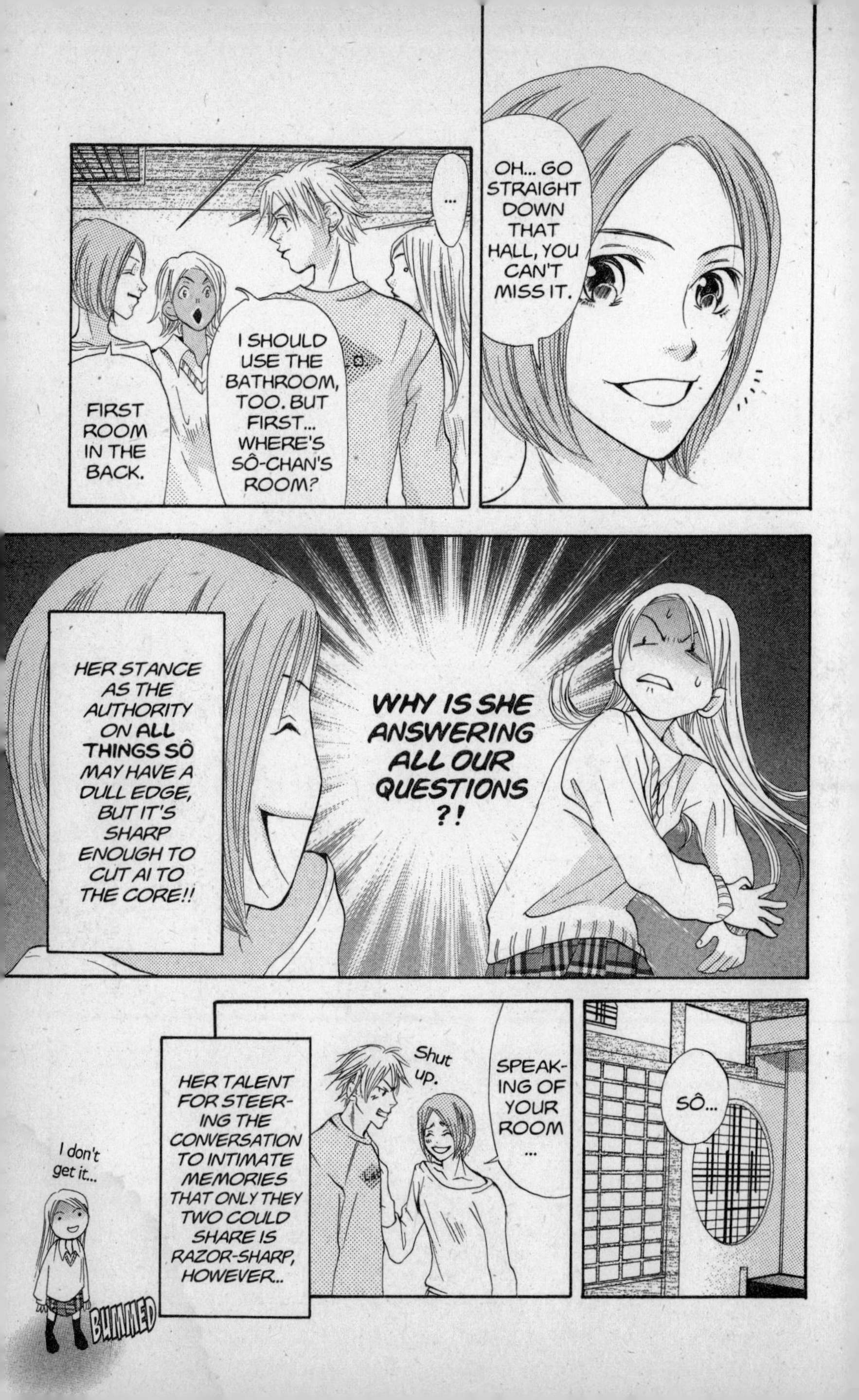
OH... GO STRAIGHT DOWN THAT HALL, YOU CAN'T MISS IT.
...
I SHOULD USE THE BATHROOM, TOO. BUT FIRST... WHERE'S SÔ-CHAN'S ROOM?
FIRST ROOM IN THE BACK.
WHY IS SHE ANSWERING ALL OUR QUESTIONS?!
HER STANCE AS THE AUTHORITY ON ALL THINGS SÔ MAY HAVE A DULL EDGE, BUT IT'S SHARP ENOUGH TO CUT AI TO THE CORE!!
SÔ...
SPEAKING OF YOUR ROOM...
Shut up.
HER TALENT FOR STEERING THE CONVERSATION TO INTIMATE MEMORIES THAT ONLY THEY TWO COULD SHARE IS RAZOR-SHARP, HOWEVER...
I don't get it...
BUMMED

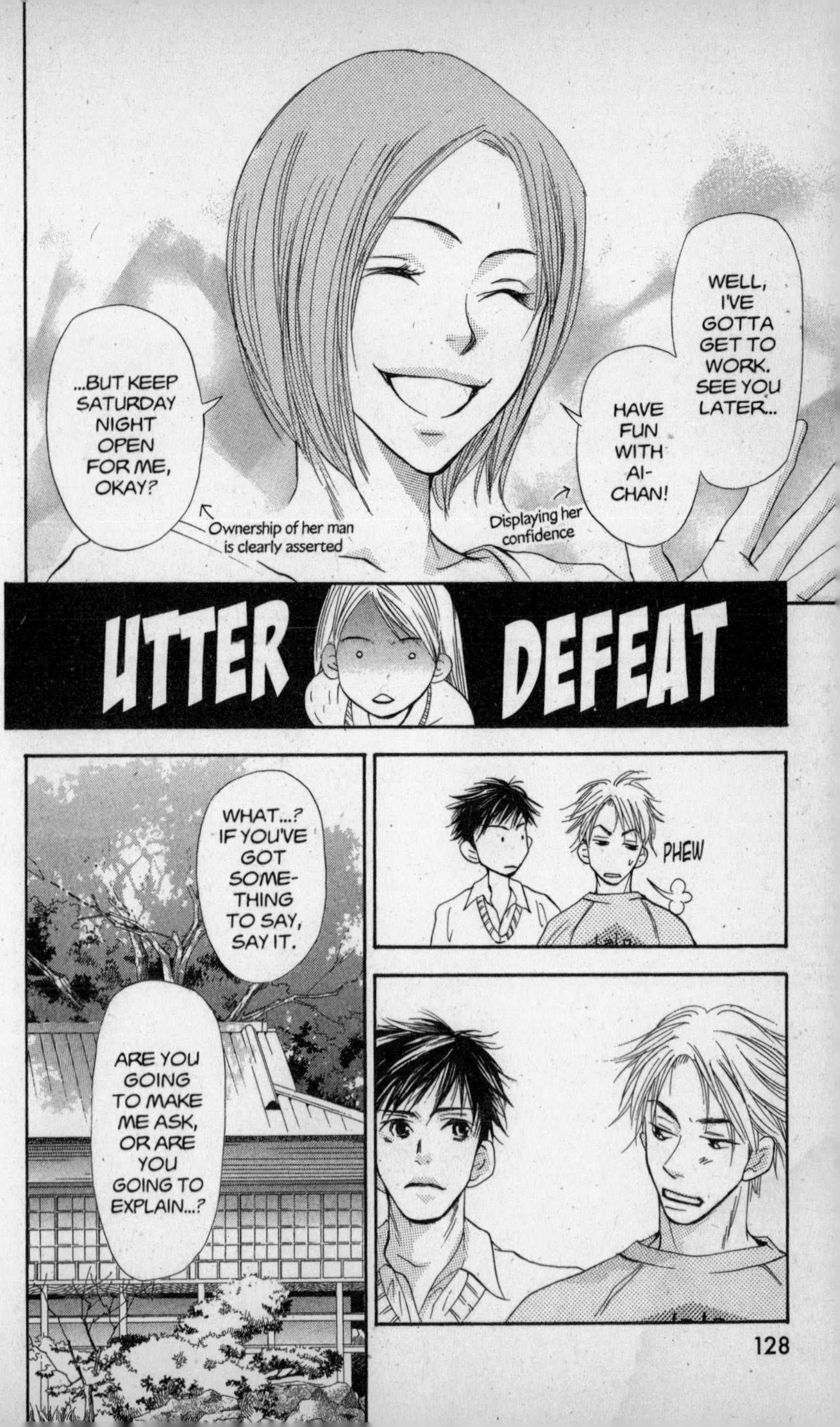
WELL, I'VE GOTTA GET TO WORK. SEE YOU LATER...
HAVE FUN WITH AI-CHAN!
Displaying her confidence
...BUT KEEP SATURDAY NIGHT OPEN FOR ME, OKAY?
Ownership of her man is clearly asserted
UTTER DEFEAT
PHEW
WHAT...? IF YOU'VE GOT SOMETHING TO SAY, SAY IT.
ARE YOU GOING TO MAKE ME ASK, OR ARE YOU GOING TO EXPLAIN...?

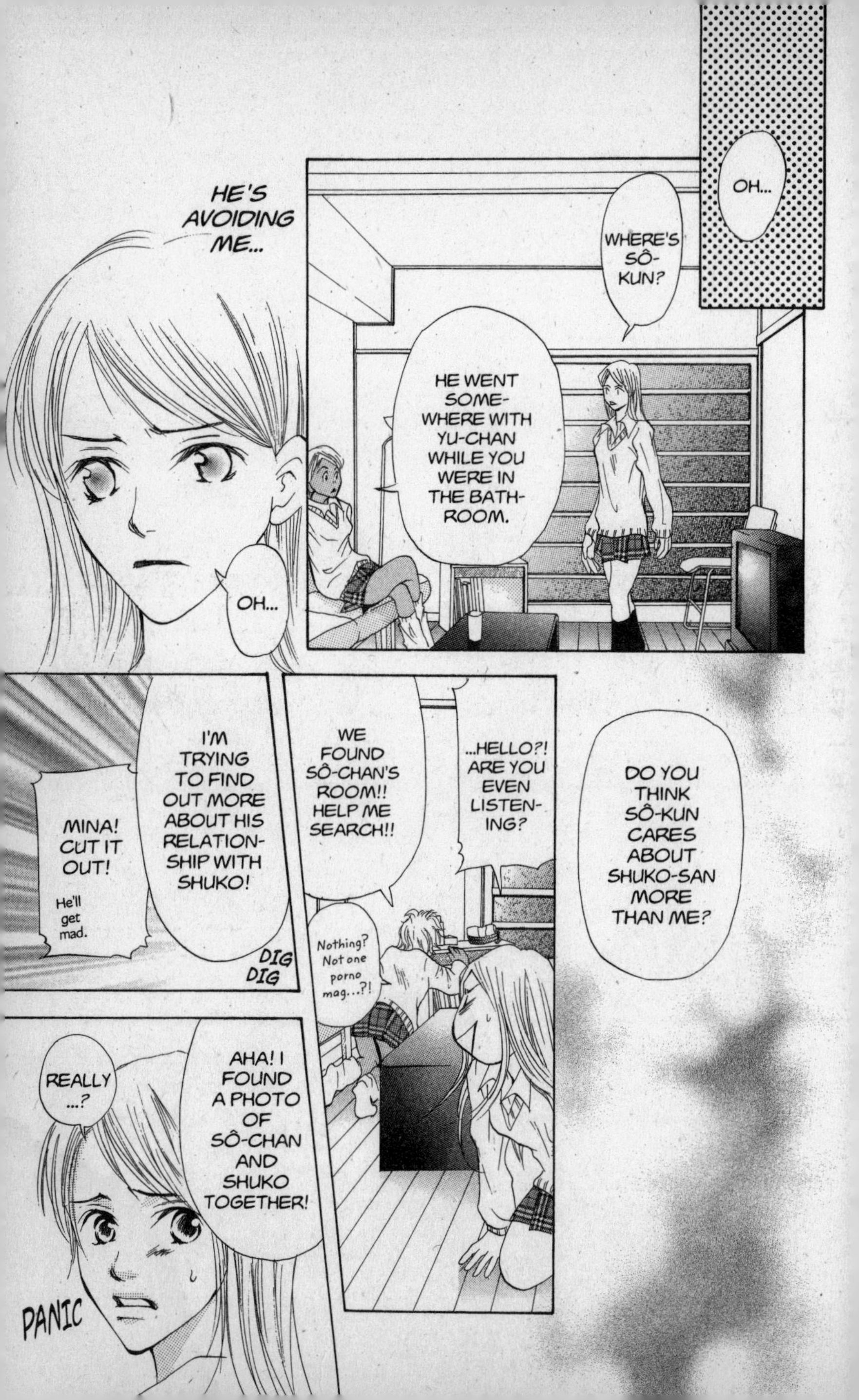
OH...
WHERE'S SÔ-KUN?
HE WENT SOME-WHERE WITH YU-CHAN WHILE YOU WERE IN THE BATH-ROOM.
HE'S AVOIDING ME...
OH...
DO YOU THINK SÔ-KUN CARES ABOUT SHUKO-SAN MORE THAN ME?
...HELLO?! ARE YOU EVEN LISTEN-ING?
WE FOUND SÔ-CHAN'S ROOM!! HELP ME SEARCH!!
Nothing? Not one porno mag...?!
I'M TRYING TO FIND OUT MORE ABOUT HIS RELATION-SHIP WITH SHUKO!
MINA! CUT IT OUT!
He'll get mad.
DIG DIG
AHA! I FOUND A PHOTO OF SÔ-CHAN AND SHUKO TOGETHER!
REALLY ...?
PANIC

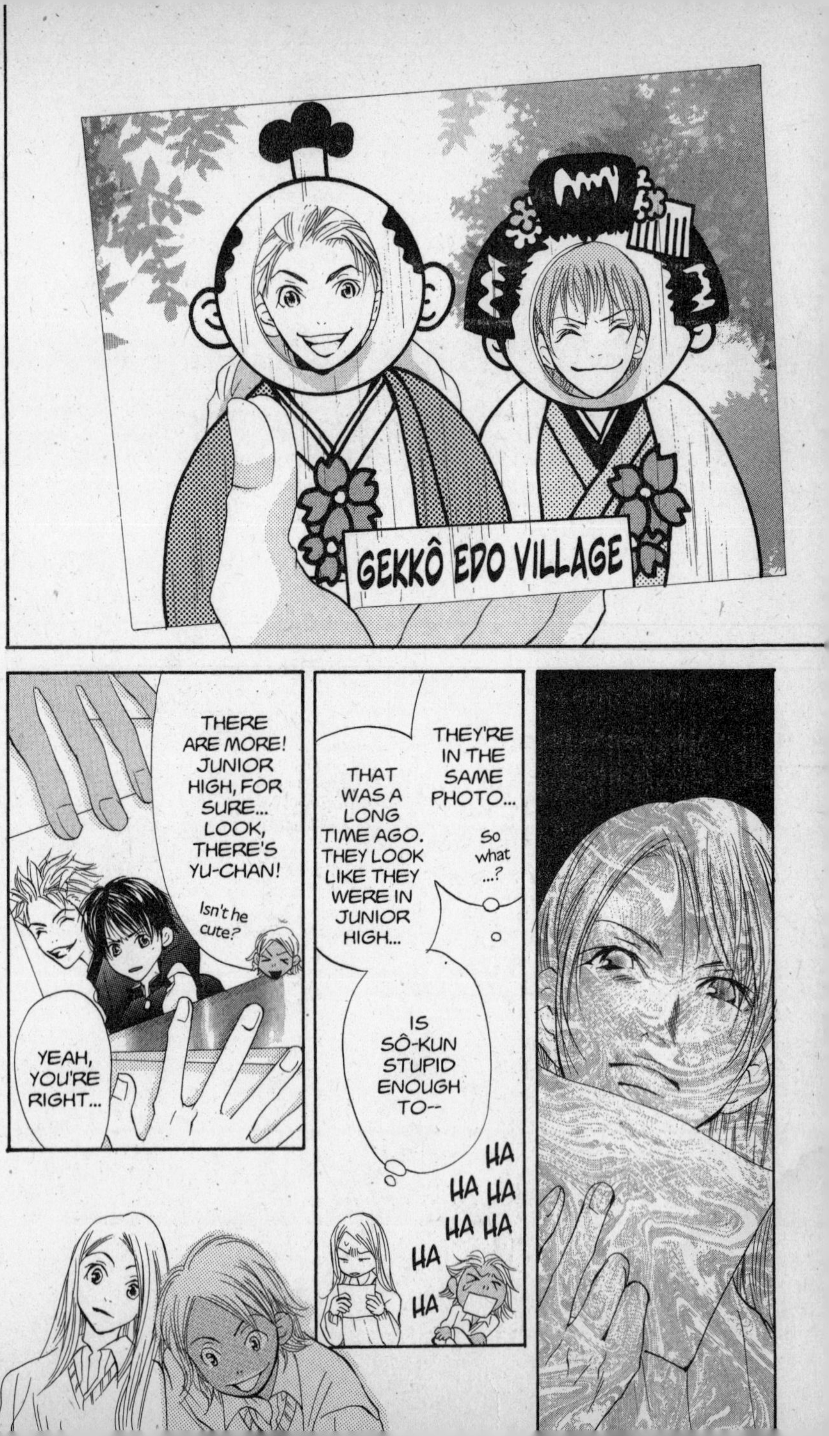
GEKKÔ EDO VILLAGE
THEY'RE IN THE SAME PHOTO...
So what ...?
THAT WAS A LONG TIME AGO. THEY LOOK LIKE THEY WERE IN JUNIOR HIGH...
IS SÔ-KUN STUPID ENOUGH TO--
HA HA HA HA HA HA HA HA
THERE ARE MORE! JUNIOR HIGH, FOR SURE... LOOK, THERE'S YU-CHAN!
Isn't he cute?
YEAH, YOU'RE RIGHT...

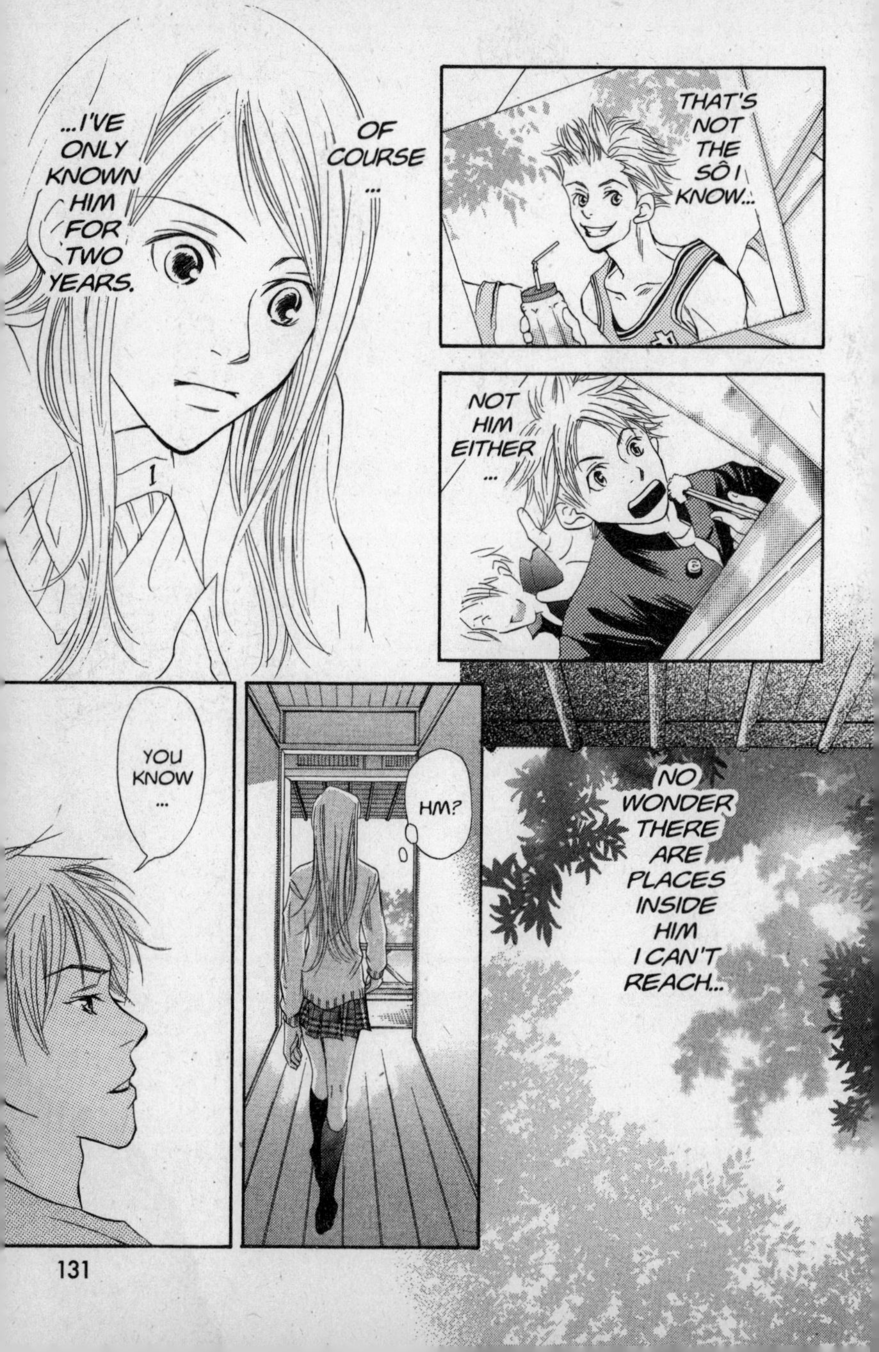

THAT'S NOT THE SÔ I KNOW...
NOT HIM EITHER...
OF COURSE...
...I'VE ONLY KNOWN HIM FOR TWO YEARS.
NO WONDER THERE ARE PLACES INSIDE HIM I CAN'T REACH...
HM?
YOU KNOW...

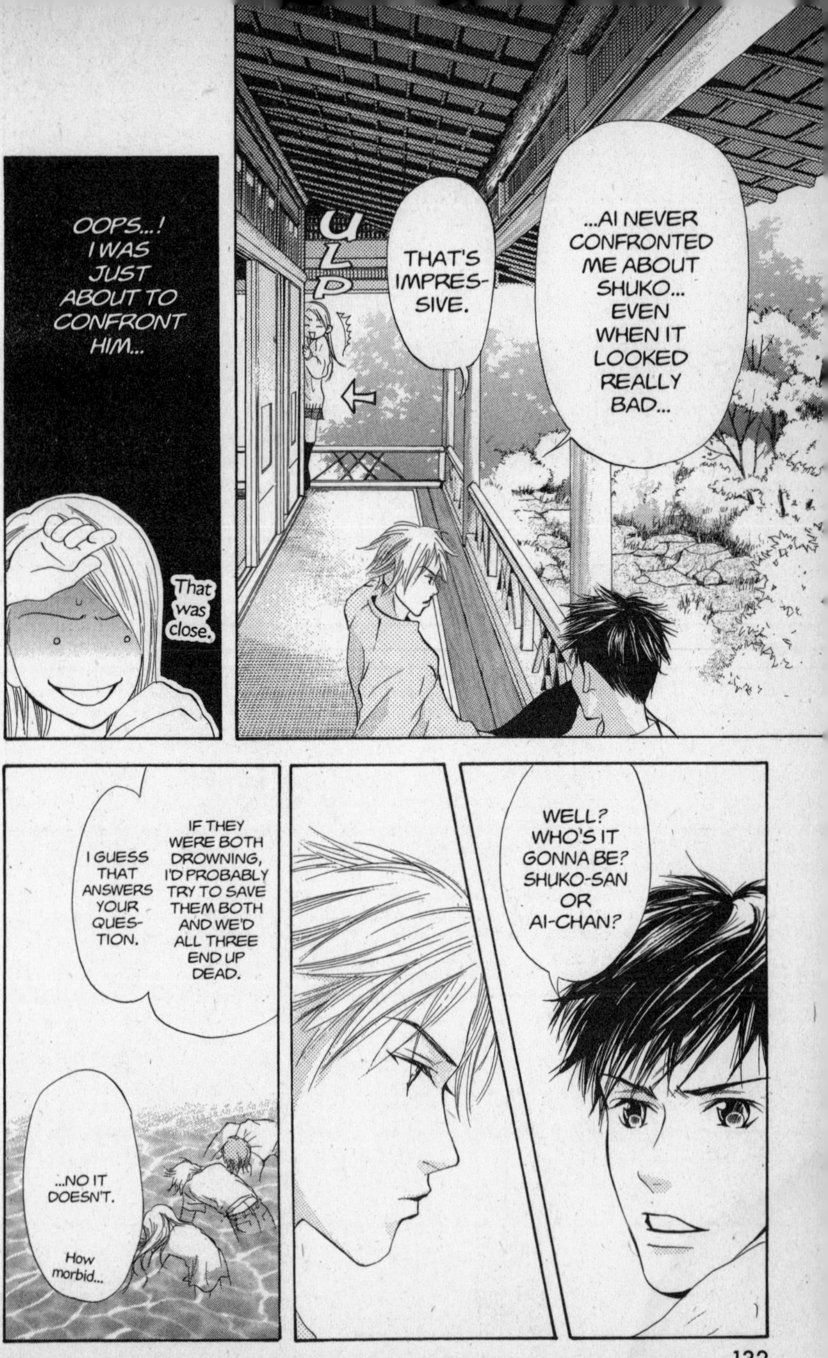
...AI NEVER CONFRONTED ME ABOUT SHUKO... EVEN WHEN IT LOOKED REALLY BAD...
THAT'S IMPRES-SIVE.
ULP
OOPS...! I WAS JUST ABOUT TO CONFRONT HIM...
That was close.
WELL? WHO'S IT GONNA BE? SHUKO-SAN OR AI-CHAN?
IF THEY WERE BOTH DROWNING, I'D PROBABLY TRY TO SAVE THEM BOTH AND WE'D ALL THREE END UP DEAD.
I GUESS THAT ANSWERS YOUR QUES-TION.
...NO IT DOESN'T.
How morbid...

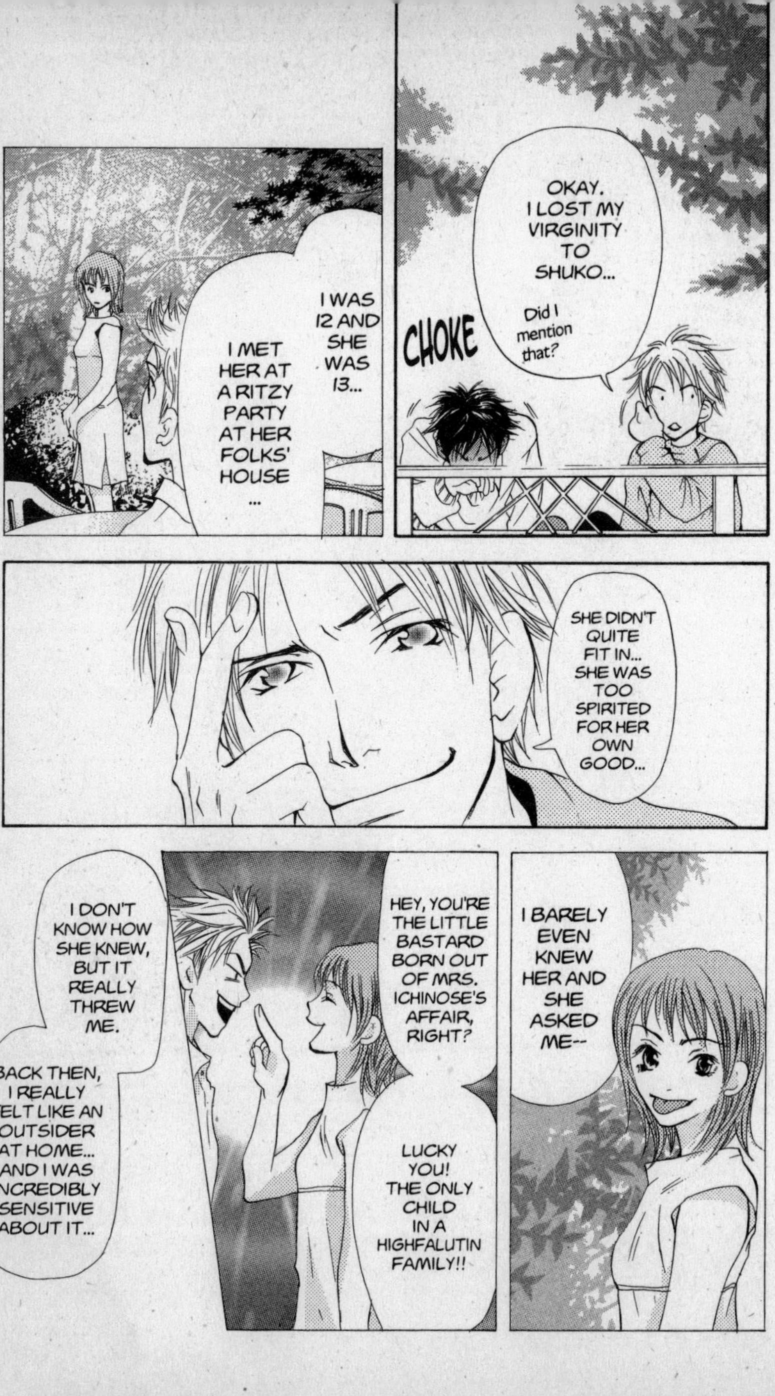
OKAY. I LOST MY VIRGINITY TO SHUKO...
Did I mention that?
CHOKE
I WAS 12 AND SHE WAS 13...
I MET HER AT A RITZY PARTY AT HER FOLKS' HOUSE ...
SHE DIDN'T QUITE FIT IN... SHE WAS TOO SPIRITED FOR HER OWN GOOD...
I BARELY EVEN KNEW HER AND SHE ASKED ME--
HEY, YOU'RE THE LITTLE BASTARD BORN OUT OF MRS. ICHINOSE'S AFFAIR, RIGHT?
LUCKY YOU! THE ONLY CHILD IN A HIGHFALUTIN FAMILY!!
I DON'T KNOW HOW SHE KNEW, BUT IT REALLY THREW ME.
BACK THEN, I REALLY FELT LIKE AN OUTSIDER AT HOME... AND I WAS INCREDIBLY SENSITIVE ABOUT IT...

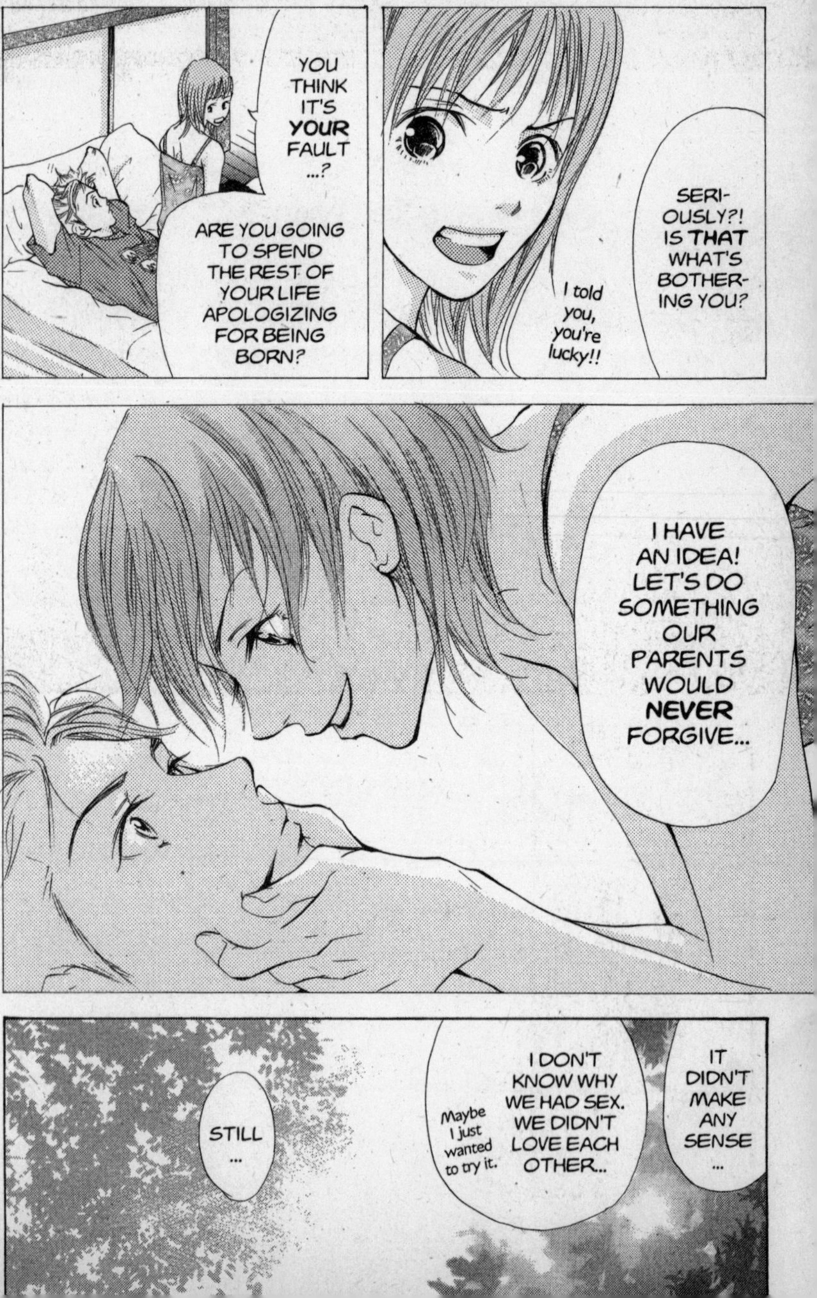
SERI-OUSLY?! IS THAT WHAT'S BOTHER-ING YOU?
I told you, you're lucky!!
YOU THINK IT'S YOUR FAULT ...?
ARE YOU GOING TO SPEND THE REST OF YOUR LIFE APOLOGIZING FOR BEING BORN?
I HAVE AN IDEA! LET'S DO SOMETHING OUR PARENTS WOULD NEVER FORGIVE...
IT DIDN'T MAKE ANY SENSE ...
I DON'T KNOW WHY WE HAD SEX. WE DIDN'T LOVE EACH OTHER...
Maybe I just wanted to try it.
STILL ...

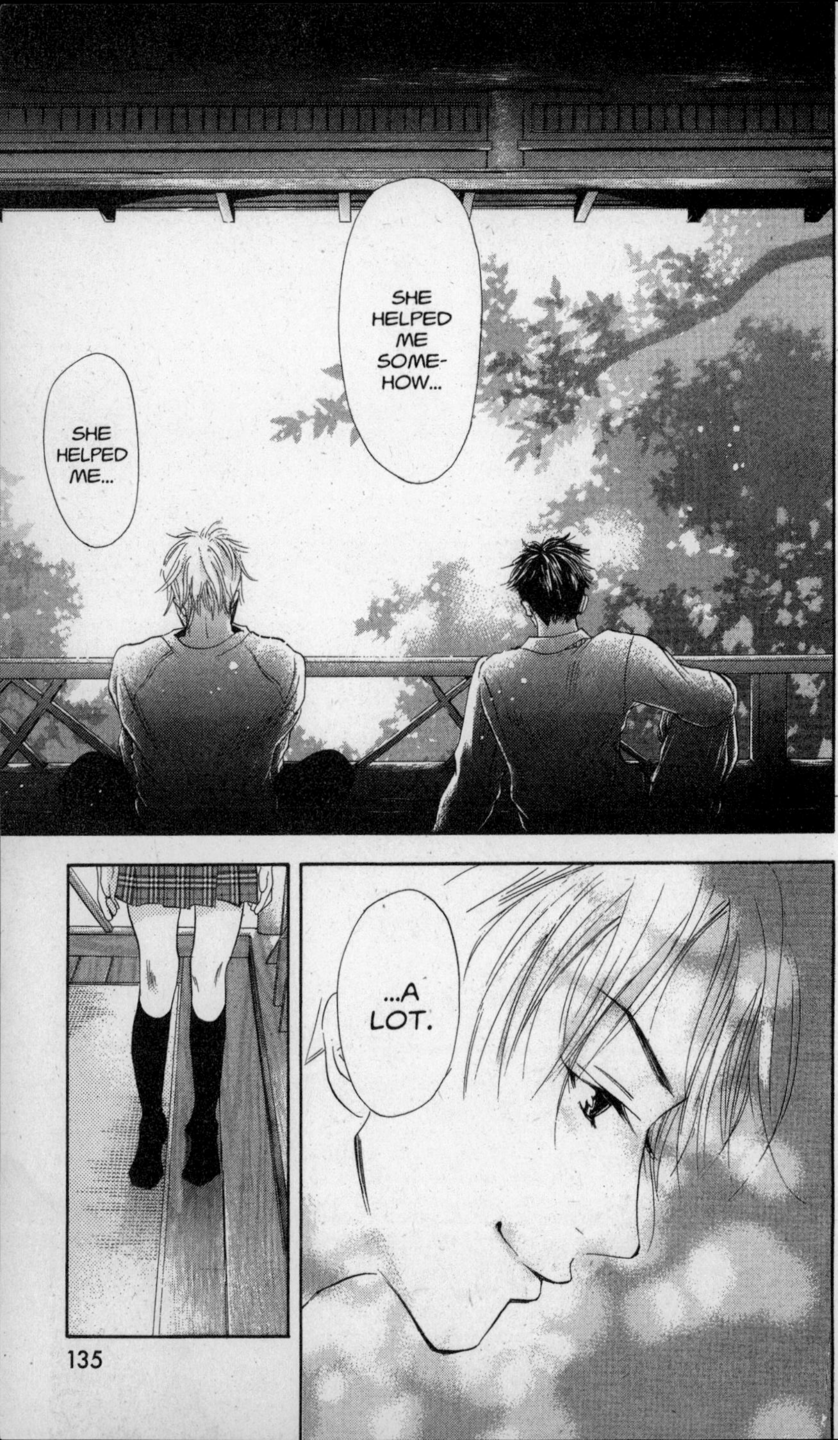
SHE HELPED ME SOMEHOW...
SHE HELPED ME...
...A LOT.

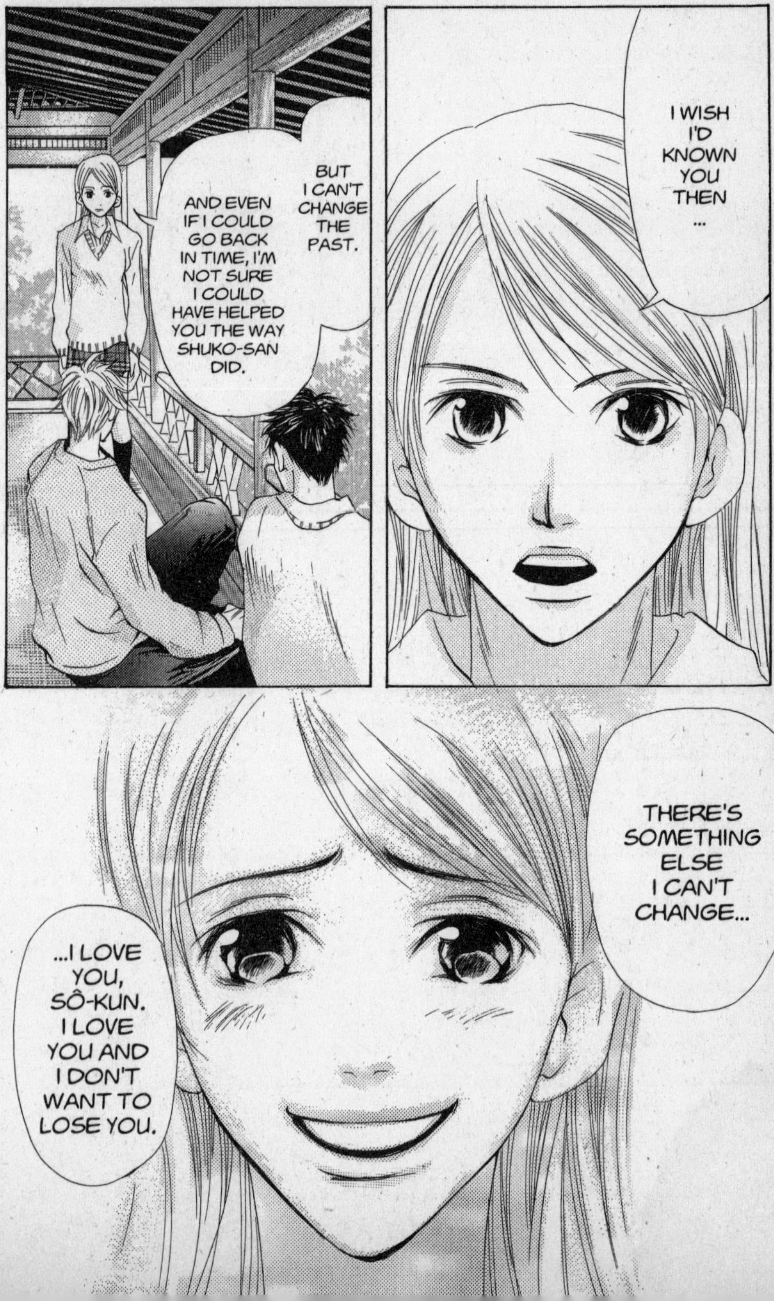
I WISH I'D KNOWN YOU THEN ...
BUT I CAN'T CHANGE THE PAST.
AND EVEN IF I COULD GO BACK IN TIME, I'M NOT SURE I COULD HAVE HELPED YOU THE WAY SHUKO-SAN DID.
THERE'S SOMETHING ELSE I CAN'T CHANGE...
...I LOVE YOU, SÔ-KUN. I LOVE YOU AND I DON'T WANT TO LOSE YOU.

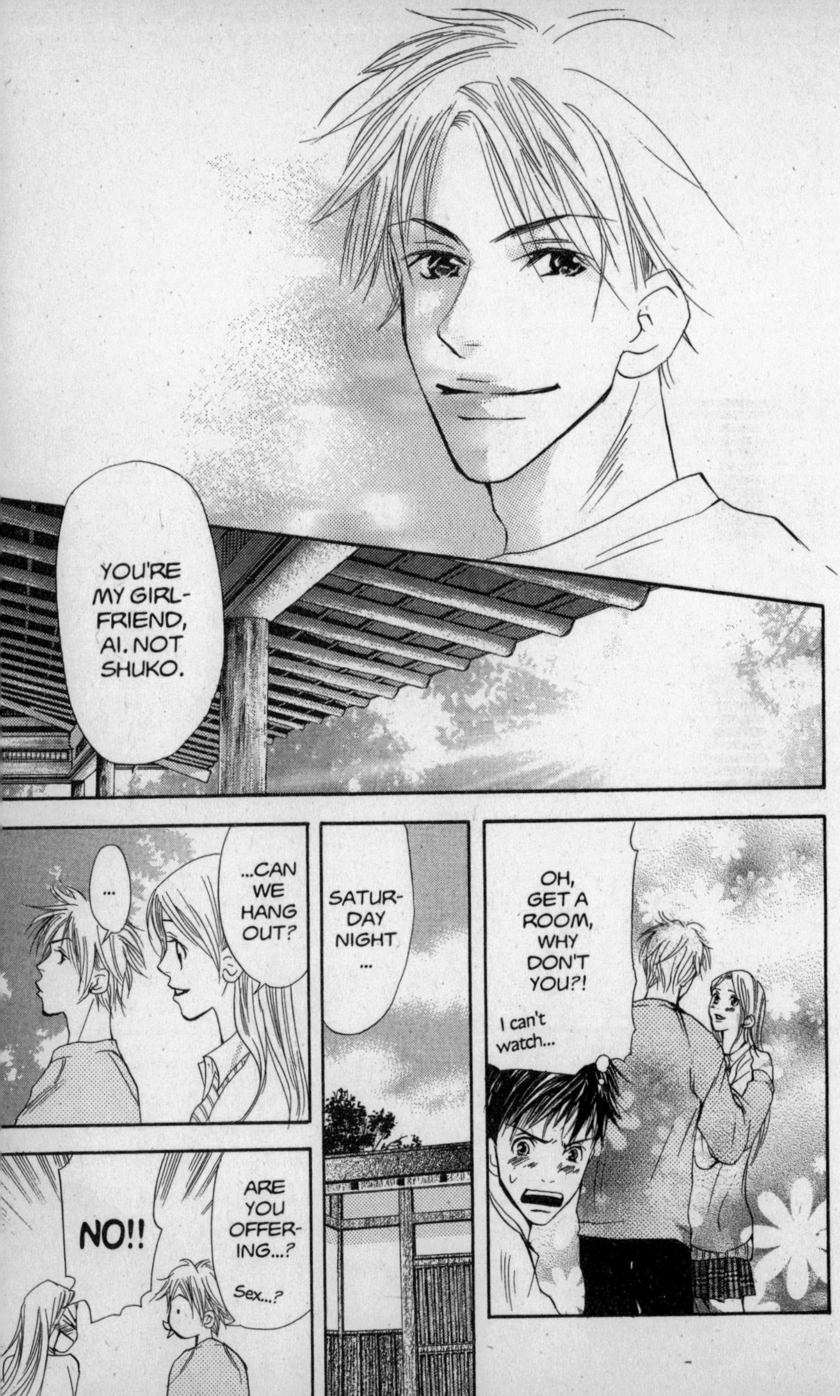
YOU'RE MY GIRL-FRIEND, AI. NOT SHUKO.
OH, GET A ROOM, WHY DON'T YOU?!
I can't watch...
SATUR-DAY NIGHT ...
...CAN WE HANG OUT?
...
ARE YOU OFFER-ING...?
Sex...?
NO!!

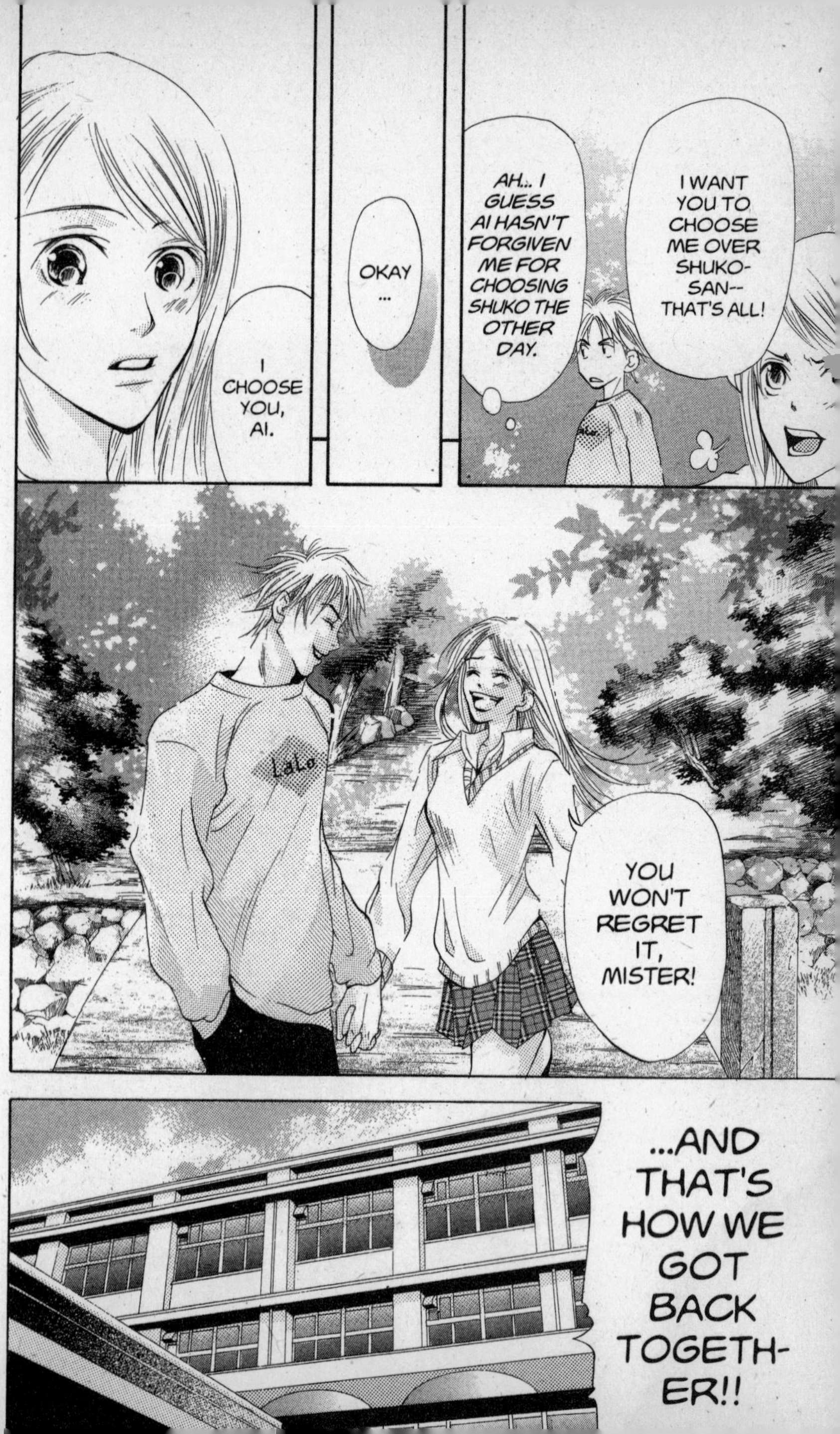
I WANT YOU TO CHOOSE ME OVER SHUKO-SAN-- THAT'S ALL!
AH... I GUESS AI HASN'T FORGIVEN ME FOR CHOOSING SHUKO THE OTHER DAY.
OKAY ...
I CHOOSE YOU, AI.
YOU WON'T REGRET IT, MISTER!
...AND THAT'S HOW WE GOT BACK TOGETH-ER!!

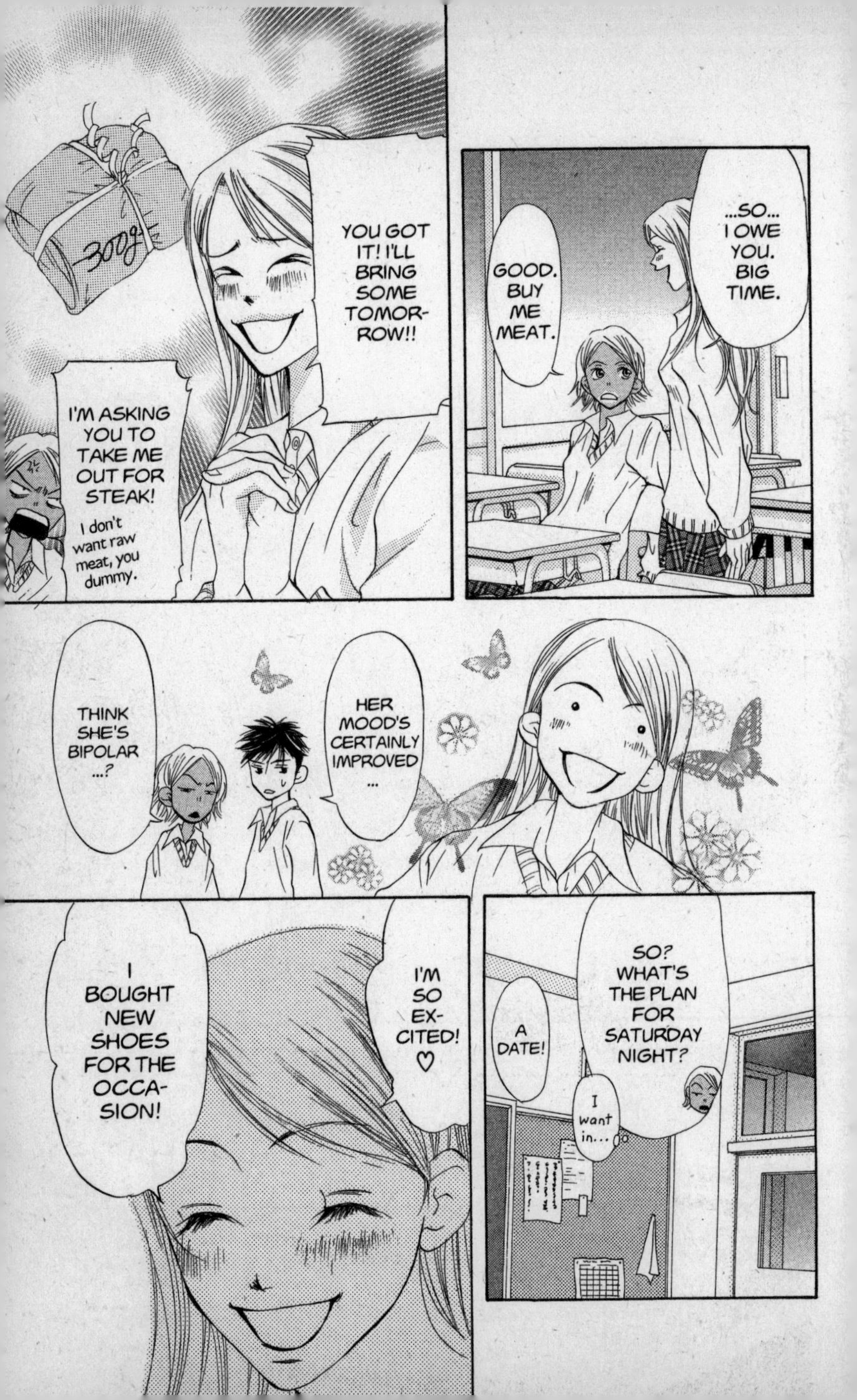
...SO... I OWE YOU. BIG TIME.
GOOD. BUY ME MEAT.
YOU GOT IT! I'LL BRING SOME TOMORROW!!
300g
I'M ASKING YOU TO TAKE ME OUT FOR STEAK!
I don't want raw meat, you dummy.
HER MOOD'S CERTAINLY IMPROVED...
THINK SHE'S BIPOLAR...?
SO? WHAT'S THE PLAN FOR SATURDAY NIGHT?
A DATE!
I want in...
I'M SO EXCITED! ♡
I BOUGHT NEW SHOES FOR THE OCCASION!

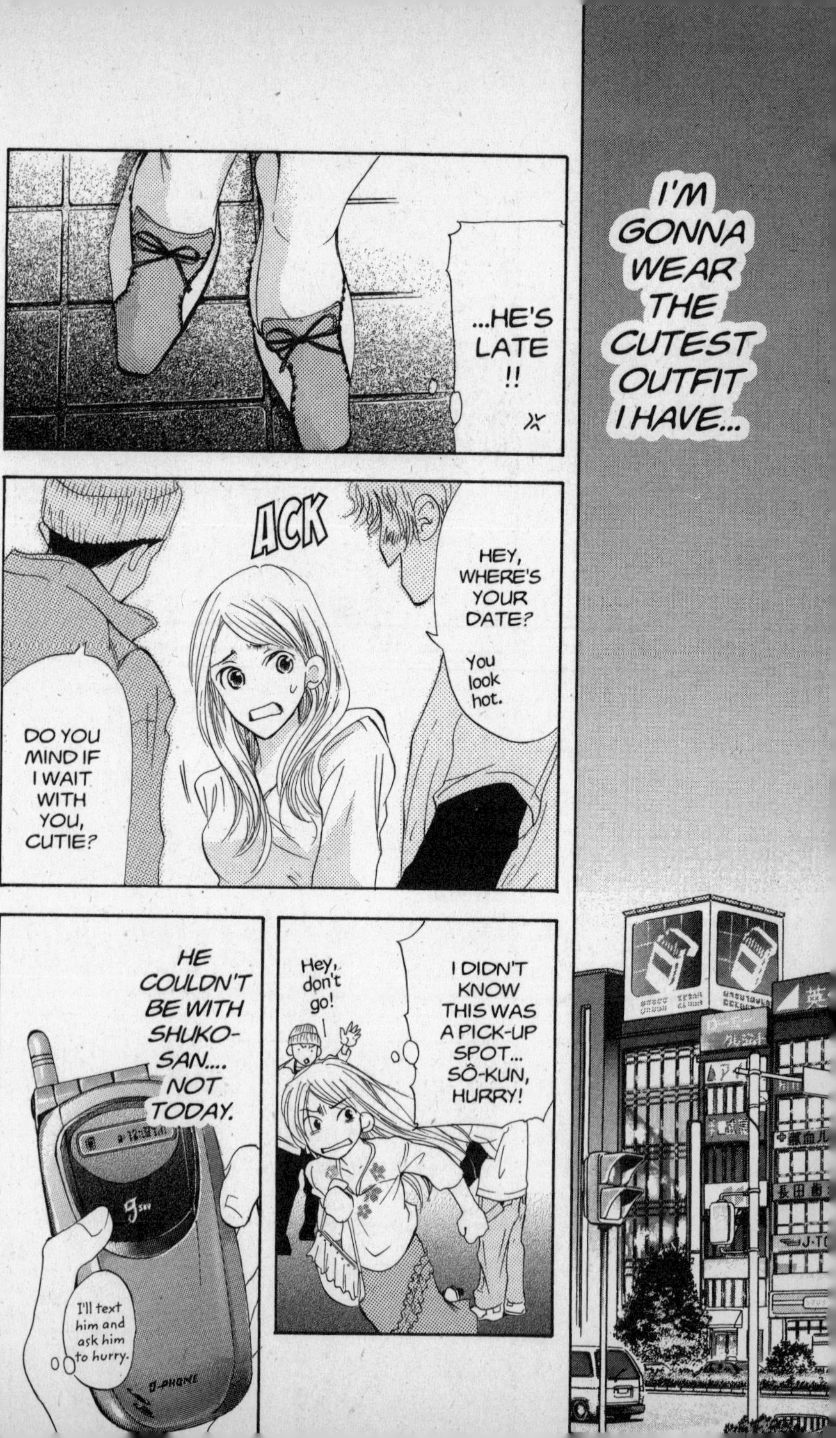
I'M GONNA WEAR THE CUTEST OUTFIT I HAVE...
...HE'S LATE !!
ACK
HEY, WHERE'S YOUR DATE?
You look hot.
DO YOU MIND IF I WAIT WITH YOU, CUTIE?
I DIDN'T KNOW THIS WAS A PICK-UP SPOT... SÔ-KUN, HURRY!
Hey, don't go!
HE COULDN'T BE WITH SHUKO-SAN.... NOT TODAY.
I'll text him and ask him to hurry.

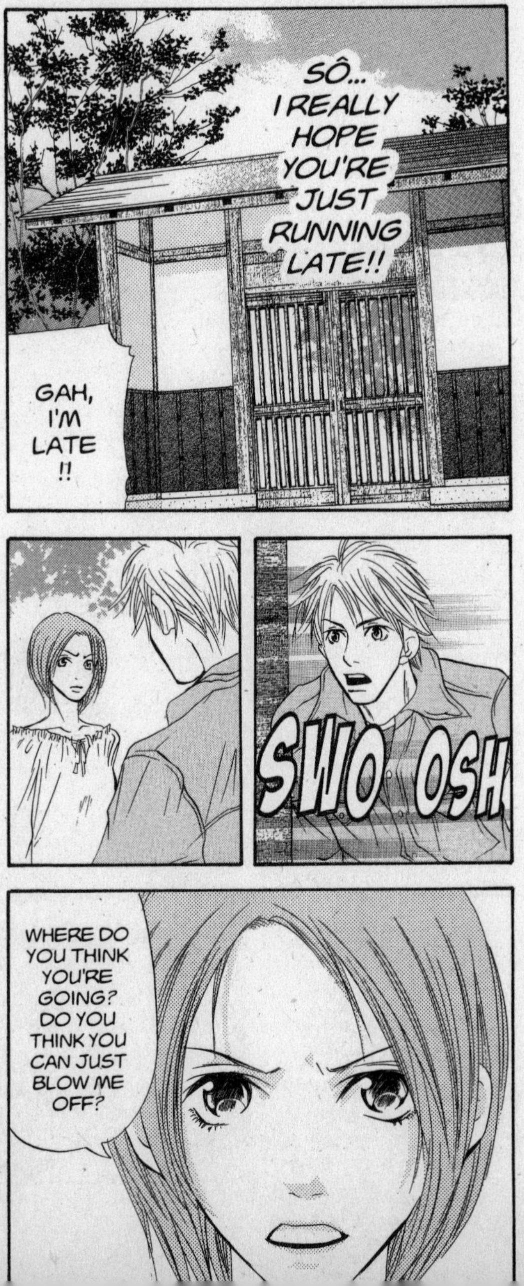
SÔ... I REALLY HOPE YOU'RE JUST RUNNING LATE!!
GAH, I'M LATE !!
SWO OSH
WHERE DO YOU THINK YOU'RE GOING? DO YOU THINK YOU CAN JUST BLOW ME OFF?

Doubt!! Backstory

Part 4

This was my first project as a professional manga artist and I didn't really understand the hierarchy. At one point, I actually asked my editor come pick up a draft from my house (!!). (I'm so sorry. That will never happen again.)

At the time, my place was a disaster, too. Not just messy-- there was a swallow's nest was on the floor of the entryway... (complete with bird poop)! I couldn't get rid of it because of the superstition that says that a swallow's nest is a good omen. Of course, I didn't tell anyone that because I'd rather they think I was messy than superstitious.

It was summer before I could make myself fess up...

By then everyone figured I was a slob.

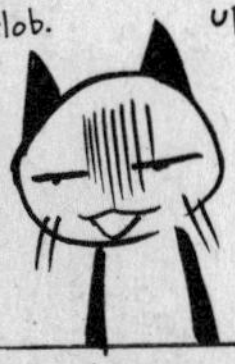

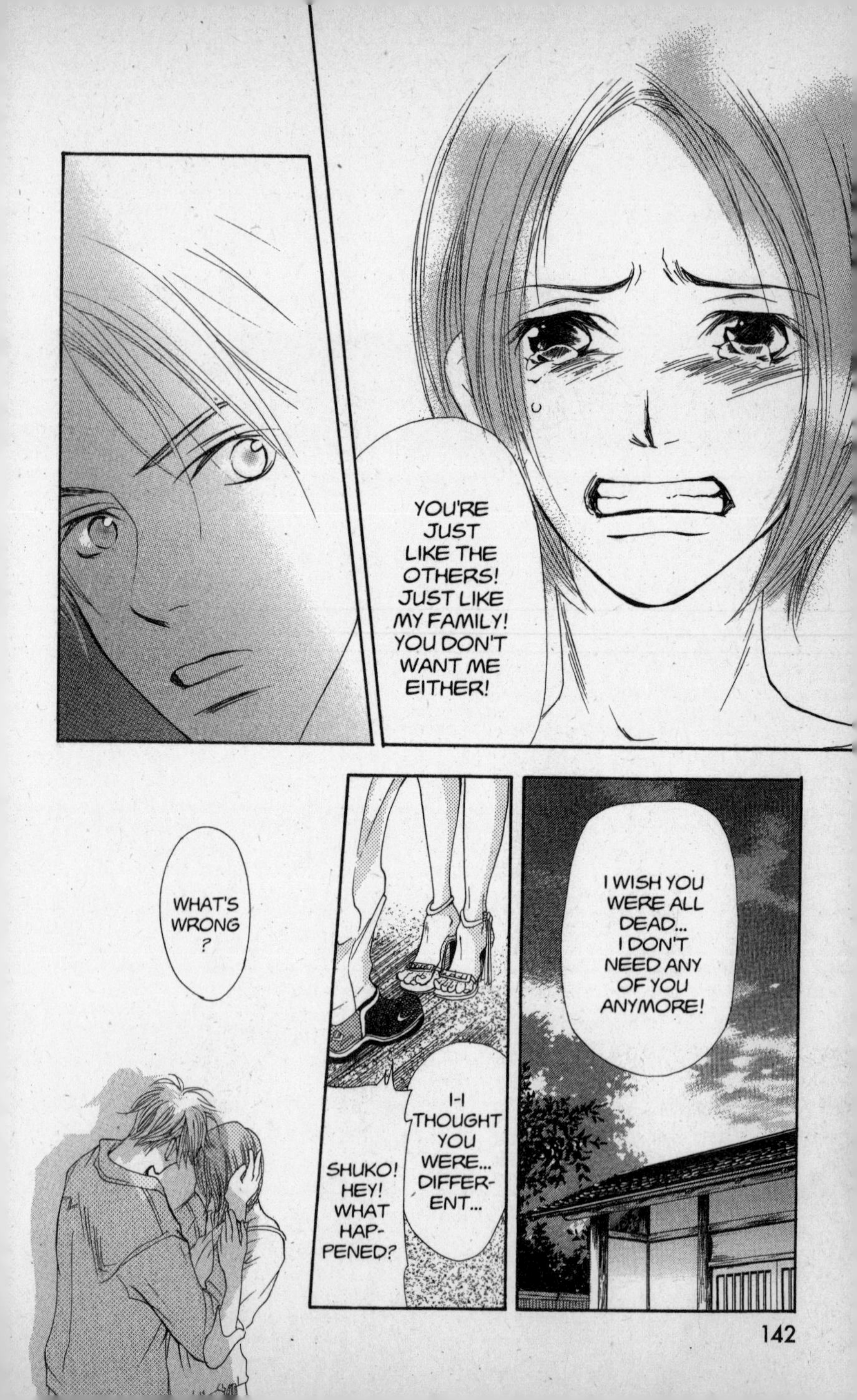
YOU'RE JUST LIKE THE OTHERS! JUST LIKE MY FAMILY! YOU DON'T WANT ME EITHER!
I WISH YOU WERE ALL DEAD... I DON'T NEED ANY OF YOU ANYMORE!
I-I THOUGHT YOU WERE... DIFFER-ENT...
SHUKO! HEY! WHAT HAP-PENED?
WHAT'S WRONG?

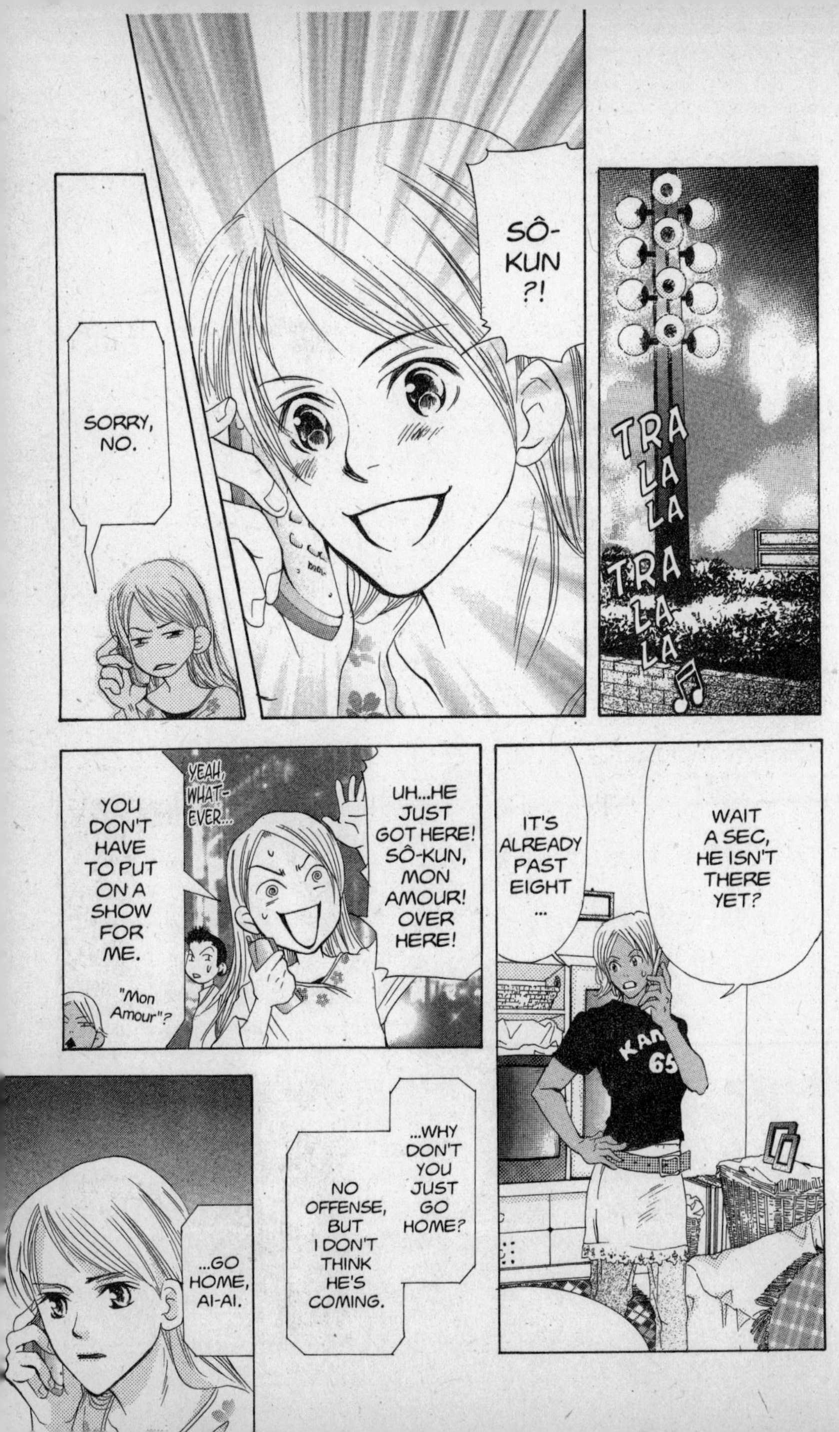
TRA LA LA TRA LA LA
SÔ-KUN ?!
SORRY, NO.
WAIT A SEC, HE ISN'T THERE YET?
IT'S ALREADY PAST EIGHT ...
UH...HE JUST GOT HERE! SÔ-KUN, MON AMOUR! OVER HERE!
YEAH, WHATEVER...
YOU DON'T HAVE TO PUT ON A SHOW FOR ME.
"Mon Amour"?
...WHY DON'T YOU JUST GO HOME?
NO OFFENSE, BUT I DON'T THINK HE'S COMING.
...GO HOME, AI-AI.

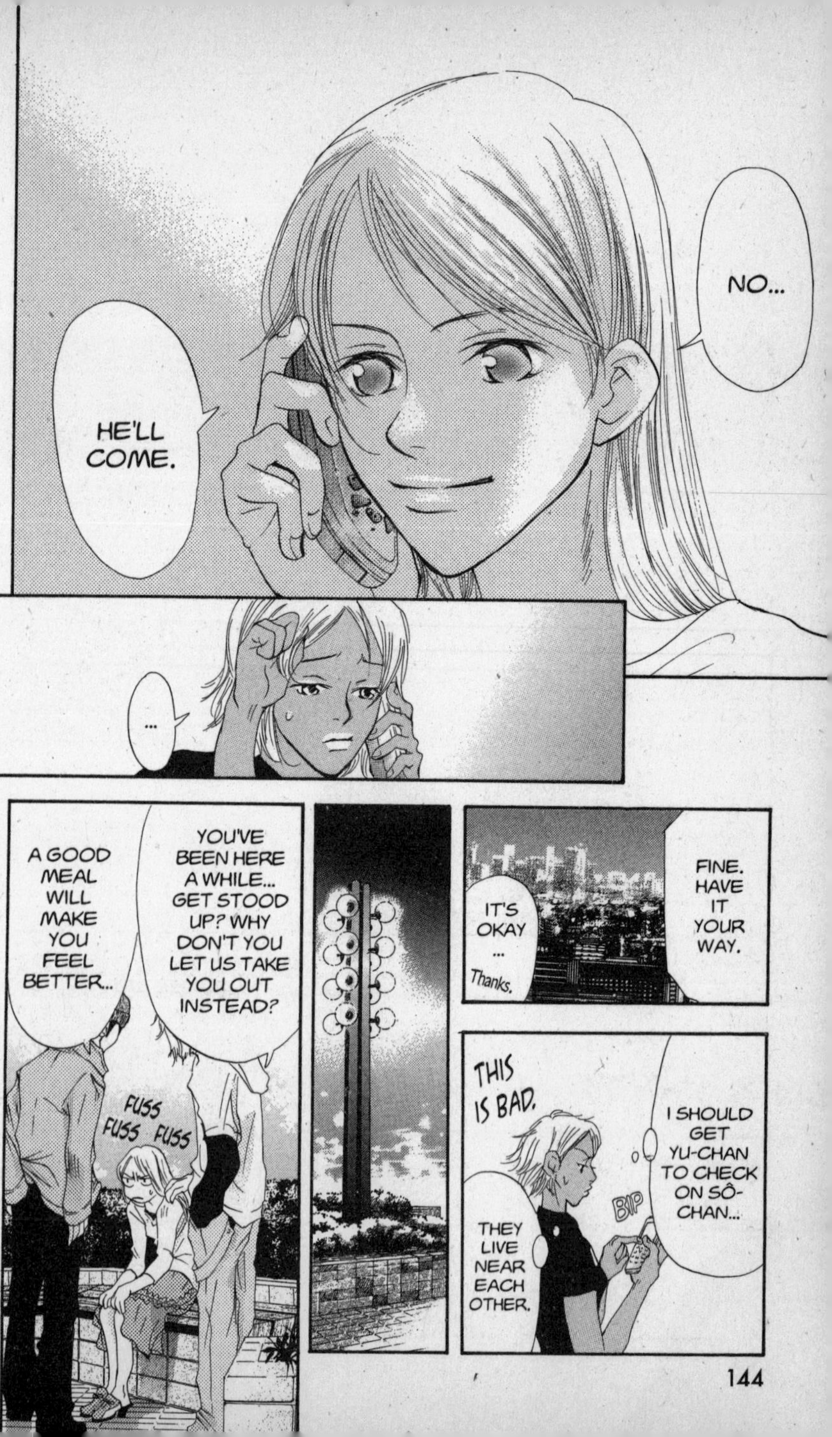
NO...
HE'LL COME.
...
FINE. HAVE IT YOUR WAY.
IT'S OKAY ...
Thanks.
I SHOULD GET YU-CHAN TO CHECK ON SÔ-CHAN...
BIP
THIS IS BAD.
THEY LIVE NEAR EACH OTHER.
YOU'VE BEEN HERE A WHILE... GET STOOD UP? WHY DON'T YOU LET US TAKE YOU OUT INSTEAD?
A GOOD MEAL WILL MAKE YOU FEEL BETTER...
FUSS FUSS FUSS

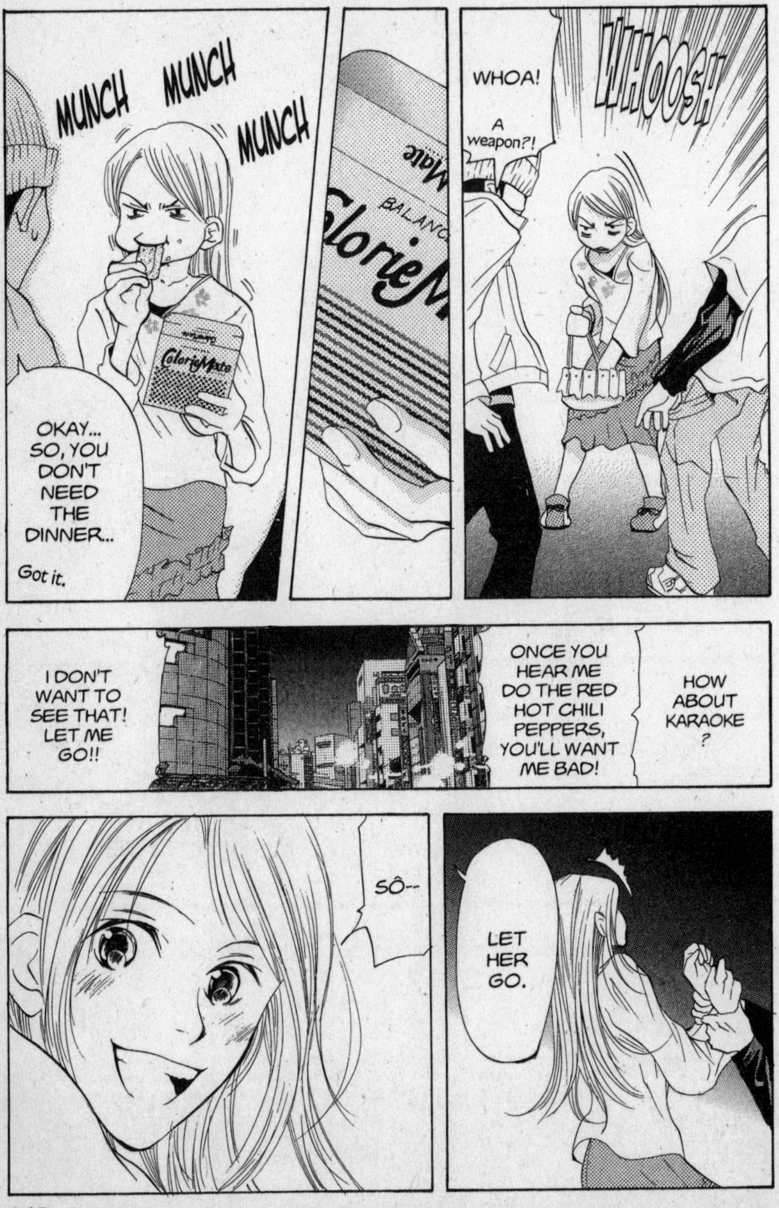
WHOOSH
WHOA!
A weapon?!
MUNCH MUNCH
MUNCH
OKAY... SO, YOU DON'T NEED THE DINNER...
Got it.
HOW ABOUT KARAOKE?
ONCE YOU HEAR ME DO THE RED HOT CHILI PEPPERS, YOU'LL WANT ME BAD!
I DON'T WANT TO SEE THAT! LET ME GO!!
LET HER GO.
SÔ--

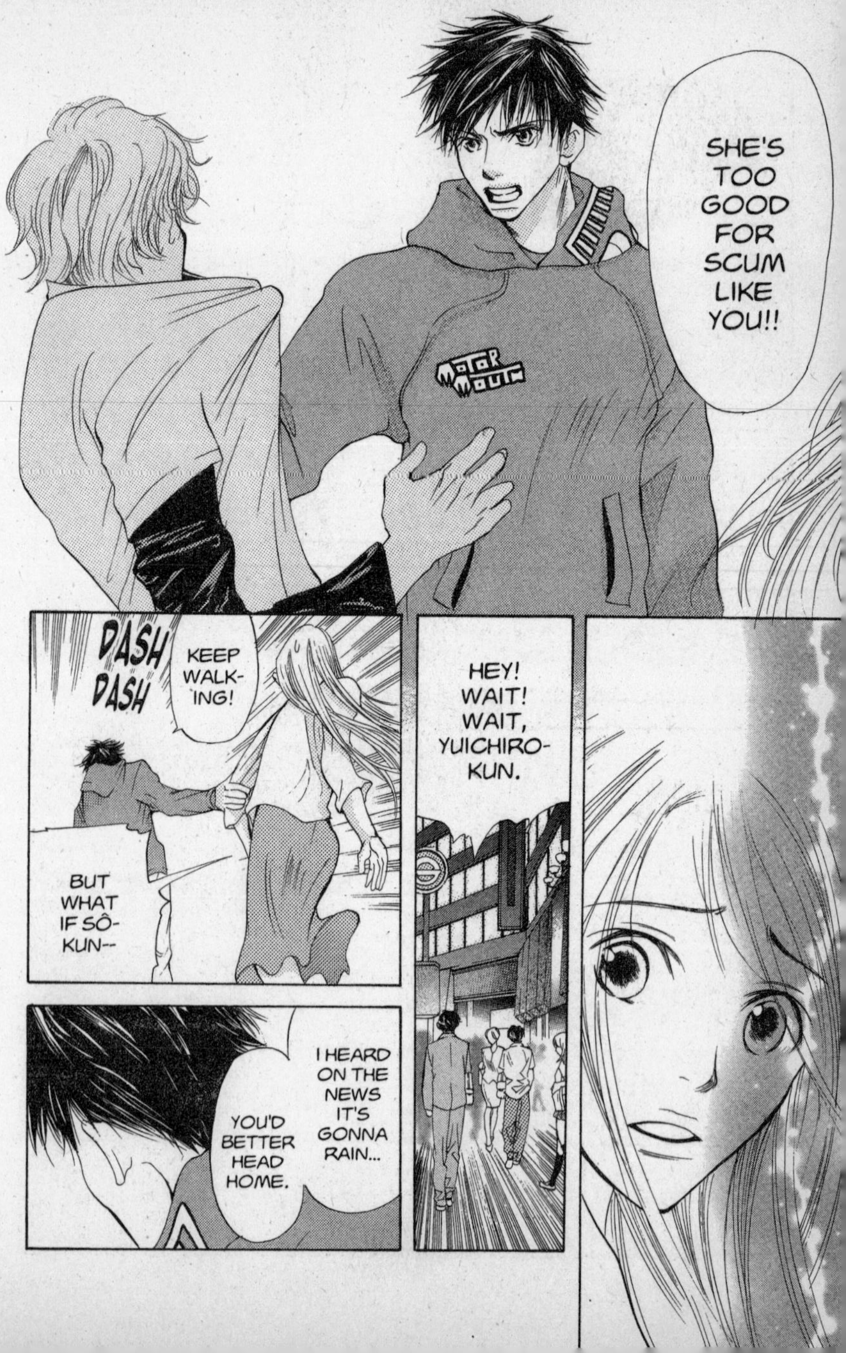
SHE'S TOO GOOD FOR SCUM LIKE YOU!!
MOTOR MOUTH
HEY! WAIT! WAIT, YUICHIRO-KUN.
KEEP WALK-ING!
DASH DASH
BUT WHAT IF SÔ-KUN--
I HEARD ON THE NEWS IT'S GONNA RAIN...
YOU'D BETTER HEAD HOME.

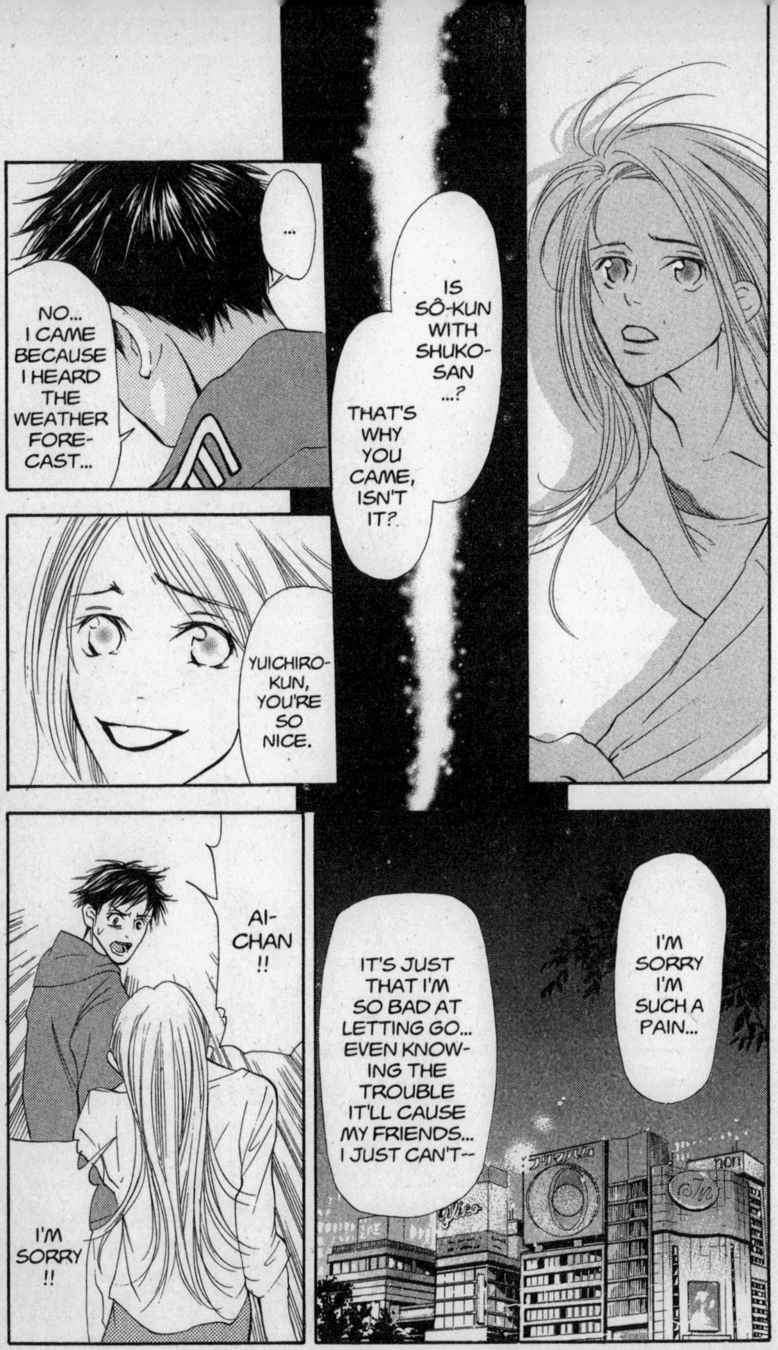
IS SÔ-KUN WITH SHUKO-SAN ...?
THAT'S WHY YOU CAME, ISN'T IT?
...
NO... I CAME BECAUSE I HEARD THE WEATHER FORE-CAST...
YUICHIRO-KUN, YOU'RE SO NICE.
I'M SORRY I'M SUCH A PAIN...
IT'S JUST THAT I'M SO BAD AT LETTING GO... EVEN KNOW-ING THE TROUBLE IT'LL CAUSE MY FRIENDS... I JUST CAN'T--
AI-CHAN !!
I'M SORRY !!

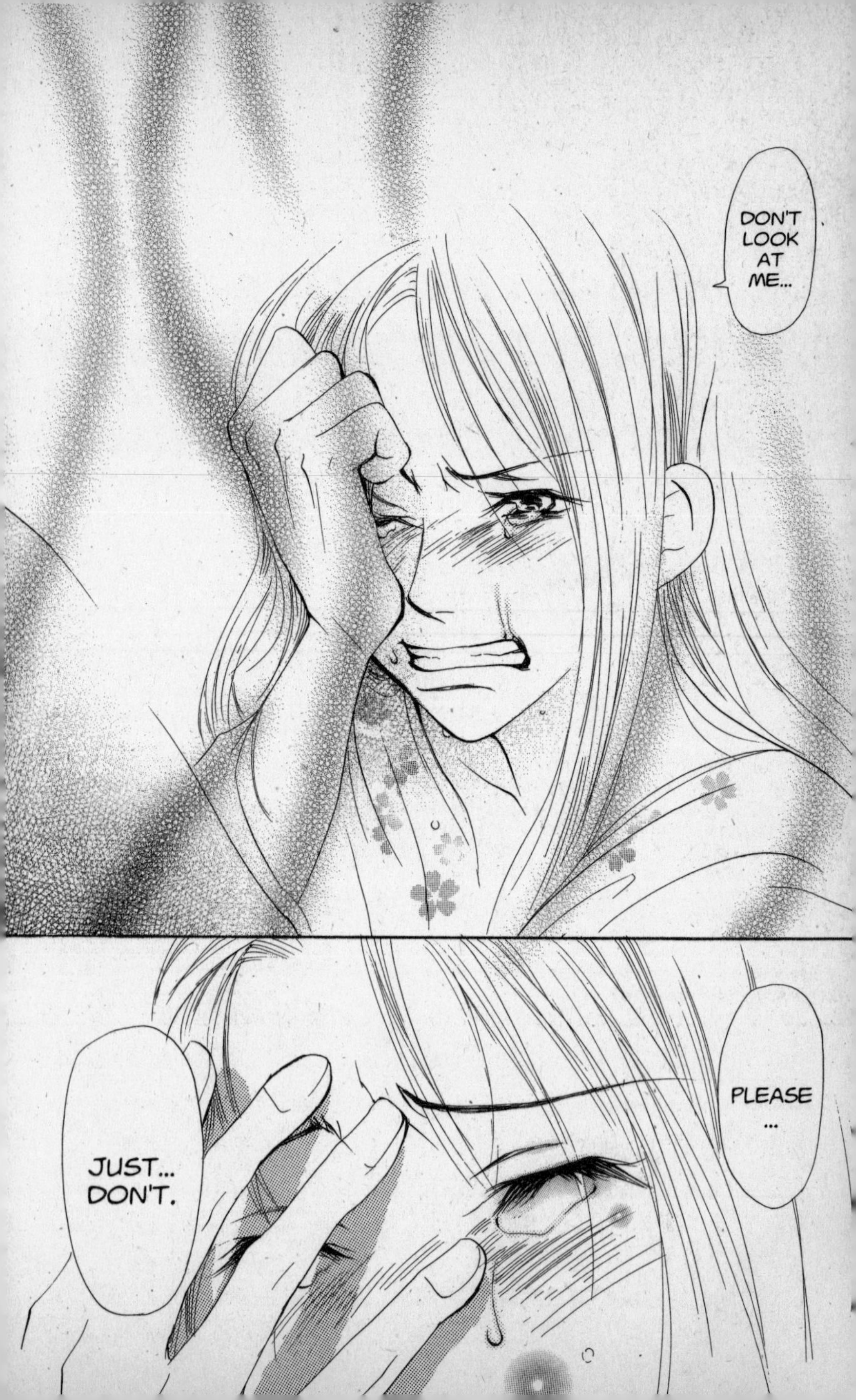
DON'T LOOK AT ME...
PLEASE ...
JUST... DON'T.

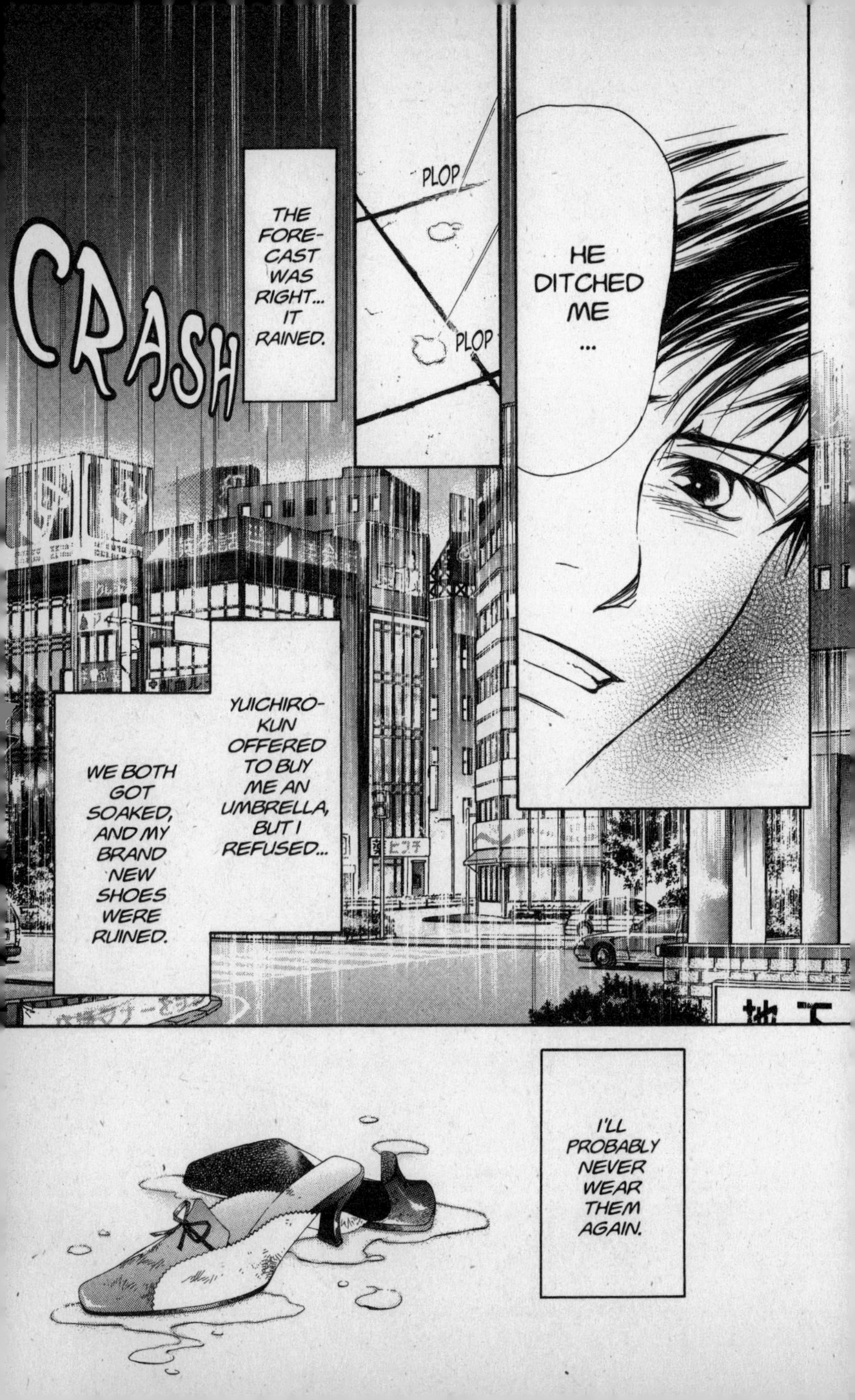
HE DITCHED ME ...
PLOP
PLOP
CRASH
THE FORE-CAST WAS RIGHT... IT RAINED.
YUICHIRO-KUN OFFERED TO BUY ME AN UMBRELLA, BUT I REFUSED...
WE BOTH GOT SOAKED, AND MY BRAND NEW SHOES WERE RUINED.
I'LL PROBABLY NEVER WEAR THEM AGAIN.

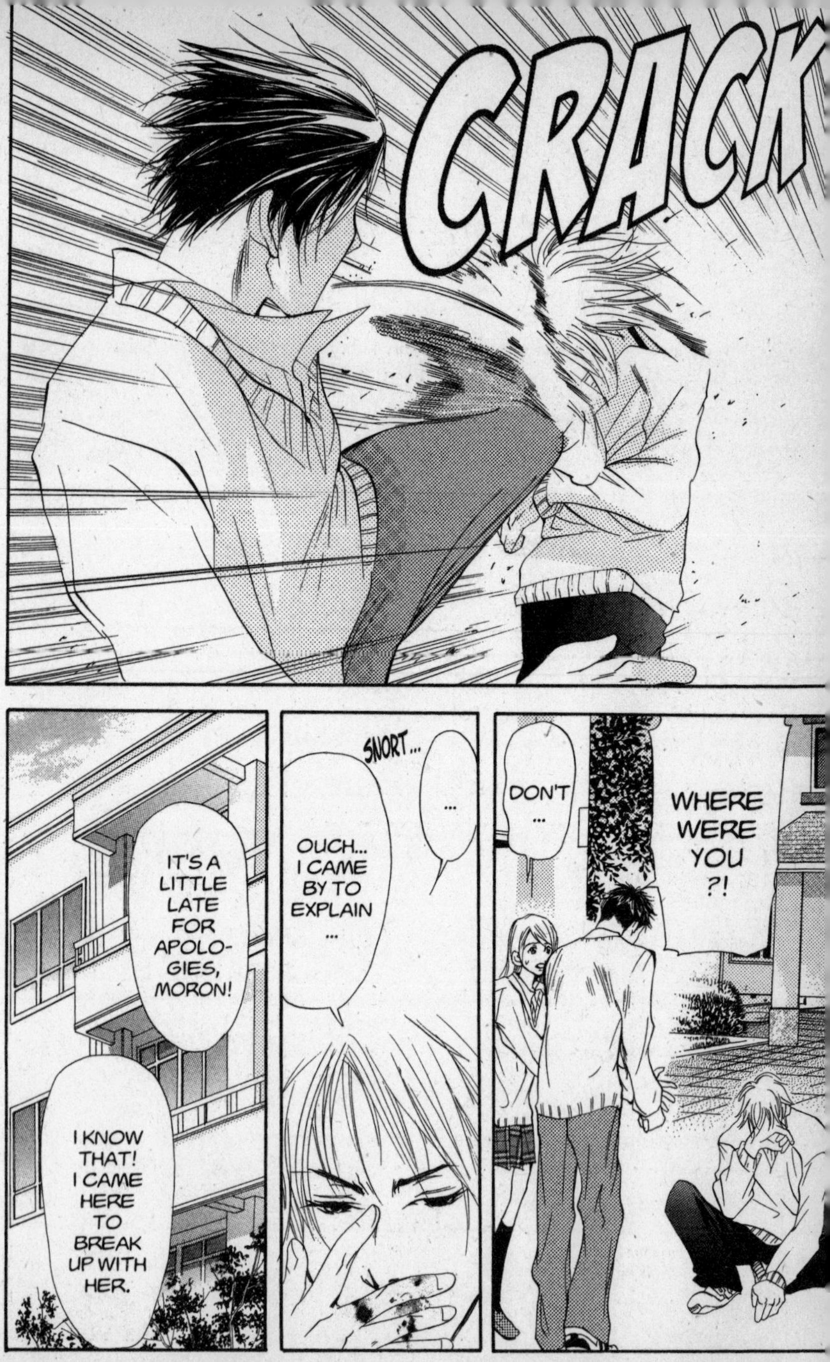
CRACK
WHERE WERE YOU ?!
DON'T ...
SNORT...
...
OUCH... I CAME BY TO EXPLAIN ...
IT'S A LITTLE LATE FOR APOLOGIES, MORON!
I KNOW THAT! I CAME HERE TO BREAK UP WITH HER.

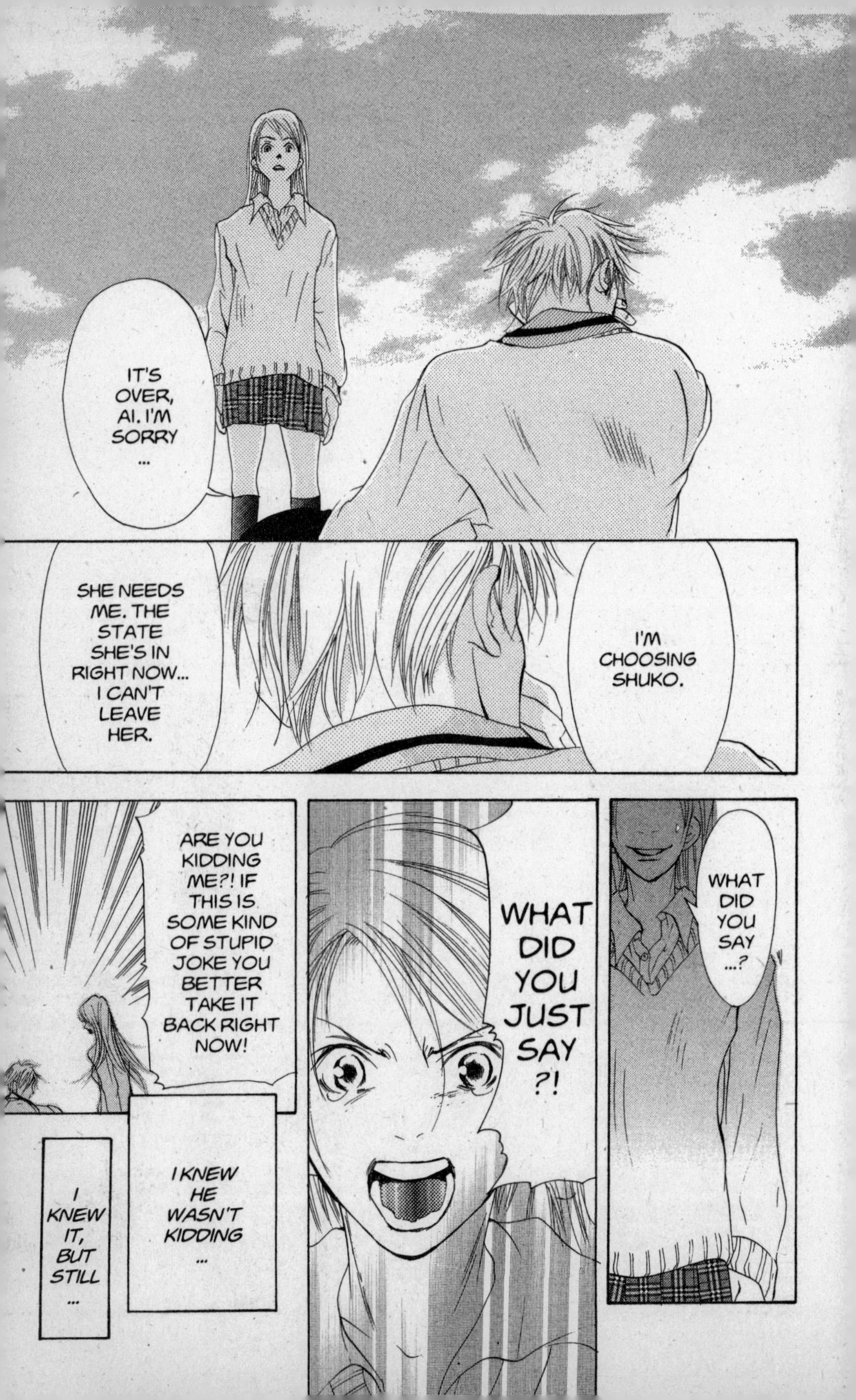
IT'S OVER, AI. I'M SORRY ...
I'M CHOOSING SHUKO.
SHE NEEDS ME. THE STATE SHE'S IN RIGHT NOW... I CAN'T LEAVE HER.
WHAT DID YOU SAY ...?
WHAT DID YOU JUST SAY ?!
ARE YOU KIDDING ME?! IF THIS IS SOME KIND OF STUPID JOKE YOU BETTER TAKE IT BACK RIGHT NOW!
I KNEW HE WASN'T KIDDING ...
I KNEW IT, BUT STILL ...

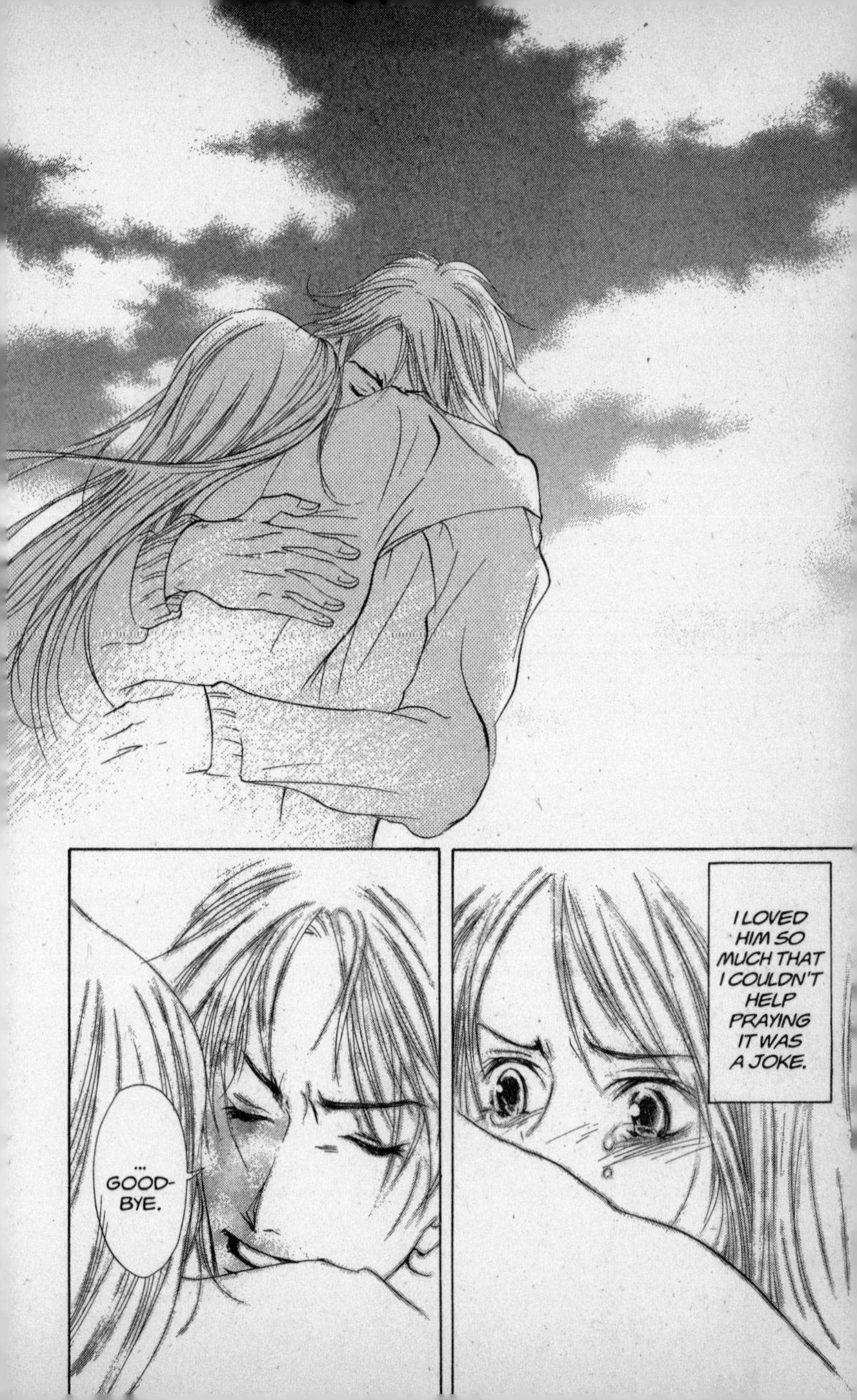
I LOVED HIM SO MUCH THAT I COULDN'T HELP PRAYING IT WAS A JOKE.
... GOOD-BYE.

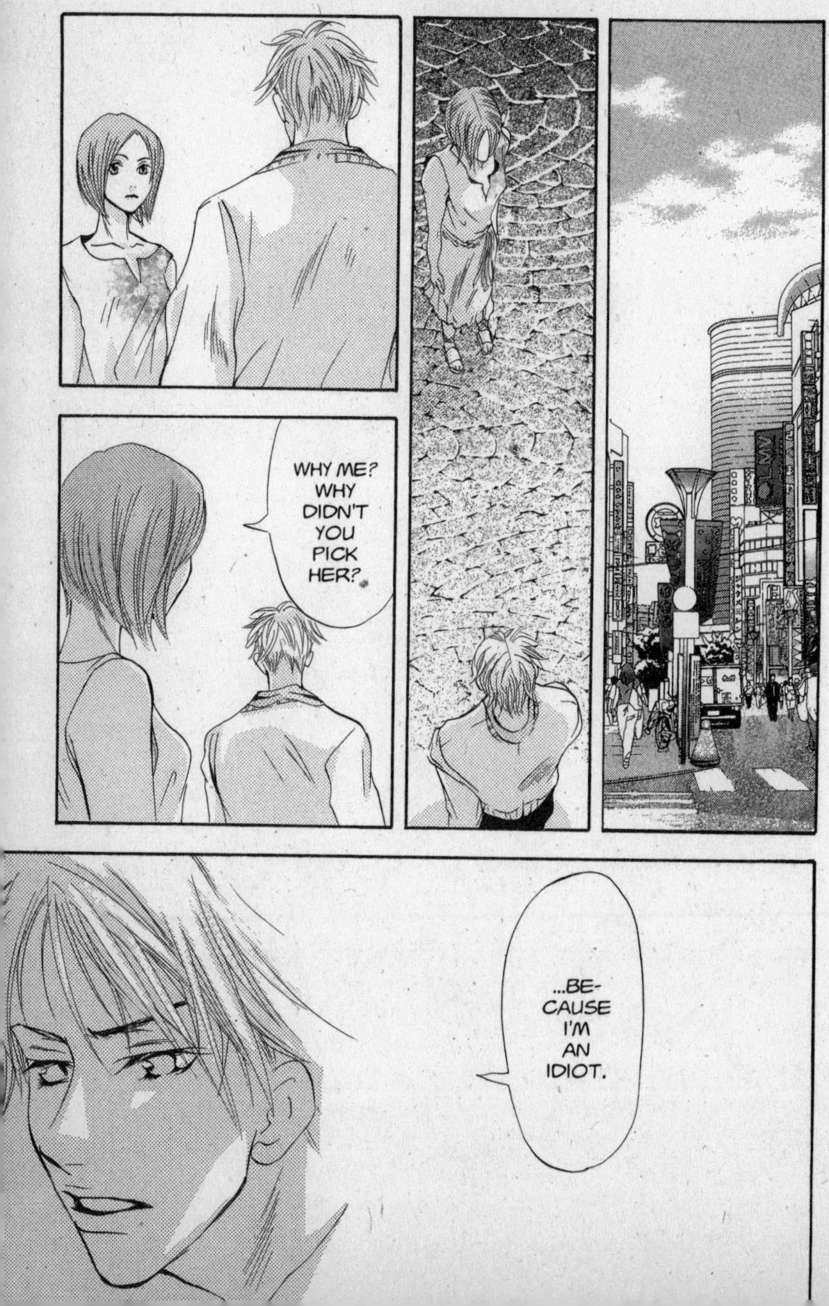
WHY ME? WHY DIDN'T YOU PICK HER?
...BE-CAUSE I'M AN IDIOT.

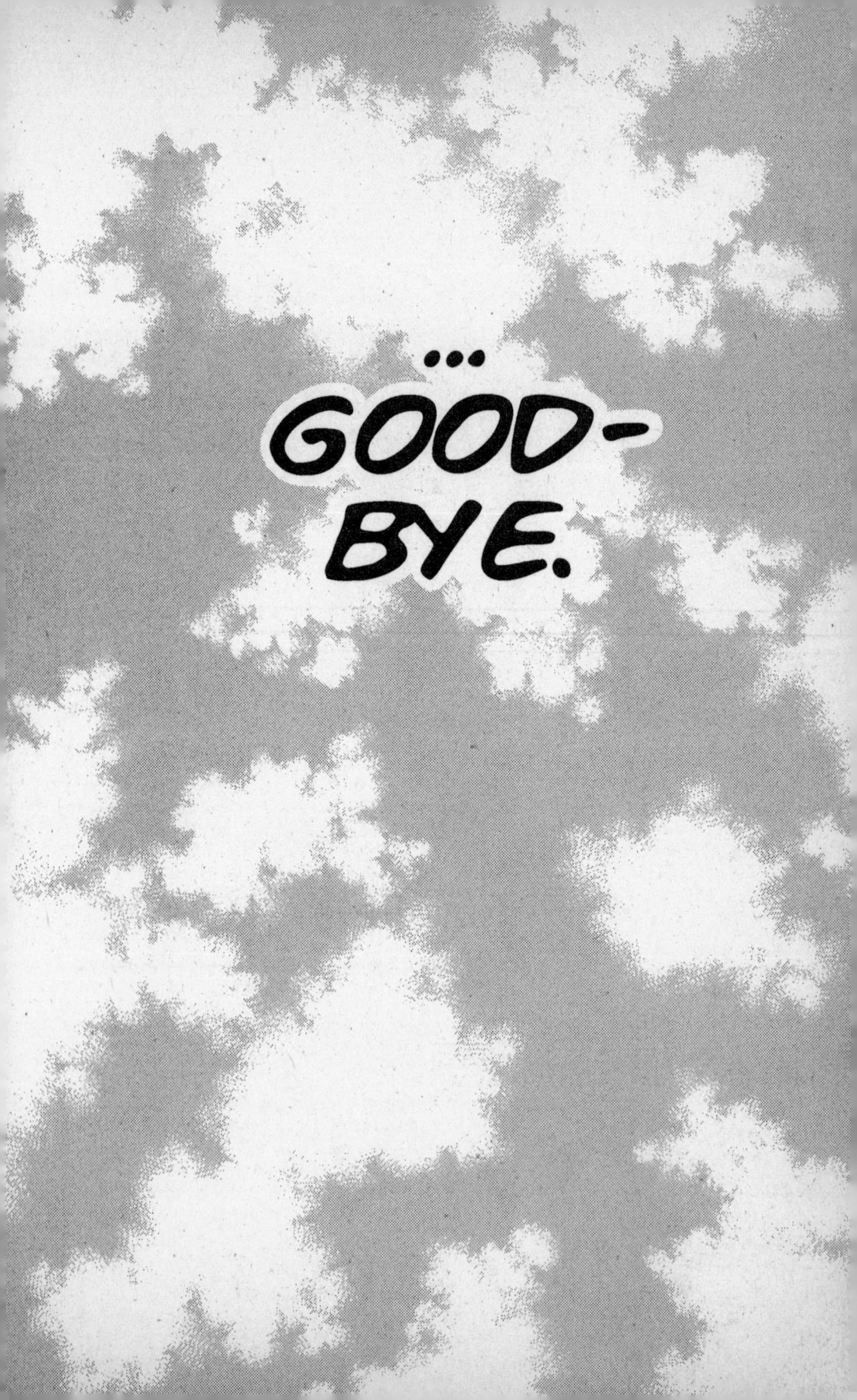
...GOOD-BYE.

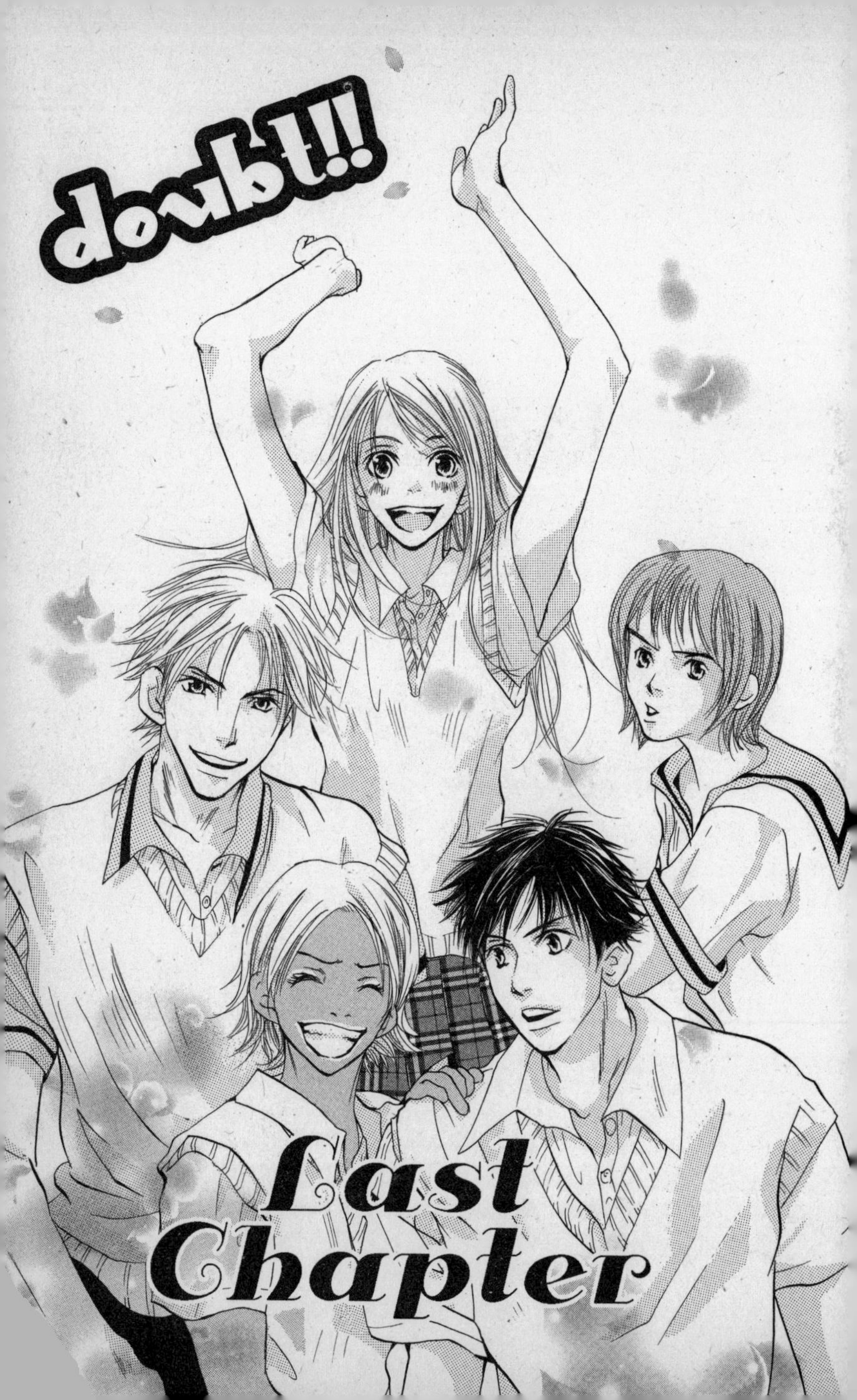
doubt!!
Last Chapter

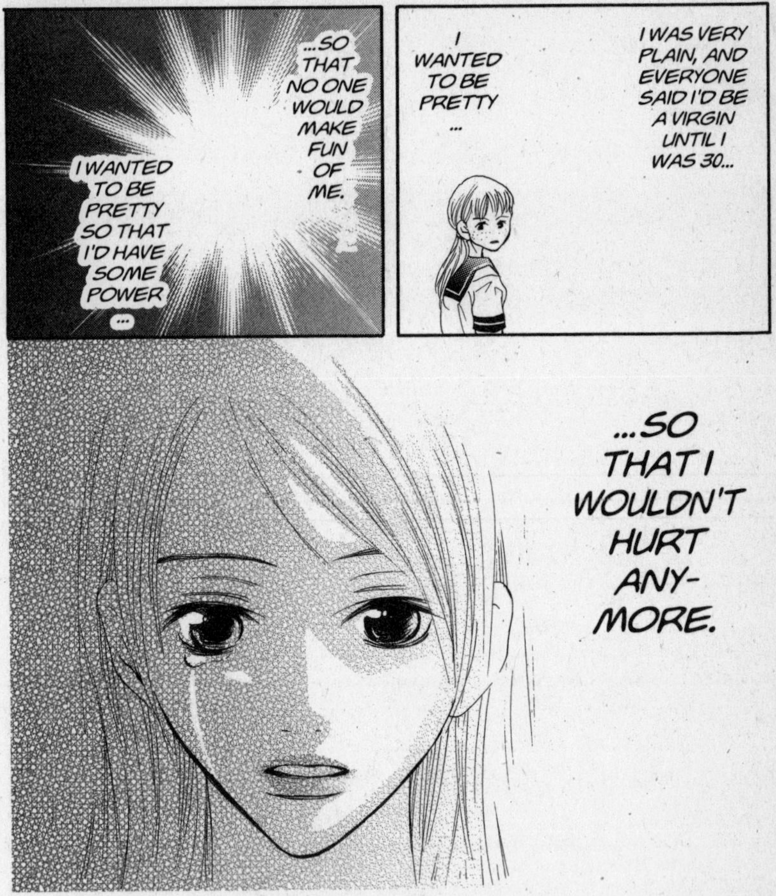
I WAS VERY PLAIN, AND EVERYONE SAID I'D BE A VIRGIN UNTIL I WAS 30...
I WANTED TO BE PRETTY...
...SO THAT NO ONE WOULD MAKE FUN OF ME.
I WANTED TO BE PRETTY SO THAT I'D HAVE SOME POWER...
...SO THAT I WOULDN'T HURT ANY-MORE.

Ai

As her creator, I meant for her to be a kind of "everygirl" -- the kind of girl who lives inside of each of us. She took on a life of her own as we moved along, though, and after working with her for over two and a half years, I find it hard to say goodbye. Nonetheless, we -- Ai and me -- appreciate your kind support all these years.

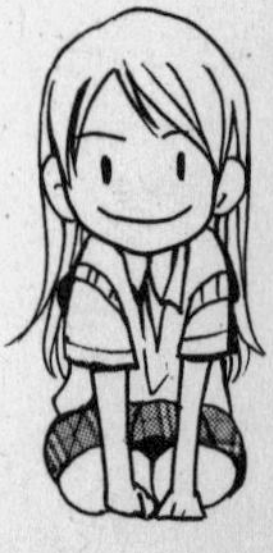

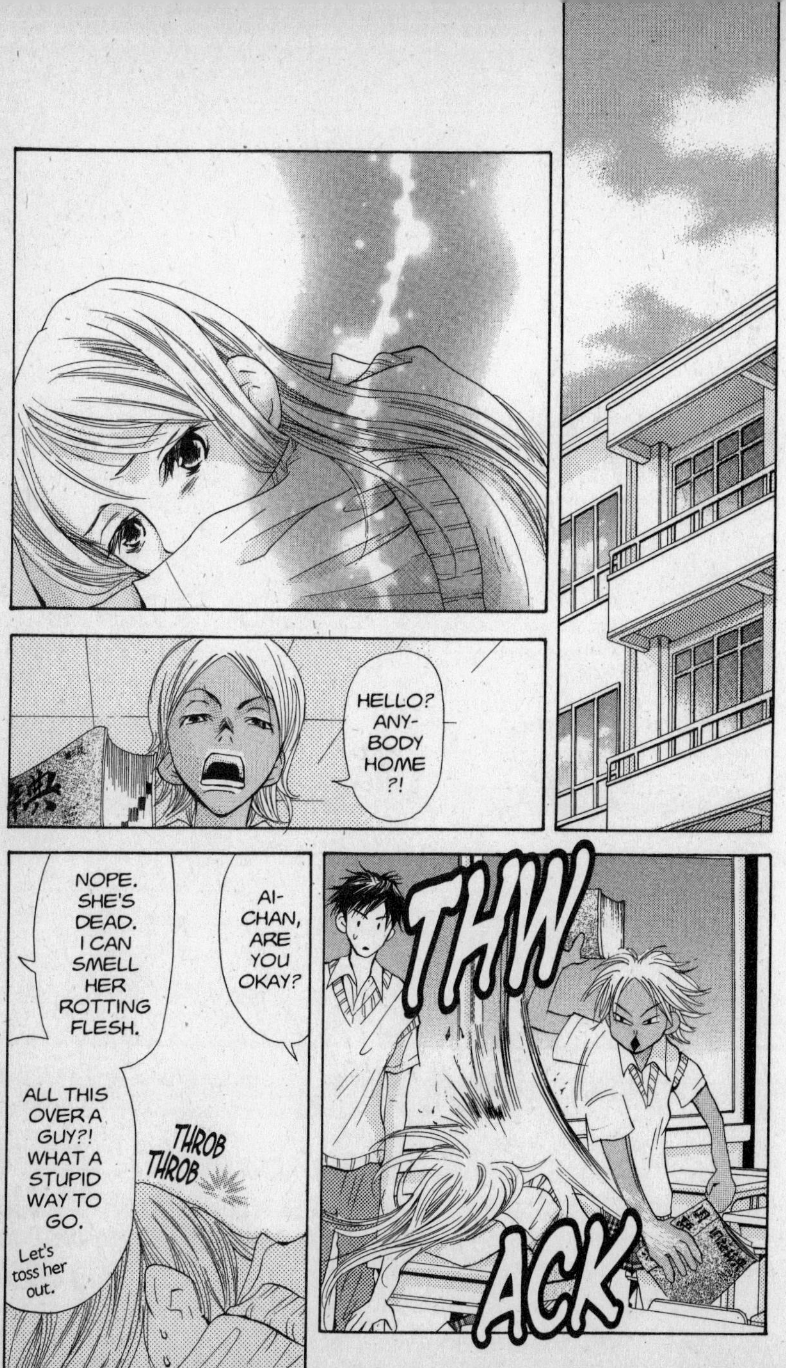
HELLO? ANY-BODY HOME ?!
THW ACK
AI-CHAN, ARE YOU OKAY?
NOPE. SHE'S DEAD. I CAN SMELL HER ROTTING FLESH.
ALL THIS OVER A GUY?! WHAT A STUPID WAY TO GO.
THROB THROB
Let's toss her out.

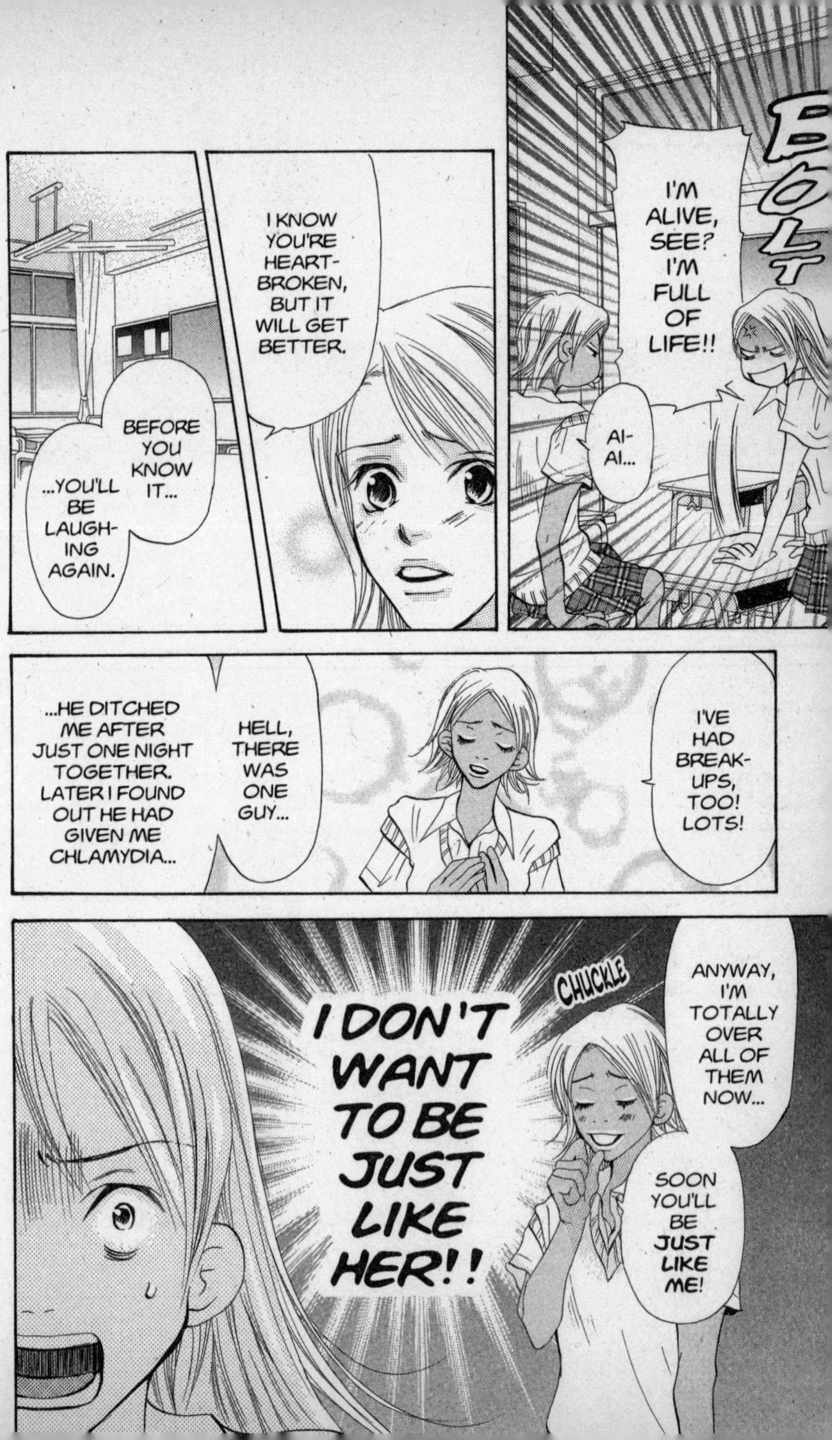
BOLT
I'M ALIVE, SEE? I'M FULL OF LIFE!!
AI-AI...
I KNOW YOU'RE HEART-BROKEN, BUT IT WILL GET BETTER.
BEFORE YOU KNOW IT...
...YOU'LL BE LAUGHING AGAIN.
I'VE HAD BREAK-UPS, TOO! LOTS!
HELL, THERE WAS ONE GUY...
...HE DITCHED ME AFTER JUST ONE NIGHT TOGETHER. LATER I FOUND OUT HE HAD GIVEN ME CHLAMYDIA...
ANYWAY, I'M TOTALLY OVER ALL OF THEM NOW...
CHUCKLE
SOON YOU'LL BE JUST LIKE ME!
I DON'T WANT TO BE JUST LIKE HER!!

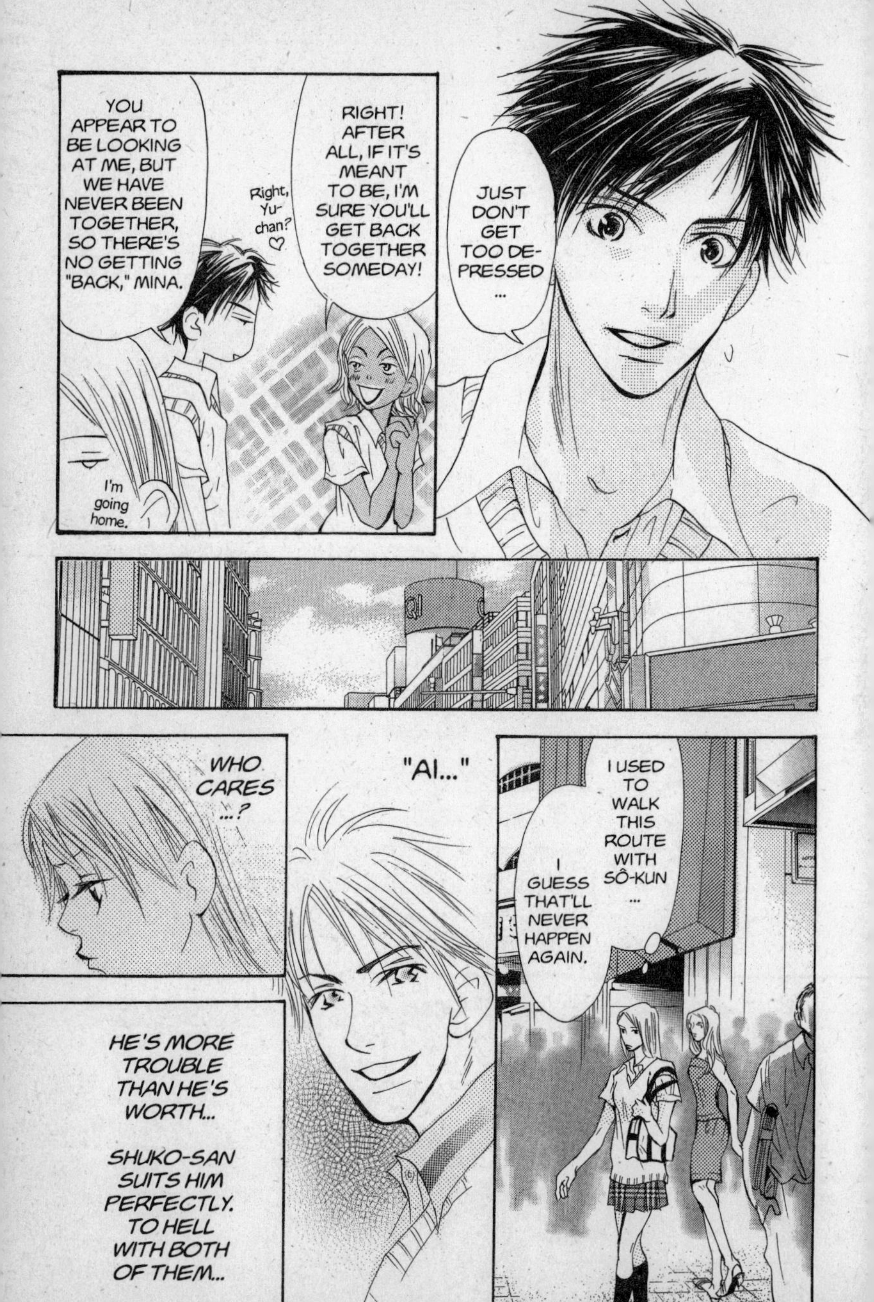
JUST DON'T GET TOO DE-PRESSED ...
RIGHT! AFTER ALL, IF IT'S MEANT TO BE, I'M SURE YOU'LL GET BACK TOGETHER SOMEDAY!
Right, Yu-chan? ♡
YOU APPEAR TO BE LOOKING AT ME, BUT WE HAVE NEVER BEEN TOGETHER, SO THERE'S NO GETTING "BACK," MINA.
I'm going home.
I USED TO WALK THIS ROUTE WITH SÔ-KUN ...
I GUESS THAT'LL NEVER HAPPEN AGAIN.
"AI..."
WHO CARES ...?
HE'S MORE TROUBLE THAN HE'S WORTH...
SHUKO-SAN SUITS HIM PERFECTLY. TO HELL WITH BOTH OF THEM...

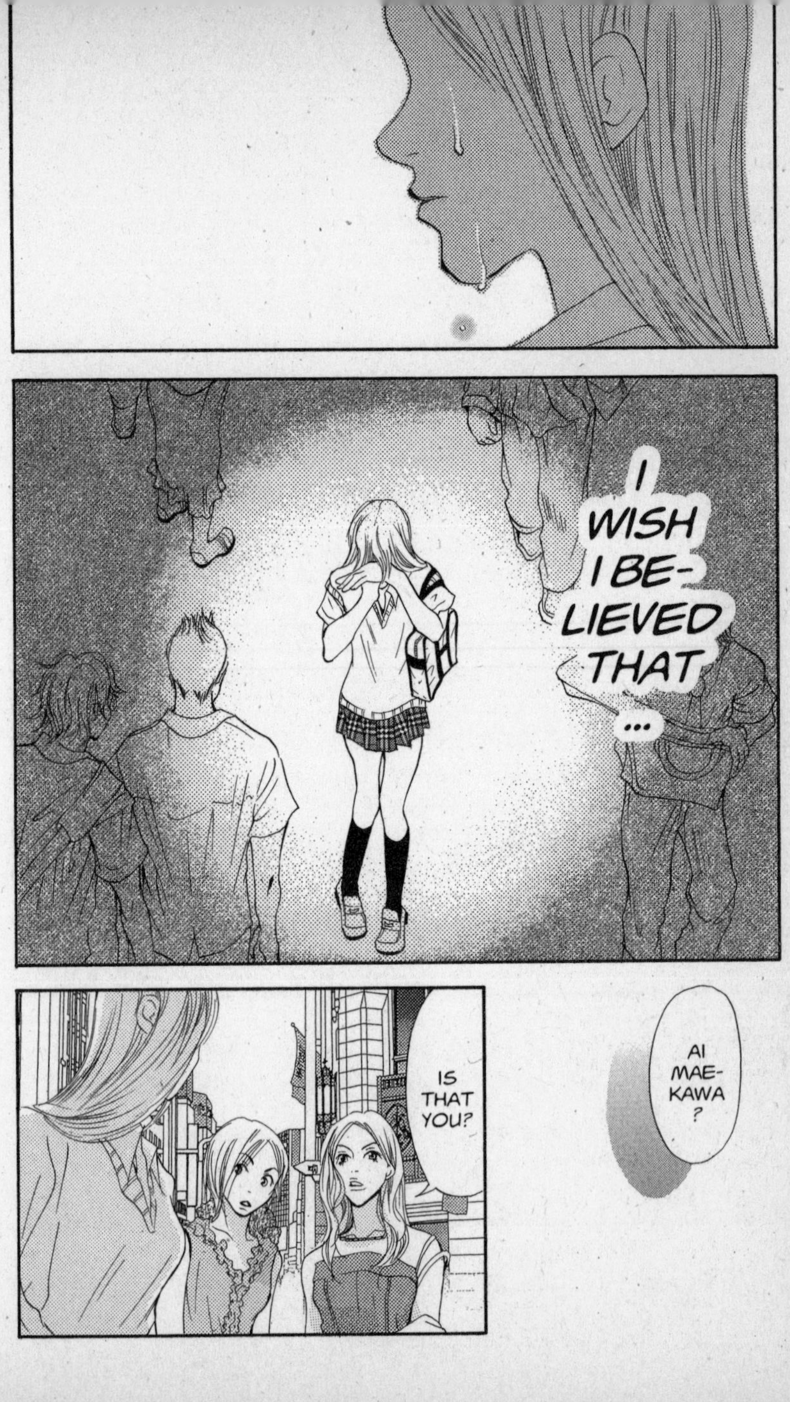
I WISH I BE-LIEVED THAT...
AI MAE-KAWA?
IS THAT YOU?

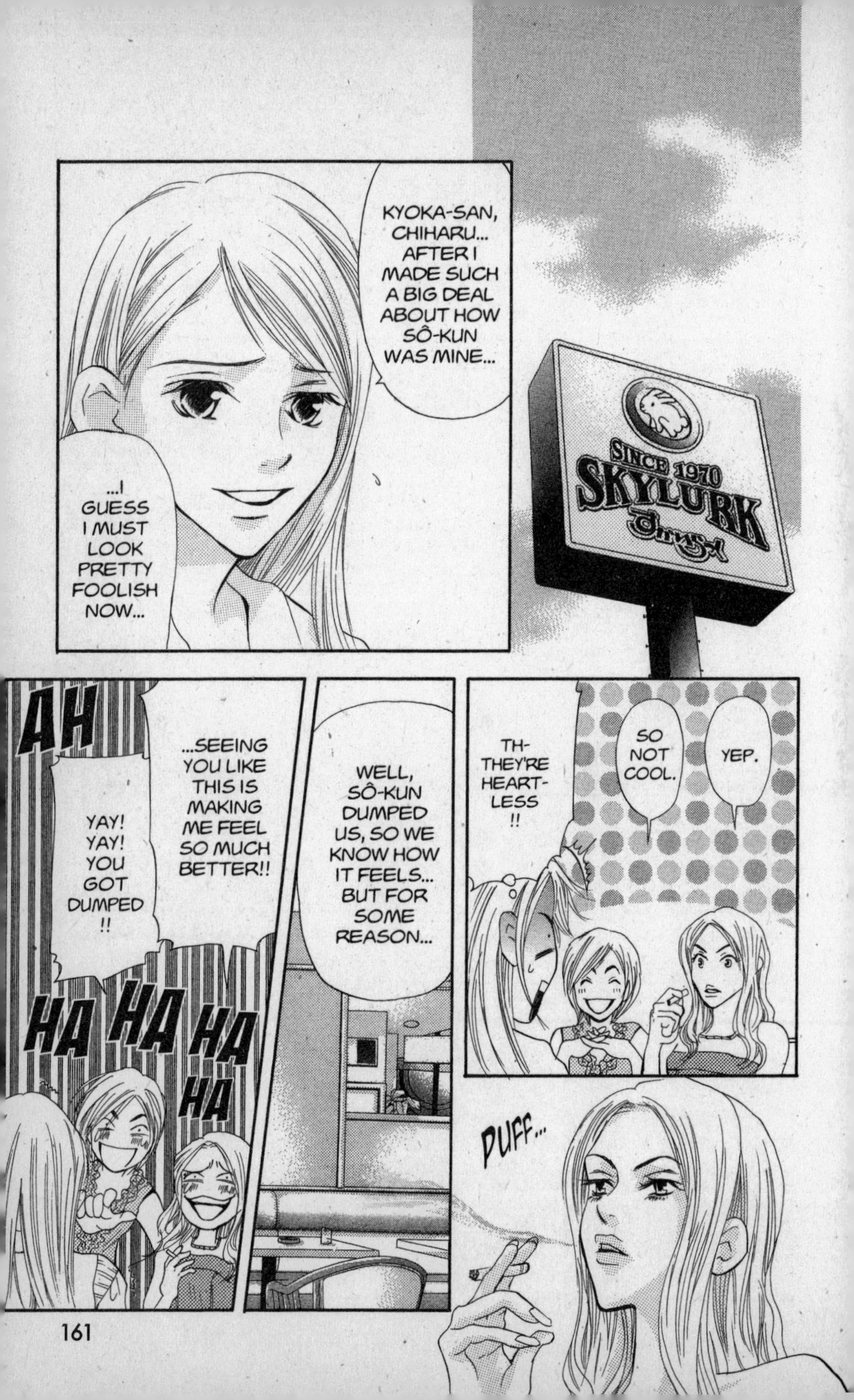
SINCE 1970
SKYLURK
KYOKA-SAN, CHIHARU... AFTER I MADE SUCH A BIG DEAL ABOUT HOW SÔ-KUN WAS MINE...
...I GUESS I MUST LOOK PRETTY FOOLISH NOW...
YEP.
SO NOT COOL.
TH- THEY'RE HEART-LESS !!
WELL, SÔ-KUN DUMPED US, SO WE KNOW HOW IT FEELS... BUT FOR SOME REASON...
...SEEING YOU LIKE THIS IS MAKING ME FEEL SO MUCH BETTER!!
AH
YAY! YAY! YOU GOT DUMPED !!
HA HA HA HA HA
PUFF...

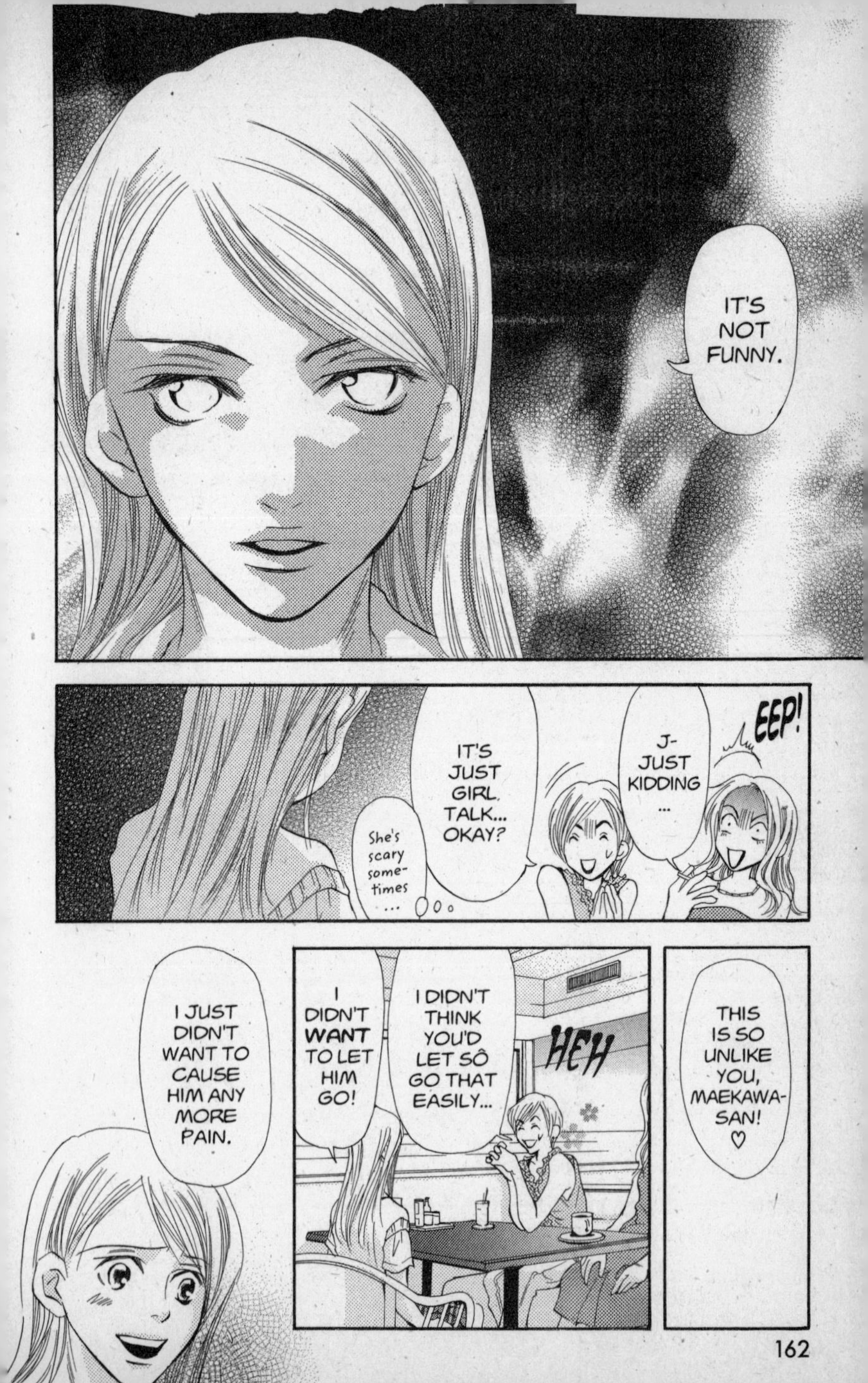
IT'S NOT FUNNY.
EEP!
J-JUST KIDDING...
IT'S JUST GIRL TALK... OKAY?
She's scary some-times...
THIS IS SO UNLIKE YOU, MAEKAWA-SAN! ♡
HEH
I DIDN'T THINK YOU'D LET SÔ GO THAT EASILY...
I DIDN'T **WANT** TO LET HIM GO!
I JUST DIDN'T WANT TO CAUSE HIM ANY MORE PAIN.

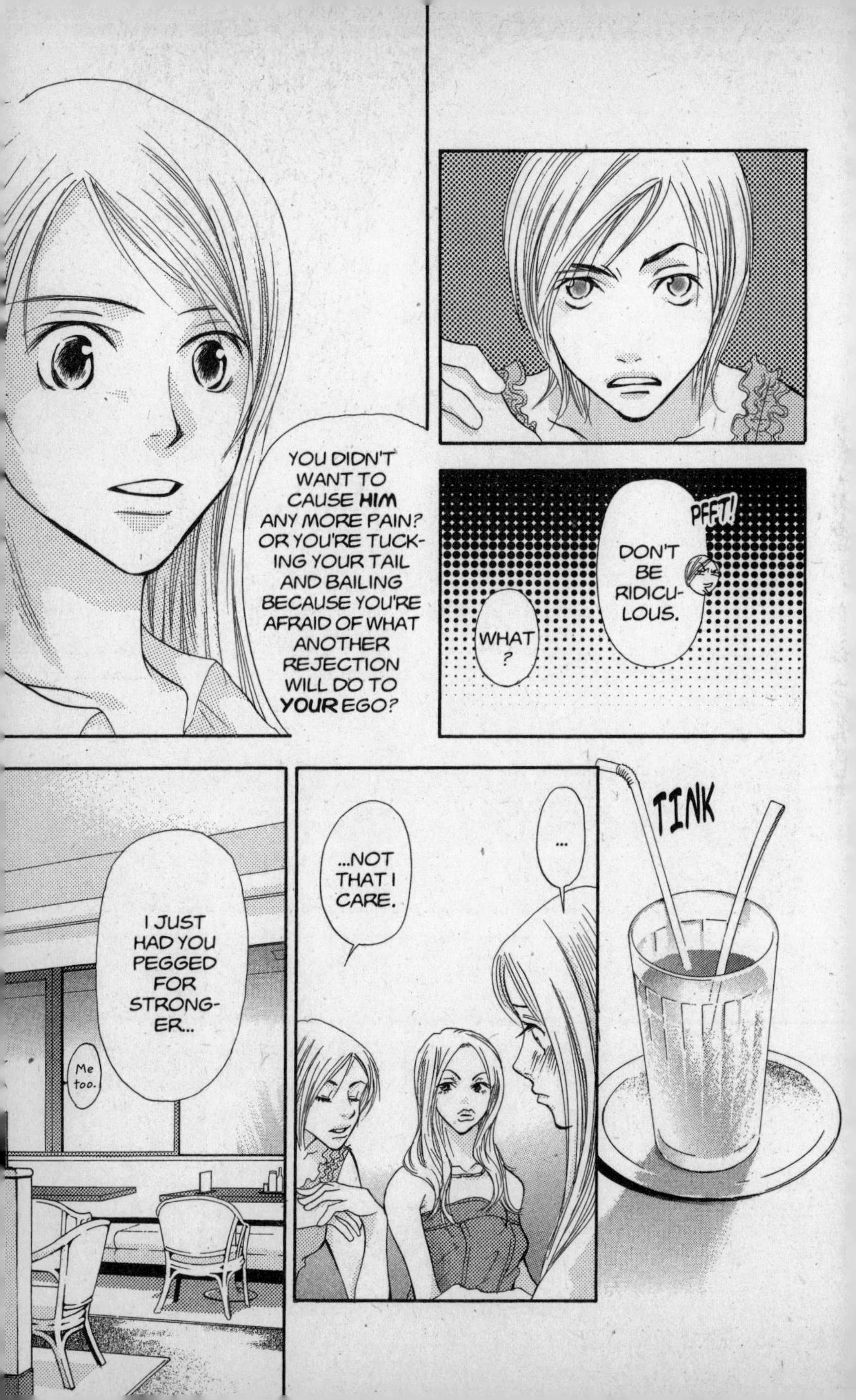
PFFT!
DON'T BE RIDICULOUS.
WHAT?
YOU DIDN'T WANT TO CAUSE **HIM** ANY MORE PAIN? OR YOU'RE TUCKING YOUR TAIL AND BAILING BECAUSE YOU'RE AFRAID OF WHAT ANOTHER REJECTION WILL DO TO **YOUR** EGO?
TINK
...
...NOT THAT I CARE.
I JUST HAD YOU PEGGED FOR STRONGER...
Me too.

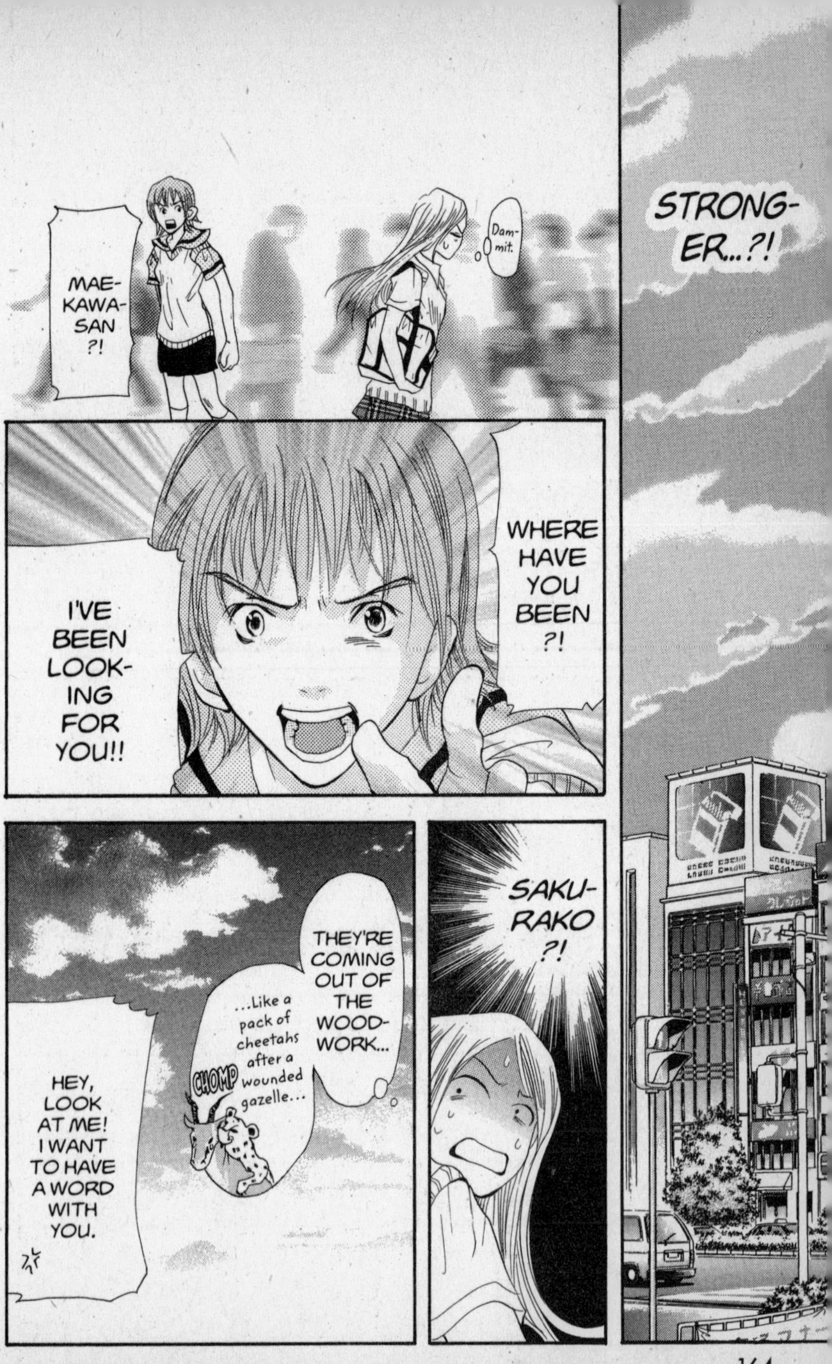
STRONGER...?!
Dammit.
MAEKAWA-SAN?!
WHERE HAVE YOU BEEN?!
I'VE BEEN LOOKING FOR YOU!!
SAKURAKO?!
THEY'RE COMING OUT OF THE WOODWORK...
...Like a pack of cheetahs after a wounded gazelle...
CHOMP
HEY, LOOK AT ME! I WANT TO HAVE A WORD WITH YOU.

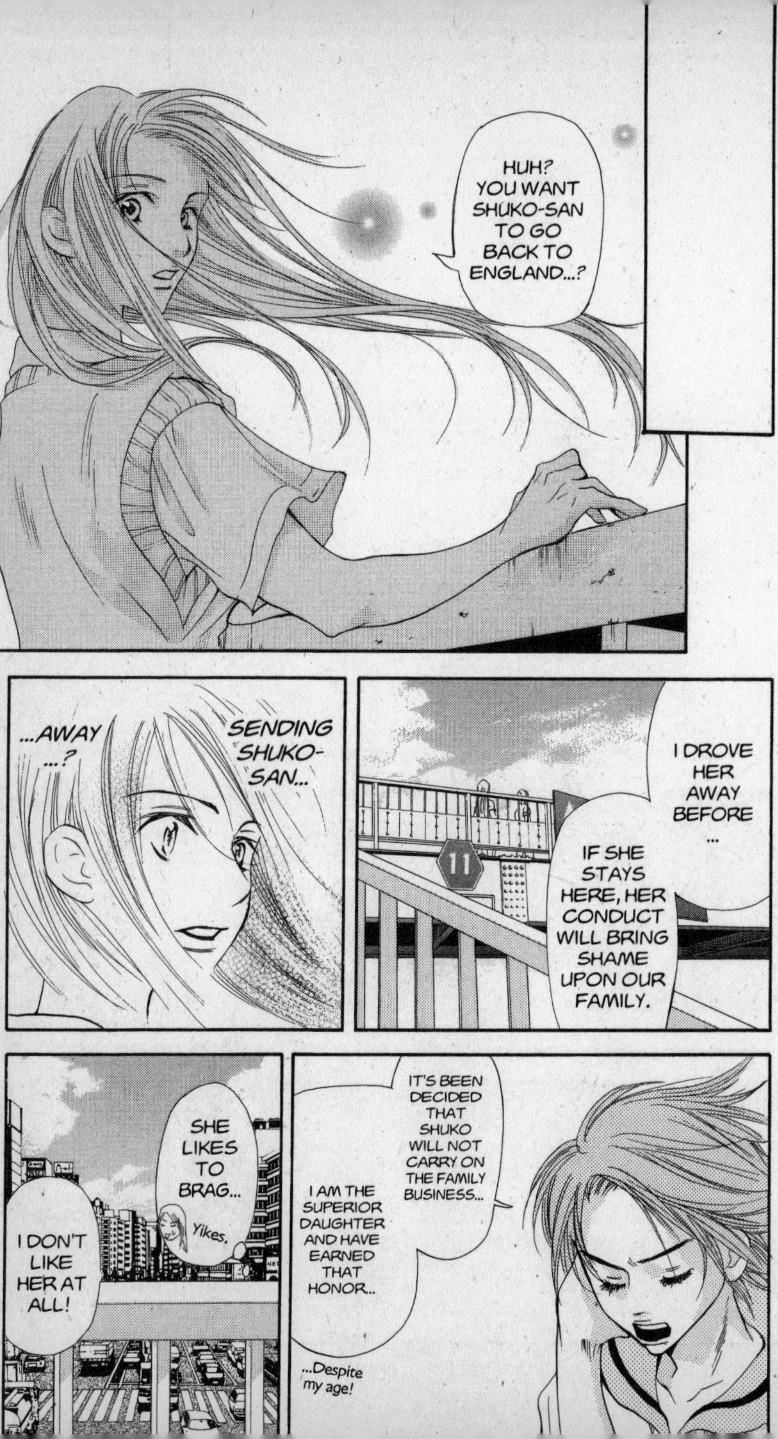
HUH? YOU WANT SHUKO-SAN TO GO BACK TO ENGLAND...?
I DROVE HER AWAY BEFORE...
IF SHE STAYS HERE, HER CONDUCT WILL BRING SHAME UPON OUR FAMILY.
SENDING SHUKO-SAN...
...AWAY...?
IT'S BEEN DECIDED THAT SHUKO WILL NOT CARRY ON THE FAMILY BUSINESS...
I AM THE SUPERIOR DAUGHTER AND HAVE EARNED THAT HONOR...
...Despite my age!
SHE LIKES TO BRAG...
Yikes.
I DON'T LIKE HER AT ALL!

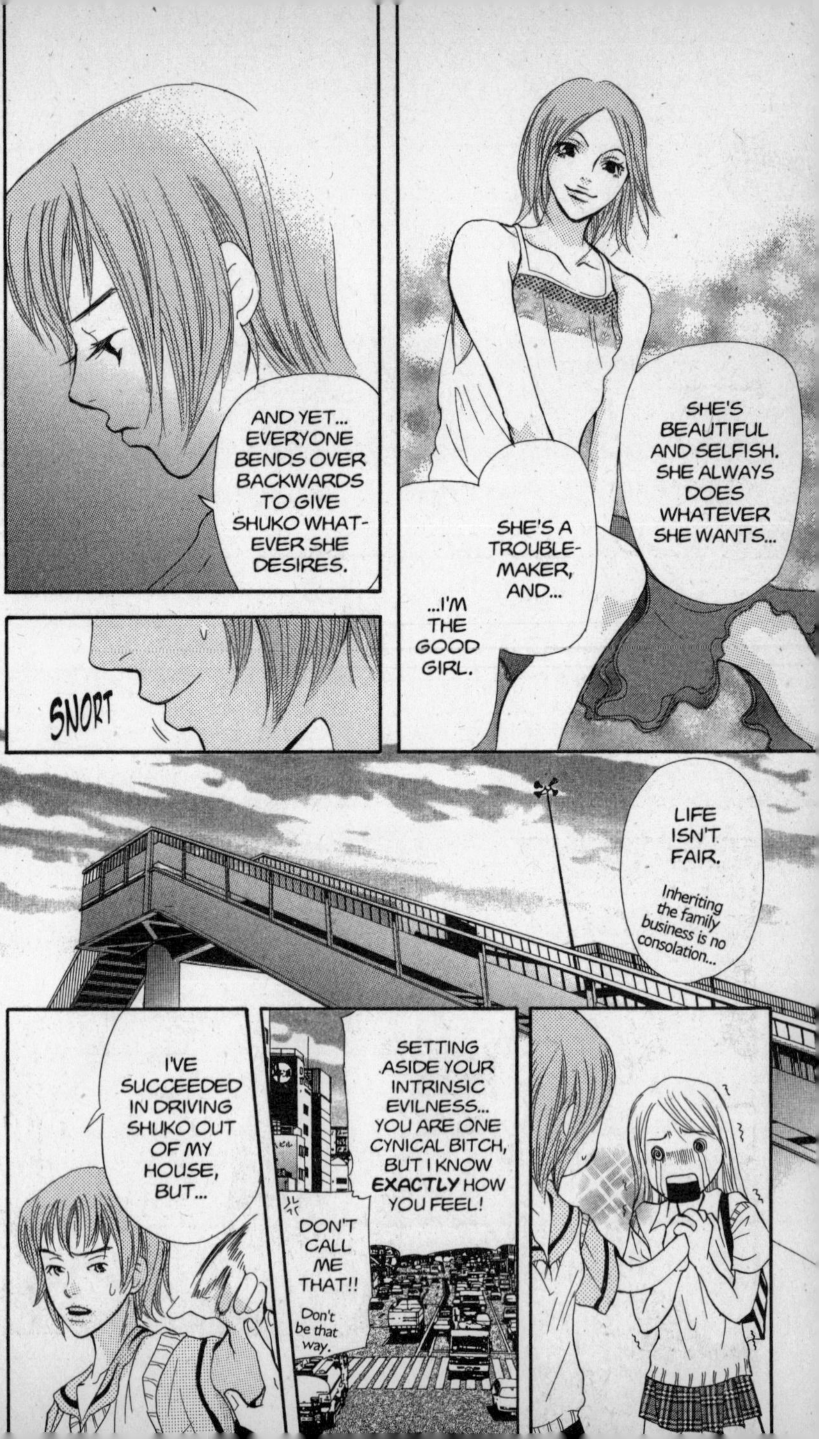
SHE'S BEAUTIFUL AND SELFISH. SHE ALWAYS DOES WHATEVER SHE WANTS...
SHE'S A TROUBLE-MAKER, AND...
...I'M THE GOOD GIRL.
AND YET... EVERYONE BENDS OVER BACKWARDS TO GIVE SHUKO WHAT-EVER SHE DESIRES.
SNORT
LIFE ISN'T FAIR.
Inheriting the family business is no consolation...
SETTING ASIDE YOUR INTRINSIC EVILNESS... YOU ARE ONE CYNICAL BITCH, BUT I KNOW **EXACTLY** HOW YOU FEEL!
DON'T CALL ME THAT!!
Don't be that way.
I'VE SUCCEEDED IN DRIVING SHUKO OUT OF MY HOUSE, BUT...

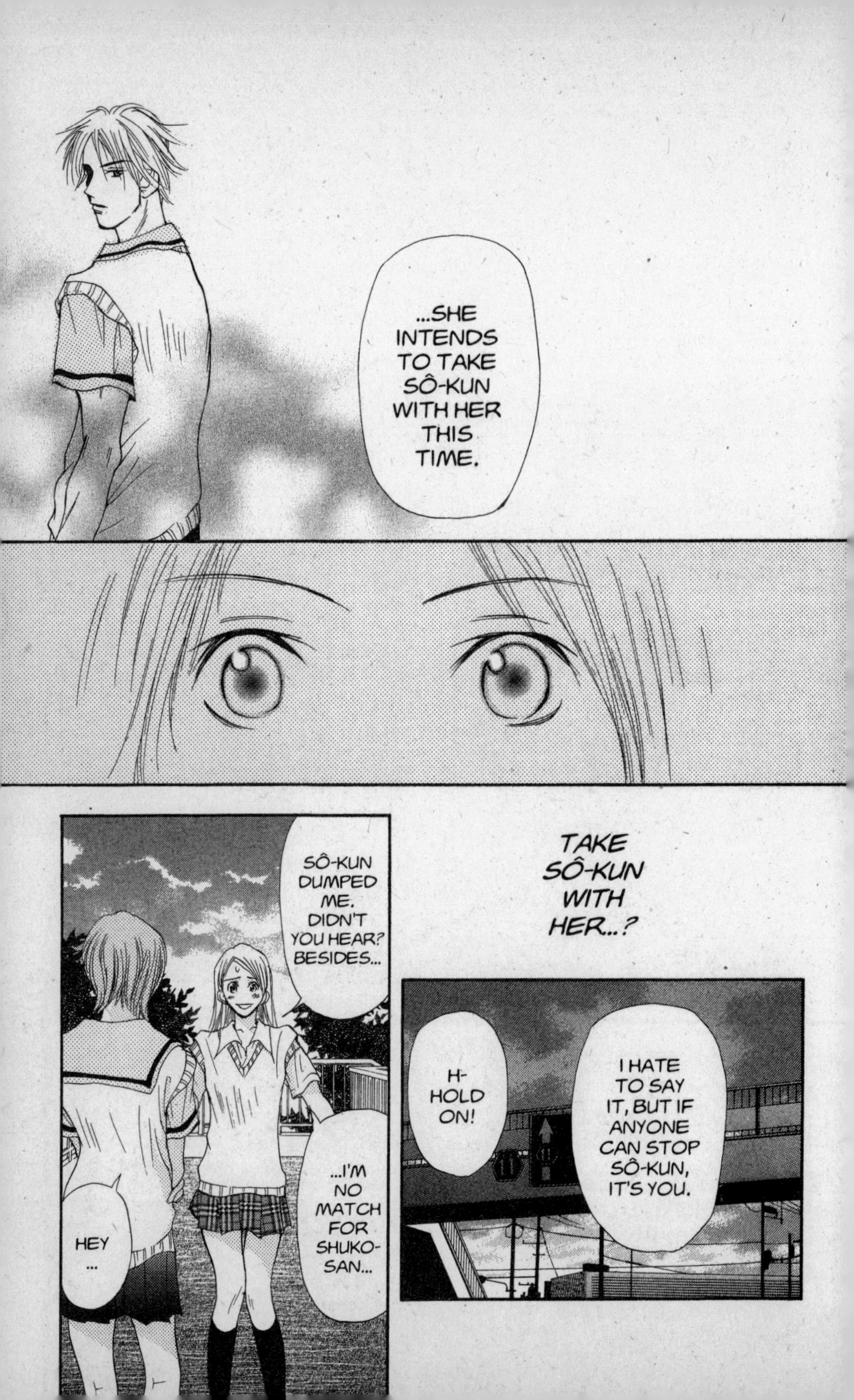
...SHE INTENDS TO TAKE SÔ-KUN WITH HER THIS TIME.
TAKE SÔ-KUN WITH HER...?
I HATE TO SAY IT, BUT IF ANYONE CAN STOP SÔ-KUN, IT'S YOU.
H-HOLD ON!
SÔ-KUN DUMPED ME. DIDN'T YOU HEAR? BESIDES...
...I'M NO MATCH FOR SHUKO-SAN...
HEY...

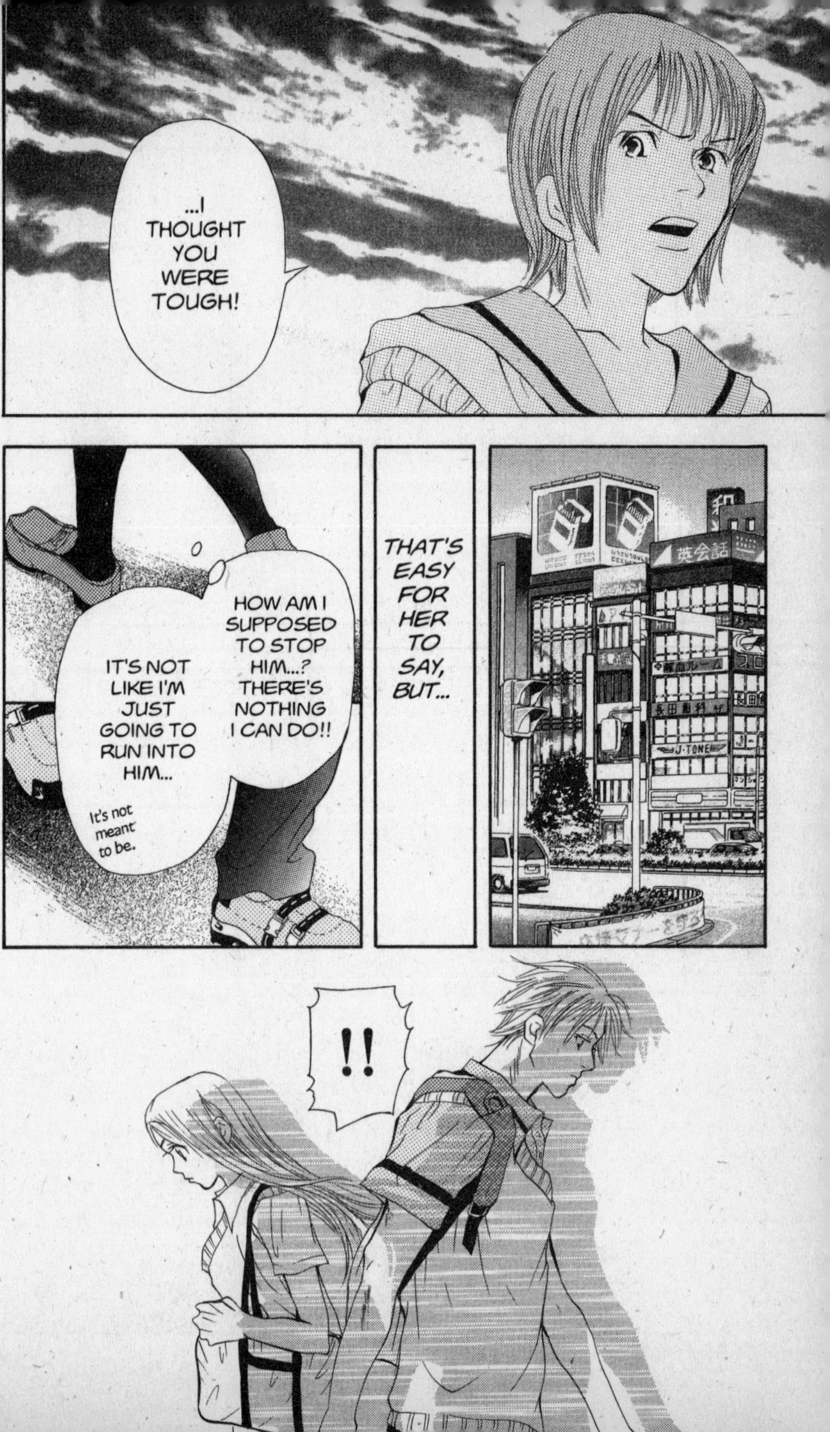
...I THOUGHT YOU WERE TOUGH!
THAT'S EASY FOR HER TO SAY, BUT...
HOW AM I SUPPOSED TO STOP HIM...? THERE'S NOTHING I CAN DO!!
IT'S NOT LIKE I'M JUST GOING TO RUN INTO HIM...
It's not meant to be.
!!

Doubt!!

Backstory

Part 5

While "DOUBT!!" was being serialized in the magazine, I suffered many hardships both in terms of my job and my private life... It was difficult to draw high-tension manga while I was depressed.

But today? I feel so fortunate to have had the chance to work on this series. Some of you have even asked for a sequel. Maybe we'll meet again someday, somewhere...? Thank you for the courage you gave me.

Many thanks to:

- Editorial staff
- Readers
- My assistants
- My friends who provided me some ideas
- and everyone else who was involved.

Thank you all!!

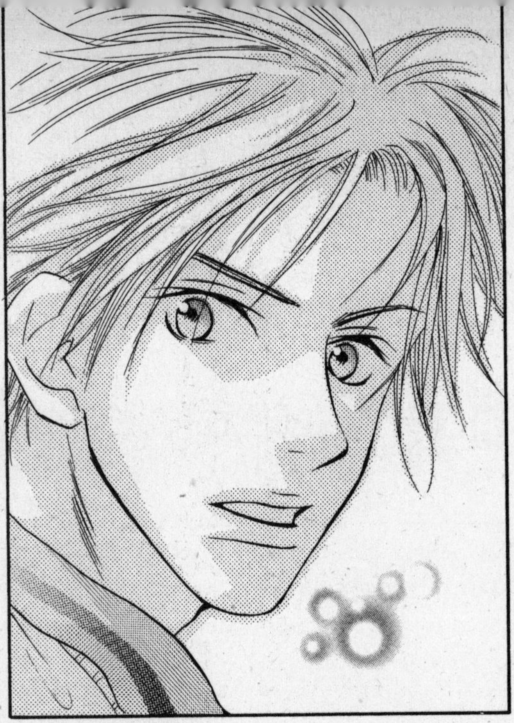

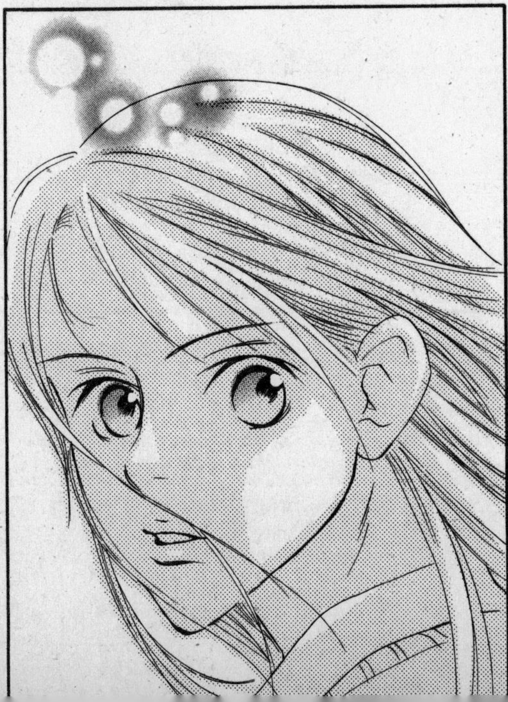

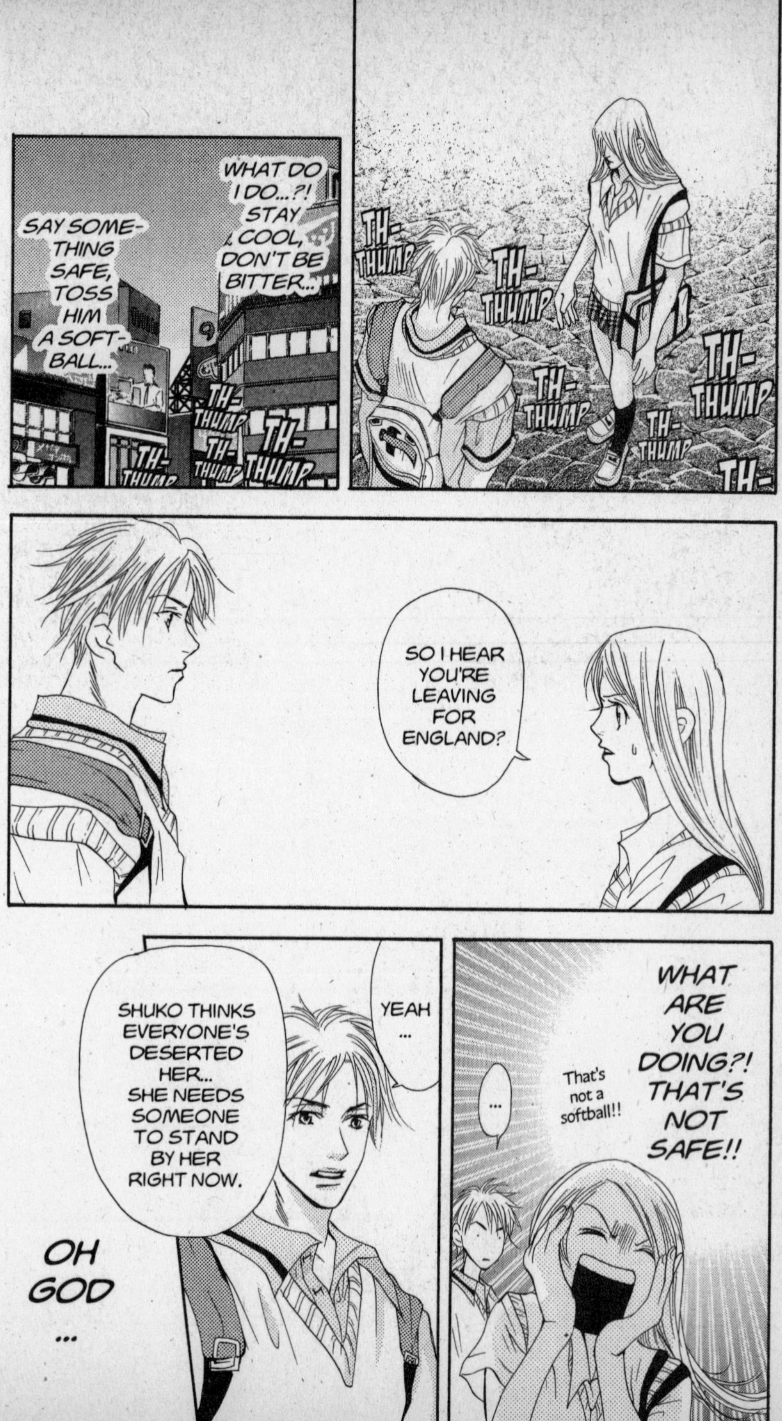
TH-THUMP
TH-THUMP
TH-THUMP
TH-THUMP
TH-THUMP
TH-
WHAT DO I DO...?! STAY COOL, DON'T BE BITTER...
SAY SOMETHING SAFE, TOSS HIM A SOFTBALL...
TH-THUMP
TH-THUMP
TH-THUMP
TH-THUMP
SO I HEAR YOU'RE LEAVING FOR ENGLAND?
WHAT ARE YOU DOING?! THAT'S NOT SAFE!!
That's not a softball!!
...
YEAH ...
SHUKO THINKS EVERYONE'S DESERTED HER... SHE NEEDS SOMEONE TO STAND BY HER RIGHT NOW.
OH GOD ...

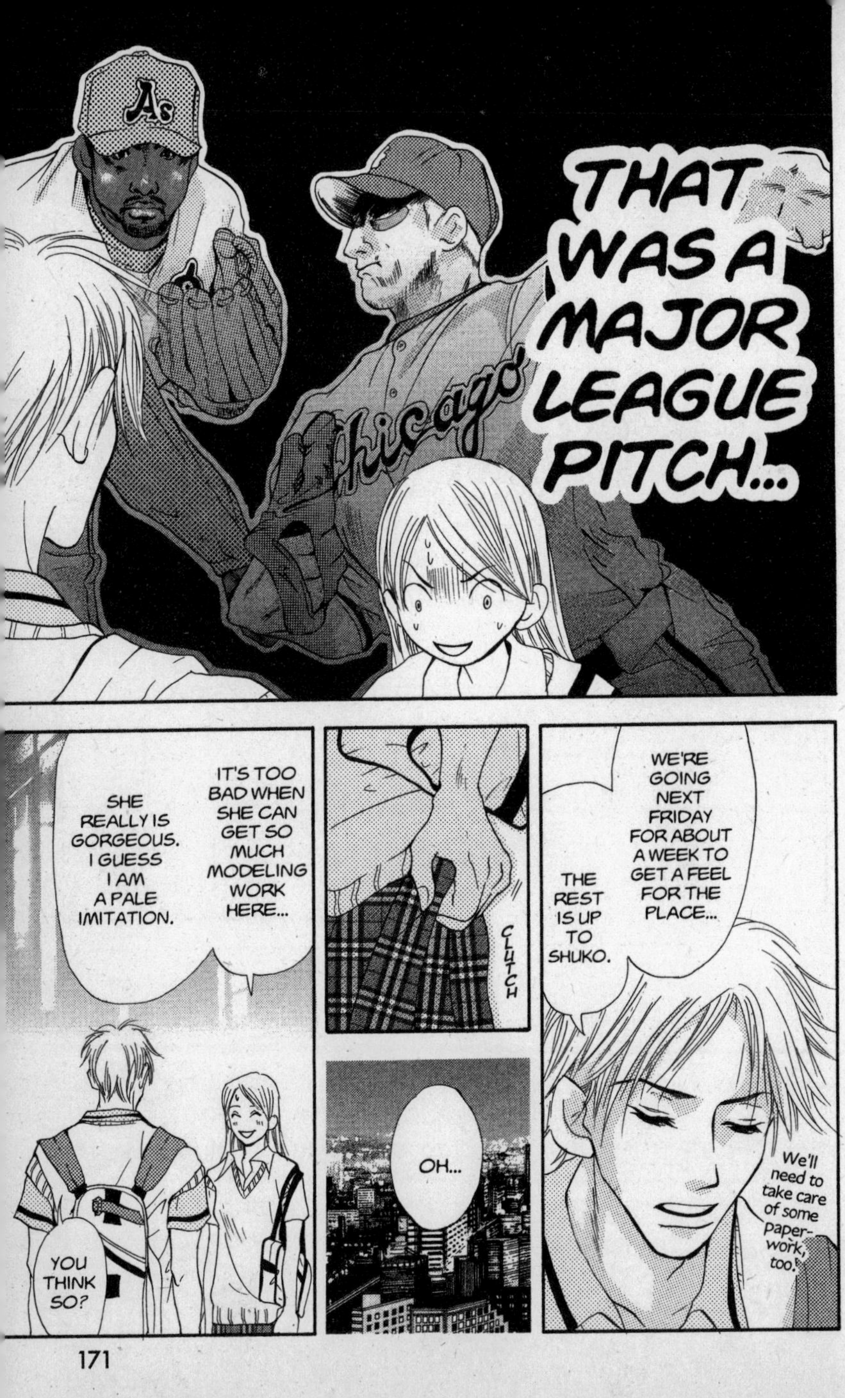
THAT WAS A MAJOR LEAGUE PITCH...
WE'RE GOING NEXT FRIDAY FOR ABOUT A WEEK TO GET A FEEL FOR THE PLACE...
THE REST IS UP TO SHUKO.
We'll need to take care of some paper-work, too.
CLUTCH
OH...
IT'S TOO BAD WHEN SHE CAN GET SO MUCH MODELING WORK HERE...
SHE REALLY IS GORGEOUS. I GUESS I AM A PALE IMITATION.
YOU THINK SO?

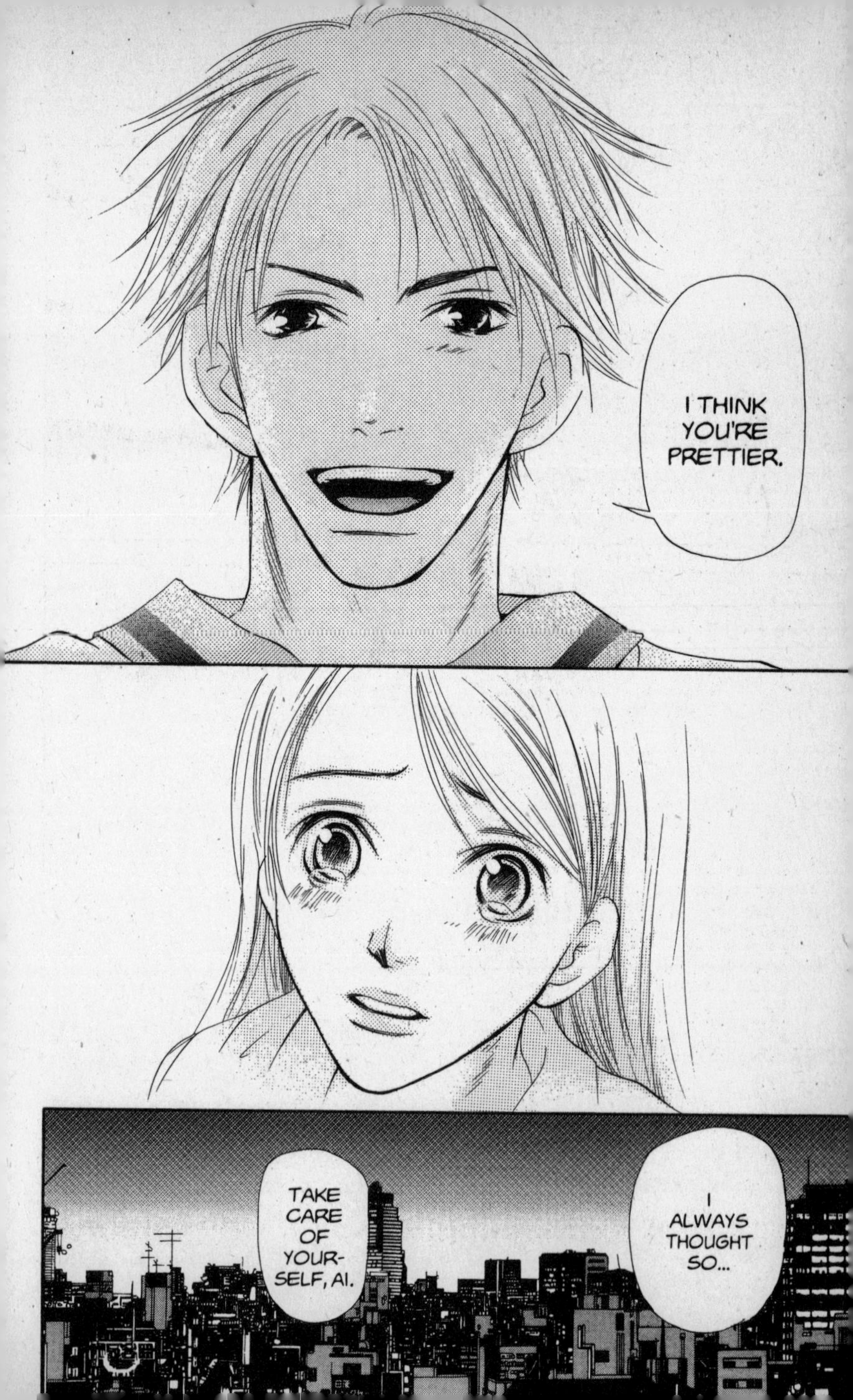
I THINK YOU'RE PRETTIER.
I ALWAYS THOUGHT SO...
TAKE CARE OF YOUR-SELF, AI.

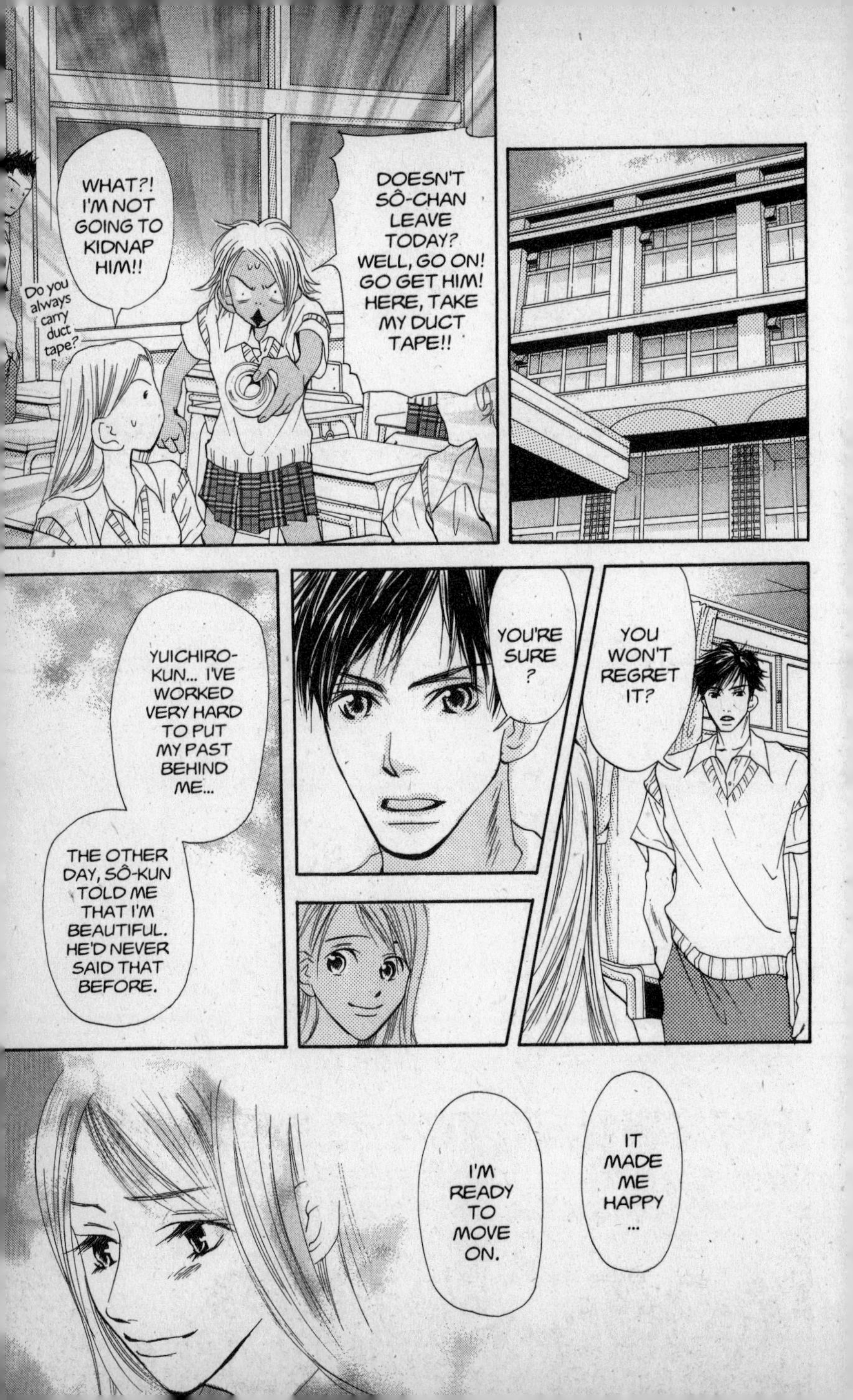
DOESN'T SÔ-CHAN LEAVE TODAY? WELL, GO ON! GO GET HIM! HERE, TAKE MY DUCT TAPE!!
WHAT?! I'M NOT GOING TO KIDNAP HIM!!
Do you always carry duct tape?
YOU WON'T REGRET IT?
YOU'RE SURE?
YUICHIRO-KUN... I'VE WORKED VERY HARD TO PUT MY PAST BEHIND ME...
THE OTHER DAY, SÔ-KUN TOLD ME THAT I'M BEAUTIFUL. HE'D NEVER SAID THAT BEFORE.
IT MADE ME HAPPY...
I'M READY TO MOVE ON.

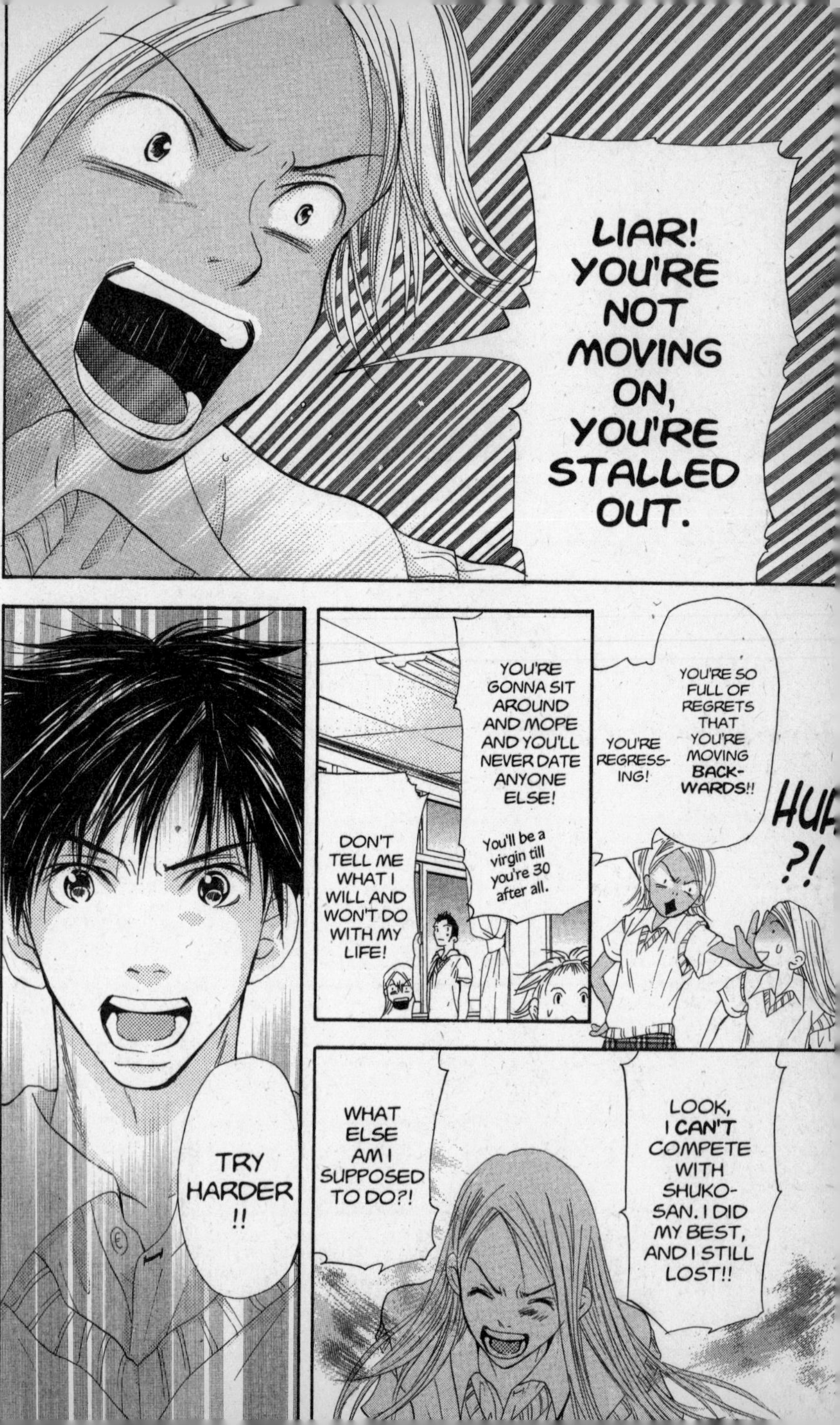
LIAR! YOU'RE NOT MOVING ON, YOU'RE STALLED OUT.
HU ?!
YOU'RE SO FULL OF REGRETS THAT YOU'RE MOVING BACKWARDS!!
YOU'RE REGRESSING!
YOU'RE GONNA SIT AROUND AND MOPE AND YOU'LL NEVER DATE ANYONE ELSE!
You'll be a virgin till you're 30 after all.
DON'T TELL ME WHAT I WILL AND WON'T DO WITH MY LIFE!
LOOK, I CAN'T COMPETE WITH SHUKO-SAN. I DID MY BEST, AND I STILL LOST!!
WHAT ELSE AM I SUPPOSED TO DO?!
TRY HARDER !!

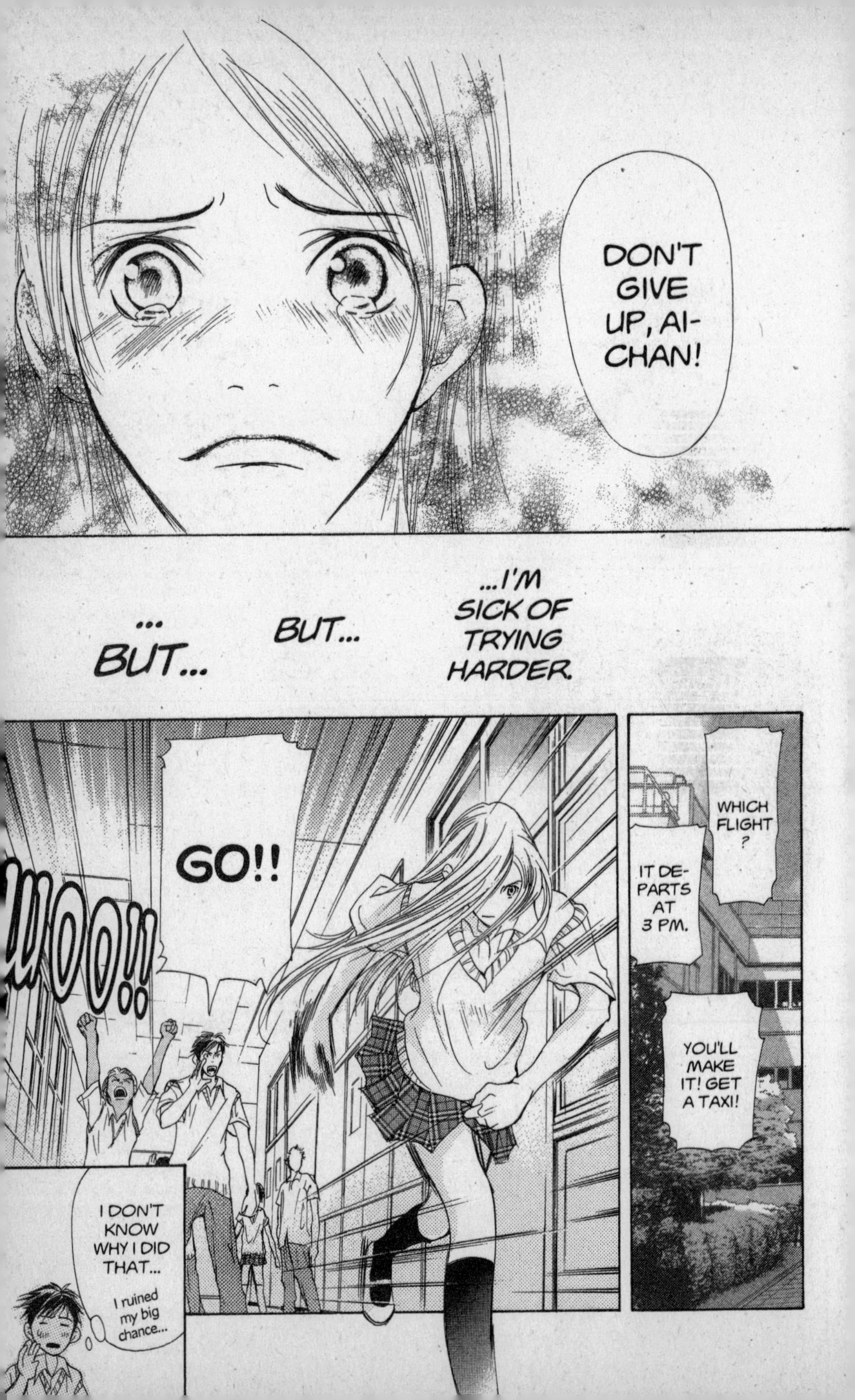
DON'T GIVE UP, AI-CHAN!
...I'M SICK OF TRYING HARDER.
BUT...
... BUT...
WHICH FLIGHT?
IT DEPARTS AT 3 PM.
YOU'LL MAKE IT! GET A TAXI!
GO!!
WOO!!
I DON'T KNOW WHY I DID THAT...
I ruined my big chance...

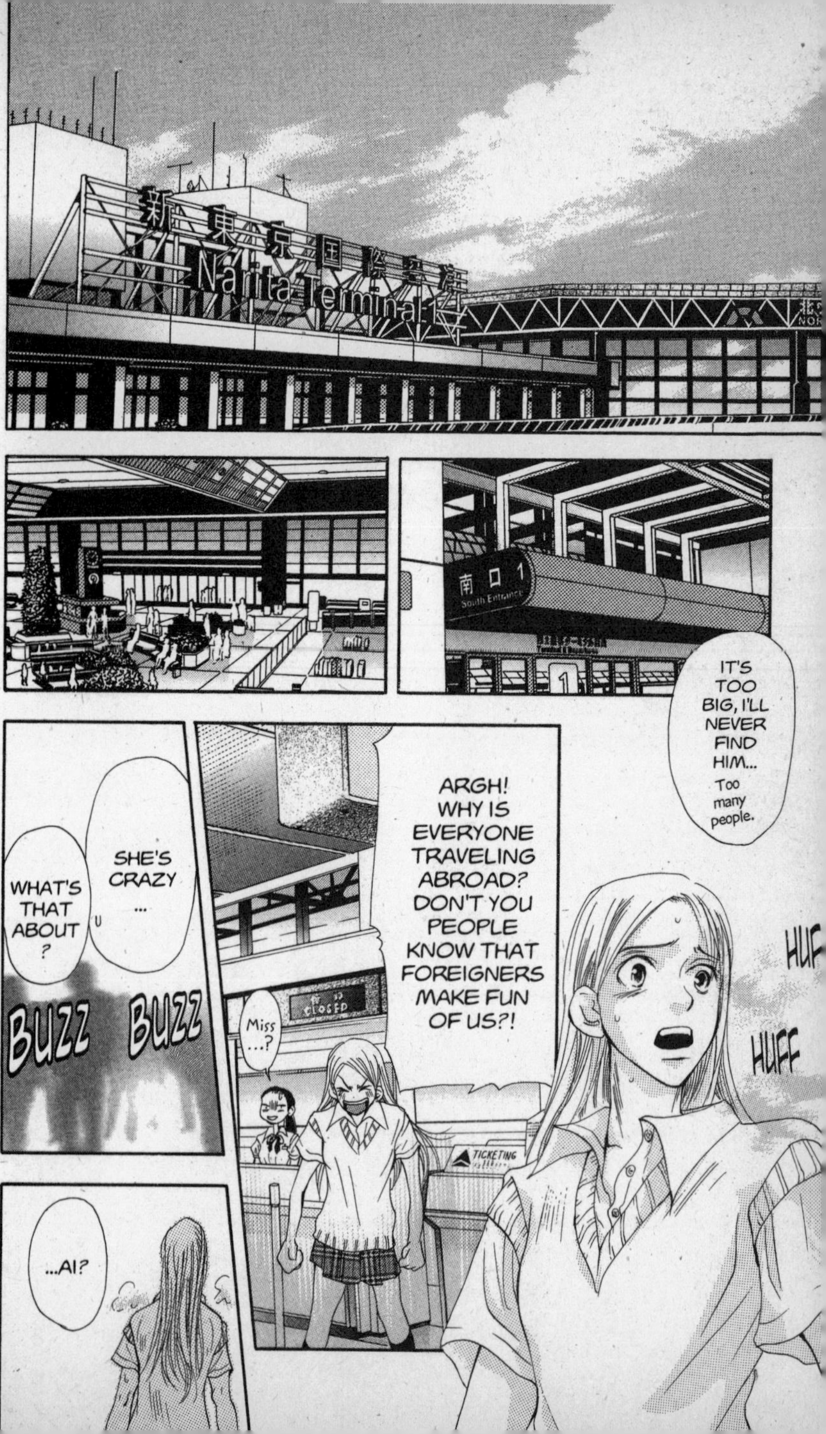
新東京国際空港
Narita Terminal 1
南口1
South Entrance
IT'S TOO BIG, I'LL NEVER FIND HIM...
Too many people.
HUFF
HUFF
ARGH! WHY IS EVERYONE TRAVELING ABROAD? DON'T YOU PEOPLE KNOW THAT FOREIGNERS MAKE FUN OF US?!
CLOSED
TICKETING
Miss ...?
SHE'S CRAZY ...
WHAT'S THAT ABOUT ?
BUZZ BUZZ
...AI?

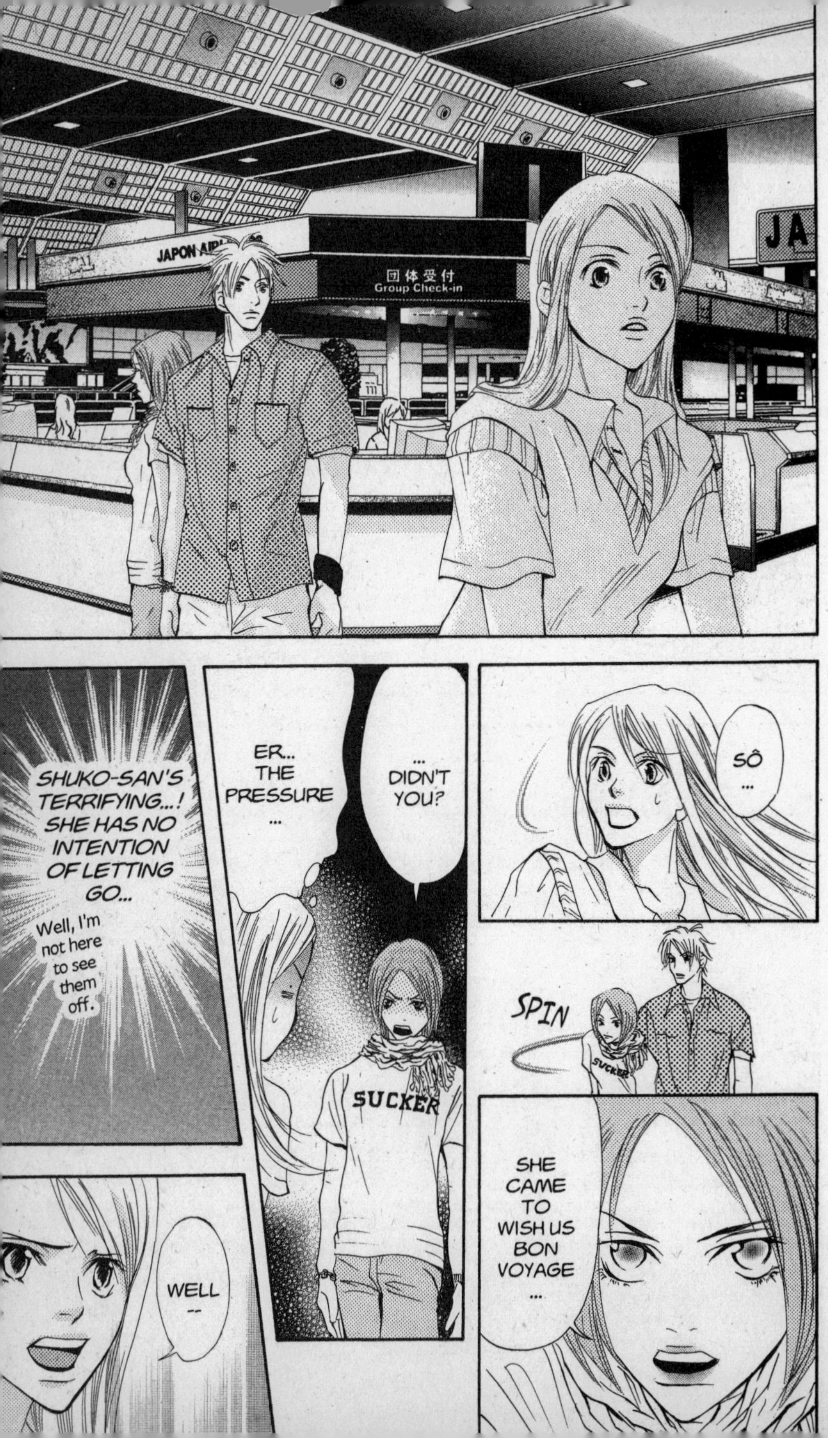
JA
団体受付
Group Check-in
JAPON AIR
SÔ ...
SPIN
SUCKER
SHE CAME TO WISH US BON VOYAGE ...
... DIDN'T YOU?
ER... THE PRESSURE ...
SUCKER
SHUKO-SAN'S TERRIFYING...! SHE HAS NO INTENTION OF LETTING GO...
Well, I'm not here to see them off.
WELL --

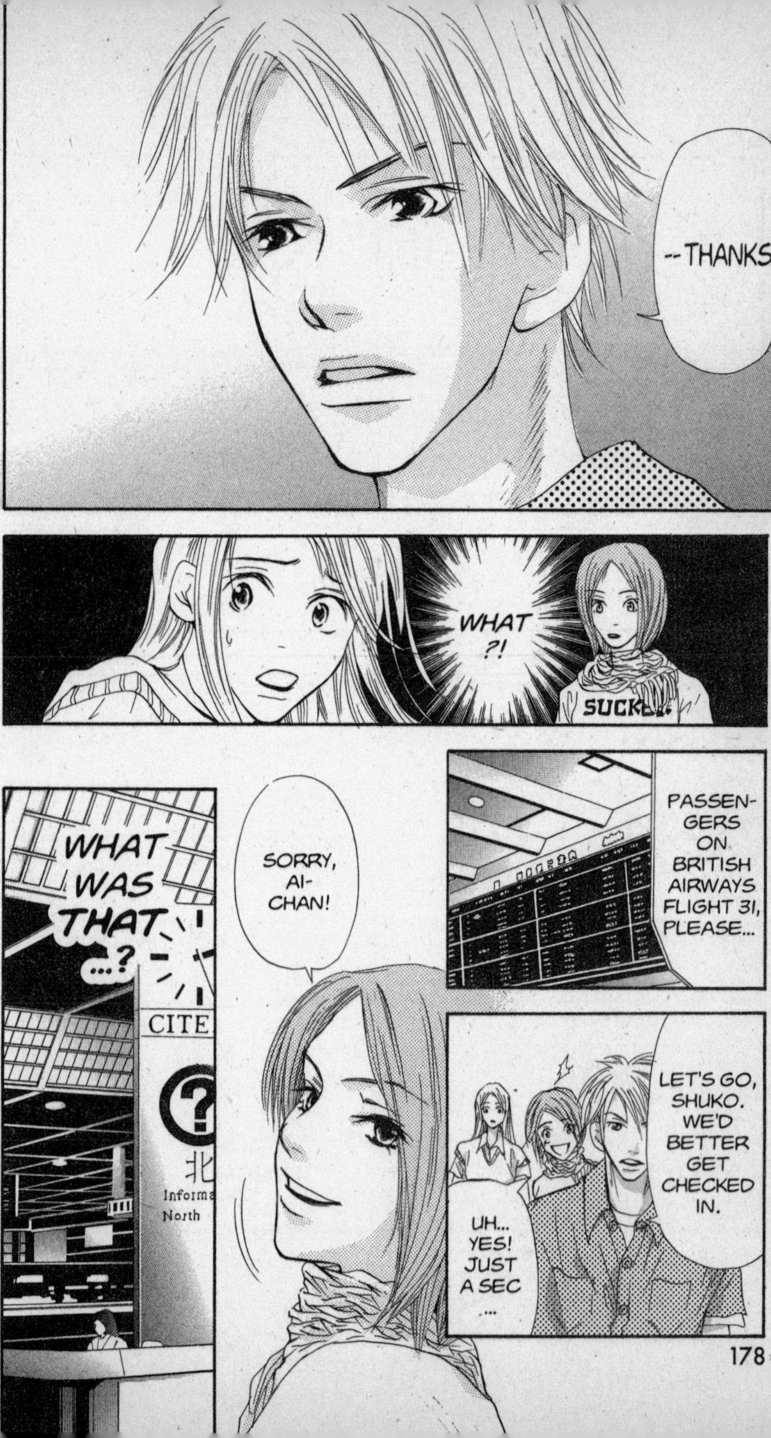
--THANKS.
WHAT ?!
SUCK...
PASSENGERS ON BRITISH AIRWAYS FLIGHT 31, PLEASE...
LET'S GO, SHUKO. WE'D BETTER GET CHECKED IN.
UH... YES! JUST A SEC ....
SORRY, AI-CHAN!
WHAT WAS THAT ...?
CITE
北
Informa
North

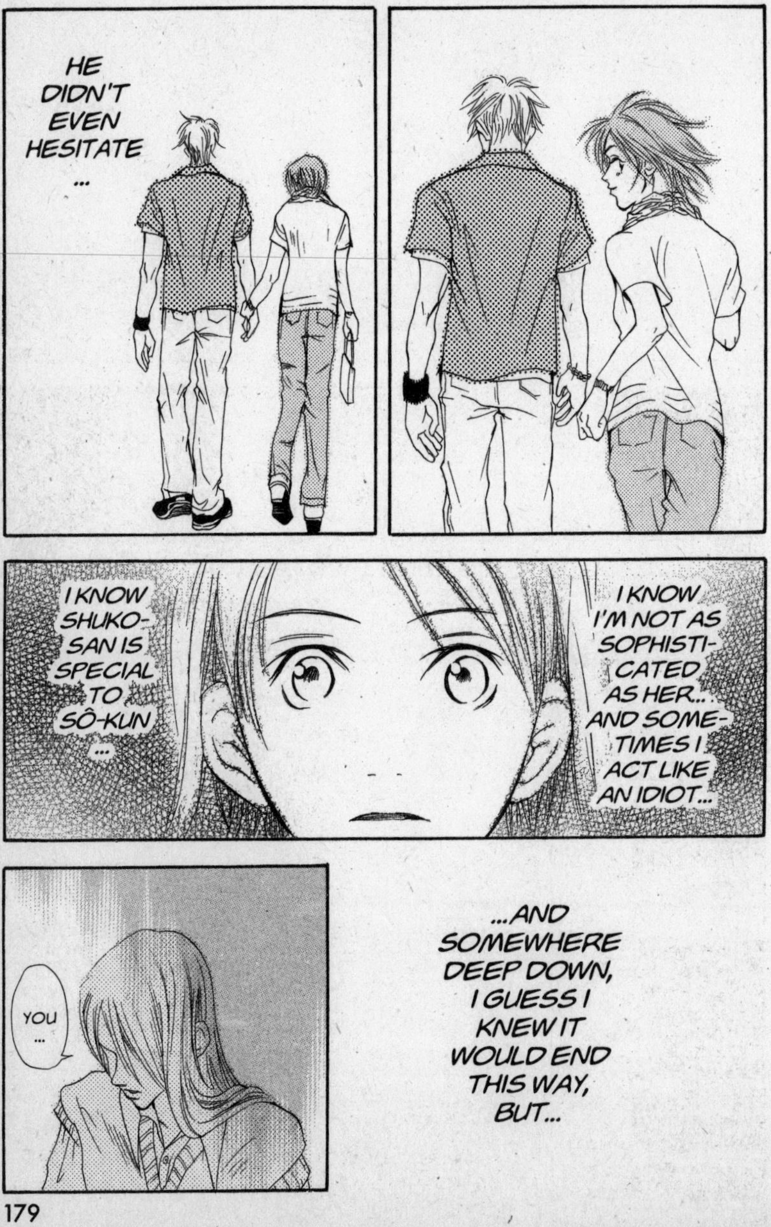
HE DIDN'T EVEN HESITATE ...
I KNOW I'M NOT AS SOPHISTICATED AS HER... AND SOMETIMES I ACT LIKE AN IDIOT...
I KNOW SHUKO-SAN IS SPECIAL TO SÔ-KUN ...
...AND SOMEWHERE DEEP DOWN, I GUESS I KNEW IT WOULD END THIS WAY, BUT...
YOU ...

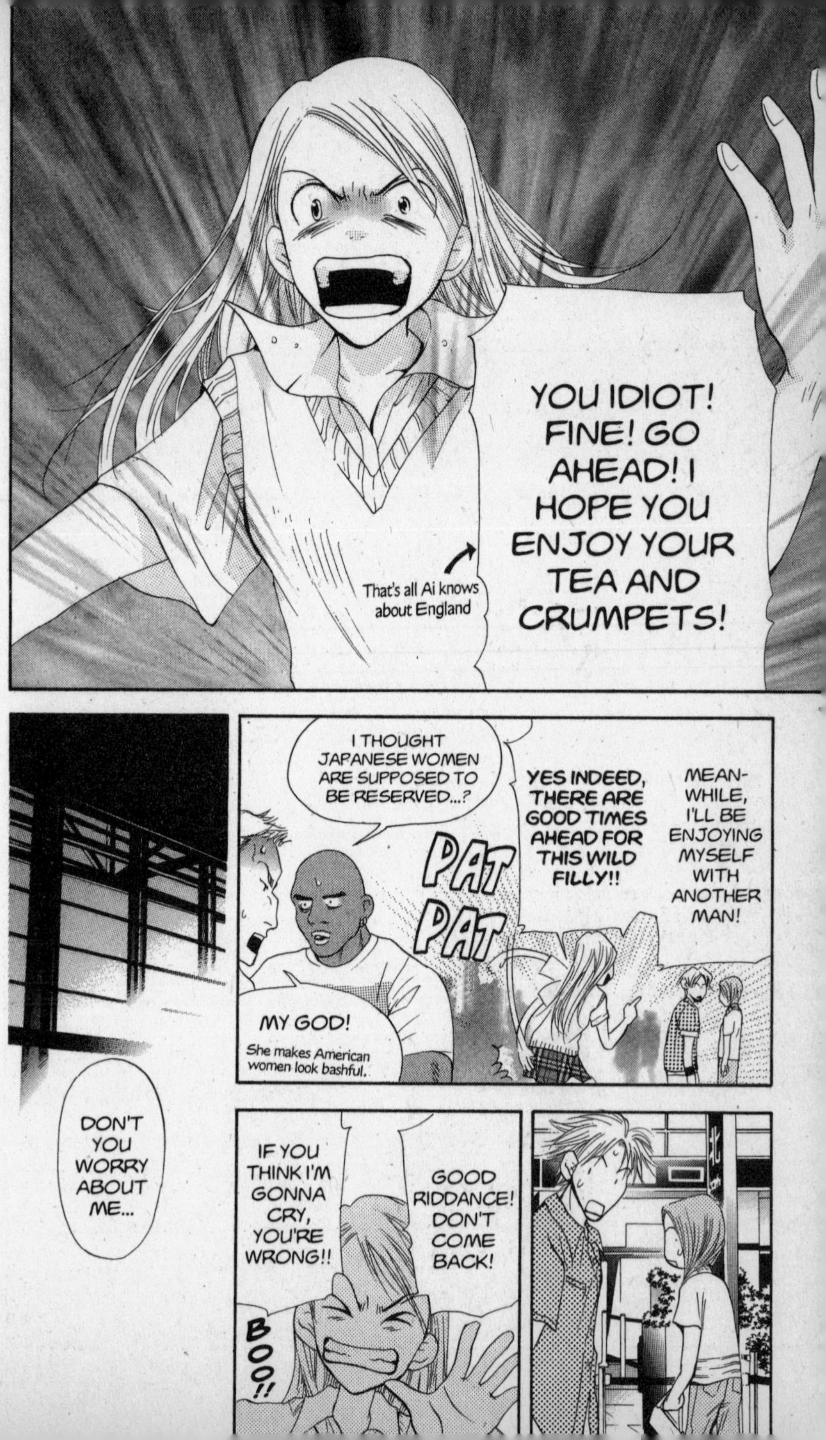
YOU IDIOT! FINE! GO AHEAD! I HOPE YOU ENJOY YOUR TEA AND CRUMPETS!
That's all Ai knows about England
MEAN-WHILE, I'LL BE ENJOYING MYSELF WITH ANOTHER MAN!
YES INDEED, THERE ARE GOOD TIMES AHEAD FOR THIS WILD FILLY!!
PAT PAT
I THOUGHT JAPANESE WOMEN ARE SUPPOSED TO BE RESERVED...?
MY GOD!
She makes American women look bashful.
DON'T YOU WORRY ABOUT ME...
GOOD RIDDANCE! DON'T COME BACK!
IF YOU THINK I'M GONNA CRY, YOU'RE WRONG!!
BOOO!!

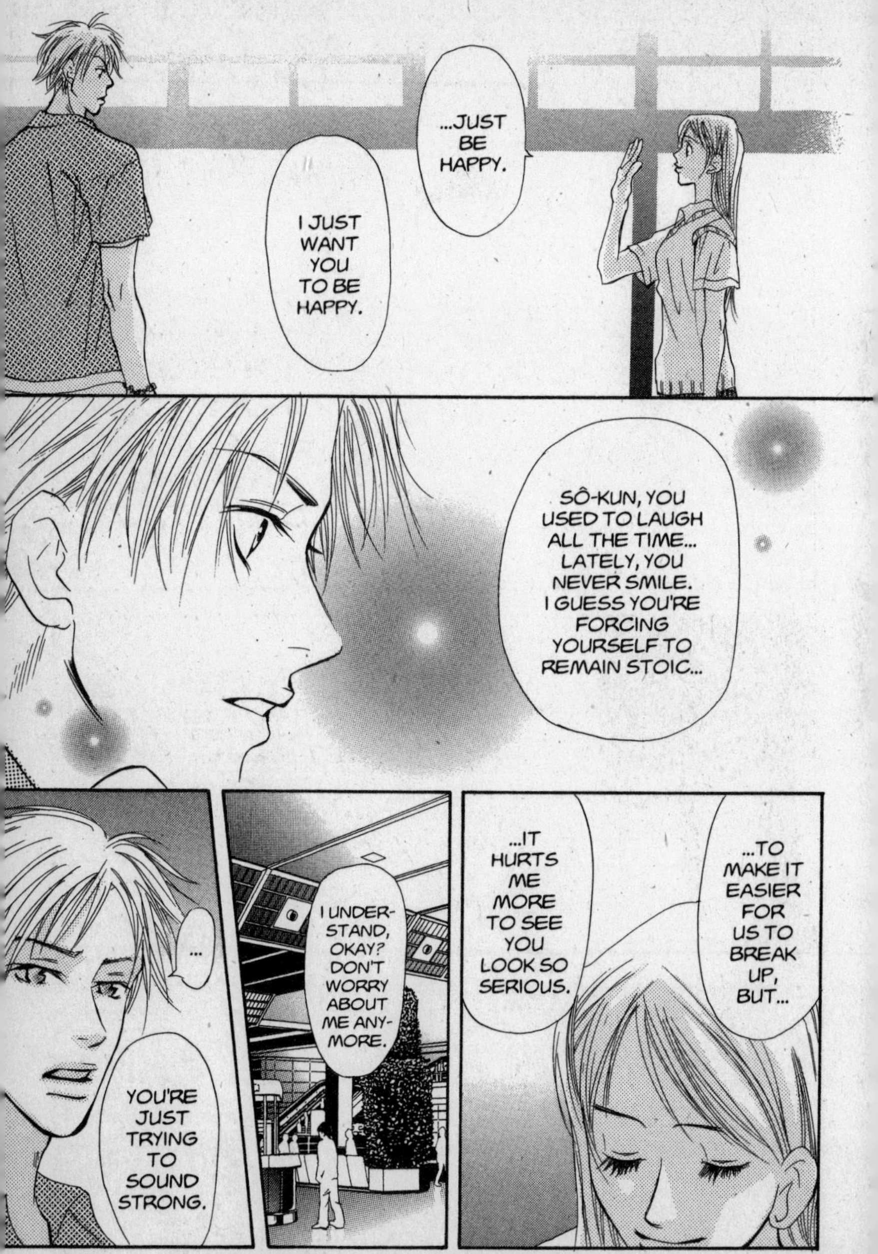
...JUST BE HAPPY.
I JUST WANT YOU TO BE HAPPY.
SÔ-KUN, YOU USED TO LAUGH ALL THE TIME... LATELY, YOU NEVER SMILE. I GUESS YOU'RE FORCING YOURSELF TO REMAIN STOIC...
...TO MAKE IT EASIER FOR US TO BREAK UP, BUT...
...IT HURTS ME MORE TO SEE YOU LOOK SO SERIOUS.
I UNDER-STAND, OKAY? DON'T WORRY ABOUT ME ANY-MORE.
...
YOU'RE JUST TRYING TO SOUND STRONG.

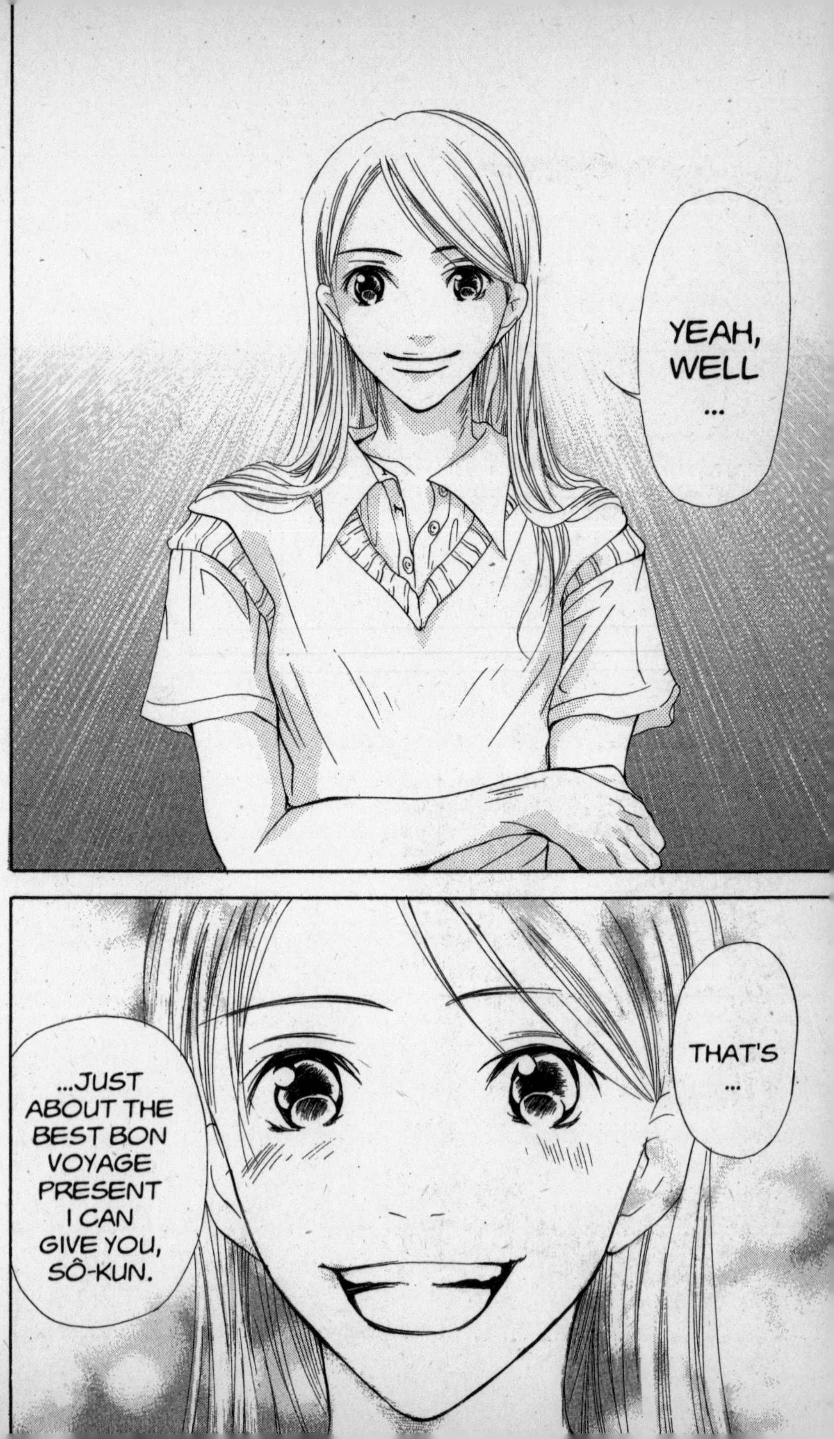
YEAH, WELL ...
THAT'S ...
...JUST ABOUT THE BEST BON VOYAGE PRESENT I CAN GIVE YOU, SÔ-KUN.

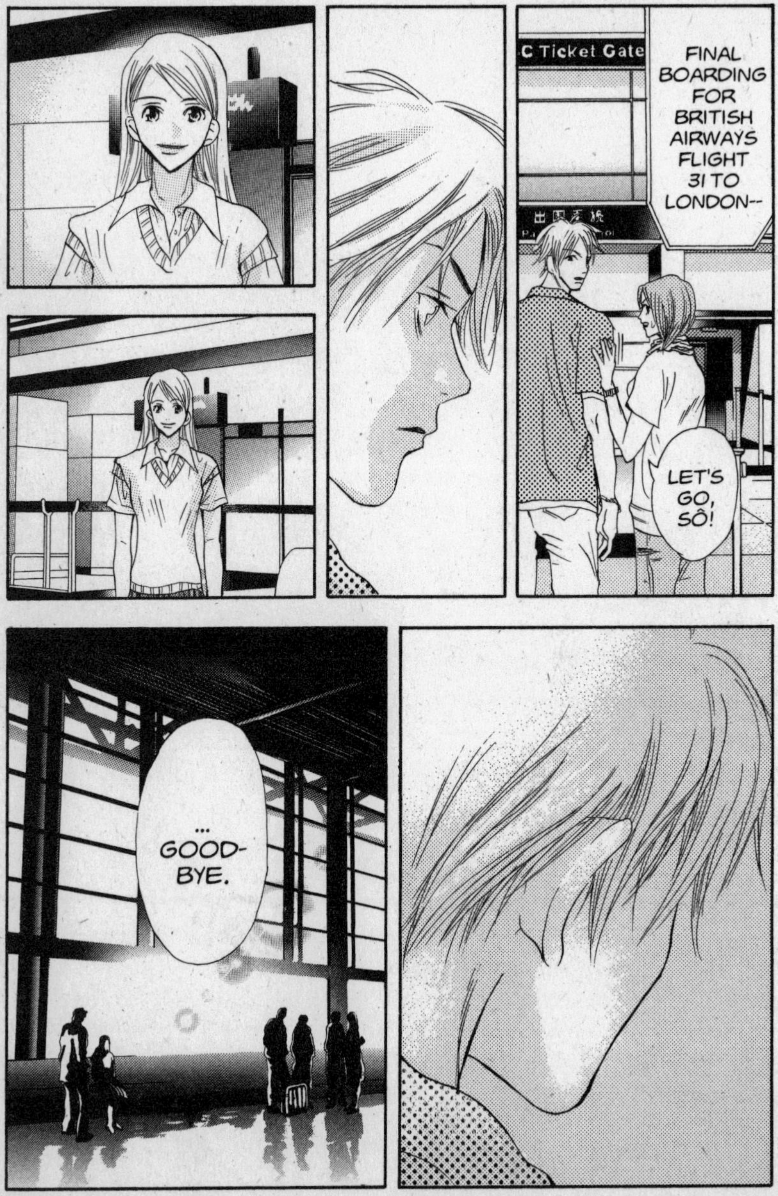
C Ticket Gate
FINAL BOARDING FOR BRITISH AIRWAYS FLIGHT 31 TO LONDON--
LET'S GO, SÔ!
... GOOD-BYE.

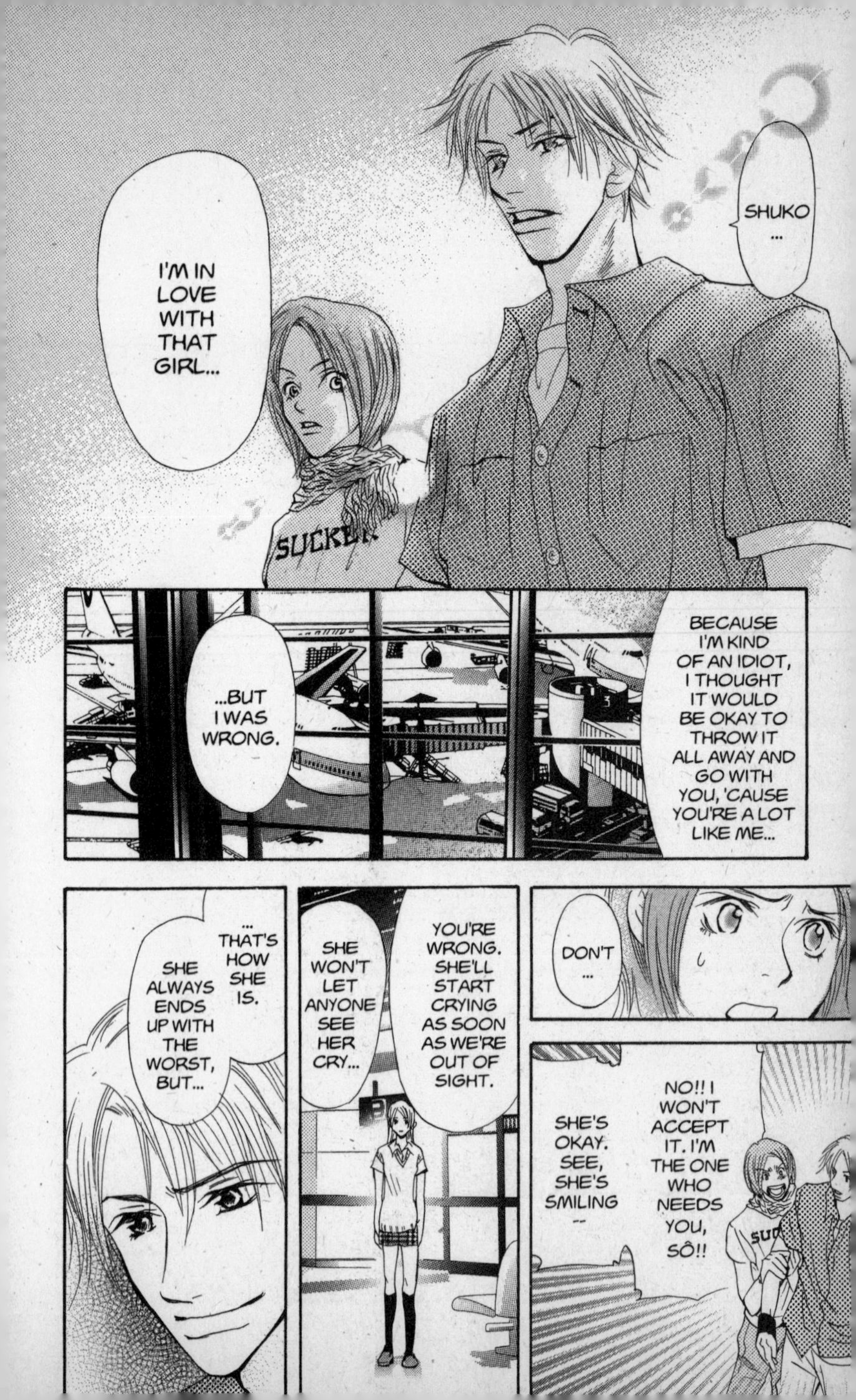
SHUKO ...
I'M IN LOVE WITH THAT GIRL...
BECAUSE I'M KIND OF AN IDIOT, I THOUGHT IT WOULD BE OKAY TO THROW IT ALL AWAY AND GO WITH YOU, 'CAUSE YOU'RE A LOT LIKE ME...
...BUT I WAS WRONG.
DON'T ...
NO!! I WON'T ACCEPT IT. I'M THE ONE WHO NEEDS YOU, SÔ!!
SHE'S OKAY. SEE, SHE'S SMILING --
YOU'RE WRONG. SHE'LL START CRYING AS SOON AS WE'RE OUT OF SIGHT.
SHE WON'T LET ANYONE SEE HER CRY...
... THAT'S HOW SHE IS.
SHE ALWAYS ENDS UP WITH THE WORST, BUT...

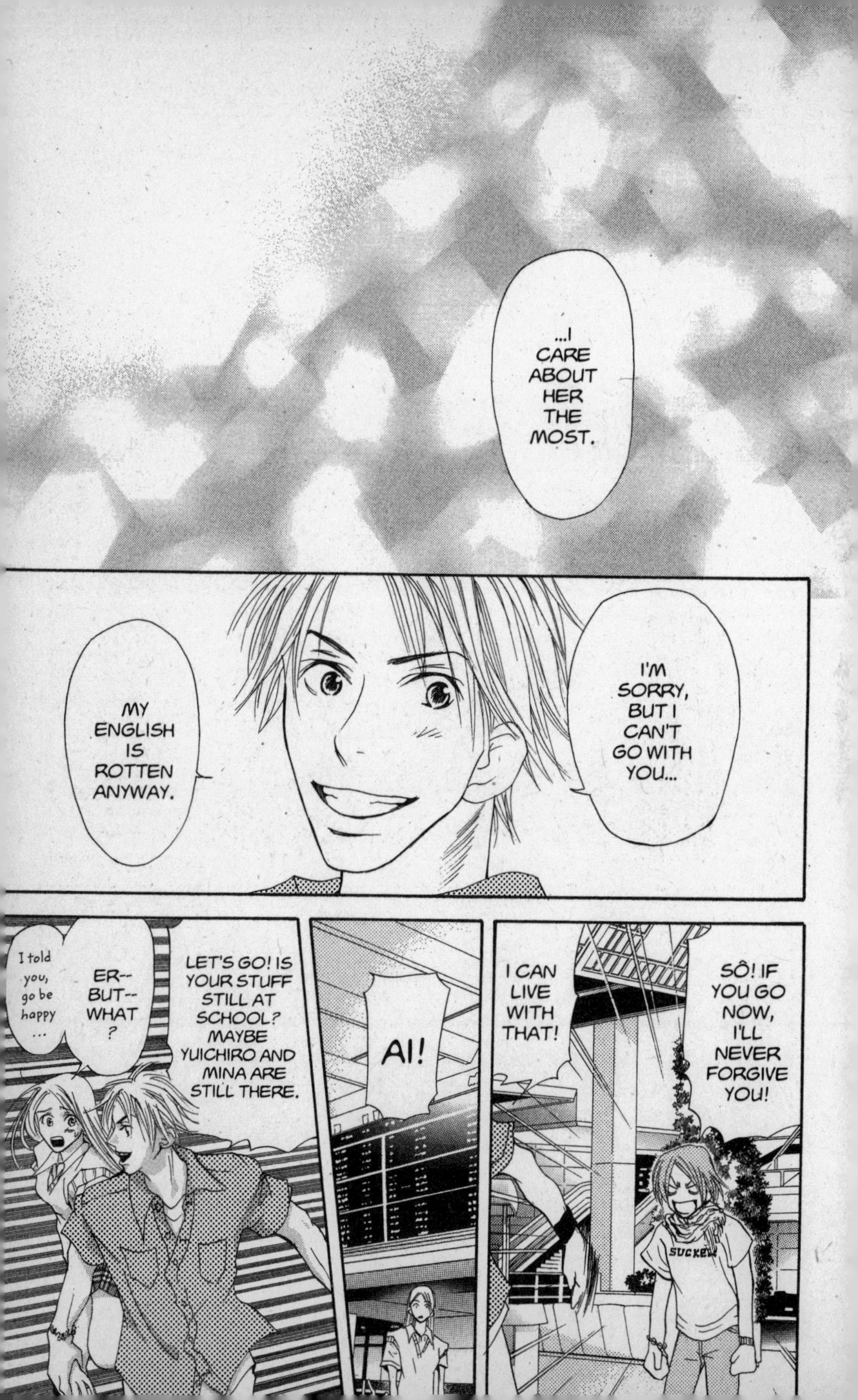
...I CARE ABOUT HER THE MOST.
I'M SORRY, BUT I CAN'T GO WITH YOU...
MY ENGLISH IS ROTTEN ANYWAY.
SÔ! IF YOU GO NOW, I'LL NEVER FORGIVE YOU!
I CAN LIVE WITH THAT!
AI!
LET'S GO! IS YOUR STUFF STILL AT SCHOOL? MAYBE YUICHIRO AND MINA ARE STILL THERE.
ER-- BUT-- WHAT?
I told you, go be happy ...

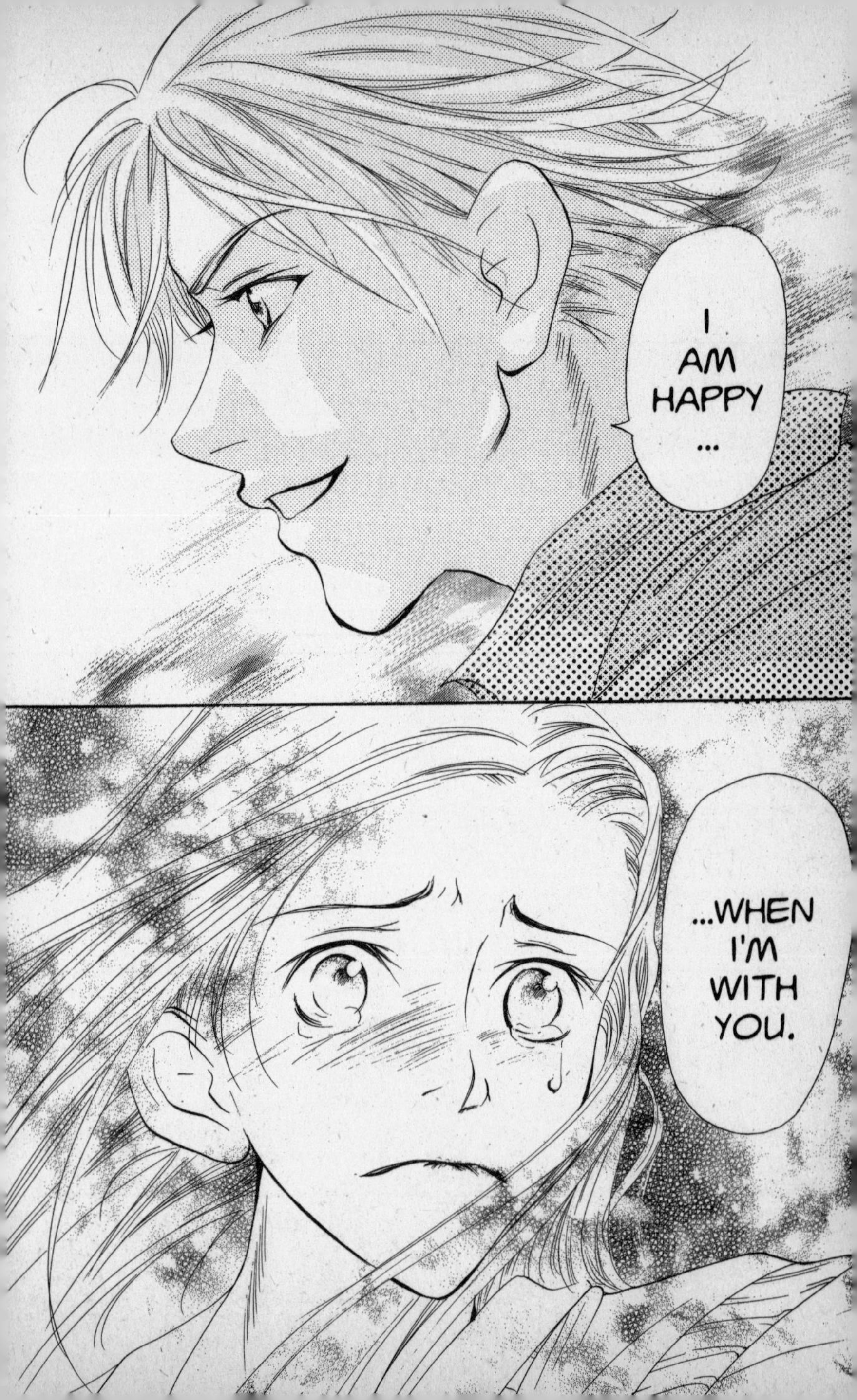
I AM HAPPY ...
...WHEN I'M WITH YOU.

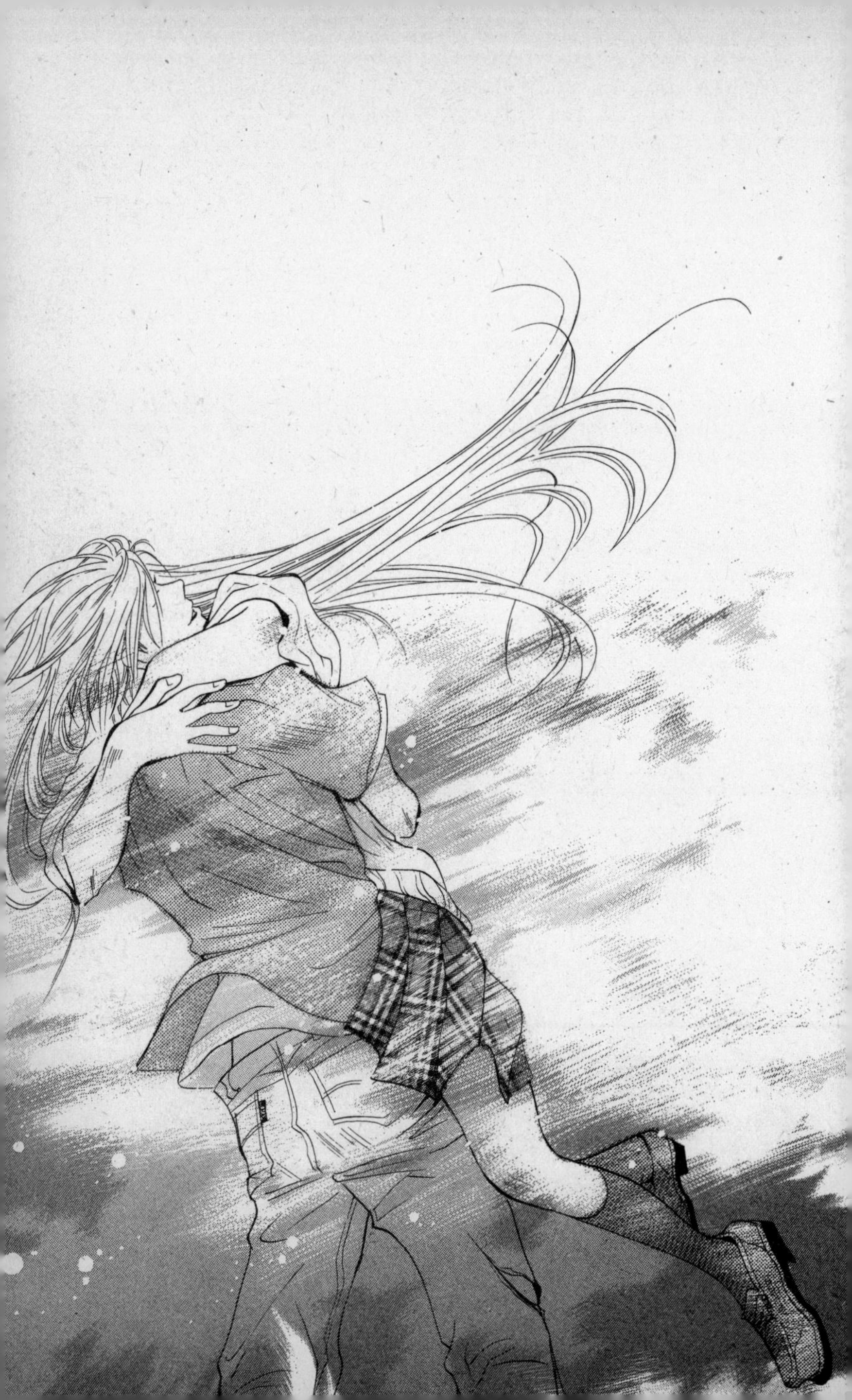

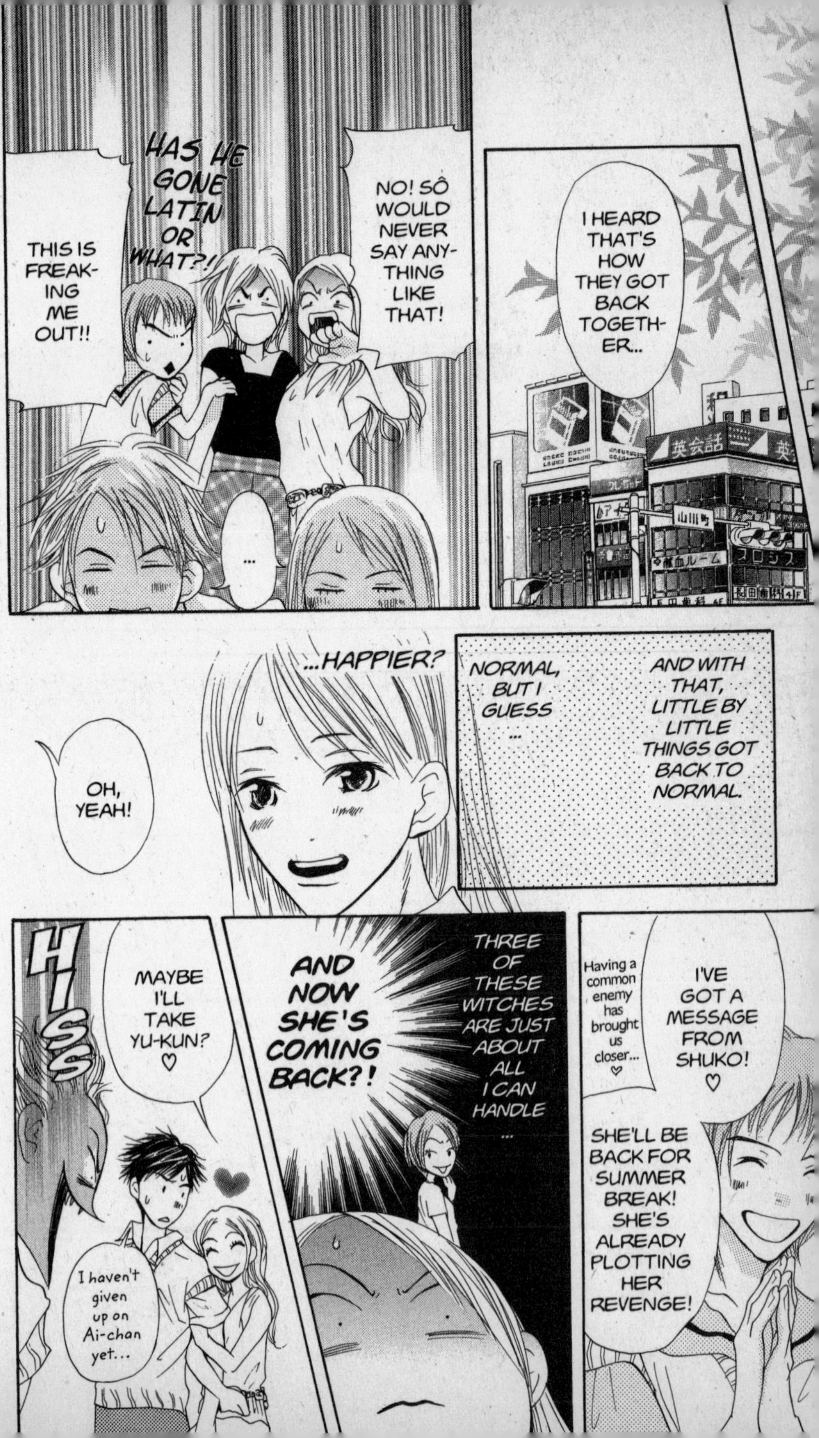
I HEARD THAT'S HOW THEY GOT BACK TOGETHER...
NO! SÔ WOULD NEVER SAY ANYTHING LIKE THAT!
HAS HE GONE LATIN OR WHAT?!
THIS IS FREAKING ME OUT!!
...
AND WITH THAT, LITTLE BY LITTLE THINGS GOT BACK TO NORMAL.
NORMAL, BUT I GUESS...
...HAPPIER?
OH, YEAH!
I'VE GOT A MESSAGE FROM SHUKO! ♡
Having a common enemy has brought us closer... ♡
SHE'LL BE BACK FOR SUMMER BREAK! SHE'S ALREADY PLOTTING HER REVENGE!
THREE OF THESE WITCHES ARE JUST ABOUT ALL I CAN HANDLE...
AND NOW SHE'S COMING BACK?!
HISS
MAYBE I'LL TAKE YU-KUN? ♡
I haven't given up on Ai-chan yet...

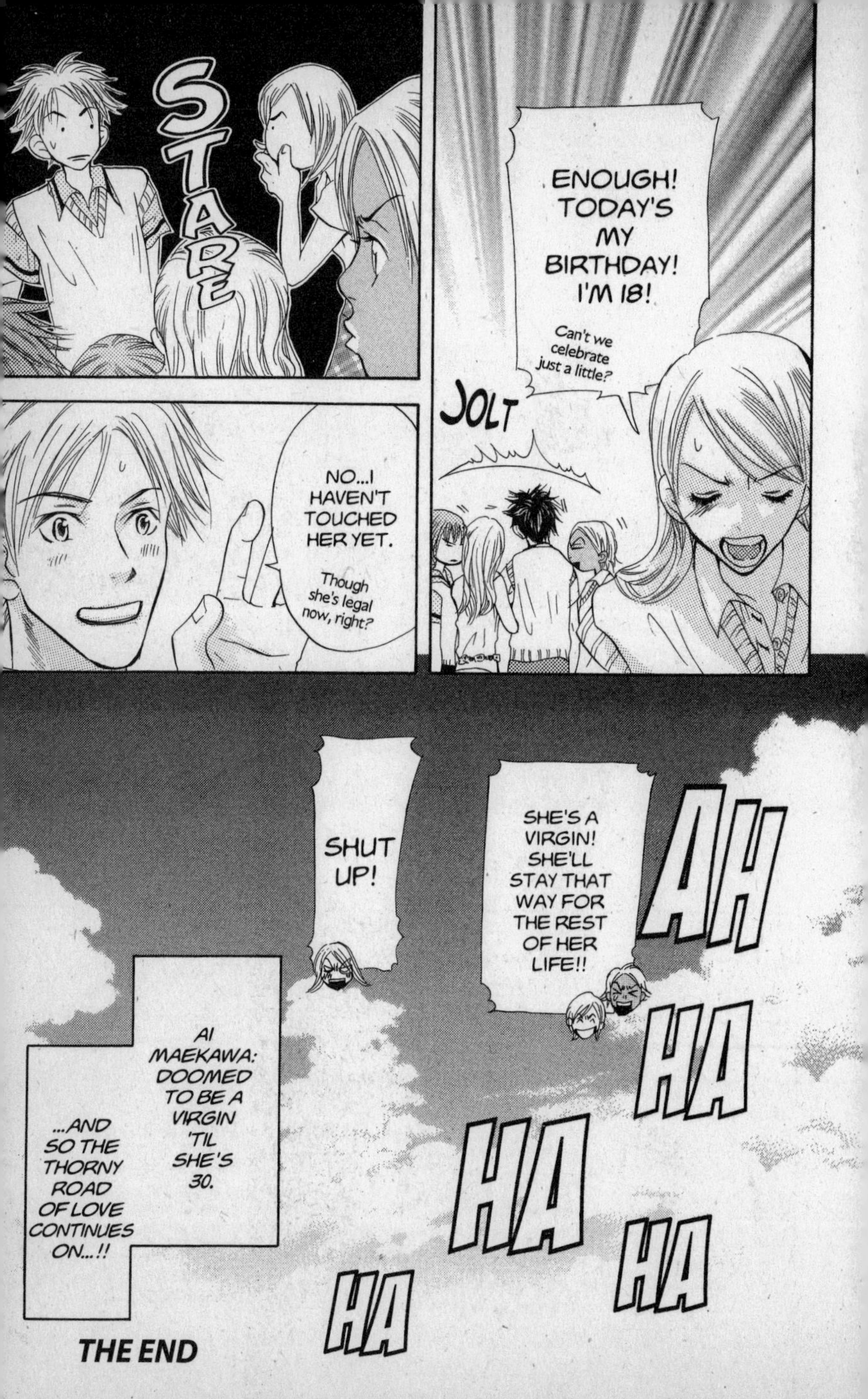
ENOUGH! TODAY'S MY BIRTHDAY! I'M 18!
Can't we celebrate just a little?
JOLT
STARE
NO...I HAVEN'T TOUCHED HER YET.
Though she's legal now, right?
AH
SHE'S A VIRGIN! SHE'LL STAY THAT WAY FOR THE REST OF HER LIFE!!
SHUT UP!
HA
HA
HA
HA
AI MAEKAWA: DOOMED TO BE A VIRGIN 'TIL SHE'S 30.
...AND SO THE THORNY ROAD OF LOVE CONTINUES ON...!!
THE END

kaneyoshi izumi

MESSAGE FROM THE AUTHOR

The last volume of *DOUBT!!* is finally here! Congratulations on making it this far, and thank you very much. I'm usually not very emotionally attached to my work, but I'm sad that this series is coming to a close. (Please don't ask, "What about the other manga you've worked on, then?!") Make sure to floor the accelerator in your hearts as you read this final volume! But keep in mind that I can't be held responsible if you speed so fast that you lose control and crash!!

ABOUT THE AUTHOR

Kaneyoshi Izumi's birthday is April 1st and her blood type is probably type A (but she hasn't actually had it checked yet). Her debut story "Tenshi" ("Angel") appeared in the September 1995 issue of Bessatsu Shôjo Comics and won the 36th Shogakukan Shinjin ("newbie") Comics Award. Her hobbies include riding motorcycles, playing the piano, and feeding stray cats, and she continues to work as an artist for Bessatsu Shôjo Comics.

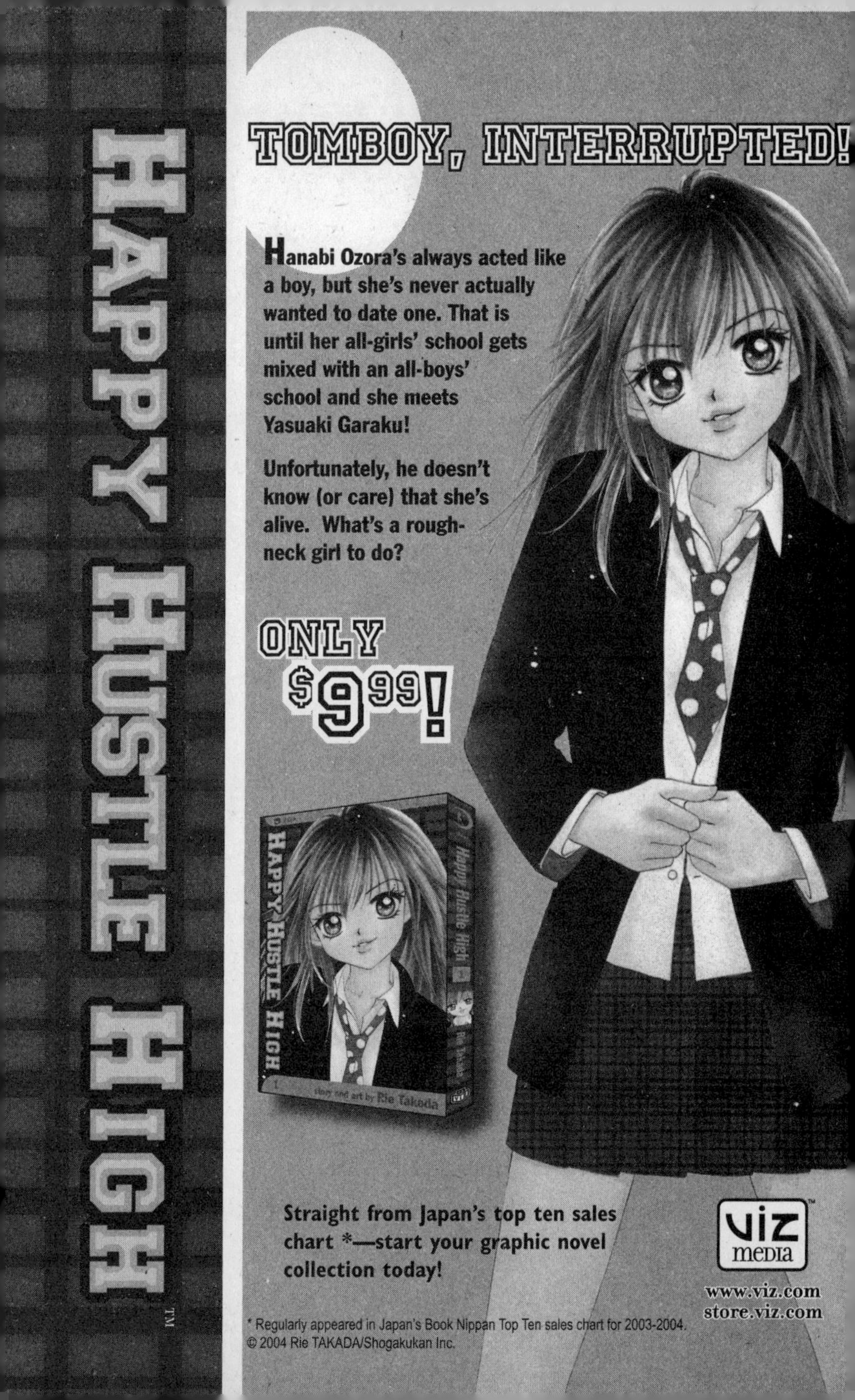
HAPPY HUSTLE HIGH™
TOMBOY, INTERRUPTED!
Hanabi Ozora's always acted like a boy, but she's never actually wanted to date one. That is until her all-girls' school gets mixed with an all-boys' school and she meets Yasuaki Garaku!
Unfortunately, he doesn't know (or care) that she's alive. What's a rough-neck girl to do?
ONLY $9.99!
HAPPY HUSTLE HIGH
Happy Hustle High
story and art by Rie Takada
Straight from Japan's top ten sales chart *—start your graphic novel collection today!
viz media
www.viz.com
store.viz.com
* Regularly appeared in Japan's Book Nippan Top Ten sales chart for 2003-2004.
© 2004 Rie TAKADA/Shogakukan Inc.

A Novel Concept

Introducing VIZ Media's new fiction line!

When we tell a story, we have the habit of giving you everything—the storyline *and* the visuals. But we're reinventing how you connect to your favorite series through our new line of full-length novels. Follow the characters you've come to love as they embark on new adventures. Except this time, we're just telling the story—we'll let your imagination do the rest.

Socrates in Love
Socrates in Love
Kyoichi Katayama
Kyoichi Katayama
Translated by Akemi Wegmüller

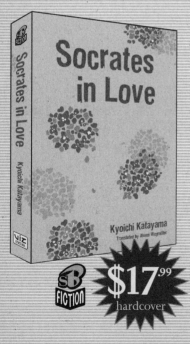

Socrates in Love

by Kyoichi Katayama

The best selling novel of all time in Japan with over 3.2 million copies sold! Finally, U.S. readers can experience the phenomenon that became the inspiration for a blockbuster movie, a hit TV show, and the Shojo Beat manga, also available from VIZ Media.

When an average boy meets a beautiful girl, it's a classic case of young love—instant, all consuming, and enduring. But when a tragedy threatens their romance, they discover just how deep and strong love can be.

SB FICTION

$17.99 hardcover

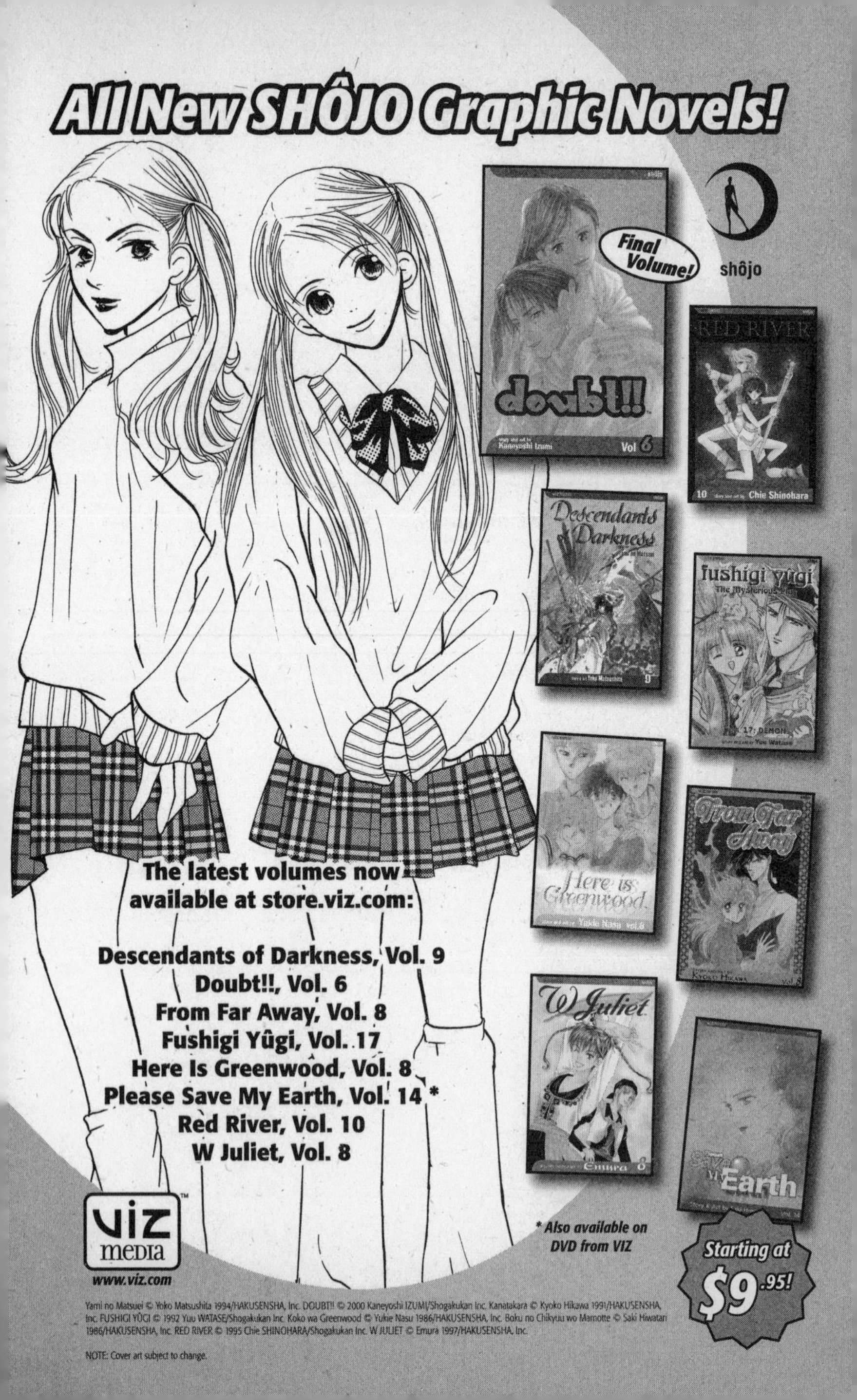

LOVE SHOJO? LET US KNOW!

☐ Please do NOT send me information about VIZ Media products, news and events, special offers, or other information.

☐ Please do NOT send me information from VIZ' trusted business partners.

Name: VICTORIA

Address: AMERICA

City: _____ **State:** _____ **Zip:** _____

E-mail: _____

☐ Male ☐ Female **Date of Birth** (mm/dd/yyyy): 3 / NO (Under 13? Parental consent required)

What race/ethnicity do you consider yourself? (check all that apply)

☐ White/Caucasian ☑ Black/African American ☐ Hispanic/Latino

☐ Asian/Pacific Islander ☐ Native American/Alaskan Native ☐ Other: _____

What VIZ shojo title(s) did you purchase? (indicate title(s) purchased)

_____

What other shojo titles from other publishers do you own? _____

_____

Reason for purchase: (check all that apply)

☑ Special offer ☐ Favorite title / author / artist / genre

☐ Gift ☐ Recommendation ☐ Collection

☐ Read excerpt in VIZ manga sampler ☐ Other _____

Where did you make your purchase? (please check one)

☐ Comic store ☐ Bookstore ☐ Mass/Grocery Store

☐ Newsstand ☐ Video/Video Game Store

☐ Online (site: _____) ☑ Other LIBRARY 50 5%

How many shojo titles have you purchased in the last year? How many were VIZ shojo titles?
(please check one from each column)

SHOJO MANGA	VIZ SHOJO MANGA
☐ None	☐ None
☐ 1 – 4	☐ 1 – 4
☐ 5 – 10	☐ 5 – 10
☐ 11+	☐ 11+

What do you like most about shojo graphic novels? **(check all that apply)**

☐ Romance ☐ Drama / conflict ☐ Fantasy
☐ Comedy ☐ Real-life storylines ☐ Relatable characters
☐ Other ______________________

Do you purchase every volume of your favorite shojo series?

☐ Yes! Gotta have 'em as my own
☐ No. Please explain: ______________________

Who are your favorite shojo authors / artists? ______________________

____

What shojo titles would like you translated and sold in English? ______________________

____

THANK YOU! Please send the completed form to:

VIZ media™

NJW Research
ATTN: VIZ Media Shojo Survey
42 Catharine Street
Poughkeepsie, NY 12601

Your privacy is very important to us. All information provided will be used for internal purposes only and will not be sold or otherwise divulged.